ANTICIPATIONS
OF THE ENLIGHTENMENT
IN ENGLAND, FRANCE,
AND GERMANY

Anticipations of the Enlightenment in England, France, and Germany

Edited by

ALAN CHARLES KORS

and

PAUL J. KORSHIN

upp

University of Pennsylvania Press

Philadelphia

Library of Congress Cataloging-in-Publication Data

Anticipations of the Enlightenment in England, France, and Germany /
edited by Alan Charles Kors and Paul J. Korshin.
   p. cm.
   Includes index.
   ISBN 0-8122-8057-1
   1. Enlightenment. 2. England—Intellectual life—18th century.
3. France—Intellectual life—18th century. 4. Germany—
Intellectual life—18th century. I. Kors, Alan Charles.
II. Korshin, Paul J., 1939–
B1302.E65A57   1987
940.2'52—dc19

87-17644
CIP

Contents

6-20-91

Contents

Editors' Note

The essays in this collection are the product of a year-long conference at the University of Pennsylvania on "The Early Enlightenment in England, France, and Germany" during the year 1981–82. As organizers of the conference, the format of which was a regular seminar, we invited the contributors, as participants, to visit the university for a week each, and to make several presentations. Those presentations included seminars with postgraduate students and a formal lecture on the subject of the early Enlightenment in Europe. The Enlightenment itself, especially in France and Germany, is the subject of intense study, but the pre-Enlightenment, the period covering the late seventeenth century and the first half of the eighteenth century, although scholars have not singled it out for much special attention, seemed worthy of special notice. Accordingly, we asked the participants to select a topic relative to the early Enlightenment in their country of interest and dealing with their subject of inquiry—whether history, history of science, philosophy, or literature—and to lecture on it. The following essays, which the participants have revised and enlarged over a period of two years or so, then, form one of the first organized efforts to address the pre-Enlightenment and some of the subjects that, in the later or high Enlightenment, hold center stage.

The conference at the University of Pennsylvania had the generous financial support of the university's Humanities Coordinating Committee, whose funds came from a National Endowment for the Humanities challenge grant. We gratefully acknowledge the assistance of the Committee, the National Endowment, our colleague in the Department of Germanic Languages, Professor John A. McCarthy, and former provost of the university Vartan Gregorian in making possible our conference and the essays in this book.

Paul J. Korshin
Alan Charles Kors

Introduction

ALAN CHARLES KORS

The Enlightenment is often described as if it had crystallized at some particular moment, often identified with some particular text, from the general
agency of prior "free thought" and "new philosophy." Usually, we presuppose rather than study the contexts and processes from which the ideas,
values, and modes of expression associated with the Enlightenment actually emerged. We too frequently ignore what Elisabeth Labrousse terms
here "the fascinating vagaries of 'influence' in the history of ideas," to
which one should add, following several of our authors, the vagaries of
influence in the history of literary forms. These essays are an effort to ex-
plore those contexts, processes, and, indeed, those "fascinating vagaries."

The organizers of the symposium that occasioned most of the papers in
this collection thought of two names for their undertaking: "Anticipations
of the Enlightenment" and "The Early Enlightenment." Both designations
involve methodological peril and both are vulnerable to charges of begging
a large number of important questions. Any enterprise that appears to
study a period in the light of its consequences invites both serious objection and caviling, for the danger of falsifying both the letter and spirit of a
philosophical, literary, and scientific generation by means of anachronism
is indeed real. Scholars who labor in the rich fields of late seventeenth- and
early eighteenth-century studies would have every right to object to any
effort that defined the primary significance of those fields in terms of their

1

relationship to the Enlightenments of France, England, and Germany. The problem predominantly addressed by these essays, however, is not any failure of seventeenth-century or early eighteenth-century studies to address the significance of the Enlightenment, but, rather, the failure of Enlightenment studies adequately to address the phenomena and complexities of the late seventeenth and early eighteenth centuries.

What continues to attract the primary interest of most scholars of the Enlightenment is the revolution of ideas associated with the eighteenth century. This in no way denigrates the "social history" of the Enlightenment, which constitutes one of the most vibrant fields of current historical studies, nor the new and fruitful modes of literary analysis, which, applied to Enlightenment texts, have yielded striking and original readings and reconceptualizations of familiar works. Nonetheless, is there any other field of study in which the intellectual historian and the literary scholar work with such interest in, comprehension of, and appreciation for each others' labors? Enlightenment studies, as the very term "Enlightenment" does more than suggest, continue to place a primary emphasis upon thought as a particularly dynamic aspect of human behavior in the Europe of the eighteenth century. The essays in this collection, however, argue that the development of ideas must be related to a longer term and more contextual framework than traditional Enlightenment studies generally have accepted. Working from such a perspective, our authors, on the whole, find far more continuity than discontinuity in the learned worlds they study.

Because Enlightenment authors themselves sought to contradistinguish their epoch categorically from the "orthodox" past, acknowledging as a source of their own ideas only, for the most part, what was most new in the seventeenth century, scholars often have begun with a similar assumption about influence. What was not a part of the "new philosophy" of the seventeenth century was somehow (however bizarre the assumption appears when stated baldly) without "positive" influence. The "sources" of the Enlightenment were to be sought in those thinkers of prior generations who most resembled *philosophes, Aufklärers* and the "modern" minds of the mid- to late eighteenth century. Most of the scholars represented here question the value of such an approach. Two claims, in particular, are virtual leitmotifs of this collection: (1) that too many historians have assumed a priori that certain movements of thought entail or preclude other aspects of belief and (2) that it is an error to read back into prior generations the sharp divisions effected by the Enlightenment.

Thus, Dale Van Kley's study identifies the contribution of Augustinian Jansenism to the most secular strains of the moral and political philosophy

2

of the Enlightenment. Elisabeth Labrousse demonstrates how arguments generated in a Calvinist context in Bayle's milieu could and would be read with such different meaning (one thinks of Pocock's notion of the "multivalence" of discourse) in the Paris of Enlightenment salons. In my own essay, the much denigrated Aristotelian scholastics of the late seventeenth century in France may be seen as influential critics of Cartesian philosophy and theology, who bequeathed a crisis in the first principles of theology to later generations. If, judging by the Enlightenment, one had deemed these Jansenists, Calvinists, and Aristotelians to have been in some bypassed backwater of history, critical aspects of the *process* of the development or emergence of major currents of the Enlightenment could not be studied, let alone understood. As John A. McCarthy writes, addressing the assumption of "decaying" literary forms prior to 1740: "In those brackish waters, . . . there was fresh life germinating." And let us put the term "brackish" in quotation marks!

There are few "clean breaks" in the intellectual and literary history described in this collection. Writing of Shaftesbury's generation, John Andrew Bernstein observes that "We exaggerate," in light of the Enlightenment's effects, "the extent to which the lines of battle were sharply drawn." Most of our authors would agree. They also appear to agree, on the whole, on several essential methodological practices: the need to re-contextualize our understanding of certain ideas and forms in the milieux from which they first emerged, the better to understand the etiology and the dynamic of the Enlightenment; the need to search more broadly for evidence and particulars than generally is done by eighteenth-century scholars, who too often, for our authors, rely on predetermined canon; a focus on the *gradual evolution* of ideational and literary phenomena; and a concern for the identity and characteristics of the *readers* as well as the authors of texts.

In conceptualizing the relationship of the late seventeenth and early eighteenth centuries to the dramatic changes in mentality and forms of expression that we associate with the later eighteenth century, our authors reach often strikingly different conclusions. Some of these differences are disagreements of substance; others arise from the variety of phenomena and questions addressed. Thus, in Van Kley's and my own studies (both focused, perhaps not coincidentally, on the sources of the French Enlightenment) the very theologies *rejected* by the later *philosophes* are shown to have been dynamic agents in the genesis of Enlightenment concepts and formulations. In the view of both essays, the creative and critical vitality of seventeenth-century French Catholicism generated important conceptions that later appear in Enlightenment thought. As Van Kley writes, "It is . . . most difficult to imagine Jansenism . . . having anticipated an ethic based upon . . . enlightened self-interest. Yet something like this happened." In John Andrew Bernstein's, Thomas P. Saine's, and Margaret C. Jacob's studies, on the other hand, a slightly different model appears. Here the implications of systems or movements of thought quite traditionalist or moderate in one context are shown to have actualized their "radical" or "progressive" potential in another. From the perspective of this latter model, however, to read back the later developments into the earlier phenomena is to falsify our understanding of the earlier period, to misstate the question of historical relationship, and to lose a sense of the complexity and particularities of eighteenth-century history.

Thus, for Bernstein, a movement generally seen as "traditionalist"—philosophical optimism—is shown to have been consistent historically with a certain progressivism. The cosmic Great Chain of Being did not have to be antiegalitarian in implication; ontological traditionalism did not have to entail political conservativism; and, in brief, there is, from the evidence, no reason to apply Basil Willey's celebrated model of the "cosmic Tory" to secular politics. Thus, for Saine, while later *Aufklärers* sought to distance themselves from Christian Wolff's philosophy, they were far more indebted to him than they could realize, and Wolff's implications went far beyond his own intended goals. Wolff emerges from Saine's essay as the would-be pious Lutheran whose conception of the will and whose notion of the relationship of philosophy and theology dramatically undermined traditional Lutheran theology. However "conservative" Wolff might be in his teleology, the "potential for radical applications of the principles themselves" was now a part of German philosophical culture. Thus, for Jacob, a scientific culture of the early Enlightenment, preponderantly concerned with practical applications of knowledge, only realized its "radical" potentials when its visions, much later in the century, became linked to social and political reform. Similarly, she writes of "the levelling tendencies" of a scientific education whose "earliest propagators self-consciously sought to reinforce the existing social hierarchy." Labrousse's Bayle is a good example of both phenomena: his Calvinism, in the context (indeed, the crucible) of the *Refuge*, generates perfectly "orthodox" arguments that when read (above all, when misread) in another time and place revealed "radical" potentials from which Bayle himself would have recoiled.

The "evolutionary emergence model" of the generation of the Enlightenment is another leitmotif of this collection. In the case of Enlightenment literary forms, if I may test your patience with extension of the metaphor, the interaction of the evolving species (the novel) with its ecological niche (the reading public) receives fresh attention. McCarthy and J. Paul Hunter, studying the transformation of literary genres, both see, in

4

Germany and England respectively, a gradual evolution of literary forms. Reading publics were not, for both scholars, what prior literary historians had assumed, and the symbiosis of literary form and an emerging "modern" mentality is subtle and complex. The needs and concerns of an increasingly secularized reading public (or at least of a stratum of that reading public) underwent a slow alteration, and authors met those changes by a gradual adaptation of the means (and indeed substance) of expression. For McCarthy, essential themes of the German Enlightenment already appear in the supposedly nostalgic "gallant novel" long before the 1740s, and there is a reciprocal influence, not antipathy, between the "old" gallant novel and the "new" periodicals, the "Moral Weeklies." For Hunter, the "emergence" of the novel occurred in the context of a disproportionately young, middling, and female audience of Londoners with new demands, cultural and psychological, upon the written word. There was no sudden creation or generation *per sautem* of some dramatically new "antiaristocratic" form; the emergence of the novel is better understood in terms of London's new literate lives and their loss of folklore, their loneliness, their need for instruction in the ways of the world. For both scholars, prior efforts to distinguish "modernity" categorically from an aristocratic past have not done justice to the richness of the phenomenon of literary change.

The role of aspects of late seventeenth- and early eighteenth-century culture more commonly linked to the emergence of Enlightenment phenomena is not ignored in this collection, however. Examining the "pioneering endeavour" of women literary authors before midcentury in Britain, Jocelyn Harris finds the influence of John Locke manifest in the texts she has studied. The critique of custom, with its dramatic implication that mere custom is tyranny, raised profound questions in many women's minds about the "customary" roles of men and women, both in social life and, in particular, in the world of letters. For Uwe-K. Ketelsen, it was the "new theology," increasingly naturalistic and emphasizing physico-theological argument (though not without its mystical side), that exercised a profound influence on German nature poetry. The new theology introduced scientific understanding to the literary culture, which in turn disseminated scientific knowledge to its own broad audience (and, Ketelsen notes, acted as a barrier to any "reductionist . . . mechanistic materialism" that might be a temptation of the new natural philosophy). For P. M. Mitchell, the Enlightenment itself, it would seem, was not far off in its own understanding of its origins. In his synthetic essay, it was indeed "the secularization of culture" that "overcame the dominance of revealed and organized religion." While recognizing the increasing appeal of rational theology to Christian minds, Mitchell stresses that the new philosophical emphasis upon "the superiority of reason" was "essential to the creation of a new culture." The revolutionary thought of the late eighteenth century was "the end product of much radical thought which had gone before," the implications of which increasingly became common property. In the intellectual world, this occasioned the displacement of theologians from a central position in the learned world, and in the literary world, in particular, it occasioned the autonomy of literature from theological concern or authority. In the political world, for Mitchell, it occasioned, in the consequences of "the new thought," "the downfall of an established, but no longer viable, political order."

Finally, let us note the modesty attendant to all of these essays, lest claims of "models" made in this introduction inflate, or worse, belie the claims actually made by our authors. Van Kley, for example, does not identify the Jansenist Nicole as the *source* of Enlightenment moral philosophy; he asserts, rather, that without Jansenist "insistence upon the social and political utility of self-love, the Enlightenment's moral rehabilitation of its indulgence would have been considerably more difficult." Bernstein, for example, ultimately finds the model of "cosmic Toryism" not entirely misleading, if properly modified by an appreciation of Shaftesbury's sense of freedom. Ketelsen, for example, while intrigued by the symbiosis of science, new theology, and literature in the German early eighteenth century, acknowledges that "it is often difficult to determine whether phenomena typical of the literature of this period are really derived from natural scientific disciplines or whether it is simply a matter of a common occurrence of enlightened rationalism." Harris's women authors excited, among their contemporaries, merely "a queer little flurry of interest." If some of these essays are correct in their criticisms of prior historiography and scholarship, a certain modesty may be an appropriate intellectual and moral quality in our field.

CHAPTER 1

Reading Pierre Bayle in Paris

ELISABETH LABROUSSE

Pierre Bayle quite often is hailed as a forerunner of the Enlightenment, but we should pause to consider how odd, in fact, the concept of "forerunner" truly is. It should be used with caution, for, by definition, it is purely retrospective; it has to do much more with later readers than with the author whom it is supposed to explain.

A "forerunner" is deemed to have exercised a powerful influence over the generations that succeeded him and that found in him one of their masters. Here again, however, caution is necessary, for in relation to ideas, an influence is never mechanical. To use an analogy, it has less to do with wax and seal than with a tennis racket and a tennis ball; that is to say, there are movement and energy on both sides. To let someone have an influence on you is, in fact, the result of an unconscious choice on your part, of a significant selection. Among the mass of books available in Paris in the 1720s, the *Historical and Critical Dictionary* occasioned a remarkable resonance in its readers: this obviously had as much to do with *their* mentality as with Bayle's.

Thus, it must be only with these reservations and nuances present in our minds that we can repeat the usual formula and say that Bayle was one of the spiritual fathers of the Enlightenment, and, in particular, a powerful influence of French thought in the eighteenth century. His *Dictionary*, in its many editions, was statistically the book most often present in private libraries of the period in France,[1] and the four folio volumes were also translated both into English and German.

Now, let us be mindful *not* to say that it was Bayle's *thought* that enjoyed this success. To be precise, it was his *works*, and it is such a corpus of books that we ought to consider here. We should not take into account the concrete behavior of the man, Bayle, as his biography shows it, a behavior that is far from allowing us to depict him as an ungodly man and disbeliever.

Indeed, in Protestant countries, the corpus of Bayle's works had not been taken universally as evidence of impiety. In 1716, the *Dictionary* was a prize given to the best theological student in Neuchâtel, Switzerland. It could have been naiveté, but Pastor Antoine Court, the principal artisan of the clandestine restoration of the Reformed churches in France, was a persistent reader and admirer of Bayle.[2] Later in the century, Count Zinzendorf, the German Pietist, was an avid reader of Bayle who never doubted the sincerity of the latter's Christian belief.

Without giving excessive weight to these isolated facts, we may still state, as a methodological principle, that the meaning of Bayle's works is ambiguous. Now, the problem we want to consider here is *not* that of deciding if the "Protestant" or the "Enlightenment" reading of Bayle is the correct or best one. The answer to such a question would depend entirely on the point of view one adopted on whether the "best" reading was the one that was closest to the author's historical impact. The question we shall pose is a more limited one: why was Antoine Court's or Count Zinzendorf's reading of Bayle never the way a Catholic Frenchman of the eighteenth century would read him?

First, let us emphasize the chronological and geographical distances that separated Bayle so significantly from his Enlightenment admirers. When Bayle was still alive, in the last years of his life, between 1700 and 1706, his renown was already established in Europe, but primarily on the basis of his broad and accurate scholarship, and his role as a high-level popularizer of philosophy and history for the educated general public. It was a generation much later than his own—nearly the generation of his contemporaries' grandchildren—that spread his reputation for unbelief in France, once his works were allowed to enter the kingdom after the death of Louix XIV in 1715.

Now, this simple fact entails significant displacements. Just to pause at one point: the Revocation of the Edict of Nantes, in October 1685, had been the central event in the lives of Bayle and his fellow refugees; for his French readers during the Regency, however, it was an old story, something far away in the past, the consequences of which were a situation taken for granted. Even those who, retrospectively, had seen it as a political blunder, such as the duc de Saint-Simon or the Regent himself, did not deem it possible to reconsider the decision taken by the Crown more than thirty years earlier. "La France toute catholique" was, for better or worse, something felt to be irreversible and to which everyone was adjusted. The tenacious and underground resistance of the Huguenots still living in France, mostly in the South, was a rural phenomenon, largely ignored by the general public. For the government, it was a thorny, quite exasperating, but clearly secondary problem, thought to be solvable either by outbursts of military brutality or by ignoring it, in the foolish hope that time would heal the wounds and that later generations would cease to favor heresy.

It would be difficult to exaggerate the naive arrogance of French culture at any period, but especially during the seventeenth and eighteenth centuries. The Parisian intelligentsia believed itself to be the center of the world. When considering foreign cultures, however, Parisians could make a certain effort of imagination, either in a condescending manner or, indeed, in a utopian and idealizing way, as in the current visions of the "good savage," the "wise Chinese," or the "meditative Englishman." They did not begin to guess, however, that a similar effort could be called for with respect to the Huguenot "Refuge" in the Low Countries. Because French was their spoken and written language, Huguenot refugees were taken to be a part of France, intellectually accessible, even if looked down upon as backward and provincial.

Frenchmen of the eighteenth century therefore believed themselves to be on the same plane as the Refuge, despite the time that had elapsed since the birth of this particular community, one that quickly had become so very peculiar in relation to French culture. Indeed, it was peculiar not only because of its fervent Protestantism (in itself enough to represent a distinctive subculture), but also because of its contacts with northwestern Europe; because of its freedoms, unheard of in France; and last, but not least, because of the political choices that made the majority of the Refugees staunch supporters, after 1688, of William III.

For example, nobody in Paris seemed to realize that there had been no censorship in the Low Countries when Bayle was publishing his books there. Parisian readers studiously looked for mental reservations, innuendoes or tricks in his works, exactly as they did in the case of an author printed in France. Above all, however, French readers had a complete and blissful ignorance about the Protestant theology that had been the framework of Bayle's discussions. To state this is by no means to take a stand about his eventual faith or lack of it. It is simply to recognize that Bayle, given his education and the circles in which he lived for practically all of his life, could not escape such a framework. The problems that he discussed most readily and most often were all theological, and it was with a theological approach that he tackled questions that later readers would be prone to think of as purely secular. Indeed, generally speaking, the seventeenth century was "theologico-political"; that is, its political doctrines were based on theological propositions. The "divine right of kings" that Bayle so consistently had advocated all of his life, for example, had a clear scriptural basis, above all, in Romans 13.

In Paris, thirty years later, no one could appreciate the ideological roots of Bayle's intense conflict with Pierre Jurieu, and there thus was born, in France, the late and absurd legend that Bayle had been Mme Jurieu's lover! People were at such a loss to comprehend why the two men, erstwhile good friends, had become bitter enemies, that they coined this little anecdote, much more in keeping with a Parisian drawing room of the period than with the possibilities of a love affair in the small Protestant town of Sedan between 1675 and 1681. In other words, Parisians reduced everything to a personal quarrel because they had not even a glimpse of the theologico-political oppositions among the Huguenot refugees. Yet, if one takes into account the specific characters of the Refuge and the moment when the struggle broke out, the complete and significant doctrinal split between the two men becomes obvious. Jurieu condemned the civil toleration that Bayle was advocating, but that was, indeed, quite alien to classical Calvinism. As for Bayle, he was indignant to see Jurieu abandoning divine right absolutism in order to authorize and sanctify the "Glorious" English Revolution. An aspect of Bayle's deep scorn for any tendency toward utilitarianism was the infamy he attached to "ambulatory doctrines," that is, to time-serving opinions that changed with the circumstances. Bayle could not forgive Jurieu—formerly, an absolutist—for his sudden change of heart, brought about by what we might describe today as common-sense political opportunism.

Indeed, the core of the matter, and that which gave such sharpness to the disagreement, was that each of the disputants—Bayle as much as Jurieu—was convinced that his adversary's stand was utterly prejudicial to the central interests of the Refugees, to this return to France for which all, at least until the Peace of Ryswick, desperately hoped. Refugees were migrants much more than settlers: they had left family and goods behind them when they escaped, convinced by wishful thinking that the Revocation ultimately would be repealed. Bayle, however, quite reasonably thought that if the Refugees were to add a political heresy to their religious one, they never would be permitted to return to France, bearers of so-called "republican" ideas about individual rights. As for Jurieu, he believed, again understandably, that an ideal of toleration, were it successful among the Huguenots, would demobilize them and make them lukewarm, just at a time when it was vital to stir up their hatred of Roman Catholicism and devote the Refuge to the service of William of Orange. Only the hoped-for victory of the Allies, he believed, would oblige the French crown to restore the Edict of Nantes.

Such a conflict between Bayle and Jurieu, however, so very clear and understandable when the problems of the Refuge are taken into account, was totally and blissfully ignored by public opinion in Paris thirty-five years later. It was not even vaguely suspected that there had been a decisive ideological opposition between the two adversaries: Jurieu was simply a fanatical villain and Bayle a noble mind.

Now, during the violent polemics of the year 1691, Jurieu had thrown pell-mell against Bayle the most deadly charges he could think of: Bayle was a traitor to the United Provinces, and he was a miscreant, if not an atheist (obviously a dreadful accusation in a community as keenly religious as the Refuge). When such indictments were known, many years later, in the Paris of the Regency, people were prone to take Jurieu's word about Bayle, often reversing its value and intent: what the theologian had wanted to be infamous was generally considered laudatory. Bayle had not even been a believer, let alone a fanatic!

From this failure to understand Bayle's Protestant context there followed, in Regency Paris, a first, fundamental distortion. In almost all of his books, Bayle had constantly assailed, directly and indirectly, the Roman Catholic Church. He criticized the Church of Rome for being complacent toward "idolatry" and "superstition," and he constantly emphasized the ferocity of its intolerance. Now in Paris, these attacks were perpetually understood as if they had been directed against Christianity itself, for indeed Roman Catholicism was practically the only form of Christianity with which Frenchmen were familiar. In other words, what had been written as anti-Catholic controversy was read as anti-Christian polemics.

Let us illustrate this by considering the famous "paradoxes" of Bayle and the interpretation they received. In 1681—four years before the Revocation, when the Huguenots still were hoping that it would not take place—Bayle stated that atheism was less dangerous a sin than idolatry. In brief, his argument ran, God would rather see his existence put into doubt than see himself clothed in infamous or ridiculous attributes. This, for Bayle, was an indirect way both to attack Rome—a Church Protestants always were taxing with being idolatrous—and to call for the toleration of "mere" heresy. Further, Bayle maintained that our theoretical opinions had no effect at all on our concrete behavior, so that atheism was not dangerous for society, whose members' actions were all equally determind by self-interest and vanity. Since heresy was perceived by everyone as a much lesser crime than atheism, Bayle implicitly was arguing that heresy was neither socially nor politically harmful. In other words, the Crown of France had no need to revoke the Edict of Nantes. Later, however, these "paradoxes" were oversimplified, and, out of context, were crudely understood as an apology of atheism.

Years later, Bayle wrote that a society of perfect Christians could not maintain itself if it were in close geographical contact with less moral neighbors. What he wanted to emphasize was the complete immorality (or amorality) of European foreign policies: international relations were purely relations of strength, and *raison d'état* was totally cynical and unethical. Bayle's argument was the statement of a moral rigorist and of a convinced pacifist, deeply sickened by the tricks of diplomacy, the cruelties of wars and the lies of the diverse national propagandas that dressed up those dire realities in hypocritical cloaks of self-jupocrification.

The example proposed by Bayle, however, was read upside down, as if he had wanted to undermine the Gospel teachings when he said that a society true to them would be rapidly conquered and destroyed. In fact, if there is one characteristic of Bayle evident everywhere in his books, it is his puritanical rigorism and loathing of utilitarianism. To him, honesty— that is, morality—is not "the best policy," because honesty is simply *not a "policy" at all*. Honesty, morality, has to do with the intention to obey one's conscience and the moral law, without any consideration for the outcome or for expediency. Bayle despised those apologies of Christianity, becoming so frequent, that presented the Christian religion as a source of happiness and success *both* on earth and in the afterlife. Thus, in this case we again meet with a complete misconception: when read by a utilitarian, the meaning of Bayle's text was precisely the reverse of what it was for a rigorist.

Even when Bayle's Parisian public were not turning his ideas upside down, even when they followed his conclusions with a certain fidelity, they still misunderstood, though unknowingly, a good part of his argumentation. Parisians generally embraced Bayle's program of religious toleration quite readily, but they ignored many of the arguments on which such a program was founded, and what they ignored were precisely Bayle's most original and most essential points.

Bayle had tried to demonstrate that persecution was uncalled for because religious intolerance created the problems that it was deemed to solve. Minorities, he had argued, in fact were loyal to the governments that treated them decently. Bayle also had sought to show that persecution was perfectly senseless, because the means it used—constraint and violence—were obviously ineffective to achieve the ends officially sought: to convince and to persuade. To the contrary, to compel someone forcibly to certain acts of religion was a sure way to strengthen the psychological resistance of some of the victims. At most, it could foster hypocrisy, linked with a bitter hatred for the religion that used such methods.

However, Bayle (his *Philosophical Commentary*, written primarily as a theological treatise, made this its central tenet) had required a *religious* respect towards individual conscience, arguing that such a respect was one with the fear of God, in other words, with piety. The use of force, in religious matters, was no less than a crime of *"lèse majesté divine,"* for each person's conscience was the seat of his personal, intimate relationship with God, on which no one should intrude. Conscience, so to speak, was God's exclusive territory; the persecutor, consequently, infringed upon nothing less than the rights of God. Although Bayle's *Philosophical Commentary* appeared just shortly before Locke's *Letter On Toleration*, Bayle was, in a way, more archaic than the English philosopher (even though more radical in his scope). For Bayle, the individual had only duties, not rights, and his foremost duty was to follow the dictates of his conscience. God was the being with "rights," and it was these divine rights that were violated by persecution.

It was not for nothing that Bayle wrote a commentary on a verse of the Gospel (Luke 14:23), "Compel them to enter." Indeed, it was of great importance to him to show that if the compulsion of consciences were legitimate and ordered by God, then all Christian denominations devoutly should use persecution, so that Christendom should be rent perpetually by internal wars. If persecution were legitimate, then what would happen to the Christian meekness so clearly favored by the Gospel that, to the contrary, so obviously forbade injustice and cruelty?

An important part of Bayle's plea for toleration, thus, was primarily the speech of one Christian directed to other Christians, but this significant aspect was quite neglected in the Paris of the 1720s. There, it was easy to be a firm partisan of religious toleration—haughtily condemning Spain or the Inquisition, for example—on the sole basis of utilitarianism and common sense. As we have seen, Bayle had not omitted this sort of argument. Nevertheless, his main originality and emphasis lay elsewhere. For his Parisian admirers, persecution was useless, absurd, and cruel. Obviously, Bayle would agree, but for him, persecution was above all wicked and impious, and this essential Baylian description was neglected in the Parisian salons.

Let us now address Bayle's celebrated discussions of "the problem of evil," for on this point Parisian misunderstandings of him become positively ludicrous. In the eighteenth century, the influence of Saint Augustine, so pervasive in French culture during the seventeenth century among both Protestants and Catholics, underwent a sudden decline. Simultaneously, the idea of "progress" became increasingly in favor, that is, the notion that the sole passage of time automatically was bringing about improvements in the human condition. Until the first years of the eighteenth century, a change most commonly had been believed to be for the worst—a decadence, a degeneration, a step further from the Golden Age. In this period, however, a striking reversal of the notion of temporal decline occurred.

For Bayle, it was a patent fact, knowable by bitter experience to a four-year-old child, that man was at the same time wicked and miserable: such a proposition was an Augustinian commonplace. For readers immersed in the optimistic idea of progress and the search for happiness, however, such stark Augustinian pessimism was not to be taken seriously. In fact, Bayle had chosen the example of "evil" to demonstrate both the incapacity of rationalistic theology and the ineluctable necessity of relying upon Revelation and faith, of eschewing our weak reason, and of trusting blindly in "the foolishness" of the Cross (I Cor. 1:23)—the Christian Revelation—despite its opacity. In this world, innocence was oppressed, sin was pervasive, and suffering and cruelty were everywhere. Consequently, optimism could only be an act of faith, a wager that the Creator of this vale of tears was, nevertheless, kind and fatherly, and would grant to his elect an everlasting happiness in another life. For eighteenth-century readers, however, keen on being happy in this life and doing their best to reach such a goal, Bayle's pages were deemed to demonstrate, intentionally, less the weakness of human reason than the fatuity of theology. As the tragic question that Bayle had discussed at length—the mystery of evil—was neglected and evaded, his texts were presumed to amount simply to a demonstration of the inanity of theological reasoning.

In many places in his works, Bayle vigorously had stated the Calvinist doctrine (whether "sincerely" or not is a moot point). In the last years of the seventeenth century, in the Refuge, however, latitudinarianism was attracting many younger theologians, called *"rationaux."* This school considered Natural Religion to be an excellent introduction to Christianity, incomplete and insufficient indeed, but not at all contradictory to Revelation. For the *rationaux*, one went smoothly from the one to the other. For Bayle, to the contrary, it required a leap of faith, a blind decision, for one to trust the traditional interpretation of the Bible; then, and only then, was the bitterness of our experience of a fallen and sinful nature counteracted in favor of a supernatural order that abolished nature. For the *rationaux*, both Natural and Revealed religions were reasonable, useful, and conducive to virtue and to an earthly happiness for the individual and the commonwealth. From this, one may well imagine the opposition to Bayle in latitudinarian circles and the accusation of unbelief thrown upon him by men who certainly were no friends of Jurieu. Surely this judgment passed upon Bayle by the latitudinarians made an impression on the Parisians some twenty years later.

In any case, how could witty and deistically inclined little *abbés* in the Parisian drawing rooms have taken seriously Bayle's exclusive reliance upon faith as opposed to reason? Thus, it was taken for granted that Bayle had been an atheist, or, at the very least, an enemy of Christianity, who took pains to depict religion as ridiculous. Some people admired, more or less secretly, such daring; many others undertook to criticize and refute Bayle, courting renown in such an effort.

The crucial question for understanding Bayle, of course, is to decide what came first in him, fideism or scepticism. Was Bayle's scepticism—his challenging the abilities of human reason to reach ultimate truths—the outcome of an initial fideistic option, or had he used fideism as a screen to make his bitter rejection of religion socially acceptable? It is for his readers to decide. What is certain, however, is that in the Paris of the 1720s the second interpretation was chosen automatically. The general atmosphere was alien to faith and fideism, in part because of the Roman Catholic hue of the culture; in part because Paris was playing tentatively and, so to speak, naughtily with incredulity; and, finally, in part because the image of miscreant Bayle was coming from so many different sides of the Refuge.

Let us sum up. The eighteenth century may well have had more than one misconception about Bayle, because it projected upon him its own mentality—a mentality at once optimistic and utilitarian, that is, quite alien to the author of the *Dictionary*. Those Parisians, however, read Bayle with gusto. He was witty, not pompous. His texts were relatively short essays. He was forever illustrating abstract considerations with concrete examples. He was humorous, ironical, and amusing, essential qualities for a generation that shrank from solemnity and hated to be bored.

The outcome of this was that Bayle's Christian apology of religious toleration was read, above all, as an apology of a condescending indifference to revealed religion and of indignation over its bursts of fanaticism. It was settled in readers' minds, once and for all, that what came first in Bayle's thought was his scepticism, his fideism being merely a cloak to hide his unbelief. Bayle's scepticism was deemed to have been the source of his hor-ror for superstition; no one stopped to consider that in the son of a Cal-vinist pastor and in a persecuted Huguenot, the feeling of horror for fanaticism and superstition very well could spring from religious motives.

When a piece of carving is subjected to oblique lighting, its aspects may change considerably according to the side the light is coming from. In the same way, read in the Paris of the Regency, a Huguenot writer of the seventeenth century well may have been turned into a "philosophe" of the Enlightenment. Such a possible misconstruction is certainly not to be la-mented: it ensured the celebrity of Bayle, and it gives to us a lesson about the fascinating vagaries of "influence" in the history of ideas.

NOTES

1. Daniel Mornet, "Les enseignements des bibliothèques privées, 1750–1780," *Revue d'histoire littéraire de la France* 17ᵉ année (1910): 463.
2. Philippe Joutard, *La Légende des Camisards* (Paris, 1977), 159–62.

CHAPTER 2

"A First Being, of Whom We Have No Proof": The Preamble of Atheism in Early-Modern France

ALAN CHARLES KORS

Eighteenth-century atheists, both the authors of the early clandestine manuscripts and later figures such as Diderot, d'Holbach, and Naigeon, believed all "proofs" of the existence of God to be flawed. They believed that neither the evidence of the natural world nor the operations of reason necessitated a belief in a Perfect Being, a Creator, or a Providence. What were the actual sources of such views, and how were they formulated and spread in the generation that preceded such explicit atheism? How and when did the particular arguments by which atheists dismissed the claims of theism—and from which an atheistic conception could emerge—enter the literature of learned society? When we address these questions historically, some intriguing phenomena come to light.

Efforts to reach atheistic conclusions from Cartesian ontological and mechanistic premises, for example, were made *not* by the Cartesians, who increasingly relied on the role of God to preserve the appearances of their system,[1] but by their Aristotelian opponents, for purposes of *reductio ad maleficum*.[2] Systems of thought devoid of creation and Providence were constructed in the seventeenth and early eighteenth centuries less by any heterodox thinkers than by perfectly orthodox classical scholars and historians of philosophy in their learned roles.[3] Refutations of proofs of the existence of God, our topic here, abounded by the late seventeenth century, not because of the emergence of actual atheists, but because of theological polemic on the issue of the proper philosophical structure for Christian doctrine. Further, the argument from "universal consent" was shattered not by any seventeenth-century dissent, but, again, we shall see, by the work of orthodox historians of thought, and, above all, by the conclusions and reports of Christian missionaries and travelers.

The lesson to be drawn may sound paradoxical, but it restores early modern minds to the fullness of their learned world: it was the orthodox culture of the seventeenth century that generated, in its debates and inquiries, the component arguments of the atheistic philosophies; the later atheists embraced and syncretized such arguments toward a different end. In this essay, I shall attempt to sketch the role of Christian theology and philosophy in the refutations of proofs of the existence of God.[4]

Consider the "problem" of Jean Meslier in this context. What has intrigued students of the atheistic "testament" left in manuscript by this obscure country priest in 1729 is the question of his "sources." The "isolated" Catholic *curé* manifested no reading knowledge whatsoever of Hobbes or Spinoza, or the *libertins*, or Bayle. He knew his Montaigne, but the references and evidence of his more contemporary reading point preponderantly to orthodox works of theology. This has led many historians to assert that he simply must have read heterodox works without leaving any evidence to that effect, or to see him as an extraordinarily original and creative mind, conceiving of atheism in an ideational parthenogenesis. Pierre Rétat refuted the mistaken assertion of a direct reference by Meslier to Bayle (it was Moréri's *Dictionnaire* that he knew), but concluded, after reviewing the critique of Providence at the heart of Meslier's system, that "if Bayle is almost [?] totally absent from the remainder of the *Testament*, here he is at the source of Meslier's reflections." In a note, he added: "[The problem] remains that Meslier does not refer to him; it seems that we are here in the presence of *souvenirs de lecture*. . . ."[5] Jean Fabre, although alleging that Meslier had read the *libertins*, concluded ultimately that Meslier's reading consisted of "only several books, and of those above all which would be found in the most modest presbytery as guarantors of the faith." This being the case, he affirmed that "this peasant and self-taught *curé*, liberated from dogma but not from scholasticism, cleared for himself the path of a merciless atheism."[6] The thesis of this essay is precisely that in the late seventeenth and early eighteenth centuries, it was works written from unimpeachable motives, to guarantee the faith, that in fact "cleared the way" for the conceivability of atheistic philosophy.

Enlightenment atheism flourished in an intellectual climate far less insistent upon formal philosophical proof—or what the seventeenth century would have termed *"évidence,"* even when purely logical—than that of the generations which immediately preceded it. Yet, just as Catholic theologians understood proof of God's existence to be a "preamble of the Faith,"[7] so did the atheists understand the refutation or dismissal of such proof to be a necessary conceptual "preamble" of any strictly materialistic system.[8] When the author of one scandalous manuscript of the early eighteenth century set forth his exposition of materialism, he dismissed matter-of-factly "a First Being, of whom we have no proof."[9] To understand the source of such confidence, we must look, above all, to the theological and orthodox philosophical community of early-modern France.

Throughout most of the seventeenth century, the universities, seminaries, and curricula of Catholic France embodied the dominant influence of Catholic scholasticism, Aristotelian in its fundamental philosophy and Thomistic in its theology. In the course of that century, two tendencies of thought would challenge that dominance: first, and most important, Cartesian and, later, Malebranchist natural philosophy and philosophical theology; and secondly, Catholic fideism, a pious scepticism about the powers of our natural faculties, without the light of faith, to make sense or system of the world. Cartesians and scholastics warred for the minds (scholastics held, for the most part, the intellectual sinecures) of Catholic France in the last half of the seventeenth century, with fideists often supporting each school in its critiques of the other's claims. Catholic (and indeed, Huguenot) theologians and philosophers agreed on the fundamental preambles of theology, in particular, on the existence of God as Perfect Being, Creator, and Providential Governor of the world. What they most emphatically did *not* agree upon, however, were the proper and compelling means of establishing such beliefs. Above all, the boisterous, prolonged, and public debates between scholastics and Cartesians, from whose perspectives each other's proofs were unconvincing, had the profoundest implications for the validity both of prevailing modes of demonstration and of all particular arguments for the existence of God.

By the late seventeenth century, there were eight proofs of God's existence especially favored by French theologians and philosophers. First, there was the classical argument from "universal consent," namely, that since all known peoples and sages believed in God's existence, it was obviously a truth of inescapable force and evidence. To most thinkers, however, while this provided "moral certainty," meaning among other things, that it took a rather perverse nature not to assent to such an argument, this "proof" was not a formal demonstration. To the scholastics, Thomas Aquinas had provided five such compelling philosophical demonstrations, all properly a posteriori, that is to say, derived from knowledge of the actual world open to our senses, and based on inductions that they believed the mind was obliged to make from its experience of the universe. The seventeenth century understood these five proofs as follows: (1) from the *contingency* of all the beings we observe, we knew there must be a *Necessary Being*, for there could be no infinite regression of contingencies; (2) from the *motion* of beings that we observe, we similarly knew that there must be a *First Mover*; (3) from the sequence of *cause and effect* in the beings we observe, we similarly knew that there must be a *First Cause*; (4) from the *degrees of perfection* in the beings we observe—for example, in goodness, in wisdom, and in powers—we knew there must be a *Supreme Perfection*, of whose absolute perfection they were partial negations; and (5) from the *benevolent purposes, harmony, and order* of the world that we observe, we knew that there must be a *Providence*, that is to say, a supremely wise and benevolent governor of the world. Seventeenth-century scholastics were committed, in epistemological theory at least, to Aristotle's dictum that nothing entered the mind except by way of the senses, and here, from our experience of the world, were five compelling demonstrations whose force, in addition, was attested to by the universal consent of mankind.

One of the Cartesian challenges to scholasticism, of course, was epistemological, in particular, the denial of the priority of sense experience in the acquisition of true and certain knowledge. To the Cartesians, our sensory experience of the world was indeed uncertain: indistinguishable in and of itself from dream, imagination, and hallucination; relative to our sense organs, location, and passions; recording impressions made on our physical being, but never penetrating to the essence and actual nature of things. For the Cartesians, truth was to be disclosed a priori, that is, as the seventeenth century understood it, by reason alone—as in geometry or logic—independently of sense experience. Descartes, his disciples believed, had offered two such purely rational proofs, both following solely from logical analysis of the idea of God as a perfect being.

Although twentieth-century philosophers and historians of philosophy debate whether Descartes advanced two or three proofs in the *Meditations*, and, indeed, whether or not these proofs were in fact "a priori," most seventeenth-century critics and defenders of Descartes believed him to have advanced two distinctly a priori demonstrations: one, from the idea of God as the most perfect being of whom we can conceive (entailing his actual existence as a necessary property of perfection); and two, from the "objective"—that is, represented—perfection of the idea of God (entailing a perfect cause of its "objective being").[10]

For some theologians, the multiplicity of proofs was a positive wealth. François Diroys, for example, in his popular *Preuves . . . de la Religion Chréstienne et Catholique . . .* (1683), employed them all, and observed that a nonbeliever "would have to want not to be persuaded," given the strength and diversity of arguments for God's being.[11] For most theologians and philosophers, however, mutually exclusive choices had to be made.

Convinced of the impossibility of a priori demonstration, scholastics subjected the Cartesian "proofs" to the most intense criticism and, indeed, ridicule, presenting them as question-begging and absurd. In Latin and French theological tomes, in formal and informal philosophical treatises, and in discussions in the more popular learned journals of the day—the defenders of the "old" philosophy maintained a steady stream of acerbic refutation. Cartesians on the whole defended Descartes's arguments as the only successful proofs of God's existence, and replied in kind to the scholastic a posteriori "demonstrations," dismissing them as unconvincing and insufficient. At the same time, classical and historical scholarship, missionary descriptions, and travel literature convinced more and more minds that the argument from "universal consent," already deemed philosophically nondemonstrative, in fact rested upon empirically false premises. While occasional voices were raised against such mutual theological fratricide, most authors defended their efforts in the same terms expressed by Dom Robert Desgabets: "It is of extreme importance to let nothing enter into proofs of the existence of God but what is utterly solid."[12] To eliminate a flawed proof, Nicolas L'Herminier explained in his *Summa Theologiae* (1701–1703), was to deny comfort to incredulity; unconvincing arguments caused the greatest harm and prejudice to theology.[13]

The result of such polemic and mutual critcism, we shall see, was indeed striking: by the early eighteenth century, every proof of the existence of God had been refuted by theologians and philosophers of impeccable orthodoxy, in works published with the theological approval and ecclesiastical *imprimatur* of superiors loyal to the respective philosophical camps. The atheistic literature of the eighteenth century embodied precisely such refutations.

Early in the patristic age, it was common for Catholic apologists to contrast the confusion and mutual contradictions of the pagan philosophers, their wars of words, to the harmony and accord of Christian thinkers. The debates and disagreements of pagan authors, it often was urged, made clear their failures as would-be teachers of truth. The harmony and accord of Christian thought, of course, if ever it had been obtained, certainly had not persisted in the early, medieval, or early-modern periods of theology, not even on issues of how best to establish the preambles of the faith. The latter debates, nevertheless, had occurred before a limited reading public, composed most disproportionately of theologians. By the last half of the seventeenth century, in an age that increasingly demanded *évidence* for belief, and in a Catholic intellectual community ostensibly bound by the Church's prior declaration that the foundations of the faith were true according to natural lights and philosophy, the acrimonious scholastic–Cartesian debates were engaging a far broader learned community, and finding their way into popular and vernacular publications. It is not astonishing that a minor current of atheism arose from such philosophical division, and we need not fabricate a history of free thought to find the source of its arguments.

What has come to be called Descartes's "ontological" proof was understood by his contemporaries as follows: what we conceive as necessarily entailed by the essence of an entity (e.g., of a triangle, three angles whose sum equals two right angles) actually belongs to it; since actual existence is necessarily entailed by the essence of the most perfect being (its nonexistence contradicting its essence as most perfect being), the perfect being actually exists.

Since Kant, most criticism of this proof has centered on Descartes's use of "existence" as a predicate, but for the scholastics, the problem above all lay in the Cartesian assumption of what in fact required proof: that we indeed had knowledge of the most perfect being. Aquinas, they believed, had identified the same "error" in Anselm's *Proslogion* and Bonaventure's *Quaestiones disputatae*.[14] Summarizing a generation of such argument, the Jesuit Gabriel Daniel, in his widely read *Voiage au Monde de Descartes* (1690; reprinted 1691), concluded that Descartes's proof was a "pure paralogism," presupposing that the idea whose necessary attributes were under examination was "a real being, that is to say, [one] which represents a real, at least a possible object." From the idea of "a knowing, feeling horse," he explained, Descartes could not deduce its actual sentience, for first, the possible and actual existence of such a horse would have to be assured. For Daniel, Descartes's "proof" precisely did not establish the *"évidence"* that the idea of God is a real rather than chimerical idea; it still lacked "the ordinary demonstrations" of the actuality allegedly represented by the idea of a supremely perfect being. For Daniel, these would require "reflection on the [external] things which prove the existence of God," for it in no way belonged to the essence of "Being" to be "supremely perfect Being." Indeed, without demonstration from the facts of the world, Descartes's idea of God seemed far more chimerical than real. One must first be convinced that God exists, and only then can one examine his essence.[15]

From the perspective of more formal scholastic analysis, Descartes had confused the nature of entities that exist as ideas of the mind (*a parte intel-*

lectus) with that of entities that exist in the actual world (*a parte rei*), failing to see that no inferences may be drawn from the former to the latter. That the *idea* of a perfect being entailed the *idea* of necessary actual existence was indubitable; that it entailed the *actuality* of necessary actual existence was precisely what could not be proven. As Bishop Pierre-Daniel Huet put the case, Descartes furtively had defined the *"est"* which pertained to the properties of an idea (known thus far to exist only in the understanding) as *"existe 'a parte rei,'"* which, alas, was the very issue in dispute. What should be added to each proposition of Descartes's proof, in Huet's view, is the phrase "in the manner that it exists," such that "if [God] existed only in the understanding, he existed necessarily only in the understanding." [16] To put the matter more simply, *if* a unicorn actually existed (which would require proof a posteriori), it must be as a creature with one horn; if God actually existed (which would require proof a posteriori), it must be as a being with necessary existence. That was all Descartes had shown.

Prevailing scholastic ontology reinforced this criticism. As Jean Du Hamel, professor emeritus of philosophy at the University of Paris, explained it, ideas were only "modifications of the mind," and thus were categorically distinct from "external objects"; a formal proof could not deduce the latter from the former. An atheist would claim, Du Hamel noted, that nothing supremely perfect could exist *a parte rei;* that the idea of such a being could exist no atheist would ever doubt. Once the actual existence of God was demonstrated a posteriori, we then could learn, of course, that the modification of our mind that was our idea of an infinitely perfect being in fact represented in some significant manner to us what was true about God the Creator. [17]

For the scholastics, proof of God from the *idea* men have of him relied upon a term ("idea") about which the Cartesians were hopelessly confused. The scholastics defined "idea" as *"species rei cognitae in mente existens,"* and believed that neither Descartes nor any of his followers had offered a consequential understanding of such mental modifications. Michael Morus, *principal* of the collège de Navarre, briefly *recteur* of the University of Paris, and, from 1701, professor of philosophy at the collège Royal, confidently wrote in 1692 that the Cartesians could not establish the innateness of ideas (the very existence of atheists demonstrating that the idea of God, in particular, was not innate), nor explain the manner of their formation and being. They had failed to understand that "the idea of a thing is its definition," and thus were incapable of a "natural knowledge of things," for they consulted not nature but merely their own definitional terms. This was the arrogant and illogical flaw at the heart of their theology. Their very use of the term "God," he argued, was not a reference to the known Supreme Being whose existence is demonstrated by the world itself, but, rather, was an ambiguous name assigned to an assumed being about whom they knew nothing.[18] The Jesuit François Perrin, in his *Manuale Theologicum* (1710), explained that the nature of all particular ideas required examination in the light of experience and authority. Men often conceived of "chimerical existence," he observed, and believed themselves "aware" of chimerical beings. What the seeker after knowledge of God required, however, was judgment a posteriori of His existence, not awareness of his own fancies.[19] François-Marie Assermet, *docteur en Sorbonne* and teacher of theology at the *grand couvent des Cordeliers* (and self-proclaimed Scotist, not Thomist), concluded, in his *Theologia-scholastica-positiva* (1713), that the Cartesians, to secure this specious proof, declared their own idea of God to be innate in all mankind. Were this so, he observed, proof would be superfluous. Descartes's disciples, however, need not be taken seriously, for all "authorities" agreed, he proclaimed, that God's existence could not be proven a priori.[20]

Descartes's "first" proof of God's existence, that the cause of the idea of infinite perfection must itself be infinitely perfect, a cause necessarily having as much perfection as its "objective"—represented—effect, was equally subjected to criticism on the grounds of a Cartesian confusion about ideas. Scholastic (and other) critics were so acerbic on the subject of the Cartesian use of the term "objective being" that the prominent Cartesian Régis was obliged to retort, in 1692, that "philosophers are free to define words as they wish, provided they are explicit about it."[21] As understood by his century, Descartes's proof from the "objective being" of the idea of God was based on the distinction between the nature of an idea as a modification of the mind (its "formal being") and as a representation of some particular entity (its "objective being"). For Descartes, one could in all instances, save one, analyze what an idea represented to us, without thereby knowing whether such a represented being had actual existence. The exception was the case of a perfect being, for on the principle that any effect must have a cause of equal or greater perfection, the cause of the objective being of the idea of infinite perfection must itself be infinitely perfect. Stated less formally, the cause (or source) of the idea of a perfect being could not be an imperfect mind or being (for they could have no infinite perfection to be represented), but only an actual perfect being. Seeing such an argument as a priori despite its causal nature, scholastics again argued against the possibility of any proof from the mere idea of God.

The most frequent scholastic objection to this Cartesian "proof" was simply that no idea in the human mind could embody in any significant ontological sense the perfection that is God. Although Gabriel Daniel believed the principle that "the cause of the idea must contain formally or eminently all [of the idea's] perfections" to be arbitrary and unproven, he argued that even were it granted, there remained a fundamental difference between "possessing" and "representing" perfection or its degrees. If the idea of perfection "possessed" actual perfection, he reasoned, Descartes's causal principle might be applicable. However, this idea merely "represented" perfection, and since no human idea "represented" anything except in a manner consistent with the imperfections of the human mind, it "represented" perfection imperfectly, and thus could have an imperfect cause of its being. In short, "the perfection of an idea is not measured by the nobility of the object it represents, but by the manner in which it represents it, which being very imperfect in the case in question, cannot be infinite."[22]

Bishop Pierre-Daniel Huet's frequently translated and reprinted *Censura philosophiae Cartesianae* (1698) described this proof as a Cartesian "game," wholly dependent on the gratuitous assumption that the "object" of an idea was identical with the actual being represented, which was precisely the question at issue. Since the manner in which men thought was imperfect, and since God's actual infinity and infinite perfections could not be embraced by any imperfect human idea, the idea of infinite perfection that we possessed required no actual infinitely perfect cause. Once one realized that "the idea of an infinite and infinitely perfect entity that is in us is finite," the absurdity of the "proof" was patent. The only Cartesian alternative was the equally absurd equation of two categorically distinct entities: the idea of God and God himself. Since ideas were merely "modifications of our minds," they all could be attributed to finite causes.[23]

Responding to Cartesian rejoinders that such criticisms would be appropriate only if the Cartesians had attempted to prove God from the "formal" rather than the "objective" being of the idea of God, Du Hamel argued that this essential Cartesian distinction was "confused" and "false." The "power [*vertu*] of representing," he insisted, could not be separated from the "formal being of ideas," since the former was merely an attribute of the latter. Indeed, he claimed, a proper conception of the "formal being" of ideas would be the power to represent and modify imperfectly; a proper conception of "objective being" would be not the active power to represent, but the passive power to be represented. The very question at issue, then, was whether we knew God himself to be represented in all his infinity and infinite perfection in any human idea. Since all Cartesians would admit that men do not know God "in an infinite and comprehensive manner," Du Hamel concluded, the question clearly must be resolved in the negative. To suppose that the "idea of God" is "the actual perception of

God" is a paralogism, for whether innate or acquired, whether represent-ing infinite perfection positively (as the Cartesians claimed) or by negation of finite imperfection (as most theologians believed, Du Hamel noted), an idea's manner of representing is always finite and imperfect.[24] When Régis replied that Descartes's proof was compelling for "a being in which we know as many perfections as we are capable of knowing,"[25] Du Hamel re-sponded scornfully that such a redefinition of infinity had nothing to do with the infinity of God. The creed, he wrote, did not announce the most perfect being of which we can conceive, but "a being in which there are infinite perfections," the divine attributes that the mind of man in no way could contain.[26] Real perfection, several theologians added, had no prior "cause" beyond its own essence; if the *idea* of God possessed real infinite perfection, it would *be* God, and thus unamenable to proof that cate-gorized it as effect.[27]

To the critics of Descartes, thus, Cartesian "proofs" were of no value whatsoever in establishing the existence of God. As Daniel bluntly put the matter: "if there were not other demonstrations of God but these [Carte-sian proofs], *there would be none at all.*" Given this, he advised disciples of Descartes not to criticize the common Thomistic proofs: "For if it were true that the other [proofs] were not more compelling in comparison to these [Cartesian proofs], one would conclude from this principle excep-tionally nefarious consequences against the existence of the First Being."[28] The drama of philosophical theology in the late seventeenth century, how-ever, was precisely that the Cartesians could no more heed Daniel's warn-ing than the scholastics could refrain from refuting Descartes.

For most Cartesians, the scholastic demonstrations suffered from the inherent weaknesses of all a posteriori argument: the errant senses could not overcome doubt with logical certainty; essences and spiritual beings were inaccessible to the senses; from finite effects, no infinite cause conceiv-ably could be inferred; from imperfect beings, no perfect cause conceivably could be known. The most celebrated Cartesian of the late seventeenth cen-tury, Pierre-Sylvain Régis, put the case quite simply: "no created thing can be the exemplary cause of the idea of God." The finite, imperfect be-ings of our unreliable sensory experience could not possess perfection, and thus could not give to us the idea of infinity and perfection, and, indeed, could be no source, ever, of any certainty. Either the idea of God was in-nate and essential to the soul and compelled belief both by its very nature and by the necessity of God alone as its author, or there could be *no* idea or knowledge of God or his existence. "The soul," he concluded, "could not form the idea of God without [first] knowing God, and if it knows Him, it has no need to form the idea of Him."[29] Proof a posteriori was impossible and absurd. Adrien Baillet's widely read *Vie de Monsieur Des-Cartes* (1691) quoted its hero as having observed, in 1637, that to win support for his manner of proof, he would have to give full force to the sceptical criticism of evidence drawn from the senses and rescue the theological mind from the sensory world. The simple truth, Baillet quoted him, was "'that it is not possible to know the certainty and evidence of reasons which prove the existence of God . . . except by remembering distinctly those [reasons] that make us see the uncertainty in all knowledge that we have of material beings.'" [30]

In 1700, in the pages of the widely circulated *Histoire des Ouvrages des Savans*, the Cartesian Huguenot theologian Isaac Jacquelot argued that the force of Descartes's rational proofs would be evident if only the senses and imagination "did not distract the understanding, and did not occupy it with corporeal objects." The Thomistic arguments for God's existence, all drawn from our observations of such "corporeal objects," might well be *consistent* with our a priori knowledge of God, but, he insisted, they were unconvincing as proofs, for they depended entirely on our prior rational knowledge of the actual existence of "necessary existence." The senses could not represent to us this necessarily existent Perfect Being, for they "represented merely material beings, which, unable to be perfect, contain *no necessary existence*. One thus must listen to reason alone. . . ." [31] The Cartesian Benedictine Dom François Lamy, in 1696, had warned the Thomists in yet starker terms. The very use of sense data in demonstration, he wrote, and, indeed, the very certainty of the faith and validity of religious knowledge, all depended on a priori knowledge of the existence of God, "in that it is necessary that [a priori metaphysics] prove for them at least that there is a God, that God is not a deceiver, and that His testimony is infallible." Without a priori truth, Lamy concluded, no certainty in natural philosophy, theology, or religion was possible. [32]

Bishop Huet, confronted by such arguments, had charged that the Cartesians were circular in proving God by logical certainty and the validity of logical certainty by the existence of a perfect God who could not be a deceiver. [33] Régis responded for the Cartesians that there indeed did exist an axiomatic certainty in rational knowledge, but that this led to knowledge of God as a perfect being who could not be a deceiver. This proof alone, he averred, made possible any knowledge drawn from our experience of the world. The implication was clear: by their very nature all a posteriori proofs were question begging and inconclusive. [34] In his *Système de philosophie* (1690), Régis appealed to the scholastics to understand that St. Thomas's "proofs" were "moral," not "metaphysical"; that is to say, that they might sound plausible and might be affectively influential, but were in no manner logically entailed and necessarily convincing. Either one proved the Perfect Being by the self-contradiction of his nonexistence and by his necessary existence as objective cause of the idea of perfection, or one "could advance no proposition that is wholly necessary to prove his existence. . . ." Régis conceded that "our mind, which is finite, cannot enclose the power of God, which is infinite," but he insisted that it was exactly this certainty that proved God from the "objective being" of such an idea, for its source could not be the imperfect world appealed to in a posteriori argument.[35] To those who found Descartes's proof "too metaphysical and too subtle," Jacquelot warned that these were the *only* certain proofs, and that "one harms truth more than one contributes to its establishment when one employs either false or captious arguments to prove it."[36] The rejection of Descartes's demonstrations, the Cartesians were urging, left theology defenseless against the would-be atheist.

Indeed, for most Cartesians, the scholastic critique of the "objective being" of the idea of God gave fatal weapons to the would-be atheist. If our idea of God were not, in fact, a clear and distinct idea of an infinitely perfect being, then we had *no* knowledge of God. The Cartesian La Coudraye, in his *Traitez de métaphysique* (1693), agreed that God is "above us," but he warned the scholastics that "they must take care that from wanting to give an exalted notion of Him, they do not make us lose sight of His true idea, which is nothing other than that of the infinitely perfect being." By saying that no idea could embody real knowledge of God's perfection (which, he granted, was not the same as full "comprehension" of God's perfection), and by limiting their "knowledge of God" to what could be represented by the imperfect world, scholastics threatened to destroy the very idea of God. What we derived from the senses were, at best, "inner sentiments, or . . . purely human opinions," and, at worst, pure chimeras, but "the real and positive perfections" alone constituted God, and these could be known only by their necessary connection to the essence of God objectively represented in the idea of God. To say that "God is," from a posteriori proof, was to posit merely *a* being; such a "proof," however, by scholastic admission, did not give knowledge of his essence, that is to say, of his perfections. Yet God *is* his perfections. The scholastics "have confused Him with a certain phantom that their imagination has formed from the collection of the negations of all that they do know [the imperfections of the world]." To avoid this awful pitfall, one must "raise oneself above all of the prejudices of the senses, the imagination and the passions, and consult, uniquely, and with strict attention, the idea of the perfect being."[37]

In short, each camp was proclaiming to the reading public that by the methods of its adversaries, God's existence could not be known. Daniel reiterated, in a new edition of his work in 1702, that nothing could save Cartesian proofs from their circularity, for "it will always be pitiable and ridiculous to want to demonstrate the existence of a God who is good and a non-deceiver, in order to convince oneself that 'what one conceives of clearly is true': since it is just so impossible to demonstrate this existence to oneself without being first convinced of this principle. . . ." Thus, he concluded, "[Descartes's] principal demonstrations of the existence of God have nothing solid and are pure paralogisms adroitly disguised as proofs."[38] Huet reminded the Cartesians that "Great philosophers in the past had examined their idea of Divinity, and concluded diversely that God was plural, corporeal, bounded by shape, mortal, or even non-existent." In light of such facts about the "idea" of God, he warned, how dare anyone believe "that God is what he thinks!"[39] To this, Régis replied directly that if our idea of the infinitely perfect were not a true idea of such a being, how could we know if any a posteriori proof established the existence of such a being? "One cannot know that a thing exists," he concluded emphatically, "without knowing in general what it is."[40] In short, then, for the Cartesians, if one did not know the perfection of God to be represented clearly in the idea of God, then no knowledge of God was possible. For the scholastics, of course, the argument was above all a question of the *adequacy* of our idea of God's essence, on which the Cartesian proofs seemed to depend. The Cartesians, however, attempted to ridicule the scholastic critique by arguing that it made any knowledge of God impossible. As Jacquelot stated it: "If [Descartes's] argument [from the idea of God] is not demonstrative, one must admit that one can no longer know any entity, nor speak of it, because we know them, judge of them and speak of them only with regard to our lights, and in conformity with the ideas that we have of them."[41]

In several ways, the emergence of Malebranchism from Cartesianism perhaps ought to have had a calming effect on this increasingly strident debate over the establishment of the most essential preamble of the faith. Malebranche conceded the need for "sensible proofs" of the existence of God, given the inattentiveness of most "sensual" minds to reason, and proclaimed that these existed in profusion, indeed, that "everything that God has done proves Him . . . everything that we see, everything that we feel proves Him."[42] Given this, he concluded, "there is no truth which has more proofs than that of the existence of God."[43] Malebranche's system of occasional causes, with its insistence that God is the only (and only conceivable) efficacious cause, appeared to constitute an independent a posteriori proof in and of itself, from the very phenomena of mental and corporeal activity. Finally, Malebranche and his disciples conceded the scholastic critique of the distinction between the "formal" and "objective" being of the "idea of God" central to Cartesian metaphysics, and claimed that purged of its general errors concerning the nature of ideas, Descartes's proof from necessary existence was enhanced and rendered incontrovertible.[44] In fact, however, Malebranchism worked to exacerbate all of the already sharp divisions of the theologians and philosophers with regard to proof of God's existence. The concessions to a posteriori proof were wholly subverted by Malebranche's epistemological principles, and he himself, we shall see, drew the appropriate conclusions concerning the task of theology. Most dramatically, Malebranche's "enhancement" of Descartes's "ontological" proof both set the defenders of a priori demonstration into a fratricidal mutual refutation of their own, and opened the a priori camp to a new set of particularly vehement objections. In short, Malebranchism would serve to discredit further the claims of a posteriori knowledge of God and to formulate the case for a priori knowledge of him in a manner that exposed it to the most outraged criticism.

When critics argued that he encouraged infidelity by establishing God's existence only by discredited a priori proof, Malebranche replied that even if he were wrong about the solidity of such metaphysical proof, he also repeatedly had offered "sensible proofs" in his works.[45] His claim indeed was correct, for in his *Conversations Chrétiennes* and his *Entretien d'un philosophe chrétien et d'un philosophe chinois sur l'existence et la nature de Dieu*, he had added such proof to that of the self-evidence of God's existence. His a posteriori demonstration followed, above all, from the ontological principles of his occasionalism, namely, the impotence of either matter or soul to exist, act, or interact of their own substantial natures. He concluded from our experience and knowledge of *any* entity that "There is thus a God, and if there were no God, I would not be pricked [by a thorn], I would not feel anything, I would not see anything, I would not know anything."[46] Nevertheless, as Malebranche made clear again and again, he agreed wholeheartedly with the central Cartesian critique of a posteriori proof, namely, that any discussion, knowledge, or a posteriori demonstration of the Supreme Being *presupposed* rational certainty of God's existence as infinitely perfect being.

Thus, in his *Entretiens sur la métaphysique* (1688), Malebranche in his own way reiterated Régis's response to Huet, insisting that prior knowledge of God was essential to any question of his being, "for otherwise, when you ask me if there is a God or infinite being, you would be posing a ridiculous question by means of a proposition whose terms you would not understand. It is as if you would ask, is there a 'Blictri,' that is to say, a certain thing, without knowing what."[47] Further, Malebranche asserted as an epistemological principle that "one can give an *exact demonstration* of a truth only by showing that it has a necessary liaison with its principle," and stated as a given that "the notion of an infinitely perfect being contains no necessary relationship to any creature."[48] Finally, Malebranche forcefully retained the Cartesian notion that only prior certainty of a God who could not be a deceiver established the grounds of any other knowledge from which a posteriori demonstrations of God could be drawn, arguing, in the *Recherche de la Vérité* (1674–75), that "All the ordinary proofs of the existence and perfections of God drawn from the existence and perfections of His creatures . . . are not convincing given [the hypothetical supposition of] a wicked demon who deceives us." He conceded that the a posteriori arguments proved "that there is a power superior to us," but, he insisted, "they do not fully demonstrate that there is a God or an infinitely perfect being."[49] Indeed, with the most ardent rationalist Cartesians, he insisted, in the very work written to demonstrate his piety, that the faith itself, and all belief through Revelation, presupposed such rational conviction, "for do you not see that the certitude of the Faith comes from the authority of a God who speaks and who cannot be a deceiver?" "If you are not thus convinced by reason that there is a God," he asked, "how will you be convinced that He has spoken?"[50] Whatever his sensitivity to charges that he had placed metaphysical philosophy *above* theology, Malebranche stood by his claim in the *Recherche de la Vérité* that "even the certitude of the faith depends on the knowledge that reason gives of the existence of God," for "the existence of God and the infallibility of divine authority are natural knowledge rather than articles of faith."[51] How did we know that God could not deceive us? It followed from certainty of his existence as infinitely perfect being. How did we achieve such certainty? "[It] is contained in the idea of the infinite. . . ."[52] So much for "sensible proofs"! True to such principles and conclusions, Malebranche advised the seeker after knowledge of God to ignore the senses, "this exterior and sensible man who is incapable of intelligence," and "learn . . . to enter into yourself and be attentive to internal truth." "Cease," he warned the would-be believer, "cease consulting your senses, if you want to hear the replies of Truth. She lives in the innermost part of reason."[53]

Malebranche and his disciples, however, did not accept the Cartesian proof from the "objective" being of the idea of God as any part of "the replies of Truth." In his ontology of ideas, of course, Malebranche was best known for his attempt to refute the conception of ideas as "modifications of the soul." For Malebranche, in his most celebrated phrase, we "saw all things in God," ideas being eternal archetypes in the Divine Being and not modal attributes or actions of the human mind. In that sense, then, first of all, the Cartesian distinction between the "formal" and "objective" being of any idea was based on a false ontological understanding. The "orthodox" Cartesians such as Régis, however, compounded their "error" by asserting, concerning the "idea of God," that an idea considered as a finite modification of the mind could represent to us the infinite perfections of God. For the Malebranchistes this was inconceivable, and the scholastics were patently correct in their criticism of a proof thus formulated. As Malebranche, we shall see, repeatedly defined the issue, it was self-evident: "nothing finite could represent the infinite."

Thus, for the Malebranchistes, any effort to prove the existence of God from the supposed representational reality of a finite modification of the mind violated the clearest principles of ontology, epistemology, and logic, and their criticisms of this particular Cartesian demonstration were as vigorous as (and, at times, indistinguishable from) those of the scholastics. In the *Recherche de la Vérité*, Malebranche wrote against the "gross error" of "those who support this proposition, that the finite can represent the infinite, and that the modalities of our soul, though finite, are essentially representative of the infinitely perfect being." It is wholly evident, he urged, "that the soul, that its modalities, that a finite thing cannot represent the infinite."[54] Almost a decade later, in reply to Antoine Arnauld's defense of both the Cartesian conception of ideas as representational modes of the human mind and Descartes's proof of God from the objective perfection of our idea of him, Malebranche charged that Arnauld was attempting to uphold "the most insupportable opinion that can be imagined, namely, that the modality of his soul is actually representative of God Himself and of infinity. . . ."[55] In 1693, replying to Régis, Malebranche reiterated his conviction that "all the modifications of a finite being are necessarily finite, for the modification of a substance [is] merely its manner of being. . . [and] our mind is finite."[56] And in 1704, ending his twenty-year debate on this issue with the now deceased Arnauld, Malebranche posed the issue with utmost clarity: "Is it indeed evident that an infinite cause is necessary to give to the soul a finite modality?" He answered his own question: it is evident that "the modalities of the soul cannot be representative of the infinite in all senses, that is to say, of God or the infinitely perfect being."[57] His disciple, Henri Lelevel, devoted the second chapter of his *La vraye et la fausse métaphysique* (1694), a critique of Régis's philosophy, to a defense of the proposition that "the soul does not have enough reality to contain the Idea of God" and a sustained criticism of the Cartesian proof of God from his necessity as cause of the objective perfection of that idea. The distinction between "formal" and "objective" being, he urged, was unintelligible and question begging. Régis could not proceed from the finite, what is "in him, what is his own," to the infinite, "what is outside of him." He should concede to the scholastics that his mind does not contain "the idea of God," but merely a finite perception.[58]

Indeed, for Lelevel, the scholastics were correct in asserting that the Cartesians "cannot boast of having invented any demonstration of the existence of God," and Régis's critic, Du Hamel, properly had placed his idea of God "in the ranks of the creatures, and judges by this idea, as by the rest of the creatures [a posteriori], that there is a God."[59] If we accepted Régis's principles, we would conclude that "the infinite being . . . exists only in the understanding and, as a consequence, has no objective reality."[60]

Malebranche, however, most emphatically did *not* agree that Descartes had formulated *no* compelling proof of God's existence. In Book IV of the *Recherche*, he offered "Descartes's proof of God" as an example of the sort of metaphysical demonstration to which all men would consent were it not for the distractions of the senses. It was axiomatic in metaphysics, he wrote, and "even more evident than the axiom that the whole is greater than its part," that "one is assured of a thing that one conceives clearly to be contained in the idea that represents it." Descartes's proof was absolute and categorically compelling: necessary existence is clearly contained in the idea of the infinitely perfect being. Just as the mind must consent to the "greater" quantity of the whole compared to the part, or to the "four angles of a square," or the valley beneath any mountain, so must it consent to Descartes's conclusion. To the scholastic charge that it was a circular argument that followed only if one *assumed* God to exist, Malebranche replied that no one added to the necessary four angles of a square the phrase "if it is *supposed* that a square has four angles." There was only one possible deduction from Descartes's demonstration: "Thus, God or the infinitely perfect being exists necessarily."[61]

The problem that Malebranche faced in defending Descartes's proof, however, arose from his criticism of the latter's notion of an "idea," and thus, of the "idea of God." How could there be an "idea of God" in Malebranchist philosophy if ideas were archetypes in God of that which he created, and, as such, if they were particular, finite entities that could not represent to us infinite perfection? What, then, was this "idea of God," for Malebranche, on which Descartes's proof depended?

Arnauld had challenged Malebranche on just this issue, charging that despite the latter's proclamation that this was "the most beautiful proof," his principle that nothing finite could be the idea of God "had ruined [it]."[62] To such charges, Malebranche replied that far from ruining Descartes's proof, his ontological clarification had enhanced it and removed the final barrier from peoples' ability to grasp its self-evidence. He had made it, he claimed, "more complete and more convincing." [63] Addressing Arnauld's criticism directly, in 1684, he averred that he always had maintained, "without difficulty" for Descartes's proof, that "with regard to the infinite, one knows it by itself, and not by an *idea*, because I know that there is no archetype on which God has been formed, and that nothing can represent God." [64] Indeed, in the very first volume of the *Recherche*, Malebranche had assured his readers that "one cannot conceive that the idea of an infinitely perfect being, which is that that we have of God, is something created," and had offered that impossibility as proof that the infinitely perfect being is known directly in itself and, thus, exists. God was known "by an immediate and direct view." [65] Forced to clarify what he possibly could mean by the "idea of God" in such a case, Malebranche, in volume two of the *Recherche*, offered a "Clarification of Descartes's Proof." Of every entity known save one, he wrote, "we do not see it in itself or by itself, . . . but only by the vision [*vue*] of certain perfections that are in God, that represent it." Thus, one can see the essence of any creature without seeing its existence, since necessary existence is not contained in the idea that represents it. In the case of the infinitely perfect being, however, "one cannot see Him except in Himself, for there is nothing finite that can represent the infinite. One cannot see God, thus, except that He exists: one cannot see the essence of an infinitely perfect being without seeing its existence." Thinking of God, then, is direct proof of "the efficacity [and existence] of His substance," for "the infinite has not and cannot have an archetype or an idea distinct from itself, that represents it." [66] Although he used the term "the idea of God," he explained explicitly what he really meant: "One sees [*voit*] that there is a God as soon as one sees the infinite, because necessary existence is contained in the idea of the infinite, *or, to speak more clearly, because one can see the infinite only in itself.*" [67] As he specified to Arnauld in 1684, "Sometimes I use the word 'idea' generally, for what is the immediate object of the mind when one thinks," but with reference to the Divinity, "this 'idea' will be God Himself." [68] In the *Entretiens sur la Métaphysique* . . . (1684), Malebranche ceased to use the term "idea" in its "general" sense, and stated the ontology of knowledge of God's existence without reservation: "God or the infinite being is not visible by means of an idea that represents Him"; God is known "without idea, . . . in Himself." [69] In 1707, he reiterated the formulation: "the idea of God can be only God, since nothing finite can represent the infinite." [70] What Huet had offered as reductio ad absurdum had come to pass as a positive claim.

Such a formulation and argument was not without its appeal, it should be noted, beyond the immediate circles of Malebranche's disciples. The eclectic theologian Jean-Claude Sommier, for example, doctor of theology at the University of Dôle, and later apostolic protonotary and archbishop of Césarée, explicitly argued in his *Histoire dogmatique de la religion* (1708– 11) that the idea of God was indeed God himself. The *Histoire dogmatique* was commissioned by and dedicated to Pope Clement XI, approved by the *docteurs-régent* of theology at Dôle, and, more remarkably, by two *docteurs* of the Sorbonne and the Jesuit *recteur* of the college d'Epinal, and bore the imprimatur of the bishop of Toul. Following Malebranche, without attribution, Sommier conflated the "objective" and "formal" being of the "idea of God," stated as axiomatic the principle that nothing finite "could represent or copy" the infinite, and concluded that our awareness of God as the most perfect being was a direct, immediate apperception of the substance of God. For Sommier, "when our soul knows and perceives the infinite being, there is nothing between our soul that knows and God who is known."[71] Such opinions would elicit a theological firestorm.

First, for the Cartesians themselves, or, more precisely, those non-Malebranchist Cartesians who maintained the concept of an idea as a representational modification of the mind, Malebranche's "clarification," as Arnauld had written, destroyed rather than strengthened Descartes's proof. What allowed Descartes to demonstrate God, Arnauld specified, was precisely that his existence was entailed by something that did *not* presuppose his existence, namely, the idea of God, distinct from God, from which his existence necessarily followed. Malebranche's proof, on the other hand, indeed "presupposed" what it must prove, namely, a perfect being "intimately united to my soul."[72] Further, for Arnauld, the very notion of knowledge without representational idea was unintelligible, and put all issues of clear and distinct knowledge into question. It fatally undermined the force and clarity of Descartes's proof, and, indeed, of all proof, and separated irrevocably the "object known" and "the perception of the object known," which could be linked only by "a representational being."[73]

In 1708, Malebranche's *Entretien d'un philosophe chrétien et d'un philosophe chinois . . .* had sought to strengthen the proof of God from consideration of infinity by giving its readers a full and clear sense of why nothing but God himself could be the object of such consideration. God is not "a particular being," Malebranche explained, "a this or a that"; rather, He is "the Being that contains in His essence all that there is of reality or perfection in all things, the infinite Being in all senses, in a word, Being." Although it is "incomprehensible" to the finite mind, he continued, God's infinity is such that He is "Being without any restriction or limitation. He contains in Him . . . all the perfections, all that there is of true reality in all beings created and possible . . . even everything that there is of reality or perfection in matter, the least and most imperfect of beings. . . ." Given this, how could anything "represent" God to us?[74]

Such formulations of God's infinity had been implicit if not quite so concisely explicit in Malebranche's theology, and Régis, for the Cartesians, already had charged him with reducing God to the general idea of universal nature and with making all beings formally parts of His essence.[75] For the Jesuit *Journal de Trévoux*, however, reviewing the *Entretien* of 1708, Malebranche at last had betrayed himself. God *is* "a particular being," the Jesuit Marquer challenged, "a this or a that," known from works whose reality was wholly distinguishable from that of the divine essence. Malebranche's consistent manner of writing about God "can well be congruent with the idea of the totality of the universe." In Malebranche's system, God is "all being" and touches our mind directly with his essence: were this the case, we would possess knowledge of all beings in all their reality, which we do not. Whatever Malebranche's intentions, his "proof from infinity" reduced itself to proof from "merely an infinity that contains in itself the reality of an infinity of things *of which our mind conceives*," which is quite distinct from any actual "infinity in all perfections . . . and by its very infinity distinguished from everything else." Such a "proof," Marquer concluded, "is not very much to advance for the existence of [the distinct and truly infinite] God." Malebranche had advanced "an idea that annihilates the Divinity by reducing it to the totality of the world."[76]

For others, the "problem" with Malebranche's proof was equally ominous, but in a different sense, and it reflected back upon the entire Cartesian enterprise. In 1687, the Huguenot theologian Pierre Poiret, who recently had been a Cartesian himself, now warned that the Cartesians were making "an idol" of "the idea of God so celebrated at the present time." It was not without "its dignity," he insisted, but "the idea of God . . . is not God Himself." Indeed, "very inappropriately posited in the place of the living God, despite its being merely the work of the creature, [the idea of God] leaves the soul truly atheistic and empty of the true God."[77] The Jesuit François Perrin's *Manuale theologicum* (1710) compared the Cartesians to "the atheists" they sought to refute, for the former also ignored the existence of the actual God known from his works, believing that they knew him when in fact they knew only an idea whose conditional nature they failed to understand.[78] When the Jesuits threatened one of the Malebranchistes of their order, Rodolphe Du Tertre, with banishment to unpleasant tasks in unpleasant places unless he recanted his philosophical apostasy, the chastened Du Tertre wrote a scathing critique of

Cartesian and Malebranchist philosophy designed to satisfy his superiors. His *Réfutation d'un nouvel système de métaphysique* (1715) denied that the finite mind, before beatitude, could have any "knowledge" of the infinite that was not merely negation of the finite, and that it was thus impossible to believe that we could, in this life, see God "in Himself by an immediate and direct vision [*vue*]." More dramatically, he charged that Malebranche and his disciples, all of whom were themselves disciples of Descartes, had substituted the idea of God for God himself, and, in the final analyis, worshipped a God who was purely "a being of [human] logic," conceived of as Being in general. He cautioned, however, against charging this new school with actual atheism.[79]

This caution was not exhibited by the doughty and eccentric Jesuit Thomist Jean Hardouin, who for a generation argued that the divinization of the "idea of God" lay at the very heart of the theology of Descartes, Régis, and Malebranche and was, in the final analysis, wholly atheistic. Hardouin's views on Cartesian and Malebranchist "atheism" were not *published* until his posthumous *Opera Varia* (1733), but he lectured all and sundry on the topic within the Jesuit milieu and circulated manuscripts on the subject. Indeed, his views were so well known that in 1715, his former disciple, later rationalist Malebranchist, then fideist, then Protestant heretic, the ex-Jesuit François de La Pillonnière, published an abstract entitled *L'Athéisme découvert par le R. P. Hardouin . . .* , which was reprinted in Themiseul de Saint Hyacinthe's *Mémoires littéraires* (1716), to explicate and clarify Hardouin's views, and to satisfy the curiosity of the public.[80]

La Pillonnière had been an intimate of Hardouin before a reading of Malebranche, at Hardouin's request ironically, converted him to Malebranchism. He communicated to Malebranche's admirer, the Jesuit Y. M. André, the lectures that Hardouin had repeated "a thousand times": "the ideas that P. M. [Malebranche] admits are in fact nothing distinct from perceptions of the mind. They are only pure chimeras, beings of reason, the universals of the schools, which are nothing *a parte rei*. His infinity, as a consequence, his idea of being in general, . . . in a word, [his] God, is not the real God."[81] In Hardouin's manuscripts and published work, he further argued that in Descartes's own philosophy, God was defined as that being represented by and causing "the idea of the Infinite." Such a being, Hardouin reasoned, is a nullity, for all philosophers save the Cartesians "taught that the idea of the Infinite is negative; and that who says 'Infinite' says simply 'that which has no limits or whose end we do not see.'" At best, Descartes and Malebranche equated God simply with human notions of "Being" or "Truth," but the only God whom the faith proclaims brought both the truth and being accessible to human understanding into existence by his will. "The goal of Descartes," Hardouin concluded, "was thus to establish that there is no other God but the being of the things that we can know," and "there," he pronounced, "is his atheism."[82] At first, La Pillonnière had felt rescued from Hardouin's critique of "rational" proofs by Malebranche's "clarifications" of Descartes, and indeed, his extreme enthusiasm for reason in *all* matters embarrassed Malebranche; by 1714, however, Malebranche could write sadly to André that while La Pillon- nière earlier "wanted no grace other than reason alone, . . . today he has embraced the opposite heresy."[83] In 1715, La Pillonnière chose to commu- nicate to the broader reading public Hardouin's reduction of claims of a priori knowledge of God's existence to atheism. For La Pillonnière, expli- cating and embellishing Hardouin, the equation of God with an idea, or with an idea or perception of truth, or with truth itself, was the diviniza- tion of mental modifications that our own minds could destroy. The God proclaimed by both Descartes and Malebranche was a "nothing, the work of the mind, the form of the understanding, an abstract and metaphysical being, a being of reason, in a word, nothing." Although such philosophers "used the word God," what they believed in was merely "this chimerical God . . . [with] nothing real, that does not exist. . . ." Where Hardouin remained committed to scholastic philosophical theology and a posteriori demonstration, La Pillonnière revealed one possible effect of having lived through a generation of such debates. Belief in God, La Pillonnière con- cluded, was an utterly supernatural gift, achieved "by faith," not natural lights.[84]

Such a position, in theory, was unutterable by Catholic theologians, although, as we shall see in our conclusion, a fideism extending even to the existence of God did emerge or sustain itself in the wake of the philosophi- cal divisions of the Catholic theological community. While a Protestant such as Poiret could recant his former belief that knowledge of God's exis- tence could be attained by natural lights, demand a complete abdication of reason in matters divine, and proclaim that faith alone could provide even the idea of God,[85] it remained the Catholic position, as Sommier reminded his readers, that "it would be a heresy to say that one cannot know the existence of God without faith."[86]

Increasingly, however, theologians were sensitive to the ravages ef- fected by Cartesian-scholastic-Malebranchiste debate. One of the leading Capuchin theologians of the early eighteenth century, Nicolas Anaclet du Havre, conceded, in a course of positive theology published for the pro- fessors and teachers of his order in 1712, that there were now "several theologians" who believed that they could "prove that one cannot demon- strate the existence of God." His explication of their arguments revealed the inroads of Cartesian-scholastic polemic. God, they claimed, could not be proven from the idea of God, because this idea was not innate, and because finite reason was inadequate to know the essence of God. Further, no proof from infinite perfection as "an effect" could be maintained, for God was defined as the First Being and First Cause, and admitted of no prior cause. Nor, they claimed, could God be proven a posteriori from the beings of the world, for a necessary cause never could be demonstrated by contingent effects nor an infinite cause from finite effects. The answers to such problems, Anaclet du Havre advised the teachers of his order, lay in the great theologians who have written on the existence of God, and he referred them to the "authorities": Saint Thomas Aquinas *and* Malebranche, Huet *and* the Malebranchist François Lamy, the traditionalist Denys Petau *and* the Cartesian Thomassin *and* the fideistic Pascal. In short, he referred them to the very problem itself.[87]

For others sensitive to this dilemma, especially those like Anaclet du Havre who did not have institutional or personal commitments to any particular mode of demonstration, the task became to find what remained standing and solid after the assaults of the diverse theological and philosophical camps against each other's citadels. The Capuchin Basile de Soissons, in his *Traité de l'existence de Dieu* (1680), wished that no one would see the need to believe in God by faith alone as "a violence against truth," but he recognized the need to aid fideistic minds. He was no admirer of Aristotle, who, he reminded his readers, believed in the independence and eternity of the visible world, and he apologized for having to use "several philosophical terms [of the School] rather barbarous in our ordinary language," but he believed that there was *one* philosophical argument that sufficed to convince the most demanding: the proof from contingent beings, from which followed all of the perfections of God.[88] The theologian and priest Michel Boutauld, whose *Le Theologien dans les conversations avec les sages et les grands du monde* (1683) was offered as an emendation of Pierre Coton's earlier apologetic work, argued that it was "a great abuse to run and ask [the philosophers] if it is true that there is a God." We had no need for "demonstrations drawn from the books of Aristotle or Saint Thomas." For the child as for the adult, simply looking at the world with an honest soul sufficed to convince one of the existence of God, for all the creatures publicly proclaimed him. One knows from faith and nature that God exists (the argument from design presented, formally, as both revealed and "moral"), and one must be content with that, for "if you want to know [it] better by speculations and convictions drawn from false logic, tomorrow you will know it no longer." "All God though He is," he concluded, "He has not had any other argument nor any other demonstration to make known His Divinity to men and convert all the nations than this one."[89] In a posthumous *Recueil* (1723) of his apologetic works, Isaac Papin, converted to Catholicism by Bossuet himself, sought to refute the Cartesian a priori proofs and to find a satisfactory demonstration of God's existence "without having recourse to the reasons of any philosopher." He claimed to have found one and only one argument for God's being that was "clear and compelling" enough "to confound the atheists," the single proof that allowed one "to be wholly persuaded of it." It was a demonstration from individual analysis of one's human nature as mortal, finite, imperfect, and not self-caused, yet grander and more perfect than any other being in nature. One *could* conceive that all other entities had existed "from all Eternity," he wrote, but knowing ourselves to be "the most admirable composition of nature," yet finite, we knew that there must be a God. He conceded, however, that a sceptic would *not* yield to this argument.[90]

Thus, even among those who rejected all a priori proof, there no longer was a consensus that the five proofs of St. Thomas were all invulnerable to refutation, and some theologians were conscious of the explicit toll taken by Cartesian-scholastic debate. In 1680, for example, the abbé Armand de Gérard addressed a Christian laity that he believed to be more and more confused and appalled by the divisions within the Catholic intellectual community. Although he favored the Thomistic arguments as illustrations for those already true theists and Christians, de Gérard opined that both Aristotelian scholasticism and Cartesian innovation stood condemned by their demonstrated inabilities to prove the God known by authority. Against the Cartesians, he argued that if God is infinite and perfect, he cannot be known by our finite and imperfect ideas. Against the scholastics, he argued that if God is spirit, he cannot be known by the corporeal senses from the beings of the corporeal world. Aristotle himself had believed the world to be eternal, and Epicurus had believed the world to be the product of the fortuitous concourse of atoms, and yet, in terms of natural lights, "these two opinions . . . are the strong conclusions of the two greatest geniuses of antiquity." This being the case, he urged, it was clear that we depended on a "recourse to faith" to know of the existence of the true God. The knowledge that the world was from God, the heart of all scholastic demonstration, was to be found neither in reason nor in nature, but only "in the book of *Genesis*," to which, in faith, we submit our minds. Only *after* so informed by faith could philosophy look at the universe and, indeed, see the evident marks of the Creator.[91] In brief, he had accepted the scholastic critique of Cartesianism, and, as well, the heart of the Cartesian critique of scholasticism, that even if one could establish a posteriori a cause of the universe, one could not know by such a means what the nature of that cause might be.

The implications of such a position were made patently and painfully clear to learned readers and students of theology in Nicolas L'Herminier's

Summa Theologiae (1701–3; 2d ed., 1718–19). L'Herminier, a doctor of theology from the Sorbonne, was an anti-Cartesian sympathetic to Jansenism who had little respect for either the scholastics or the new philosophy. In his *Summa*, he rejected Descartes's proofs of God (and all attempts to prove God a priori or by "necessary conjunction") as question begging, agreeing with scholastic critics that such demonstrations indeed presupposed the very object of their proof. He further agreed that the formally finite nature of the idea of God obviated any proof from its "objective" cause, and that the very existence of atheists, for whom the idea of God was neither innate nor self-evident, refuted the premises of Descartes's chain of argument. The idea of God, he concluded, came to us either by instruction or by reasoning from the evidence of the senses.[92] When he turned to St. Thomas's five proofs, however, L'Herminier revealed the profound influence on his theology of the Cartesian argument that unless an a posteriori proof established the existence of a "perfect" being, it had failed to establish the existence of God against the objections of would-be atheists. His atheists were atomists whose possible objections to Aquinas he saw as forceful indeed.

St. Thomas's proofs from contingent being, from motion, and from efficient cause, L'Herminier reasoned, were *not* demonstrative. No one, he argued, conceivably denied that there was a necessary being given contingency, a prime mover given motion, or a first cause given efficient causes, but Aquinas had begged the issue entirely of whether or not the necessary prime mover and first cause had to be a *perfect* being, that is to say, God. Assume, L'Herminier wrote, eternally existing atoms with inherent essential motion, and one has assigned just as plausibly to such atoms the status that St. Thomas had assigned to God. If the issue were whether or not *any* cause existed of contingent being, motion, and the sequence of cause and effect, St. Thomas would triumph; atheists, alas, demanded further demonstration that such causes could be found only in a perfect being, and St. Thomas presupposed what was in fact the very issue in dispute. Turning to St. Thomas's proof from degrees of perfection, L'Herminier concluded that it too begged the central issue in dispute. If there were "degrees of perfection," they must have a perfect cause; St. Thomas proved *that*. The argument, however, would be wholly inefficacious, L'Herminier decided, against the thinker who claimed that the very use of the term "perfection" begged the issue, seeing all things as merely the result of the chance arrangements of atoms, and seeing human judgments about such things as merely the arbitrary pronouncement of how entities affected our physical senses and well-being. Such an atheist could not be persuaded by St. Thomas's argument that what he observes and judges depends upon an infinitely perfect being. Further, the argument from "negations" told us merely what "God" was *not*. Only the argument from providential governance of the world triumphs, L'Herminier concluded, for only the benevolent purposes, order, and harmony of the universe demonstrated the existence of qualities—intelligence, goodness, and will—that could not be attributed to imperfect corporeal entities.[93] As we shall see, however, proof of God from providential order and governance was, of St. Thomas's five proofs, the most widely if indirectly imperiled in the orthodox culture of the late seventeenth and early eighteenth centuries.

As already noted, of course, Cartesian epistemology itself constituted a formidable objection to proof of God's existence from the phenomena of nature, since prior knowledge of God was necessary in the Cartesian system both to know that an external world existed apart from our dreams, imagination, or chimeras, and to establish the validity of any putative knowledge of that material world. Further, Cartesian mechanism, with its antifinalism, its denial of natural inductive knowledge of ends or purposes, militated against the entire foundation of proof *ex gubernatione rerum*. For the Cartesians, and, indeed, most Malebranchistes, proof of God's "Providence" (apart from faith) could only be deductive from his essence as perfect being. Congratulating Leibniz on his proof a priori of the world's providential excellence, Malebranche had written of the immense dangers of attempting to establish Providence a posteriori, "because we are only too given to judging God by ourselves [i.e., our human standards], and to judging the plan of his work, although we know almost nothing of it." In such a state, Malebranche had feared, we drew analogies based on the duties of men toward each other, and so judged, Providence was open to all the "apparent reasons [objections]" of thinkers such as Bayle.[94] Indeed, Malebranche once had even urged that Descartes's theory of the automatism of animals followed compellingly from rational analysis of God's essential Providence, since "animals suffer pain, each more miserable than the other. Now, they have never sinned. . . . Thus, [given the scholastic supposition of animal-souls] God is unjust."[95]

In theory, to be sure, there need have been no conflict between a priori and a posteriori proofs *of* God's Providence, since from any of Saint Thomas's other demonstrations one could attempt to deduce the Providence of the necessary being, and since rational knowledge of Providence could induce a search for the actual manifestations of what one knew a priori to be the ordered condition of the creation. In fact, however, many a priori theologians believed that in the midst of confused and confusing sensory evidence, a priori deduction was the *only* source of certainty of God's Providence, and many believed that this circumstance itself demonstrated the necessity and utility of their philosophical method. It followed from such a position, however, that natural sensory knowledge could not establish that Providence of God which could constitute an a posteriori proof of his existence.

Thus, the rationalist Carthusian monk, Alexis Gaudin, in his *La distinction et la nature du bien et du mal* (1704), stressed the priority of rational certainty of Providence over any inferences one might be tempted to draw from sensory experience. The philosophical debates of our age, Gaudin argued, had raised this issue to urgent prominence, for from experience, man believed himself to know of "evils" and "imperfections" in the world. Fortunately, we knew with certainty from our idea of God that he existed as a perfect being, and thus that evil and imperfection could not be his work. Imperfections in a work, he reasoned, could only arise from indifference, ignorance, caprice, malice, or impotence on the part of its creator, and such "defects," logically, "could not be found in the great worker of the world, in the Creator, who can be conceived only as an infinitely perfect being." If one trusted to the senses, one would admit "imperfections" as real qualities in the world, and atheism would follow as a consequence. "Will we remove existence to God," he asked rhetorically, "to give it to evil?" Just as God's nonexistence would contradict his essence, however, so would such defects, and thus one knows with certainty that what we term "imperfection" or "evil" must be mere privation. Both the atheists and the Manicheans could be defeated by reason, a priori, alone.[96]

The Huguenot theologian, Jacques Bernard, put the matter more simply in his discussion of reason's role, in his *De l'excellence de la religion* (1714; new ed., 1732). Our experience of the world, he wrote, is of a universe of endless confusion, suffering, pain, uncertainty, and shadow. Just as in human affairs "the most excellent machines easily break down," so in the world open to our gaze "I see, every day, certain parts of this world that perish . . . [and] others that appear to me to leave their appropriate order and place." "The more lights and knowledge I have," he confessed, "the more I see of examples of this disarray." Sunspots, he confided, made him fear that the sun was unstable and one day would be extinguished. Further, "thunder, lightning, storms, winds, tempests, too-frequent rains, overly long droughts, earthquakes, sterility, plague, war, the malice of the wicked, all of that terrifies me. . . ." "Every creature," he added, "can do me harm; how can I be reassured?" Fortunately, he replied, reason suffices to calm the doubts that all men might have concerning Providence, for the truth of God's Providence does not depend upon our sad experience of the sensible world, but follows from logical consideration of the nature of God. A being of infinite perfection *must be* a being of infinite wisdom and infinite goodness. One may not discern the Providence of God in nature, but one may know with certainty that it is there.[97]

The problem, of course, is that Gaudin's and Bernard's arguments are compelling only if one has a priori or independent a posteriori proof of the existence of the perfect being. Gaudin was writing explicitly against Bayle, Bernard implicitly; the irony is that for those in search of some unassailable a posteriori proof, such rationalist "proofs" of Providence against Bayle entailed, in effect, the *refutation* of the demonstration *ex gubernatione*. When the abbé Claude-François Houtteville, in his *Essai philosophique sur la Providence* (1728), opined that whatever the empirical claims for and objections to Providence, this divine attribute was nonetheless deductive with certainty from the infinite perfection of God, the Jesuit *Journal de Trévoux* asserted that Houtteville's statement of such objections would carry the day over his response to them.[98] In earlier reply to all such rationalist proofs, and explicitly against Malebranche, the *Journal de Trévoux* had written that all attempted a priori demonstrations of the providential beauty and harmony of the world were in effect assaults on the liberty of God to create and govern however he would, and that ultimately there was only one acceptable demonstration of Providence: "that the world with its alleged defects bears in its beauty and its constant arrangement the marks of an infinite power and wisdom, that the discomforts we would rather not feel serve to exercise the good and punish the wicked; that, finally, God knows how to draw a greater good from what appears to us an evil." It was the task of theology and philosophy to demonstrate these claims a posteriori.[99]

The question of Providence was a thorny one for orthodox Christians of the late seventeenth and eighteenth centuries. There were, of course, all the problems posed by Cartesian rationalism and antifinalism to be confronted. In addition, there were a host of particular controversies, over occasionalism, premotion, and prescience, for example, that often required attention. Above all, however, the question of Providence was problematic because it intersected two very different issues. First, there was a question of dogmatic theology: how do we reconcile the content of the Christian faith with the phenomena of the observable world? Secondly, there was a question of natural theology: what are the reasonable inferences to be drawn by natural lights from the observed world concerning the existence of God (the issue of Aquinas's fifth way)? Most theological commentary, in fact, occurred in the first mode, in that literature of piety and consolation that far exceeded in quantity the works of philosophical theology. The question was, "How could there be both Providence and the world of disorder and pain?" and Christian theology, assuming God, the fall, sin, Christ, salvation, and damnation, answered confidently according to the doctrines of the faith. For theologians focusing on *natural* proof of the existence of God a posteriori, however, the "argument from governance" could make no such *scriptural* assumptions.

In the wake of the increasing mathematical order and anatomical-ecological harmony that men believed the natural philosophers to have disclosed, however, such natural theologians often seemed increasingly confident of such a proof "from governance." Indeed, by the early eighteenth century L'Herminier was not alone, to say the least, in endorsing it as, if not the sole, at least the most persuasive argument. As Malebranche had observed, however, human beings tended to think of Providence less in terms of divine architecture, and more in terms of models of human equity and love. The "pastoral" theologians spoke to *that* reality, and what opened the door to the profoundest doubts about the efficacy of the proof *ex gubernatione rerum* was less, it would appear, the theoretical arguments of Cartesians and others than precisely the arguments of those who sought to reconcile Christian Revelation and the natural order for the spiritual peace of the faithful. Framed, on the whole, to stress our dependence upon and consolation from the revealed truths of the supernatural faith, such arguments constituted in and of themselves a formidable objection to the natural induction of the Providence of God. Pierre Bayle did not create the "problem" of Providence in the late seventeenth century. He merely saw what many others saw: that if belief in Providence required faith in Christian Revelation, such belief could not be offered as a natural inference from natural phenomena. In the mid-eighteenth century, David Hume would argue that theology proceeded at cross-purposes when it claimed *both* that the disorders and injustices of the natural world, given a perfect being, entailed a belief in an afterlife *and* that the facts of this life entailed a belief in a perfect being, given the order and harmony of the natural world.[100] He was merely describing the manifest behavior of a Christian intellectual community, some of whose finest minds and sensibilities were drawn at times to the claims of a consoling faith and some of whose finest minds and sensibilities were drawn at times to the claims of a natural theology. In a culture whose most favored proofs of God were all under assault from competing philosophical camps, the most celebrated of those proofs was a victim not only of such philosophical critique, but also of the implications, dramatic in context, of the meditation of Christian piety on Providence and the mysteries of the faith.

The Jesuit Louis Bourdaloue, one of the most celebrated preachers of the late seventeenth century, in an analysis of the etiology of incredulity, saw doubts concerning Providence as the final, decisive phase in the formation of "atheists." "Reflections that they make on the events of the world," he explained, "make them doubt if there is a Providence . . . [and] no longer knowing if there is a Providence, they no longer know if there is a God. . . ."[101] In a later sermon on the "accord of reason and faith," he urged the Christian never to fear reason, for the order of nature, its arrangement and utility, established the existence of God beyond any shadow of doubt. There well might be other convincing proofs, he concluded, "but here is one above all others that is wholly sufficient."[102] In Boutauld's *Théologie dans les Conversations* (1683), God's Providence visible without demonstration in nature was termed the only proof written by God himself; reliance upon it allowed the theologian to say "that my method and my fashion of reasoning on divine existence is the method of God Himself."[103] In a more formal mode, Petiot's *Demonstrations Théologiques* (1674) urged that the argument from providential order was the one proof accessible to and compelling for all minds, especially since this order manifestly had been made uniquely for the benefit of man. For Petiot, all evidence constituted natural proof of Providence. Not only "the perfection and beauty" of the universe in all its parts, but, likewise, "movements so bizarre and ravages so horrible on the earth, so frequent and in so many places" effected the same proof. Floods increased the fecundity of the soil; storms swept away the poisons of the plague; earthquakes served "to punish the wicked and destroy criminal homes and cities"; monsters, toxic herbs and plants, deserts, savage beasts, thistles, and snakes all added beauty and proportion to the creation and all "had their use and their utility." In short, the entire spectacle of nature and man's place within nature could only be understood as "the visible effects of Providence," constituting "the good of the universe."[104] Petiot spoke for a legion of theologians.

Generally, such arguments are contrasted to the more heterodox (if less widely circulated) views of naturalistic antifinalists, Baylian "pyrrhonists," or would-be neo-Epicureans, as if all Christian theology were in agreement on the beauty and utility of the natural world. There was a Christian tradition of no small influence and standing, however, which had taken a quite different view of the world open to our gaze, and described it as part of the very wages of Adam's sin. Jacques de Jant's 1666 translation of Osorio de Fonseca's *de Vera Sapientia* (Lisbon, 1578), the *Théologie curieuse*, referred to this tradition in its essay on "the perfection of the world," arguing that Saint Basil had been wrong to argue that without Adam's fall roses would not have thorns, nor the world "disorders." What such Christians took to be imperfections, he declared, were in fact "perfections" that could be explained knowledgeably: monsters both had beauty and set in relief the beauty of others; venomous plants and snakes were more aids to animals and useful to man than harmful. In short, "what is not good for one use is good for another," and once that is understood, one sees that "it is impossible that [God] could have made the world more perfect than we see it."[105] One did not have to reach a similar conclusion concerning nature, however, to draw an equally reassuring inference from it concerning Providence. The theologian d'Abillon had conceded that the world, indeed, "would be more beautiful if there were not so many monsters, infirmities, pains, poverties, miseries, . . . changes, and perpetual vicissitudes," and, thus, that it was manifestly imperfect. In fact, d'Abillon wrote, it was so imperfect "that it appears more a rough draft than a final effort and a perfect masterpiece of [God's] power." However, God manifestly had done this so that man might never believe in the perfection of natural forces, but always recognize nature's and his dependence on a higher cause. In *that* sense, God's Providence was visible in the structure of nature.[106] Saint Basil was both right and wrong.

While for some Catholic theologians knowledge of Providence as an inference from nature was the very route to God, for others, such as the formidable Henri-Marie Boudon, *grand archdiacre* of Evreux, *submission to* Providence was the very test of having reached a proper relationship with God. The problem, he wrote in 1678, was *not* to judge Providence, but to adore it. The miracle of faith and the witness of the New Testament were the basis of our belief, and our duty was to submit to the Providence which these revealed.[107] In two of Bossuet's sermons "On Providence," he commented that doubts concerning Providence were the major cause of doubts concerning the existence of God himself. The problem of looking at nature without aid, in order to find God's Providence, was that we often saw only what appeared to be the confusion of the world, in the manner of those who look at "trick paintings" whose coherence is manifest only from one place and one angle. When the secret is revealed, all falls into place. For Christians the place and angle of proper perspective on the world are found in the New Testament alone. We know of God's Providence from that Revelation, without fathoming its design, for its design relates to eternity. Only in the light of God's promise of "eternal felicity" does the world make final sense. Only with "faith" in Providence does one come neither to admire, nor condemn, nor fear anything which is merely of this present finite life. Only from the perspective of the last judgment are our final difficulties resolved.[108] Again, such arguments might well provide consolation for the faithful, but they did not establish from the evidence of the natural order the preamble of such faith. Indeed, when the virtue and necessity of faith were stressed beyond Bossuet's notion of a perspective then satisfying to natural lights, such "consolations" might demand the positive rejection of *any natural proof* of providential governance. Let us examine what the most pious literature of Christian consolation might contribute to undermining St. Thomas's final proof.

In 1679 and 1680, we have seen in part, the abbé de Gérard recalled for his readers that Epicurus did not believe in God's Providence and that Aristotle did not believe that it extended to the earth. That these great minds had reached such conclusions "having only reason as their guide," he appealed, demonstrated that our faith in Providence was founded only on Revelation, and that a Christian must always think on this topic with that faith as his guide, knowing that his consolation was to be found only in Christ and in God's justice in eternity.[109] In 1683, Diroy's *Preuves . . . de la Religion Chréstienne* concluded that the proof of Providence was inseparable from the Revelation of the true religion. Doubts about Providence, he argued, were "based on the disorders which appeared [to men] to be in the world and everything that one sees occur there." The folly of such judgments, he warned, was that they ignored the true, revealed *teleos* of man, the true locus of his happiness, and falsely assumed that God's conduct should be related to this present world, which bears witness to our sins and our revolt against God. "If the world were regulated as the majority of men would wish," he admonished, "the good would be too attached to it." The end of man was in the world to come, and God, "whose essential goodness and wisdom do not necessarily have to do what appears to us more in conformity with justice and goodness," exercised his Providence in a manner revealed in Scripture to offer us a blessed eternity.[110] In 1684, the *Quatres Dialogues* of the abbés Dangeau and Choisy replied to the question "Why is the world so badly regulated if God indeed wishes to take the trouble of involving Himself with it?" Their answer was a pious one: suffering is a blessing, for given the unimportance of this natural world compared to the glory of the next, adversities and illnesses were "favors" from God in preparation of eternal reward; the prosperity of the wicked doomed them to "nothingness" and eternal punishment, and they served as "executioners of God's justice . . . , rods which God uses to chastise his people."[111] In 1690, the philosopher Lelevel's *Entretiens sur ce qui forme l'honneste homme et le vray scavant* revealed that even a Malebranchist could abandon his natural rationalism on the issue of Providence. He argued that only Christian premises and Christian education could unite our understanding to the ways of God. The corruption of nature entailed the need for a "redeemer," and only grace through union with Christ and his Catholic Church both redeemed nature and allowed us to know God in truth. In Christian revelation alone was the efficacious antidote to the "impiety of the Epicureans" concerning Providence.[112] In that same year, the Sorbonniste Pirot approved the publication of pious *Réfléxions et Maximes Chrétiennes* that began the discussion of Providence from the premise that the imperfections of the world and the suffering of man in nature were occasions for the virtue of faith and submission. If one truly believed in God through Christ, one understood that all of his actions were infinite in sanctity, charity, and purpose. The Christian should "rejoice" in "the pleasure that He finds in our pains," for it is the pleasure he takes in our faith. Indeed, one cannot find the perfection of God in his works, but only in him, and his works are *not* to be admired in their structure and qualities, but only in the fact, known by faith, that his will is manifest in them. "You have lost all that was most dear to you: your son is dead; your goods have been seized," the *Réfléxions* affirmed; "rejoice at what God, who can not fail, has permitted to be your fate; all that God does, He does with infinite holiness." In short, "let us learn," by faith, "to second the designs of God by our consent; our patience is the greatest thanks that we may offer Him." [113] In the abbé Jean Rousseau's *Traité . . . de Providence* (1694), the seventeenth century was condemned as "blind" and rebellious in its effort to order and comprehend God's ways. Scripture, he maintained, teaches us always to trust God and to suffer the world with Christian courage and supernatural virtue. Given the existence of God, what is "reasonable" is to submit to his Providence, instead of complaining about our experience of this natural world as "miserable, laborious and painful; about poverty, the persecution of the just, and a thousand other things that never could be understood." We indeed find, in the natural order, "monsters that terrify," but the antidote to doubts concerning Providence lies not in natural knowledge, but in trust in God through Christ and Church, and in our Christian awareness that all that is and occurs must be with his choice. With such faith, one understands Providence under the aspect of eternity, salvation, and damnation, and not in the light of our misleading knowledge of the natural order. [114] The Huguenot Cartesian Pierre Villemandy, in his *Traité des causes secondes* (1696), wrote that it was perfectly comprehensible that *before the clarification of Revelation*, "almost all the world was in this error, that God had very little part in what occurred in nature." Without knowledge of Scripture, man could not know that "[God's] sovereignty presides over all events." In short, "without the lights of grace," he wrote, one quickly falls into atheism. The enlightenment of grace, unknown from the study of nature alone, is precisely, he specified, the knowledge that there exists a God of intelligence, that man has sinned and is being judged, and that there is a purpose to the universe and to history. [115] In Dom André Rose's *Nouveau sistême par pensées sur l'ordre de la nature* (1696), the philosophical monk argued that only Adam could have reasoned by philosophy alone from nature and human life to the Providence of God. Theology errs egregiously when it listens to the voice of philosophy; in our fallen state, theology must be "based purely and simply on Holy Scripture and Tradition."[116] What Scripture teaches us is that God is wholly free, and free, thus, to create what he would, by the means he would, and for ends he would, and free, thus, to deal with and indeed destroy his creatures when and how he would. The natural philosophy of the seventeenth century is blasphemous when it speaks of the "perfections" of this world. God could have created another world "infinitely more beautiful" than this, and could have done so by means "incomparably more fecund." Saint Basil was correct: God created monsters and disorders in this world to punish the sins of man, which he foresaw. The argument from design is theologically absurd: "One must not regard the world as a work that God made to make Himself admired by minds, by disposing things this or that way." Further, one must not believe "that there is not the least irregularity in any effect considered in particular except so that the whole should thereby be supremely beautiful, delightful, charming." To the contrary, "God formed the world to punish a man whom He foresaw would rebel against Him. . . ." No wonder, he concluded, that men are able "to convict God (as the impious do) of having lacked wisdom in creating and arranging the world such as we see it." Given the reality of the Fall, we deserve the creation in which we find ourselves.[117] In 1706, the editor of the late apologist Louis Ferrand's *De la connaissance de Dieu* believed that the latter's defense of Providence required strengthening. "To deny Providence," he explained, "is to deny the existence of God," and man must recognize that God's Providence aims not at our well-being in *this* world, but prepares us for the life to come. Ultimate good and evil, he warned, and the ultimate *teleos* of all things, are not known to man, but to God alone, and relate to revealed issues of salvation and damnation above all.[118] Providence, the great preacher Massillon reminded his Christian auditors, is known to us in terms of a world beyond nature and the present life: "all the visible world itself is made only for the age to come."[119] In short, there was another Christian voice in early-modern France besides that of the natural theologians, and it had a message of august heritage to repeat: the ways of the world do not lead us to knowledge of God: rather, knowledge of God, supernaturally revealed and known by faith, leads us to an understanding of the world. It was an orthodox reminder that was manifestly chilling in its effect on the equally orthodox effort to prove beyond doubt by natural lights the existence of God from his governance of the creation. Every mind exposed to the latter arguments had read or heard that reminder countless times, and such would have been the case had Pierre Bayle never written a single word.

As for the argument from "universal consent," by the late seventeenth century it was in shambles, as evidenced by the many recorded uses of "atheists" by scholastics against the alleged innateness of the idea of God. St. Augustine had written that there was no people so barbarous that they had no sentiment of divinity, and his argument long had been incorporated into Christian demonstrations of God's existence. While, indeed, many travellers and missionaries wrote in support of such a claim, the seventeenth century nonetheless witnessed a dramatic flowering of travel literature, much of it by missionaries themselves, that provided a rich basis for refutation of this demonstration. There was, of course, the celebrated controversy over the beliefs and rites of the Chinese, best understood, perhaps, as a chapter of ecclesiastical and missionary rivalries within the Catholic Church, but with profound implications for this particular proof. While critics of the Jesuits often stressed the "atheism" of Chinese thought in general, important Jesuit works themselves proclaimed that atheism had made inroads among the Chinese "men of letters." [120] Responding to widespread charges that the atheism of China was far more extensive than the Jesuits had allowed, the Jesuit Le Comte asked his critics to consider "[if] the libertines will not take advantage of the avowal that is made to them that in so vast and so enlightened, so solidly established, so flourishing an empire . . . the Divinity never has been known? What will become of the arguments that the Holy Fathers, in proving the existence of God, drew from the consent of all peoples?" [121] Yet the work of those who denied the atheism of the fundamental doctrines of Chinese philosophy was condemned by Rome and the Sorbonne in formal censure. [122]

The undermining of "universal consent," however, went far beyond the problems of the Jesuits in China. From Léry's *Voyages* of 1578 to the dawn of the Enlightenment, a host of pious authors noted that "despite Cicero's argument," they had observed whole peoples and nations without any belief in any God whatsoever. Such characterizations were offered by travellers to the New World of the Indians of Brazil, [123] the Indians of Florida, [124] most of the Indians of New France, [125] and, in particular, the Indians of Cape Breton [126] and the Hurons, [127] and, finally, the Indians of the Massachusetts coast. [128] Similar claims of atheism were made concerning the inhabitants of Madagascar, [129] of the Isle de Cayenne, [130] and of the Isle de Maragnan. [131] By 1670, when Abraham Roger's study of the Orient was translated into French, its editor felt obliged to add a lengthy footnote explicitly disputing Roger's earlier claim that travellers confirmed the universal consent to belief in God. [132] Sir Paul Rycaut's study of the Ottoman Empire, translated into French in 1670 and frequently reprinted, expressed his amazement at discovering a significant intellectual movement there that explicitly denied God and embraced formal atheism, and he noted that it included some of the most learned savants of the Ottoman world. "Until now," he confessed, "I could not believe that there was genuine atheism in the world." [133] Although Gervaise's *Histoire de Siam* (1688) had claimed that the Siamese, despite believing that the world was eternal and arranged by chance, still knew of God, however false their views of him, La Loubère's *Du Royaume de Siam* (1691) assured his readers that the Siamese did not worship false gods, but knew of "no Divinity, neither true nor false."[134]

Indeed, some missionaries and travellers made a special point of commenting on the honesty and decency of "atheistic" peoples they had encountered. The missionary Jean-Baptiste Du Tertre, for example, discussing the black slaves he had met in the Antilles, noted that they were not even idolators, but "worshipped no God, and never had had the slightest thought that there was a God." He was struck, nevertheless, by "the love they have for one another," and by their "tenderness" and "compassion."[135] This was not an uncommon theme.[136]

In terms of the idea of "universal consent" within the Western tradition, by the early eighteenth century this notion had been shattered by a generation of classical scholarship and history of philosophy, much of it emanating from German universities, but widely read (in Latin) and discussed in France. Despite occasional warnings that their conclusions would lead the faithful to think that half the wise men of the world had been atheists, scholars increasingly had concluded in favor of attributing systematic atheism to more and more prior sages, and, indeed, to whole celebrated schools of thought.[137] Among the moderns, Pomponazzi, Cardan, Ficino, Campanella, Bruno, Machiavelli, Vanini, Rabelais, Hobbes, Spinoza, and Toland were more likely than not to be so categorized. More dramatically, given the culture's reverence for the ancients, similar conclusions were reached concerning almost all of the pre-Socratic philosophers, and entire movements of Greek philosophy, including, for many, all the Eleactics. Some went so far—and not merely malicious Cartesians among them—as to argue that Aristotle himself, correctly understood, betrayed, at least by implication, an atheistic philosophy.[138] By the time Buddeus's scholarly study of atheism appeared in 1717 (widely read in France and later translated into the vernacular by the Sorbonniste Louis Philon), its author felt obliged to rescue Plato, Heraclitus, Hippocrates, Plutarch, Cicero, and Pliny from the charges of atheism made by learned colleagues, many of whom had attempted to demonstrate that these thinkers had had no idea whatsoever of the *perfect* being or of a Providence. Buddeus himself, however, agreed with the verdict of guilty against most of the Ionic philosophers, most of the Greek sceptics, Strato, the Cynics, most Stoics, and the entire "Eleactic sect." Further, he declared that the case against Aristotle was plausible, but not conclusive as yet.[139]

In arguing for the atheism of so much classical thought, it should be noted, these scholars often explicated—correctly or not is irrelevant—world views that conceived of the universe without the idea of God. They stressed the absence of any idea of creation ex nihilo in antiquity and the pervasiveness of belief in the eternity of matter. They proposed, in effect, that most Greek and Roman philosophers believed the world explicable—in theory, at least—in terms of material and natural forces alone. They emphasized that for most ancient thinkers, even the mind and will of man were conceived in wholly corporeal terms, and that for many, the passage from life to death was merely and solely the dissolution of material aggregates into new arrangements. In a culture increasingly relying on the somehow manifest nature of the argument from design, they insisted that there were broad currents of ancient thought open to explanation of the world by the fortuitous concourse of material bodies alone. Indeed, they often attempted to explicate such views with cogency and coherence, so that their audience might appreciate in full the chasm between pre-Christian and Christian ways of thought. Without ever reading or encountering a single libertine, materialist or atheist, the early modern learned mind could find abundant grounds for rejecting even the "moral" persuasiveness of the argument from universal consent.

The cumulative effect of all of these disputations of particular proofs of the existence of God was neither the emergence of a "school" of early-modern French atheism nor even the appearance of a significant number of individual atheistic authors. Indeed, at the height of the Enlightenment, decades later, atheism remained a minor, circumscribed current of thought. Yet, as the manuscripts of the early eighteenth century reveal, the possibility of atheistic thought in a culture formerly so uniformly theistic had been effected, and a new chapter in the history of human speculation had begun. To think atheistically, some perspective was necessary at the outset from which one could no longer believe oneself to be compelled by demonstrations of the being of God. Even among French Catholic thinkers for whom the natural demonstrability of God was a prescribed article of belief, the confidence that such demonstration was secure had been, in many cases, shattered.

   Although the Catholic church consistently had condemned the opinions of medieval theologians such as Pierre d'Ailly and William of Ockham that full, evident demonstration of God's existence was not obtainable by natural lights, sincere Catholic minds of the early-modern world were reaching similar conclusions. If there is a God, Pascal had written, he is so incomprehensible to us that we are incapable of knowing either what he is or even if he is, except through Jesus Christ and grace: "Through Jesus we know God. All those who have claimed to know God and prove His existence without Jesus Christ have had only futile proofs to offer."[140] Huet's *Traité philosophique de la faiblesse de l'esprit humain* reached conclusions as profoundly sceptical about knowledge a posteriori as his earlier *Censura* had been concerning knowledge a priori.[141] At the end of Desgabet's defense of Malebranche's proof of God's existence, the Benedictine philosopher had granted that it was beset by theoretical objections and difficulties, but he pleaded that "there being no other argument but this one that is proportioned to everyone's capacity, . . . there would be peril to disparage it and combat its solidity." Perhaps, he conceded, it convinced us only because God first had revealed himself to us in Scripture, and that "men corrupted by sin would never have taken it upon themselves to think of God . . . if God first had not made Himself known to man, and if this knowledge had not been passed down from father to son by means of instruction. . . ."[142] In the catechism prepared by Eustache de la Conception in 1699, the Carmelite theologian had included the existence of God among the mysteries of the Christian religion and had written that we knew both God as Creator and God incarnate in Christ only "by faith." Indeed, he defined faith as "a gift of God by means of which we believe in [that] God."[143] In Gaspart Langenhert's *Philosophus Novus* (1701–2), it was argued that a Christian philosopher can only be sceptical and could embrace neither Platonic, Epicurean, Aristotelian, nor Cartesian systems. All "science," Langenhert urged, including knowledge of God's existence, "presupposes faith, which . . . cannot . . . be demonstrated by the sole lights of nature." He who wishes to know anything whatsoever of God, he specified, must first believe "by faith" that there is a God. *All* sciences *assumed* their objects of study to exist: the mathematician cannot "prove" points and lines to exist; the physicist cannot "prove" bodies to exist; the theologian cannot "prove" God to exist! This shows, he concluded, the wisdom of the Christian injunction to faith.[144] In 1728, the abbés Blondel and Louail proposed that belief in God was achieved by faith alone, and that "the first sacrifice that one owes Him is that of the mind and all of its lights." Man is ignorant and the world a place of shadows, and it is only by virtue of "this man-God" Christ that we learn of an "infinitely perfect being," a Creator, and a Providence.[145]

We have scant knowledge of Meslier, but we do know that he had been drawn to Cartesian thought while at the seminary, that he became a friend of and presumably read the work of the Jesuit Claude Buffier, and that the latter prevailed on him to read the abbé Houtteville's treatise on Christianity. He also read the Jesuit Tournemine's unauthorized preface to a reprinting of Fénélon's treatise on the existence of God.[146] Buffier's and Tournemine's furious recapitulations of the scholastic critiques of Cartesian proofs of God may well have disabused Meslier of any a priori grounds of belief.[147] What else might Meslier have found in the thought of his friend Buffier and in the recommended treatise by Houtteville? In the latter, Houtteville had praised Pascal's emphasis on the need for faith to know God, his understanding, in Houtteville's words, that "it is not by metaphysical and abstract proofs" that men should "be led to perfect conviction." Natural demonstrations, Houtteville had urged, "depend too much on the imagination and the senses to extend to first principles, sources of all truth." It was not by means of reason or the senses, but "by the heart," that God's existence could be known.[148] In Buffier, Meslier encountered a Jesuit thinker who, for all the force of his refutation of Cartesian and Malebranchist proofs of God, was also aware of the force of rationalist critiques of scholasticism. In Buffier's system, one cannot prove with "absolute evidence" that nature exists, that we know true things from it, or that God exists. All a priori proof is question begging, and all a posteriori proof depends not on "complete demonstration," but on the *assumption* of "first truths," principles which are not demonstrable themselves, but without which no other demonstrations are possible. These nondemonstrable "first truths" are acquired "by way of sentiment," "a natural sentiment," and include one's own existence, the existence of bodies, the principle that what is known by "sentiment" and "experience" by "all men" must be received as true, and the principle that order "could not be the effect of chance." It is impossible, indeed malicious, Buffier concluded, to ask for "certain proof" of these "first truths," for they are *presupposed* by human thought and not amenable to demonstration.[149]

In short, we need not detach the first speculative atheists of the French eighteenth century from the learned and orthodox culture that engendered them. When the eighth session of the Fifth Lateran Council reaffirmed, in 1513, the Church's doctrine that "[philosophical] truth never contradicts [revealed] truth," and commanded Christian philosophers, at the universities or elsewhere, to refute philosophically all non-Christian objections to the foundations of Christian belief, Cajetan de Vio, the leading Dominican spokesman, complained that this would lead to a fearful confusion of philosophy and theology, and one bishop refused to sign the bull, disturbed that matters of faith and matters of human intelligence would be removed from their proper spheres.[150] Perhaps Saint-Evremond, in 1662, had seen yet more clearly the irony of Christian apologetic disputation on the strengths and weaknesses of proofs of the most essential preamble of the faith: "We burn a man unfortunate enough not to believe in God," he wrote, "and yet we ask publicly in the schools if He exists."[151]

NOTES

1. See the particularly astute discussion of this phenomenon in Richard A. Watson, *The Downfall of Cartesianism 1673–1712: A Study of Epistemological Issues in Late 17th Century Cartesianism* (The Hague, 1966).

2. Jean-Baptiste de La Grange, Oratoire, *Les principes de la philosophie, contre les nouveaux philosophes Descartes, Rohault, Regius, Gassendi, le P. Maignan* . . . (Paris, 1675), passim, esp. 1–175; Gabriel Daniel, S.J., *Voiage au Monde de Descartes* (Paris, 1691), 144–53 (first published in Paris and Amsterdam, 1690); Jean Du Hamel, *Reflexions critiques sur le système Cartesien de la philosophie de Mr Régis* (Paris, 1692), passim, esp. 220–25, 330–44; J. Galimard, *La philosophie du prince, ou La veritable idée de la nouvelle et de l'ancienne philosophie* (Paris, 1689), 53–216; Rodolphe Du Tertre, S.J., *Réfutation d'un nouveau système de métaphysique*, 3 vols. (Paris, 1715), 1 and 2, passim, directed principally against Malebranche and, by extension, against Descartes.

3. Much of this literature was the product of German scholarship, but read and widely cited in France. See, for example, Johann Franz Buddeus, *Theses theologicae de atheismo et superstitione variis* . . . (1st ed., Jena, 1717; reprint, Jena, 1718; 2d ed., Jena, 1722; 3d ed., Trajecti ad Rhenum, 1737; in French, *Traité de l'Athéisme et de la Superstition*, trans. Louis Philon, ed. J.-C. Fischer, Paris and Amsterdam, 1740); Ralph Cudworth, *The True Intellectual System of the Universe*, part 1, (London, 1678), presented to a French audience by Le Clerc in his periodical *Bibliothèque choisie* (1703), 1:63–138, 2:11–77; Jacques-Parrain, baron Des Coutures, ed. and trans., *Lucrèce, De la Nature des Choses, avec des remarques sur les endroits les plus difficiles de Lucrèce*, 2 vols. (Paris, 1685); Johannes Henricus Foppius and Wuldebrandus Vogt, *De Atheismo Philosophorum Gentilium Celebriorum* (Bremen, 1714); Nicolas Hieronymus Gundling, *Observationum Selectionum ad Rem Litterrarium Spectantium*, vol. 1 (Frankfurt and Leipzig, 1707); Jenkin Thomas Philipps, *Dissertatio Historico-Philosophica de Atheismo* . . . (London, 1716); Jacob Friedrich Reimmann, *Historia Universalis Atheismi* . . . (Hildesiae, 1725); Anton Reiser, *De Origine, Progressu et Incremento Antitheismi* . . . (Augsburg, 1669); Abbé Dominique Réverend, *La physique des anciens* (Paris, 1701); Fridericus Philippus Schlosserus, *Spicilegium Historico-Philosophicum de Stratone Lampsaceno* . . . (Wittemberg, 1728), which defended Strato from the charge of atheism, but referred readers to the multitude of texts and sections of texts that articulated such a claim; Theophile Spizelius, *De Atheismi Radice* . . . (Augsburg, 1666) and *De Atheismo Eradicando* . . . (Augsburg, 1669). Many today would add Bayle's *Dictionnaire* to a list of such "well-intentioned" efforts. See also the discussion of the rather eccentric

work of Jean Hardouin and François de La Pillonnière, below, and nn. 80–84, and the summary of such scholarship, below, and nn. 137–39.

4. On the absence of any philosophical atheism before the seventeenth century in France, see Lucien Febvre, *Le problème de l'incroyance au XVIe siècle, la religion de Rabelais* (Paris, 1942; rev. ed., Paris, 1947).

5. Pierre Rétat, *Le Dictionnaire de Bayle et la lutte philosophique au XVIIIe siècle* (Paris, 1971), 239–42.

6. Jean Fabre, "Jean Meslier, tel qu'en lui-même . . . ," *Dix-Huitième Siècle* no. 3 (1971): 107–15.

7. See the learned discussion of the concept of "preamble of the faith" by S. Harent in A. Vacant et al., eds., *Dictionnaire de Théologie Catholique*, art. "Foi," sect. 6 ("Préparation rationelle de la Foi"), 6:171–237.

8. See, for example, the attention paid to formal proofs of the existence of God in d'Holbach's *Système de la Nature*, 2 vols. (Amsterdam, 1770) and in Jacques-André Naigeon's *Philosophie Ancienne et Nouvelle*, 3 vols. (Paris, 1789–93).

9. Bibliothèque de l'Arsenal, MSS. 2558, no. 2, "Essais sur la recherche de la vérité," 101–2.

10. On conflicting modern analyses and interpretations of Descartes's proofs, see M. Guéroult, *Descartes selon l'ordre des raisons*, vol. 1: *L'âme et Dieu* (Paris, 1953); the response to this by H. Gouhier, "La preuve ontologique de Descartes (A propos d'un livre récent)," *Revue Internationale de Philosophie* 8, no. 29 (1954): 295–303; and the reconsideration by Guéroult, *Nouvelles reflexions sur la preuve ontologique de Descartes* (Paris, 1955). See also E. M. Curley, *Descartes Against the Skeptics* (Cambridge, Mass., 1978), 125–69; A. Kenny, *Descartes* (New York, 1968), passim; L. J. Beck, *The Metaphysics of Descartes, A Study of the Meditations* (Oxford, 1965), 231–37; B. Magnus, "The Modalities of Descartes' Proofs for the Existence of God," in B. Magnus and J. B. Wilbur, eds., *Cartesian Studies: A Collection of Critical Studies* (The Hague, 1969), 77–87; W. Doney, "The Geometrical Presentation of Descartes' A Priori Proof," in M. Hooker, ed., *Descartes, Critical and Interpretive Essays* (Baltimore, 1978), 1–25; H. Gouhier, *La pensée métaphysique de Descartes* (Paris, 1962), 143–61; J. Rée, *Descartes* (London, 1974), 135–40, 162–64.

11. François Diroys, *Preuves et préjugez pour la Religion Chrétienne et Catholique contre les fausses religions et l'Athéisme* (Paris, 1683). The work was frequently reprinted. Diroys (1620–1691) was a doctor of theology of the Sorbonne and canon of Avranches. Bossuet and Fénélon, who both sought to be independent of any particular school of natural philosophy, also should be counted among the "eclectic" theologians in terms of their demonstrations of the existence of God, as should Bishop Jean-Claude Sommier.

12. Dom Robert Desgabets, Benedictine, *Critique de la Critique de la Recherche de la vérité, où l'on découvre le chemin qui conduit aux connaissances solides* (Paris, 1675), 86.

13. Nicolas L'Herminier, *Summa Theologiae ad usum scholae accommodata*, 3 vols. (Paris, 1701–3), 1:40–44.

14. See Aquinas, *Summa Theologiae*, Ia, q. II, art. I and *Summa Contra Gentiles*, I, X, xi.

15. Daniel, *Voiage*, 163–75.

16. Pierre-Daniel Huet, *Censura philosophiae Cartesianae* (Paris, 1689), cap. 4, art. 8. By 1694, the *Censura* was in its fourth edition.

17. Jean Du Hamel, *Lettre de Monsieur Du Hamel, ancien professeur de philosophie de l'Université de Paris, pour servir de réplique à Monsieur Régis* (Paris, [1699]), 7. This was written in response to an earlier response to Du Hamel's criticism by Pierre-Sylvain Régis, *Réponse aux Reflexions critiques du M. Du Hamel sur le système Cartesien de la Philosophie de M. Régis* (Paris, 1692). See also Jean Du Hamel, *Reflexions critiques*. Jean Du Hamel was a *licencié* in theology of the Maison et Société de la Sorbonne and had served as professor of philosophy at the collège de Plessis-Sorbonne of the University of Paris. He should not be confused with Jean-Baptiste Duhamel (or Du Hamel), the academician.

18. Michael Morus, *De Existentia Dei et Humanae Mentis Immortalitate Secundùm Cartesii et Aristotelis Doctrinam Disputatio* (Paris, 1692), 56–79, 196–313.

19. François Perrin, S.J., *Manuale Theologicum sive Theologia Dogmatica et Historica ad usum seminariorum* (Toulouse, 1710), 5–9.

20. François-Marie Assermet, *Theologia scholastico-positiva ad S.R. Ecclesiae mentem elucubrata*, vol. 1: *In Quo Tractatur De Theologiae Principibus, Prolegomensis, De Deo Uno, Ejusque Attributis* (Paris, 1713), 111–12. This despite Duns Scotus's perhaps analogous argument from the idea of God to God's existence in *De Primo Principio*, 3:2: "Si potest esse, potest esse a se, et ita est a se." Leibniz, of course, thought the absence of the "si potest esse" and any proof of that possibility a fatal flaw in Descartes's argument.

21. Pierre-Sylvain Régis, *Réponse aux Reflexions*, 5–8. See n. 17, above.

22. Daniel, *Voiage*, 174–75. See also Morus, *De Existentia Dei*, 292–93.

23. Huet, *Censura philosophiae*, cap. 4, arts. 1–7, 9. See also Morus, *De Existentia Dei*, 71–79, 238–47, 292–313. This issue will be joined again in our discussion of Malebranche.

24. Du Hamel, *Reflexions critiques*, 12–16, 68–78. See also Perrin, *Manuale Theologicum*, 5.

25. Régis, *Réponse aux Reflexions*, 40–42.

26. Du Hamel, *Lettre*, 7.

27. Assermet, *Theologia*, 111–12; Etienne Petiot, S.J. *Demonstrations Théologiques pour établir la foy chrestienne et catholique . . .* (Metz, 1674), 19; Guillaume Dagoumer, *Philosophia ad usum scholae accommodata*, vol. 3: *Metaphysica* (Paris, 1703), 235–39. Dagoumer was a professor of philosophy at the collège d'Harcourt, and early in his career was suspected of sympathies for Cartesianism. His scholastic fidelity established, he enjoyed a brilliant academic career, serving as *recteur* of the University of Paris for the unusually long periods of 1711–13 and 1723–25, and as *proviseur* (administrative head) of the collège d'Harcourt from 1713–30.

28. Daniel, *Voiage*, 174–75 (emphasis added).

29. Régis, *Réponse aux Reflexions*, 71–79.

30. Adrien Baillet, *La Vie de Monsieur Des-Cartes*, 2 vols. (Paris, 1691), 2:284–85; see also 1:181 and 2:507.

31. *Histoire des Ouvrages des Savans* 16 (1700): 220–22 (emphasis Jacquelot's). Hereafter cited as *H.O.S.*

32. Dom François Lamy, Benedictine, *Le nouvel athéisme renversé, ou réfutation du sistême de Spinosa . . .* (Paris, 1696), 5–8. François Lamy should not be confused with the abbé Bernard Lamy of the Oratoire.

33. Huet, *Censura philosophiae*, cap. 4, art. 10.

34. P.-S. Régis, *Réponse au livre qui a pour titre P. Danielis Huetii . . . Censura Philosophiae Cartesianae. Servant d'éclaircissement à toutes les parties de la philosophie, sur tout à la métaphysique* (Paris, 1691), 247–51.

35. P.-S. Régis, *Système de Philosophie*, 3 vols. (Paris, 1690), 1:59, 79–87.

36. *H.O.S.*, 16:199–200.

37. Denis de Sallo, sieur de La Coudraye, *Traitez de métaphysique demontrée selon la méthode des géometres* (Paris, 1693), "Préface" [unpaginated: xxii–xxviii]. La Coudraye (or Sallo) was a man of letters with many contacts in the world of philosophy, and the founder and first publisher of the *Journal des Savans*. Although he is generally treated as a Malebranchist and he did admire Malebranche, his posthumously published *Traitez* offered a more "orthodox" Cartesian proof, and relied on the representational power of the idea of God.

38. Daniel, *Voiage*, new ed. (Paris, 1702), 524–25.

39. Huet, *Censura philosophiae*, cap. 4, art. 9.

40. Régis, *Réponse aux Reflexions*, 219–51.

41. *H.O.S.*, 16:217–18.

42. Malebranche, *De la Recherche de la vérité*, livre 2, Ière partie, chap. 6, in André Robinet, ed., *Oeuvres Complètes de Malebranche* (hereafter cited as *O.C.*), 21 vols. (Paris, 1958–70), 2:19; on the inattentiveness to reason, see ibid., livre 4, chap. 11, sects. 2 and 3, in *O.C.*, 90–104.

43. Ibid., 103–4.

44. Ibid., 93–106.

45. Malebranche, *O.C.*, 19:841–42.

46. Malebranche, *Conversations Chrétiennes*, entretien 1, in *O.C.*, 4:14–30; see also *Entretien d'un philosophe chrétien et d'un philosophe chinois sur l'existence et la nature de Dieu*, in *O.C.*, 15:11–18.

47. Malebranche, *Entretiens sur la métaphysique et sur la religion*, in *O.C.*, 12:56.

48. Ibid., 137–38; the emphasis is Malebranche's,

49. Malebranche, *Recherche*, livre 6, IIème partie, chap. 6, in *O.C.*, 2:371.

50. Malebranche, *Conversations*, entretien 1, in *O.C.*, 4:14.

51. Malebranche, *Recherche*, livre 4, chap. 6, sect. 2, and livre 6, IIème partie, chap. 6, in *O.C.*, 2:52, 372.

52. Ibid., 372.

53. Malebranche, *Conversations*, entretien 1, in *O.C.*, 4:11–12, 36.

54. Malebranche, *Recherche*, livre 4, chap. 11, sect. 3, in *O.C.*, 2:96–101.

55. Malebranche, *Réponse au Livre des vraies et fausses idées*, in *O.C.*, 6:169.

56. Malebranche, *Réponse au Livre*, chap. 2, in *O.C.*, XVII^1:283.

57. Malebranche, *Réponse . . . à la Troisième Lettre de M. Arnauld . . . touchant les idées . . .* , in *O.C.*, 9:947–50.

58. Henri Lelevel, *La vraye et la fausse métaphysique, où l'on réfute les sentimens de M. Régis, et de ses adversaires, sur cette matière* (Rotterdam, 1694), 22–39.

59. Ibid. For Lelevel, in his published course of philosophy, the correct a posteriori proof was from Malebranche's system of occasional causes, namely, the inefficacity and impotence of both mind and matter, and, the consequent necessity of God given the activity and powers of any entity in general, and, in particular, given the harmony of body and soul: see Lelevel, *Conférences sur l'ordre naturel et sur l'histoire universelle . . .* (Paris, 1699), xiv–xvi, 1–8, 108–10, 374–82; he did, however, in this same work, offer his audience, without criticism, the arguments from necessary being given contingency and the argument from design (ibid., 401–56).

60. Lelevel, *La vraye et la fausse*, 22–39.

61. Malebranche, *Recherche*, livre 4, chap. 11, sect. 2, in *O.C.*, 2:90–95.

62. Antoine Arnauld, *Des vraies et des fausses idées, contre ce qu'en enseigne l'auteur de la Recherche sur la vérité* (Cologne, 1683), 285–88; and *Troisième Lettre . . . au R. P. Malebranche* (1698), published in Malebranche, *O.C.*, 9:1027–41.

63. Malebranche, *Réponse à la Troisième Lettre*, in *O.C.*, 9:947–48.

64. Malebranche, *Réponse aux vraies et fausses idées*, in O.C., 6:165.

65. Malebranche, *Recherche*, livre 2, I ère partie, chap. 6, in *O.C.*, 1:441–42; see also livre 3, II ème partie, chap. 7, in *O.C.*, 1:449–50.

66. Ibid., livre 3, chap. 11, sect. 3, in *O.C.*, 2:96–101.

67. Ibid., livre 6, II ème partie, chap. 6, in *O.C.*, 2:371–72 (emphasis added).

68. Malebranche, *Réponse aux vraies et fausses idées*, in *O.C.*, 6:166–67.

69. Malebranche, *Entretiens sur la métaphysique*, entretien 2, in *O.C.*, 12:53–54.

70. Malebranche, *Traité de l'amour de Dieu . . .* , in *O.C.*, 4:11–12.

71. Jean-Claude Sommier, *Histoire dogmatique de la religion; ou La religion prouvée par l'authorité divine et humaine, et par les lumières de la raison*, 3 vols. (Paris, 1708–11), 1:23–35. The approbations of Pissonat of the collège Royal, Rouget of the Sorbonne and the Jesuit Maucervel, *recteur* of Epinal, reinforce one's sense that peer review, when reputations were already established and time was dear, could be as lax in the seventeenth and eighteenth centuries as in the twentieth.

72. Arnauld, *Troisième Lettre* in Malebranche, *O.C.*, 9:1031ff.

73. Arnauld, *Des vraies et des fausses*, 285–88.

74. Malebranche, *Entretien d'un philosophe chrétien et d'un philosophe chinois*, in *O.C.*, 15:3–7.

75. P.-S. Régis, *Seconde Réplique de M. Régis à la Réponse du R. P. Malebranche . . . touchant la manière dont nous voyons les objets qui nous environnent* (Paris, 1694), art. 23.

76. *Journal de Trévoux*, juillet 1708, art. 89, 1134–43 and décembre 1708, art. 160, 1985–2004.

77. Pierre Poiret, *L'Oeconomie Divine, ou Système universel et démontré des oeuvres et des desseins de Dieu envers les hommes*, 7 vols. (Amsterdam, 1687), 2:568–73. For

Poiret's prior Cartesianism, see the *first* edition *only* of his *Cogitationes rationales de Deo, anima et mâlo* (Amsterdam, 1677).

78. Perrin, *Manuale Theologicum*, 5–9.

79. Rodolphe Du Tertre, S.J., *Réfutation d'un nouveau système métaphysique proposé par le P.M. . . . Auteur de la Recherche de la Vérité*, 3 vols. (Paris, 1715), 1 : 277–319; 2 : 11–99, 139–220.

80. On Hardouin's manuscripts and activity, see the contemporaneous accounts of Malebranche's hard-pressed Jesuit supporter Y. M. André, in Malebranche, *O.C.*, 19 : 840–42 and 20 : 213–14, and Hardouin's admonitory and menacing letter to André (25 Nov. 1712), in ibid., 19 : 823, where he wrote of several years of trying to convince André and Du Tertre that "Malebranchism . . . was atheism"; Hardouin's manuscripts on Malebranche and Descartes can be found among those in the collection Bibliothèque Nationale, MSS.: *Fonds français*, 14705–14706. For the publication of Hardouin's views, see his *Athei Detecti*, in Hardouin, *Opera Varia* (Amsterdam, 1733), 1 : 243, and his "Reflexions importantes," in ibid., 249–73. See also La Pillonnière's letters to Malebranche, written during his period of discipleship, concerning Hardouin's ongoing imputation of atheism to Cartesianism and Malebranchism in Malebranche, *O.C.*, 19 : 772–76. On La Pillonnière, see his *L'Athéisme découvert par le R. P. Hardouin, jésuite, dans les écrits de tous les Pères de l'Eglise et des philosophes modernes* (s.l.n.d. [1715]), reprinted in Thémiseul de Saint-Hyacinthe, *Mémoires littéraires*, 2 vols. (La Haye, 1716), 2 : 403–35. See also his letters to and from Malebranche, and the accounts of his life by André and others, assembled in Malebranche, *O.C.*, 19 : 758–60, 772–76, 780–81, 797, 801, 881, 889–90; 20 : 213–14, 356. Hardouin (1646–1729) was arguably the most idiosyncratic scholar of the early-modern world. He believed that most "ancient" literature had been composed in the thirteenth century by a conspiracy of heretical monks, and that Jesus and the disciples spoke only Latin. He was compelled by his order to retract such views, but nonetheless remained all of his life a respected scholarly figure. He served as professor of theology at the collège de Louis-le-Grand from 1683 to 1714, and in 1687, the Assemblée du Clergé de France commissioned him to edit a new collection of the councils of the Church. His *Athei detecti* conflated Saint Augustine (whom he took to be pseudo-Saint Augustine), the neoplatonic and Platonic Fathers (also forged, in his view), Jansen, Arnauld, Pascal, Nicole, Descartes, Régis, and Malebranche into one school of (pseudo-)Augustinian-Jansenist-Cartesian atheists who worshipped not God, but truth or the idea of truth. It had to please more than a few Jesuits and Thomists in France. He awaits his definitive biographer. La Pillonnière's tale would be of almost equal interest.

81. In Malebranche, *O.C.*, 19 : 841.

82. On Malebranche, see Hardouin, *Opera Varia*, 43–104; on Descartes, see ibid., 200–243, 249–73.

83. Malebranche to Y. M. André, 8 juin 1714, in *O.C.*, 19 : 881.

84. La Pillonnière, *L'Athéisme découvert*, passim.

85. P. Poiret, "Discursus praeliminaris de fide divina et ratione humana," added

to the *second* edition of his *Cogitationes rationales de Deo, anima et malo,* new ed., aug. (Amsterdam, 1685). In an "Appendix" to that edition, Poiret claimed that he was allowing a new edition to be issued so that he could add the "Discursus praeliminaris" and demonstrate how far he previously had erred in trusting to reason. Among his later efforts, he edited the spiritual works of Bourignon, Sainte Cathérine de Gênes, Madame Guyon, and Fénélon.

86. Sommier, "Dissertation Préliminaire, ou Apologie de la raison et de la foy contre les pyrrhoniens et les incrédules" (1708), in *Histoire dogmatique,* 1 : i–iii.

87. N. Anaclet du Havre, Capuchin, *Sujet de conférences sur la théologie positive, où l'on propose les questions dogmatiques et historiques, qui concernent la religion, tant en général qu'en particulier, avec la citation des auteurs qui traitent de ces matières. A l'usage des capucins.,* 3 vols. (Rouen, 1712), 1, III ème partie, 61–62 ("Reasonings of several theologians to prove that one cannot demonstrate the existence of God. . . ."); the authorities to whom he refers his readers can be found in 1, III ème partie, 48–49 ("on the existence and the essence of God") and 2, I ère partie, 1–2 ("the truth of the existence of God"). In his own proofs, which he labels necessary only for "the atheists," since the Christian can know God by faith, he favors those theologians who have argued for God from design, first cause, motion, thought, and universal consent (ibid., 2–6), but he later cautions that any philosophical or theological argument not drawn from infallible ecclesiastical authority or from Scripture is not binding in any manner whatsoever, and warns that our attachment to the opinions of mutually contradictory particular theologians has led to "so many opinionated disputes and contestations" (ibid., 2, II ème partie, 409–10). For Petau's Thomistic proofs, see Denys Petau, S.J., *Theologicorum Dogmatum,* vol. 1: *De Deo Uno, Deique proprietatibus agitur* (Paris, 1644); for Thommassin's Cartesian and Malebranchiste proofs, see Louis Thommassin, Oratoire, *Dogmatum Theologicorum . . . ,* 3 vols. (Paris, 1684–89), vol. 1: *Dogmatum theologicorum de Deo . . .* (Paris, 1684), and vol. 3, part 1: *De Prolegomenis theologiae* (Paris, 1689).

88. Basile de Soissons, Capuchin, "Traité de l'Existence de Dieu. Où il est prouvé par la raison naturelle qu'il y a un Dieu, ou qu'il n'y a rien du tout. Aut Deus aut nihil. Contre les Infidelles et les Athées de notre siècle," paginated separately (45 pp.) at the end of vol. 1 of his *Fondement inébranlable de la doctrine Chrétienne . . . ,* 3 vols. (Paris, 1680–83).

89. Pierre Coton and Michel Boutauld, *Le théologien dans les conversations avec les sages et les gens du monde* (Paris, 1683), 16–47. This work was in its third edition and fourth printing by 1696.

90. Isaac Papin, *Recueil des ouvrages composés par feu M. Papin en faveur de la religion . . . Nouvelle édition, augmentée de plusieurs manuscrits posthumes et dediée à M. L'Evêque de Blois,* 3 vols. (Paris, 1723), 2 : 423–42.

91. Abbé Armand de Gérard, *La philosophie des gens de cour* (Paris, 1680), "Epître" and "Préface" (both unpaginated), and 1–54, esp. 33–35, where he argues that one must not be *a* philosopher seeking truth, but a *Christian* philosopher seeking *Christian* truth. On a Christian a posteriori theology, see 116–86. On

page 186, he denies the right to use Copernicus's theory in any argument from design, since it is "too opposed to Holy Scripture."

92. Nicolas L'Herminier, *Summa*, 1:24–40, 49–55. The *Summa* enjoyed a second edition (Paris, 1718–19).

93. *Summa*, 40–63. L'Herminier (1657–1735) taught theology at Paris from 1699 until 1707, when he was called to high position in the diocese of Mans. His Jansenist views on free will and grace, however, eventually caused him ecclesiastical difficulty, and he ended his career among the Jansenist circles of Paris. Cf. Jean Meslier, *Oeuvres Complètes de Jean Meslier*, 3 vols., ed. J. Deprun, R. Desné, and A. Soboul (Paris, 1970–1972), 2:207–8, where the atheistic curé argues that both the atheist and the believer reject an infinite chain of causes and effects, and agree that "there is an unproduced first cause which must be, as a consequence of itself, independent of any other cause." Where the atheists name such an entity "nature" or "natural being," however, the theists, Meslier observed, name such a being "God," and assign it the powers of omniscient, omnipotent, and voluntary creation and governance: "It is in that, principally, that they are opposed." One can see, thus, in both Meslier and L'Herminier, the essential nature of the debate over "Providence" for those who denied the necessity of concluding in favor of perfection or excellence from mere consideration of the "absurdity" of infinite sequence.

94. Malebranche, *O.C.*, 19:813.

95. Malebranche, *Défense . . . contre l'Accusation de M^onsr De la Ville . . .* (Cologne, 1682) in *O.C.*, XVIII^I, 513–18.

96. A. Gaudin, Carthusian, *La distinction et la nature du bien et du mal, Traité où l'on combat l'erreur des Manichéens, les sentimens de Montaigne et de Charron, et ceux de Monsieur Bayle* (Paris, 1704), preface and 1–160. Gaudin's work was published with the approbation of the Oratorian and Sorbonniste La Marque Tilladet. Gaudin cited neither Descartes nor Malebranche in support of his views, but Saint Augustine.

97. Jacques Bernard, *De l'excellence de la religion*, 2 vols. (Amsterdam, 1714), 1:94–100. There was a second edition published at Amsterdam in 1732.

98. Abbé Claude-François Houtteville, *Essai philosophique sur la providence* (Paris, 1728), 51ff.; *compte rendu* in the *Journal de Trévoux*, août 1728.

99. *Journal de Trévoux* (juillet 1708): 1134–43.

100. David Hume, *An Inquiry Concerning Human Understanding*, sec. 11: "Of a Particular Providence and of a Future State."

101. Louis Bourdaloue, S.J., *Oeuvres de Bourdaloue*, 16 vols. (Paris, 1826) [a reissue of the *Oeuvres* of 1703–34], 3:196–97.

102. Ibid., 14:135–43.

103. Coton and Boutauld, *Le théologien*, 27–47; the quotation is from 46–47.

104. Petiot, *Demonstrations Théologiques*, 120–303.

105. Hieronymous Osorio de Fonseca, *Théologie curieuse contenant la naissance du monde. Avec douzes questions belles et curieuses sur ce sujet*, trans. Jacques de Jant (Dijon, 1666), 71–98.

106. André d'Abillon, *La Divinité défendue contre les athées* (Paris, 1641), 84–95.
107. Henri-Marie Boudon, *Oeuvres Complètes de Boudon, Grand Archdiacre d'Evreux . . .*, 3 vols., ed. J.-P. Migne (Paris, 1856), 1:367–424.
108. Jacques-Bénigne Bossuet, *Ouevres de Bossuet*, 4 vols., ed. Institut de France (Paris, 1849), 1:414–17; 2:715–24.
109. de Gérard, *La philosophie*, 33–35; and his *Le véritable Chrestien qui combat les abus du siècle, ou maximes et reflexions chrestiennes, sur quelques points de la religion* (Paris, 1679), 76–117.
110. Diroys, *Preuves et Préjugez*, 25–33.
111. Abbé de Choisy and abbé Dangeau, *Quatres Dialogues* (Paris, 1684), 142–55.
112. Henri Lelevel, *Entretiens sur ce qui forme l'honneste homme et le vray sçavant* (Paris, 1690), 61–98, 221.
113. *Reflexions et maximes sur divers sujets de morale, de religion et de politique* (Paris, 1690), 84–91. (Bibliothèque National, Imp.: R.18657).
114. Abbé Jean Rousseau, *Traité moral de la divine providence envers ses créatures, dans tout les états de la vie* (Paris, 1694), 80–348.
115. Pierre Villemandy, *Traité de l'efficace des causes secondes contre quelques philosophes modernes, dans lequel on prouve cette efficace par des principes également clairs et solides . . .* (Leiden, 1686), 4–5. For Villemandy, denial of Providence was atheism.
116. Dom André Rose, *Nouveau sistême par pensées sur l'ordre de la nature* (Paris, 1696), "Avertissement," and 20–21. Rose was a Benedictine.
117. Ibid., 1–20.
118. Louis Ferrand, *De la connoissance de Dieu. Par feu Monsieur Ferrand. Avec des remarques de M**** (Paris, 1706), 319–440. The author of the 'remarques' added to every subsection was anonymous; see the latter's explanation of the need to strengthen apologetic works in the light of early eighteenth-century thought in his preface [i–viii, unpaginated].
119. J.-B. Massillon, *Oeuvres complètes*, 4 vols., ed. Abbé E. A. Blampignon, (Bar-le-Duc, 1865), 1:111–19. Massillon was bishop of Clermont.
120. See, for example, Ricci's *De Christiana expeditione apud Sinas* (1615): *L'Expedition Chrétienne de la Chine tirée des commentaires de Riccius*, ed. P. Trigault (Lyon, 1616), 166–69, 188, which argued that Confucianism was theistic, but that there indeed were many learned atheists in China; Longobardi's *Traité sur quelques points de la religion des chinois* new ed. (Paris, 1701), passim, which stressed the atheism of Chinese men of letters; and Philippe Couplet's "Proemialis declarationis," in Couplet et al., *Confucius, Sinarum philosophus, sive Scientia sinensis latine expositata studio et opera Prosperi Intercetta, Christiani Herdtrich, Francisci Rougemont, Philippi Couplet* (Paris, 1686–87), part 2, which spoke of a secret cult of atheism among the learned.
121. L. Le Comte, S.J., *Eclaircissement sur la demonstration faite à N.S.P. le Pape des nouveaux mémoires de la Chine* (s.l., 1700), 14.
122. See A. de Lionne, *Observationes in quaesita sinarum imperatori a patribus S.J. proposita et illius ad ea responsionem circa Coeli, Auroum, et Confucii cultum . . .*

(s.l.n.d. [1704]), which gloats over these events. De Lionne was bishop of Rosalie.

123. Jean de Léry, *Histoire d'un voyage fait en la Terre du Brésil*, ed. Michel Contat ([1578]; Lausanne, 1972), 187–207 (Léry's *Histoire d'un Voyage* was first published in La Rochelle in 1578, and was reprinted in 1580, 1585, 1595, 1599, 1600, 1611, 1642, and 1677); Jean Mocquet, *Voyages en Afrique Asie, Les Indes Orientales et Occidentales . . .* , 2d ed. (Paris, 1617), 133. (Mocquet's *Voyages* were first published in Paris in 1616; the second edition was reprinted in Rouen in 1645 and 1655).

124. René Laudonnière, *L'Histoire notable de la Floride . . .* (Paris, 1586), in the critical edition published as *Three Voyages*, ed. and trans. Charles E. Bennet (Gainesville, 1975), 11–13; and Marc Lescarbot, *Histoire de la Nouvelle France . . .* (Paris, 1609), 683.

125. Lescarbot, *Histoire*, 3d ed. (Paris, 1617), vii, 92, 709–24.

126. Paul Le Jeune, S.J., *Relation de ce qui s'est passé en la Nouvelle France en l'année 1635* (Paris, 1636), 210–213. Le Jeune was "astonished" by this discovery, he explained; he previously had argued, in his *Relation de . . . 1633* (Paris, 1634), 75–79, that attributions of atheism were both inaccurate and "a great mistake."

127. Samuel de Champlain, *Voyages et Découvertes faites en la Nouvelle France, depuis l'année 1615 jusques à la fin de l'année 1618* (Paris, 1619) in *The Works of Samuel de Champlain*, 6 vols., ed. H. P. Biggar (Toronto, 1922–35), 3:15–16, 51–52, 143; 4:319–20. This work was reprinted in 1620 and 1627, and was included in the two printings of Champlain's works in Paris of 1632.

128. Ibid., 3:407.

129. François Cauche, "Relation de l'Isle de Madagascar," in *Relations véritables et curieuses de l'Isle de Madagascar et du Brésil . . .* , ed. Claude Morisot, (Paris, 1651), 45.

130. Antoine Biet, *Voyage de la France Equinoxiale en l'Isle de Cayenne . . .* (Paris, 1664), 360–62.

131. Claude d'Abbeville, Capuchin, *Histoire de la Mission des Pères Capucins en l'Isle de Maragnan et terres circonvoisines* (Paris, 1614), 328.

132. Abraham Roger, *La porte ouverte, pour parvenir à la connaissance du* PAGANISME *caché . . .* , ed. and trans. Thomas La Grue (Amsterdam, 1670), 139–40n.

133. Paul Rycaut, *Histoire de l'état présent de l'Empire Ottoman . . .* trans. M. Briot (Paris, 1670), 237–39. This was first published as *The Present State of the Ottoman Empire . . .* (London, 1668). A second edition of the French translation was released in the year of its publication, in Paris and Amsterdam, 1670; it was reprinted in Amsterdam in 1671; in Rouen in 1677; and in La Haye in 1709.

134. Nicolas Gervaise, *Histoire naturelle et politique du Royaume de Siam* (Paris, 1688), 157–239; Simon de La Loubère, *Du Royaume de Siam, par Monsr De La Loubère, envoyé extraordinaire du Roy auprès du Roy de Siam en 1687 et 1688*, 2 vols. (Amsterdam, 1691), 1:188, 394–95, 405–28. La Loubère, *Du Royaume,*

370, 396–99, 404–5, also believed in the atheism of the "men of letters" of China, and, *Du Royaume*, 380–81, in the atheism of India. La Loubère's work was reprinted in Paris in 1691 and in Amsterdam in 1714. He was a member of the Académie française from 1693.

135. Jean-Baptiste Du Tertre, O.P., *Histoire générale des Antilles habitées par les français*, 4 vols. (Paris, 1667–71), 2:499–502. He should not be confused with the Jesuit Rodolphe Du Tertre.

136. Le Jeune's atheists of Cap Bréton were described as modest, intelligent, serious, agreeable, exceptionally clever, honest and decent in *Relation*, 210–13; Lescarbot's atheistic Indians of North America, in *Relation*, 3d ed., passim, were praised throughout his account for their virtues and nobility, leading him to argue (709–724) that atheism is far better than idolatry; Léry, *Histoire d'un voyage*, 96, described his atheistic natives of Brazil as a physically and emotionally healthy people, without "defiance . . . avarice . . . envy and ambition. . . ."; La Loubère, *Du Royaume*, 1:222–23, praised his atheistic Siamese for their goodness, purity of morals, conjugal fidelity, and respect of elders, and, despite what he described as their tendencies to theft, avarice, and boastfulness, declared that their moral moderation compared favorably to the ways of the Europeans; Rycaut, *Histoire de l'état*, described his atheists as "mutually loving and strongly protective, obliging and hospitable, . . . frank and generous towards each other, and prompt to do each other services even to excess."

137. For what follows, see the authors cited in n. 3, above. On those who warned of the dangers inherent in the tendency of seventeenth-century classical commentary to find atheism prevalent among the ancients, see, for example, Michel Morgues, *Plan théologique du Pythagorisme et des autres sectes sçavantes de la Grèce* . . . , 2 vols. (Toulouse, 1712), passim; Benjamin Binet, *Idée générale de la théologie payenne* . . . (Amsterdam, 1699), 30–85; Laurent Bordelon, *Théatre philosophique, sur lequel on représente par des dialogues* . . . *les philosophes anciens et modernes* . . . (Paris, 1692), 153–58, which does, however, leave the question of Epicurus unresolved, 36ff.; R. W. Boclo, *Dissertatio philosophica, de Gentilium Philosophiae Atheismi Falso Suspectis* . . . (Bremen, 1716), passim; Johann Ch. Wolff, *Dissertatio de Atheismi falso suspectis* (Hamburg, n.d.), passim; V. E. Loescher, *Praenotiones Theologicae contra Naturalistarum et Fanaticorum omne genus Atheos, Deistas, Indifferentistas, Anti-scripturarios, etc.* (Wittenberg, 1708), 1–24. (Loescher believed in the reality of atheism, but saw great dangers in the overextension of the philosophical definition beyond what so described a few "truly stultified" minor figures, and a handful of manifest atheists such as [he believed] Spinoza.)

138. Jenkin Thomas Philipps argued in 1716 that Aristotelian philosophy led ineluctably to atheism, and that Descartes had rescued theology from its dangers and implications, in his *Dissertatio Historico-Philosophica de Atheismo* . . . (London, 1716), 6–22, and, in particular, 8, 9–13, 17–19. See also Valerianus Magnus, Capuchin, *Principia et specimen philosophiae axiomata; ens non factum, lux mentium; vacuum; vitrum marabiliter fractum; incorruptibilitas aquae;*

atheismus Aristotelis; soliloquia animae cum Deo (Cologne, 1652); Samuel Parker, *Disputationes de Deo et providentia divina* . . . (London, 1678), diput. 1, sect. 24; Jean de Launoy, *De varia Aristotelis in Academia Parisiensi Fortuna* (Paris, 1653), cap. 14. Anton Reiser, *De Origine, Progressu et Incremento Antitheisme* . . . (Augsburg, 1669), 226–382, after criticizing those who failed to distinguish between false belief and disbelief concerning God, argued that Aristotle, Epicurus, and all the Stoics should be placed among those convicted of the latter. Jacob Friedrich Reimann, *Historia Universalis Atheismi et Atheorum falso et merito suspectorum* . . . (Hildesiae, 1725), 133–270, thought it clear that Aristotle himself was no atheist but claimed that some of the later Greek peripatetics appear to have been such; he did classify Zeno, all the Greek sceptics, Galen, Lucretius, Varro, Pliny (and a host of lesser figures) among "the atheists," noting that *many* more of the ancients *may* have been such. J. H. Foppius and W. Vogt, *Exercitatio I: De Atheismo Philosophorum Gentilium Celebriorum* (Bremen, [1714]), found the early Eleactic and Ionic schools "irreproachable," but saw a "degeneration" of Greek philosophy to atheism.

139. J. F. Buddeus, *Traité de l'Athéisme et de la superstition* . . . , trans. Louis Philon, and ed. J.-C. Fischer (Amsterdam, 1740). Philon, in his "Avertissement," called Buddeus's work the deepest and most extensive on the subject. On Plato, see 16, n. 2; on Heraclitus, Hippocrates and Plutarch, see 39–45; on Cicero and Pliny, see 47–50. On the atheism of ancient thought, see 9–10 (the Ionics); 17–20 (the sceptics); 23–24 (Strato); 27–29 (the cynics and stoics); 29–39 (the Eleactic "sect"). On Aristotle, see 20–23 and 108–14. Among the modern atheists he included, 52–68, Bruno, Vanini, Campanella, Machiavelli, and Césalpin. Buddeus regretted that Descartes had been placed by many among the atheists, but utterly rejected Descartes's proofs of God, and argued that the Cartesian rejection of final causes was "strongly to the atheists' taste," destroying the means by which to make "the best arguments to demonstrate the existence of God," 72–75.

140. Pascal, *Pensées*, no. 547 (ed. Brunschvicq). For Pascal, it should be noted, the fulfillment of prophecies did constitute a proof of sorts of the Divinity.

141. Huet, *Traité philosophique de la faiblesse de l'esprit humain* (Paris, 1723): translated into Latin as *De Imbecillitate mentis humanae libre tres* (Amsterdam, 1738).

142. Desgabets, 86–89.

143. Eustache de La Conception, Carmelite, *Instructions en forme de catéchisme sur tous les mystères de la religion, par demandes et réponses* (Paris, 1699), 3–4; the *Instructions* were published with the approbation of the Sorbonniste Pirot.

144. Gaspard Langenhert, *Philosophus Novus. Le Noveau Philosophe* [in Latin, with French translation by abbé Regnier Desmarais] (Paris, 1701–2), 1:13–73. The *Philosophus Novus* bore the approbation of La Marque Tilladet.

145. Abbé L. Blondel and abbé J. Louail, *L'Idée de la religion chrétienne où l'on explique tout ce qui est nécessaire pour être sauvé* (Paris, 1728), 1–4.

146. Bibliothèque de l'Arsenal, MSS. 2588, no. 1, 1–5.

147. See Claude Buffier, S.J., *Elémens de métaphysique* . . . (Paris, 1725), 39–79, for his clearest exposition of the errors of Cartesian proofs; and René-Joseph

Tournemine, S.J., "Reflexions . . . sur l'athéisme, sur la démonstration de monseigneur de Cambray, et sur le système de Spinosa," in Fénélon, *De l'Existence de Dieu* (Paris, 1713). Tournemine was the editor of the *Journal de Trévoux*. Unbeknownst to Fénélon, he added these "Reflexions" to a 1713 edition of Fénélon's treatise that he edited and published, claiming (quite falsely) that Fénélon had used a priori arguments (in addition to a posteriori arguments) merely ad hominem, to lead "the Cartesians and Malebranchistes" to God, recognizing that such proofs were not of themselves demonstrative. In addition to assailing the a priori proofs, Tournemine accused Malebranche of Spinozism. Forced by the King's confessor, Le Tellier, to give Malebranche satisfaction, Tournemine wrote in the *Journal de Trévoux* (novembre 1713): 2029–30, that he "never had thought of casting any suspicion of Atheism on this virtuous priest," but could not resist concluding that "God said, 'I am that I am.' God did not say, 'I am all that is (I am the being in general).'"

148. Abbé Claude-François Houtteville, *La religion chrétienne prouvée par les faits. Avec un Discours historique et critique, sur la méthode des principaux auteurs qui ont écrit pour et contre le christianisme depuis son origine* (Paris, 1722), cliii–clviii.

149. Buffier, *Elémens*, 79–132.

150. Charles-Joseph Hefele, *Histoire des Conciles d'après les documents originaux*, trans. Cardinal J. Hergenroether, (Paris, 1917), vol. 8, Ière partie, 420–22.

151. Charles de Saint-Evremond, *Oeuvres mêlées*, 5 vols. (Amsterdam, 1706), 1: 184–85.

CHAPTER 3

Pierre Nicole, Jansenism, and the Morality of Enlightened Self-Interest

DALE VAN KLEY

The notion that a movement so secular as the French Enlightenment might have had other than purely secular origins would have until recently raised scholarly eyebrows. With the spectacular exception of Carl Becker's provocative thesis that the Enlightenment took much more from Christianity than it acknowledged or of which it was consciously aware, the regnant explanations have instead pointed to such obvious candidates as the scientific revolution, the geographical discoveries, the skeptical tradition or more generally the influence of classical antiquity as mediated by the Renaissance and seventeenth-century "free-thought."[1] The agency granted to the theological and religious movements of the preceding era has been at most that of an indirect facilitator: that by their internecine conflicts they weakened each other, opening a breach eventually exploited by forms of rationalism, naturalism, and religious skepticism. Catholics versus Huguenots, Gomarists versus Arminians, Jansenists versus Jesuits—the parties to these conflicts succeeded only in exposing to full view the precarious nature and socially disruptive effects of their mutually exclusive claims to truth, and in leaving a battlefield littered with casualties of religion's own making.[2] The fact that the Jansenist-Jesuit controversy dragged ingloriously on under the high noon of the eighteenth century accentuated this effect in France particularly.[3]

Research since the Second World War has cumulatively modified this picture. As early as 1939 Robert Palmer, a student of Carl Becker writing obviously under his influence, insisted convincingly upon the thematic proximity between Jesuit or Molinistic theology and many Enlightenment emphases. By rehabilitating human nature and its freedom of will as well as by minimizing the role of divine grace and restricting sin to conscious violations of divine commands, Palmer argued, French Jesuits facilitated the acceptance of Enlightenment naturalism and went more than half way in their zeal to communicate with philosophies once these appeared upon the scene.⁴ Before becoming a solvent of confessional loyalties, the revived classical skepticism of Pyrrho and Sextus Empiricus, Richard Popkin demonstrated in 1960, served mainly as an auxiliary in the cause of Catholic fideistic apologetics against Protestantism.⁵ Pierre Bayle, long regarded as the most prototypical of the forerunners of the Enlightenment, startlingly emerged in 1963 from Elisabeth Labrousse's scholarly studio in markedly Calvinistic tones, with the result that any contribution made by him to the formation of Enlightenment thought appears, mutatis mutandis, as a contribution by seventeenth-century Calvinism.⁶ More recently, Quentin Skinner, in his magisterial study of the foundations of modern political thought, has demonstrated how the crucible of religious conflict gave rise to the major themes of modern political thought—natural-rights popular sovereignty versus natural-law absolutism—by the close of the sixteenth century, leaving the Enlightenment the task of composing comparatively minor variations on these themes.⁷

But however many and devious the roads from the Church to Enlightenment, the movement of Catholic Augustinianism known as Jansenism would seem to represent a recalcitrant dead end. Jansenists neither blushed to perform miracles in full view of urbane Paris in the 1730s nor hesitated, in their party's weekly *Nouvelles ecclésiastiques*, to oppose Enlightenment naturalism in all its ways, shapes, and forms throughout the "century of lights."⁸ It was in view of their many theological concessions to Enlightenment naturalism that the Jesuits, too, found themselves the objects of Jansenist harassment during this same century. Against the Jesuits' rather favorable estimate of man's capacity to know and choose the good even after Adam's fall, the Jansenists insisted upon the morally debilitating consequences of this catastrophe: without God's grace man was a prisoner of concupiscence and could only do evil. And against the Jesuits' "sufficient" grace which the sinner was free to appropriate or reject, the Jansenists pitted an "efficacious" grace that omnipotently rescued the will from the dungeons of concupiscence and bore it up on the wings of "charity." Charity or concupiscence—these were the only states or "delectations" available for fallen man. Neither condition could he really be said to have chosen for himself.⁹

Jansenism's morally severe, ascetically otherworldly and militantly antisecular character becomes even clearer in comparison to Calvinism, its seventeenth-century Augustinian cousin. Sharing with Calvinism the Augustinian doctrines of divine predestination and reprobation and efficacious or irresistible grace—and with these the denial of human free will—Jansenism was strenuously opposed to the Calvinistic doctrines of justification by faith alone and to the way the Synod of Dordrecht (1618–19) articulated the doctrine of the perseverance of the saints. What the Jansenists objected to in this formulation was not the proposition that God's elect persevered to the gates of heaven—this held true by definition—but rather to the doctrine that anyone who had ever been justified or in a state of grace necessarily persevered and so lived in the certainty of his election. For the Jansenist the polarities "just-unjust" and "elect-reprobate" were simply not interchangeable, with the result that among the "just" many did not persevere and that, even among those who did, most would neither have known that they would nor necessarily have found themselves in a state of justification at any given point in their lives. God sometimes momentarily withdrew efficacious grace even from the saints in order to humble them, to put them in their place, as it were; Saint Peter's spectacular denial of Christ was a case in point. This doctrinal difference in turn hinged on Jansenism's quite Catholic—and Augustinian—view of the state of justification: namely, as the objective presence of "charity" or the works of righteousness in the believer, which he might lose by God's withdrawal of the efficacious grace that alone enabled him to perform these works. This view stands in marked contrast to the Calvinist believer's unmerited and purely "imputed" righteousness which he had appropriated by means of a faith definitively given to him by God's grace.[10]

The doctrine of divine election could therefore never function as a doctrine of comfort for the Jansenist as it often did for the Calvinist. Condemned doctrinally to navigate uncertainly in this life between the Scylla of "presumption" of one's salvation on the one side and the Charybdis of despair at the prospect of damnation on the other, the Jansenists salvaged the best of this shipwreck by making virtues of "salutary fear" and "holy trembling." Nothing more appalled them than the Calvinists' smug certainty and damnable "false assurance" that enabled them to maintain that King David never ceased being justified even as he slept with the wife of a man he caused to be killed; nor was anything closer to the heartbeat of Antoine Arnauld's nine-hundred-page polemic against Calvinism than its concluding section entitled "the utility of fear demolished."[11] To banish fear was to destroy the fine balance of the Christian life, which was to maintain the elements of hope, fear, and trembling in a state of precarious balance. Although Jansenists held up the ideal of performing even the most secular and indifferent of actions in a spirit of "charity" or love for God, secular involvement came to them "accompanied by too many dangers" of losing charity for them to have developed a Catholic counterpart to Calvinism's frank ennoblement of secular vocations; pristine Jansenist conversions hence typically took the form of full or partial withdrawal from secular commitments.[12] By the same token, Jansenist asceticism was altogether too *craintif* to have become entirely this-worldly; whatever the merits or demerits of the Weber thesis, it could hardly have arisen in connection with Jansenism. It is therefore most difficult to imagine Jansenism ever accommodating, much less having anticipated, an ethic based upon anything so secular—and "enlightened"—as the pursuit of enlightened self-interest.[13]

Yet something like this happened. Not only did seventeenth-century Jansenism anticipate this hallmark of the French Enlightenment's ethical thought, but the Jansenist Port-Royalist who most clearly did so, Pierre Nicole, at least widely disseminated if he did not actually coin the phrase "enlightened self-love."[14] Ironically, the anticipation in question occurred, not because of any softening of or deviation from the "hard" Jansenist line, but precisely because of what was most severe, otherworldly, uncompromising—in a word, Jansenist—about Jansenism: namely, its quantitative restriction of salvation to the divinely predestined "elect" and its preoccupation with the only sort of (efficacious) grace that really counted, that necessarily engendered charitable works on the part of the "just." Forced by the combination of their stingy distribution of grace and their low view of man without it to account for the apparent orderliness and civility of the world in terms other than grace or the residual goodness in man, some Jansenists did so in terms of sin or "concupiscence" itself. Now for the Jansenist, the essence of "concupiscence" was the preferment of self or self-love to God.[15] To explain order and civility in terms of concupiscence was therefore to explain it in terms of self-love which, however much an impediment to one's salvation in the hereafter, became by the same token indispensable to the smooth running of the world here below. Having importantly contributed to the creation of the morality of enlightened self-interest, Jansenists had only to see it and declare it good. This additional step, however, they never took.

The Jansenist who most clearly exemplifies this process is Pierre Nicole, author of the widely read *Essais de morale;* the essays that most clearly contain this anticipation are those entitled "De la Grandeur" and "De la charité et de l'amour propre," although important fragments of Nicole's argument abound in many of the other essays as well. In the very first paragraph of the latter essay Nicole forthrightly announces his paradoxical thesis, that "although nothing is more opposed to charity which relates everything to God than self-love (*amour propre*) which revolves entirely around the self, yet there is nothing more similar to the effects of charity than those of self-love. So closely does it follow the same paths that one could hardly do better in marking those to which charity should lead us, than to discover those actually taken by enlightened self-love. . . ."[16] To explain this paradox is the remainder of the essay's goal.

Nicole's first premise is an authentically Jansenist statement of the nature of fallen man (that is, human nature subsequent to Adam's fall) bereft of the aid of divine grace, and hence necessarily motivated entirely by concupiscence or self-love. Thus motivated and left entirely to his own devices, fallen man loves only himself "without limits or measure" because such is the character of self-love "at basis and in its first instincts," that is, in its undisguised and naive condition. It implants in man's heart the "tyrannical disposition" of wanting to "dominate over everything," rendering him "violent, unjust, cruel, ambitious, flattering, envious, insolent, and querulous," to name only these few. "Such is the monster," Nicole concludes, "which we harbor within us. . . . It is the principle of all our actions which have no other basis than fallen corrupt nature."[17]

Self-love's primitive passion to "dominate" over everyone and everything is inhibited by this inconvenience, however, that all other selves are animated by precisely this same passion, with the result that to the precise degree that the passion to dominate strikes one as legitimate and adorable where he himself is concerned, it appears illegitimate and contemptible as manifested in others. Everyone is therefore motivated, not only by a desire to tyrannize over others, but to prevent others from tyrannizing over him. Whence there arises a Nicolean state of nature plagued by "all men in arms against each other," which differs from Thomas Hobbes's more famous "war of every man against every man" not so much in judgment of fact as in that of value. For if by this description the Sage of Malmesbury had "wished only to depict . . . the disposition of men's hearts in relation to each other without pretending to render it just and legitimate, he would have said something as conformed to the truth and experience as that which he (actually) said is contrary to reason and justice."[18] And for Nicole as well as for Hobbes, the political state derives from this condition of war. Reduced by their mutually exclusive desires for domination to a preoccupation with elemental self-preservation, men were driven to form defensive unions with each other; faced with internal as well as external threats to these unions, they invented laws, crimes, "wheels and gibets" to give them teeth. "The fear of death," concludes Nicole, "is therefore the first bond of civil society and the first rein on *amour propre.*" [19] Nicole differs from Hobbes, not in his description of the empirical origin of sovereignty—even if conferred by popular agreement it remains for the one as for the other an irrevocable concession—but in his insistence that only divine sanction can ultimately render it legitimate. Louis XIV was not Nicole's sovereign for nothing. [20]

But the fear of death was only the beginning of society. Forced by others and the political order to renounce physical domination, yet far from resigned to complete impotence or nullity, amour propre hit upon the device of giving the better to receive, of employing flattery or making itself serviceable in order to obtain what it desired. "Gross" cupidity or material interest is therefore Nicole's second bond of society; it is the source of all commerce whether in goods and money or in "works [*travaux*], services, assiduities, and civilities. . . ." And what wonders does it not perform! For it is by means of "this commerce that all the needs are in some fashion fulfilled, without charity playing any role whatsoever," so that "in states where it has no place because the true Religion is banished from them, one lives in no less peace, security, and comfort, than if one were in a republic of Saints." [21] Indeed, Nicole goes so far as to suggest that amour propre thus enlightened does better at providing for material needs than what he calls "communal charity." "What charity would it be," for example, "that built an entire house for another, that furnished it, carpeted it and gave it the key?" Yet the cupidity of the innkeeper "will do so happily." Or again, "what charity [would be willing] to go look for remedies in the Indies, to abase oneself before the vilest ministers, and to render to others the lowliest and most tiresome of services? Cupidity does all of that without complaining." [22] And so on.

By themselves, however, fear and interest would neither suffice to account for all the varieties of human sociability nor exhaust concupiscence's ingenuity in imitating charity. Yet a third concupiscent motive is necessary to complete Nicole's antitrinity, and this he identifies as the desire to be esteemed, respected, and admired, but above all loved. By far the "most general" if not the strongest of the social passions, the desire to be loved is also by far the "subtlest and finest," Nicole thinks, in counterfeiting the movements of charity. For whereas it is often easy enough to distinguish "human fear" and "gross interest" from a genuine movement of charity, it is simply not possible to track this "quest for the love and esteem of men" by reason of the "marvellous dexterity" with which it effaces "all the traits and characters of concupiscence." This latter chameleonlike capacity self-love developed because, knowing full well that to reveal its true colors would only elicit others' aversion, it chose rather to imitate charity in order to elicit their affection. The result is an inclination so mobile that there is "nothing into which it cannot slither," and simultaneously so perfect in its imitation of charity that it is "practically impossible to know precisely what distinguishes them from each other." Yet a motivational chasm separates the two. Whereas charity is inspired by love for God spilling over into love for others, self-love aping charity produces only the morality of "human decency" [*l'honnêteté humain*], at its basis concupiscent and corrupt.[23]

Nicole goes on to illustrate these points with reference to self-love's capacity to imitate charity's various ramifications as outlined by Saint Paul in his first epistle to the Corinthians.[24] Take humility, for example. The charitable man is naturally humble because, loving divine justice and hating injustice, he perceives the radical injustice of desiring or accepting people's admiration, whether for certain "human qualities" which are "sinful, vain and frivolous," or for genuinely good ones, which are undeserved gifts of God. Far from soliciting vain praises, charity rather "joyfully embraces every humiliation and abasement" and "thus restricts itself to an exact modesty." "Yet there is nothing in these," Nicole insists, "that self-love does not imitate perfectly." For knowing well that other selves would correctly perceive a gaudy display of his supposed virtues as a poorly disguised attempt to win their praise, the decent [*honnête*] man wisely renounces not only such "gross and base vanities" but even the subtler "detours" and "little artifices" employed to the same effect. Nicole appeals to the examples of the generals Condé and Turenne who, though merely *honnête*, spoke of their military exploits with as much or more indifference and modesty as Saint Louis might have employed in describing his crusading activities in Egypt—"so much do saintliness and *honnêteté* resemble each other in their external actions, . . . having only this difference between them, that whereas saintliness is struck by vanity's injustice in relation to God, decency [*honnêteté*] is moved by its baseness in relation to men."[25]

It is the same with charity's other manifestations. Acknowledging one's faults? Charity does so "not only with joy, but with avidity," valuing even the accompanying pain as a necessary medicine for the disease of *amour propre*, which as the dominant principle is full of resentment towards others' admonitions, but which nonetheless takes the same tack as charity in order to disarm criticism in advance and make a lovable candor out of what it knows it cannot hide.[26] Responding to unjust accusations? Charity does so "modestly," "gently," and with a view towards the salvation of the unjust accuser, while "enlightened *amour propre*," although mainly concerned "to efface these injurious suspicions and reestablish [its] reputation," follows precisely the same procedure.[27] Giving credit to others where credit is due? Charity does so all the more willingly because in so doing it need not fear its own soul's "vanity and complaisance" whereas amour propre, although inwardly "malign, jealous, envious, full of venom and spite," nonetheless adopts the same external course in order to "acquire friends, disarm enemies, and get on well with all the world."[28] Exercising patience? "Charity is patient amidst injuries . . . in order to satisfy God's justice whereas amour propre, impatient at basis, is not incapable of a "*patience d'intérêt et de vanité*, which produces the same outward effects." *Bienfaisant*, grateful, faithful, unambitious—there is not one of these characteristics of charity with which enlightened self-interest does not cloak itself, although motivated by diametrically opposed considerations.[29] Nicole goes so far as to suggest that by "sensing something base and despicable" about undue subservience to sensual pleasures, an *amour propre sage et éclairé* can fashion for itself a life of moderate asceticism, which effectively counterfeits charity's own aversion to the flesh, motivated in its case by a desire to remain attached to God alone. Not only can amour propre seek ascetic silence and practice austerities, but it can even suffer death joyfully to its own advantage, there being "martyrs of vanity as well as of charity."[30]

So effectively does self-love imitate charity that it quite suffices, in Nicole's opinion, for the perfect running of society. "To reform entirely the world, that is, to banish from it all vices and gross disorders," he audaciously concludes, "it suffices in the absence of charity, to give men an *amour propre éclairé* which knows how to discern its true interests, and tends towards those by ways which right reason discovers. However corrupt," he adds, "that society internally and in the eyes of God, nothing would be externally better regulated, more civil, just, peaceful, *honnête* or more generous, and what is even more admirable is that, although it were animated and moved by amour propre alone, amour propre would not be visible, and though entirely devoid of charity, one would see only the forms and character of charity."[31]

If this were not enough, and lest the pious console themselves with the thought that this temporal interchangeability between charity and amour propre is limited to externals alone, Nicole pulls even this prayer rug from beneath his knees. Although infinitely inimical, leading either to eternal life or damnation, the principles of charity and *amour propre* are no more introspectively distinguishable than they are in their external effects. Behind "formal and express reflections" flit "transitory thoughts," "confused ideas" as well as "imperceptible movements of the heart," which escape conscious attention and render one unaware of the complexity of one's own motivations. Charity and amour propre are therefore often found mingled together in one's motivations "without his being able to know for certain which of the two prevails." Consequently "one seeks both God and the world" without always being able to distinguish between the two; nor can one ever be sure of a given action that it "is entirely exempt from all *recherche propre*."[32]

Yet far from legitimizing impiety, spiritual skepticism, or despair, even this introspective dimension of Nicole's mixed-up state of affairs boasts a providential design. Were things otherwise, the children of light would be easily identifiable, a nation apart, a situation destructive of the "state of faith" by which God resolved to save some and not others. The evil ones, knowing that they could not attain the standard of the blessed, would not even attempt it.[33] Moreover, this state of affairs is not without advantages for the just themselves in that it powerfully combats pride and dangerous presumption:

> It is useful for the just not to know themselves, and not to see their own justice. For that would be capable of making them fall [*déchoir*]. Man is so weak, even in his strength, that he would not be able to bear its weight. And by a strange reversal which has its source in the corruption of our hearts, although our good consists in the possession of virtue and our evil in being full of faults, it is nonetheless more dangerous for us to know our virtues than our faults. The knowledge of our humility makes us proud, and the knowledge of our pride makes us humble. We are strong when we know ourselves to be weak, and we are weak when we think ourselves strong. Thus this obscurity which prevents us from seeing clearly whether we act from charity or *amour propre*, far from being detrimental to us, is salutary. It does not deprive us of our virtues, but prevents us from losing them, by holding us always in *humility* and *fear* [my italics], by making us suspicious of all our works, and by throwing us upon the mercy of God alone.[34]

A more impeccably Jansenist lesson from all the foregoing could hardly have been drawn.

It is hence Nicole's Jansenism, rather than any diminution or attenuation of it, which is the key to his argument that enlightened self-love or concupiscence is by itself quite sufficient for the smooth running of the world. Nor is it easy to imagine how it could have turned out otherwise. The combination of a low view of human nature after the fall and a stingy distribution of grace in the fallen state leaves Nicole little else besides fallen nature or concupiscence itself with which to explain the apparent order and harmony in society and the state. That this paradox is credited to God's marvelous providence hardly alters the fact that it is by the manipulation of sinful nature itself that God achieves the appearance of charity and the reality of societal order. Suggestions such as Nannerl O. Keohane's to the effect that Nicole's vision of an autonomous terrestrial society exists in spite of, or in uneasy juxtaposition to, his Jansenism are somewhat off the mark.[35] The fact that his analysis of such a society led Nicole straightway to the Jansenist ethic of "humility and fear" is indication enough that, in his mind at least, the two have everything in—as well as outside—the world to do with each other.

This is not of course to deny that Nicole's Jansenism is tempered by a certain "humanism," a begrudging respect for some unaided human capacities, or that he was temperamentally less polemical or extreme in his formulations than some other Port-Royalists. In opposition to Arnauld he developed a doctrine of "general grace" which, akin to Calvin's "restraining grace," remained as an aid to all men after Adam's fall, enabling them to attain partial knowledge of God as well as of eternal and natural law.[36] Unlike Pascal, therefore, Nicole allowed for human reason's capacity to perceive natural law and approximate divine justice, and he had a limited use for traditional Thomistic arguments for God's existence.[37] Nicole's role in suppressing certain of Pascal's more extreme formulations in the first edition of the *Pensées* is well known.[38]

Yet it is not these "humanistic" mitigations in Nicole's thought that are responsible for the line of argumentation in question, but rather what is most Jansenist about his Jansenism. It is Nicole's very Augustinian hostility to humanistic naturalism that ironically produces a naturalism of a purely descriptive and novel sort.[39] For unlike the traditional concept of natural law with its strong ethical content and relatively optimistic estimate of human reason's capacity to perceive it, the sort of natural law that emerges from the premises of Nicole's argumentation is purely behavioral and descriptive in character, lending itself perfectly to formulation in terms of corpuscular Cartesian physics:

> As little bodies . . . unite their forces and movements they form great masses of matter . . . called whirlpools, which are like estates and kingdoms. Since these whirlpools are themselves crowded and confined by other whirlpools, as by neighboring kingdoms, little whirlpools form in each larger one, which, while following the general movement of the larger bodies propelling them, do not

cease, however, to have a movement of their own, which in turn forces smaller bodies to revolve around them. Similarly great personages of state, while following the general movement, have their own interests providing centers for quantities of people attached to them. Finally, as all little bodies propelled by whirlpools also turn around their own centers, so little people, who follow the fortunes of the great and those of the state, do not cease in all the duties and services they perform for others to think of themselves and to have their own interests continually in view.[40]

By the same token, however, it is misleading to talk as Lionel Rothkrug does about Nicole's "desire to establish the supremacy of the human intellect" and his tendency to identify "reason with the divine."[41] For if in the context of the present argument Nicole's "reason" can be said to play the role of guide, it is in the realm of means and not of ends. In this latter domain it is passion or concupiscent amour propre who is queen; reason is at best her handmaiden.

Not only is the argument altogether compatible with Nicole's Jansenism, but it is quite compatible with Jansenism generally. In addition to the glimmerings of natural law "amidst the shadows which amour propre has cast," the beneficent effects of amour propre itself figure among the causes which the Jansenist jurist Jean Domat recognized as "contributing to the preservation of the society of men by men themselves."[42] Jacques Esprit similarly expressed wonderment at amour propre's role in the formation and continuance of the political order as well as in producing such apparently disinterested and socially beneficial sentiments as pity.[43] Pascal himself, in some respects more Jansenist than the Jansenists, marveled at "the grandeur of man amidst concupiscence itself, in knowing how to derive from it such an admirable order and in having made of it an image of charity."[44] Nor is the argument a stranger to seventeenth-century Augustinianism more widely construed. Beginning with the Calvinistic premises of the "total depravity" of fallen man and the numerically few recipients of "irresistible grace," Pierre Bayle in his *Pensées diverses sur la comète* followed a similar line of argumentation to a very similar conclusion. Elisabeth Labrousse, who has done Pierre Bayle scholarship the immense favor of taking his Calvinism seriously, has likewise insisted upon Bayle's Augustinian hostility to traditional naturalism as the key to his providentialist rehabilitation of the passions and the more behavioristic naturalism thus entailed.[45]

Finally, the example of Pierre Nicole throws a brilliant light on the Protean nature of political Augustinianism. In a classic thesis, H. X. Arquillière has intriguingly argued that Saint Augustine's rhetorical imprecisions and hyperbolic denigration of human nature, reason, and justice eventually led, in the hands of lesser followers at a time of increasing Christianization, to a denial of the secular state's independent reason for existence and therefore to the medieval absorption of the temporal by the spiritual and the natural by the supernatural. This "political Augustinianism" constituted the indispensable intellectual background to Pope Gregory VII's claims on behalf of papal power over temporal potentates.[46] If that is so, it remains paradoxically the case that, formulated even more sharply in the sixteenth and seventeenth centuries amidst gradual deChristianization, "political Augustinianism" in the hands of Nicole and Bayle had more spectacularly secularizing consequences than the natural law tradition championed especially during this period by Arminians and Jesuits.[47] Of course, neither Nicole nor Bayle ventured to pronounce the pursuit of self-love morally good. To the best of my knowledge, no Jansenist ever did. When at mid-eighteenth century Claude-Adrien Helvétius in *De l'esprit* audaciously stood Nicole on his head by christening the passions generally and self-interest particularly as productive of "true virtue" and "acts of the most enlightened *charity*," [my italics] contemporary Jansenists could not find words suitably strong—"horrible," "abominable," "scandalous," to name just a few—with which to characterize this "travesty of vices into virtues."[48] The irony is that without their seventeenth-century spiritual forebears' insistence upon the social and political utility of self-love, the Enlightenment's moral rehabilitation of its indulgence would have been considerably more difficult.[49]

NOTES

1. Carl Becker, *The Heavenly City of the Eighteenth-Century Philosophers* (New Haven and London, 1932). On this subject in general, see Ira O. Wade's chapter on "Theories on the Enlightenment's Origins" in *The Intellectual Origins of the French Enlightenment* (Princeton, 1971), 28–57. Wade himself seems to put most stress on science, humanism (including free thought and skepticism) and religious reform, although he does not neglect travel literature, 361–91. Among some recent historians of the Enlightenment not mentioned in Wade's discussion, Franklin L. Baumer, in *Modern European Thought: Continuity and Change in Ideas, 1600–1950* (London and New York, 1977), esp. 30, lists the new science, the Renaissance and its revival of skepticism, the mutually destructive character of the religious wars and European exposure to alien cultures; Peter Gay, in *The Enlightenment: An Interpretation*, 2 vols. (New York, 1967–69), 1:313, points to "classicism plus science"; Norman Hampson, *The Enlightenment*, vol.

4 of *Penguin History of European Thought* (Baltimore, 1968), 15–40, underscores the Renaissance, scientific, and geographical discovery, plus continental rationalism and English empiricism; and for J. H. Brumfitt, *The French Enlightenment* (London and Basingstake, 1972), 27–59, it is Cartesian rationalism, Lockean empiricism, and scientific discovery, aided and abetted by the "breakdown of absolutism." On skepticism specifically, see Richard H. Popkin, *The History of Skepticism from Erasmus to Spinoza* (Berkeley, Los Angeles, and London, 1979); on French free thought more generally, see J. S. Spink, *French Free Thought from Gassendi to Voltaire* (London, 1960), and René Pintard, *Le libertinage érudit dans la première moitié du XVII siècle* (Paris, 1943). On science and the Enlightenment, see Herbert Butterfield, *The Origins of Modern Science* (New York, 1968); and on literature and the Enlightenment, see esp. V. Pinot, *La Chine et la formation de l'esprit philosophique, 1640–1740* (Paris, 1932), updated by *Les rapports entre la Chine et l'Europe du temps des lumières*, Actes du II Colloque International de Sinologie (Paris, 1980). Paul Hazard's classic *La crise de la conscience européenne* (Paris, 1935), 5–29, remains one of the best general treatments.

2. Lest Wade's attention to "religious reform" be construed as an acknowledgment of a positive contribution on religion's part, he specifies that "this fragmentation of the Church into very dynamic religious sects squabbling with each other offered a fertile ground for the rise of religious skepticism which inevitably contributed to a further weakening of religion." (Wade, *Intellectual Origins*, 132). The same is roughly true of Baumer's mention of the Reformation, the mainly indirect and negative role of which was to have challenged and weakened the principle of authority (Baumer, *Modern European Thought*, 30). The present essay, however, is most specifically opposed to Hugh H. Trevor-Roper's "The Religious Origins of the Enlightenment," in *The European Witch-Craze of the Seventeenth Century and Other Essays* (New York and Evanston, 1969), 193–236, which, despite its title, denies to religion and especially to Calvinism any role whatsoever and argues that even the various seventeenth-century heterodoxies, such as Arminianism, extreme Molinism, and Socinianism, were only new manifestations of Erasmianism assuming the form of religious heresies. For Trevor-Roper, the Enlightenment is above all the resumption of the Renaissance after having been interrupted by a century and a half of theological bigotry and religious civil war.

3. However valid it might be, the thesis that the Jansenist-Jesuit controversy facilitated the triumph of the Enlightenment in France originated as a theme in the propaganda of the philosophies themselves. See, for example, Voltaire, *Précis du siècle de Louis XV* in *Oeuvres complètes de Voltaire*, 92 vols. (Kehl, 1785–89), 25:399–437; and Jean Le Rond d'Alembert, *Sur la destruction des Jésuites en France, par un auteur désintéressé* (n.p., 1765), 191–206.

4. Robert Palmer, *Catholics and Unbelievers in Eighteenth-Century France* (Princeton, 1939), 23–102.

5. Richard H. Popkin, *The History of Skepticism from Erasmus to Spinoza, passim*. It could of course be argued that this is not so much a positive contribution as a

negative and indirect one, demonstrating how a device first used in interconfessional squabbling eventually boomeranged against fideism of any and all confessional varieties.

6. Paul Dibon, *Pierre Bayle, le philosophe de Rotterdam* (Paris, 1959); and Elisabeth Labrousse, *Pierre Bayle*, 2 vols. (La Haye, 1963–64). For an older view, see H. Robinson, *Bayle the Sceptic* (New York, 1931).

7. Quentin Skinner, *The Foundations of Modern Political Thought*, 2 vols. (Cambridge, 1978). The second volume subtitled *The Reformation* is most relevant to this point. Although more widely recognized than in other areas, the eighteenth century's debt to the *political* thought of the Reformation and Counter-Reformation is not the focus of this paper. For Jansenism's contribution to eighteenth-century political thought and to the Revolution, see Rene Taveneaux, *Jansénisme et politique* (Paris, 1965); and D. Van Kley, *The Jansenists and the Expulsion of the Jesuits from France, 1757–1765* (New Haven, 1975); and "Church, State, and the Ideological Origins of the French Revolution: The Debate over the General Assembly of the Gallican Clergy in 1765," *Journal of Modern History* 51 (Dec. 1979): 629–66.

8. Robert Kreiser, *Miracles, Convulsions, and Ecclesiastical Politics in Early Eighteenth-Century Paris* (Princeton, 1978); and Jan Christiaan Havinga, *Les Nouvelles Ecclésiastiques dans leur lutte contre l'esprit philosophique* (Amersfoort, 1925).

9. Treatments of Jansenist theology by way of contrast to Molinism are legion. Suffice it to mention, somewhat arbitrarily, Alexander Sedgewick's *Jansenism in Seventeenth-Century France: Voices in the Wilderness* (Charlottesville, Va., 1977); and Louis Cognet's *Le Jansénisme, Que sais-je* series (Paris, 1964). Walter E. Rex's brief description in *Pascal's Provincial Letters: An Introduction* (London and Sydney, 1977) are especially lucid and helpful.

10. Treatments of Jansenism in relation to Calvinism are not so numerous. The most helpful work in this regard remains Jean La Porte's *La Doctrine de la grace chez Arnauld* (Paris 1922), and *La morale d'après Arnauld* (Paris, 1952). Pascal's *Ecrits sur la grace* in *Oeuvres complètes*, ed. Lafuma (Paris, 1963) is a characteristically lucid if an obviously biased source on this subject.

11. Antoine Arnauld, *Le renversement de la morale de Jésus Christ, par les erreurs des Calvinistes, touchant la Justification* in *Oeuvres complètes*, 42 vols. (Lausanne, 1775–83), esp. 59, 85, 104, 260, but in general 644–756. Although Arnauld often refers to "*frayeur salutaire*" and "*crainte salutaire*" (645, 649), these quotations are taken from Pierre Nicole, "De la crainte de Dieu" in *Essais de morale, contenus en divers traités sur plusieurs devoirs importants*, 3 vols. (Paris, 1715), 1:133–35.

12. The quotation is from Nicole, "Des moyens de conserver la paix avec les hommes," in *Essais de morale*, 1:234–35. For examples of fine balance between hope and fear, see "De la crainte de Dieu," ibid., 1:117–19, 135–38, 145–48; "De la connoissance de soi-même," in ibid., 3:100–2, where he talks about the importance of holding our "âme dans un juste équilibre"; and "Des diverses manières dont on tente Dieu," in ibid., 3:174–76.

13. Elinor Barber, in *The Bourgeoisie in Eighteenth-Century France* (Princeton, 1955),

43–45, has this matter more or less right, as does Bernard Groethuysen, *Die Entstehung der bürgerlichen Welt-und Lebensanschauung in Frankreich*, 2 vols. (Halle/Salle, 1927), passim.

14. Nicole, "De la charité et de l'amour propre," *Essais de morale*, 3:103, 126, 139. Neither A. J. Krailsheimer's *Studies in Self-Interest from Descartes to La Bruyere* (Oxford, 1962) nor Albert O. Hirschman's *The Passions and the Interests: Political Arguments for Capitalism before its Triumph* (Princeton, 1977) uncovers the origin of the phrase, while Nannerl O. Keohane's *Philosophy and the State in France: The Renaissance to the Enlightenment* (Princeton, 1980), 310, uncovers a slightly later use of the phrase by Nicolas Malebranche in his *Traité de morale*, ed. Michel Adam, in *Oeuvres complètes*, 20 vols. (Paris, 1962–67), 11:38, 44–45, 269–71.

15. See, for example, Nicole, "De la civilité chrétienne," in *Essais de morale*, 2:92–96, and "De la connoissance de soi-même," 3:7–10.

16. Nicole, "De la charité et de l'amour propre," in *Essais de morale*, 3:103.

17. Ibid., 104.

18. Ibid., 105. For Hobbes's quotation, *Leviathan*, (Indianapolis and New York, 1958), 106.

19. Ibid., 106–7.

20. Nicole, "De la grandeur," in *Essais de morale*, 2:122–23.

21. Nicole, "De la charité et de l'amour propre," in ibid., 3:107–8, 113.

22. Nicole, "De la grandeur," in ibid., 2:135–36.

23. Nicole, "De la charité et de l'amour propre," in ibid., 3:110–14.

24. 1 Corinthians 13:1–13.

25. Nicole, "De la charité et de l'amour propre," in *Essais de morale*, 3:114–18.

26. Ibid., 122–26.

27. Ibid., 127–28.

28. Ibid., 130–31.

29. Ibid., 132–34.

30. Ibid., 135–37.

31. Ibid., 139. In other words, God contrives to maintain civility in human society stricken by the Fall by means of the Fall's worst consequences.

32. Ibid., 140–42.

33. Ibid., 143–44.

34. Ibid., 144–45. In the event that this reflection may be regarded as untypical on Nicole's part, see his "De la connoissance de soi-même," in *Essais de morale*, 3:98–100; and "Des diverses manières dont on tente Dieu," in ibid., 3:172–74.

35. Keohane, *Philosophy and the State in France*, 294–95.

36. See E. D. James, *Pierre Nicole, Jansenist and Humanist: A Study of his Thought* (The Hague, 1972), 7–31. Or see Pierre Nicole, *Traité de la grace générale*, 2 vols. (n.p., 1715).

37. For references to natural law, see, for example, Nicole, "Des moyens de conserver la paix avec les hommes," in *Essais de morale*, 1:205–6; and "De la connoissance de soi-même," in ibid., 3:56–63. For his arguments for the existence of God, see "Discours contenant en abrégé les preuves naturelles de l'existence de Dieu, et de l'immortalité de l'âme," in ibid., 2:20–35.

38. Jean Mesnard, *Pascal* (Paris, 1962), 126–54.
39. I take minor issue here with E. D. James's *Pierre Nicole*, 148–61.
40. Pierre Nicole, "De la charité et de l'amour propre," in *Essais de morale*, 3:109. I have borrowed Lionel Rothkrug's translation in *Opposition to Louis XIV: The Political and Social Origins of the French Enlightenment* (Princeton, 1965), 52.
41. Rothkrug, *Opposition to Louis XIV*, 84.
42. Jean Domat, *Les loix civiles dans leur ordre naturel. Traité des loix*, 2d ed. (Paris, 1695), xli, and quoted in René Taveneaux, *Jansénisme et politique* (Paris, 1965), 86.
43. Keohane, *Philosophy and the State in France*, 307–8.
44. Pascal, *Pensées*, in *Oeuvres complètes*, no. 211, p. 529. See also nos. 106 and 118, pp. 512, 518. I fail to see that Pascal's unmasking of sublimated concupiscence in these later two fragments differs in any significant respect from what Nicole does in "De la charité et de l'amour propre." I part company here with Keohane in *Philosophy and the State in France*, 297.
45. Labrousse concludes, concerning Bayle's analogous argument in *Pensées diverses sur la comète*, that although it is "son opposition decidée à toutes formes de naturalisme qui nous semble en être la ligne maitresse," his antinaturalisme is so extreme that it results, "sur un plan subordonné," in a "semblant de naturalisme," and that Bayle's eighteenth-century readers such as Voltaire were quite mistaken in seeing him as one of their precursors. Nonetheless, it seems to me that the contribution of neo-Augustinianism is essential to the full-blown naturalisms of the eighteenth century in that, without it, these latter would have found it more difficult to see goodness and beneficence where the Christian tradition had always seen evil and concupiscence. Now seventeenth-century Augustinianism such as Nicole's undoubtedly facilitated this transition.
46. H. X. Arquillière, *L'Augustinisme politique: Essai sur la formation des théories du moyen age* (Paris, 1955), esp. 31–46, 119–201.
47. For a similar insistence upon the secularizing consequences of Augustinianism, particularly during the Renaissance, see William J. Bouwsma, "The Two faces of Humanism: Stoicism and Augustinianism in Renaissance Thought" in Heiko A. Oberman and Thomas A. Brady, eds., *Itinerarium Italicum: The Profile of the Italian Renaissance in the Mirror of its European Transformations* (Leiden, 1975), 3–60. Augustinianism's emphasis upon man's intellectual imitations, Bouwsma argues, "points to the general secularization of modern life, for it implied the futility of searching for the principles of human order in the divine order of the cosmos, which lay beyond human comprehension. Man was accordingly now seen to inhabit not a single universal order governed throughout by uniform principles but a multiplicity of orders: for example, an earthly as well as a heavenly city, which might be seen to operate in quite different ways. On earth, unless God had chosen to reveal his will about its arrangements unequivocally in Scripture, man was left to the uncertain and shifting insights of a humbler kind of reason, to work out whatever arrangements best suited his needs. Hence a sort of earthy practicality was inherent in this way of looking at the human condition," 45.

48. *Nouvelles écclésiastiques*, (12 and 18 Nov. 1758): 181–88; and Claude-Adrien Helvétius, *De l'esprit* (La Haye, 1759), four "discours" paginated separately; as well as D. W. Smith, *Helvétius: A Study in Persecution* (Oxford, 1965), 122–25. I am not aware that Helvétius quotes Nicole directly, but he was undoubtedly acquainted with the *Essais de morale*. Moreover, he does cite and defend François de la Rochefoucauld's *Maximes de morale* (*De l'esprit*, 1:35), which is both chronologically and spiritually close to Nicole's "De la charité et de l'amour propre."

49. On the rehabilitations, first of self-interest, then of the passions more generally, and the gradual fusion between the two, see Albert O. Hirschman, *The Passions and the Interests: Political Arguments for Capitalism before its Triumph* (Princeton, 1977), as well as Thomas A. Horne's *The Social Thought of Bernard Mandeville: Virtue and Commerce in Early Eighteenth-Century England* (New York, 1978); and Keohane's *Philosophy and the State in France*, passim. All these treatments similarly insist upon the Enlightenment's ethical debt to the seventeenth-century French and Augustinian *moralistes*.

CHAPTER 4

Shaftesbury's Optimism and Eighteenth-Century Social Thought

JOHN ANDREW BERNSTEIN

The eighteenth century saw the modern belief in progress rise steadily in importance. More static, traditionalist conceptions of life and society, however, remained extremely powerful. The basic question that I want to answer in this essay is where cosmic optimism, the belief in a Providential world order, stood in relation to progressivism on the one hand and traditionalism on the other. In stating my question in terms of optimism in general rather than of Shaftesbury in particular, I want to focus upon the relationship of Shaftesbury to other optimist thinkers and the relationship, in turn, between optimism and the Enlightenment, both of which can best be discerned in connection with the progressive-traditionalist dichotomy. I hope to show that optimism was less overwhelmingly conservative in its implications than Basil Willey has suggested with his famous phrase designating it as "Cosmic Toryism," and that Shaftesbury in particular, in spite of a recent contention to the contrary, cannot profitably be understood as a Cosmic Tory.[1] I also hope to show that a wider lesson is suggested by these convictions, namely, that the conflict between progressivists and traditionalists in eighteenth-century England was less sharp than it sometimes appears to have been. Because my intention is to illuminate Shaftesbury by placing him in context and in comparative perspective, it will be necessary to refer to many other writers and necessary, also, to reflect upon some of the ambiguities inherent in eighteenth-century optimism in general.

Perhaps the simplest way of approaching these ambiguities is to note that optimism's meaning could vary, and was supposed to vary, according to the intended recipient of the doctrine. People who were looked upon as possible rebels received an explanation of Providence designed simply to stifle their allegedly unreasonable and dangerous expectations. In this spirit, Soame Jenyns, understandably Basil Willey's favorite example of a Cosmic Tory, argued that, in the best of all possible worlds, any form of possible government was of necessity more or less bad.[2] Much earlier in the century, Jonathan Swift, specifically addressing the poor in a well-known sermon, counseled resigned submission, as countless preachers had done before him.[3]

It does not follow, however, even for these writers, that the message of optimism for the privileged was intended merely as a guilt-soothing anodyne that blithely instructed them to be "resigned" to the utter misery of the many. There is no major figure, not Shaftesbury, Swift, Pope, Bolingbroke, not Jenyns, whose optimism can be demonstrated to have such a meaning. Even at its most conservative and hierarchical, optimism was part of a comprehensive system of duties designed to elevate the virtue of the upper classes and refine their social concern fully as much as it was designed to check the ambitions of the many. It was not even a mere effusion of people expressing how wonderful it was to be alive, rich, and titled, but was dominated by a subtle, certainly a nonrevolutionary, reformist impulse.

It may be difficult to see how a doctrine that holds, to use again the famous formulation of Shaftesbury's contemporary and admiring reader, Leibniz, that this is "the best of all possible worlds" could be an inducement to reform as opposed to an invitation to absolute complacency. But the very act of propounding the doctrine changes its meaning, and it becomes: this is the best of all possible worlds, and it would be still better if only everyone knew it, because so much of the world's evil springs from a lack of the right inspiring faith among classes high and low. This reformulation does not refute optimism as self-contradictory, but it does pinpoint the ineradicable tension within optimist writing between elevated complacency and reformist zeal, a tension that invites misunderstanding. Even the *rhetoric* of the optimists sometimes betrays this tension, especially in Pope's *Essay on Man*. Pope is widely admired as a poet, while few defend the intellectual content of the *Essay on Man*. But it may be that the rhetorical manner of the *Essay* is occasionally more misconceived than the ideas. The problem is in part that his dogmatisms are at variance with his professed uncertainties.[4] But a more serious problem is that, when Pope descends to wielding his heroic couplets like a lash applied to the backs of galley slaves, calling them "fools" in the bargain, the harshness of his manner conflicts with the harmony of his matter, and the high-minded gentleness he would inculcate. The result is paradoxical. Pope's defiant pomposity betrays his conviction that the world as it is on the human level is at variance with the world as it should be on the divine level, while the same pomposity creates the impression that Pope is simply trying to brow-beat the lowly into greater submission; and that is far less than the whole truth. Shaftesbury understood far better than either Pope or Bolingbroke the need for lyricism and a gentle mode of persuasion designed to evoke an erotic attachment to the cosmic order. But even Shaftesbury would not have taught his optimism at all without the conviction that much in the world's morals urgently required the amendment such an attachment could effect. Many of his observations on the concrete realities of life, which can be quite acerbic, show this conviction well enough. God's be-neficence, exhibited in the Cosmic Order, was supposed to be a model for man. But man needed to be induced to follow the divine model, and until he did, the best of worlds would remain improvable because of evil at all levels of society.

But this raises a formidable political question. If optimism teaches a comprehensive system of duties binding and interrelating high and low, does that mean that the submissiveness of the ruled should be contingent upon the worthiness of the rulers? Few of the optimists raised this ques-tion explicitly, and none ever gave a comprehensive and well-defined an-swer to it. Had they done so, their political intentions would have been far less ambiguous. There is nevertheless abundant reason to deny that eigh-teenth-century English optimism stood for unconditional passive obe-dience. Even Soame Jenyns specifically asserted the right to change a truly tyrannical government.[5] Shaftesbury gave a clear indication that the resig-nation which can be asked of the lowly is contingent upon liberty and genuine legal authority, if certainly not upon equality of condition, in one of his few passages that deals explicitly with class. The "spirit of tragedy," he wrote,

> can ill subsist where the spirit of liberty is wanting. The genius of this poetry consists in the lively representation of the disorders and misery of the great; to the end that the people and those of a lower condition may be taught the better to content themselves with pri-vacy, enjoy their safer state, and prize the equality and justice of their guardian laws. If this be found agreeable to the just tragic model, which the ancients have delivered to us, 'twill easily be con-ceived how little such a model is proportioned to the capacity or taste of those who in a long series of degrees, from the lowest peas-

ant to the high slave of royal blood, are taught to idolise the next in power above them and think nothing so adorable as that unlimited greatness and tyrannical power, which is raised at their own expense and exercised over themselves.[6]

If, in spite of passages of this sort, it is all too easy to see the essence of optimism as residing in a repressive hierarchicalism, the reason is to no small degree the ubiquitous presence of the notion of the Great Chain of Being in optimist writing.[7] This doctrine, which held that reality is ordered in an infinite hierarchical system from God to the smallest particle, is easily merged with the advocacy of pious acceptance of God's Providence, thus giving the distinct impression that optimism has little point except to justify social and political inequality. Although it is indeed indisputable that none of the optimists wanted to abolish the peerage or give the vote to one and all, it remains true that the social and political meaning of the Great Chain is very different from what it is sometimes taken to be.

One should remember, first of all, that the Chain of Being did not concern society directly at all. For this reason, writers indisputably egalitarian by the standards of their respective eras, such as John Locke and Thomas Jefferson, were perfectly comfortable with the idea.[8] In the Middle Ages, to be sure, it was common practice to draw an analogy between human society and cosmic society, and to use the cosmic as a model for the human. But this particular kind of analogy seems to have faded, though it had not disappeared, by the eighteenth century. Shaftesbury, Pope, and even Bolingbroke all used the Great Chain to assert the unity of mankind within the variety of the cosmos, *not* the stratified plurality of mankind upon the cosmic model. Man as a whole was always seen by them as occupying one rank in the *scala naturae*. As a result, the resignation they sought to inspire was a resignation of the human race as a whole to the inevitable limitations of finite existence, not a resignation in the face of tyranny.[9]

If, furthermore, we seek examples of the postmedieval use of the Great Chain or a definite political purpose by British writers, we indeed shall find them in many sixteenth- and seventeenth-century texts; but we also shall find that these examples are only incidentally relevant to the aristocracy whom the Cosmic Tories were allegedly writing to support. The primary significance of the analogy between society and cosmic hierarchy among these earlier writers was that it strengthened the position, not of the aristocracy, but of the *king*.[10] This was entirely natural; for if anyone's position of power in the Chain was clear, it was God's; and if anyone's position on earth was analogous to God's in a nation that had repudiated the pope, it was the king's, be the positions of seraphim, cherubim, dukes, and earls what they may. Yet no one contends that eighteenth-century optimism should be read as a defense of thorough-going divine-right monarchy, for which there is no evidence whatever. In light of these considerations, the likelihood that the analogy between the cosmos and society possessed a serious sociopolitical meaning in the Enlightenment is inherently improbable as well as hard to justify by the sources. Those who did employ the old analogy did so as a mere imaginative expression adopted for a particular purpose, a purpose which might be neither especially royalist nor aristocratic in nature. For such men, the Chain did not determine the thought but merely gave color to it. One such writer, incidentally, was Daniel Defoe, often viewed as the antithesis of all that the optimists stood for. But when Defoe denied he was a leveller, and added that there was a hierarchy in heaven and on earth,[11] he did so, surely, because he believed in the sanctity of property rights, not because of a devout adherence either to the *Celestial Hierarchy* of the Pseudo-Dionysius or to the aristocracy. An unfortunate consequence of undue emphasis upon the Great Chain in studies of eighteenth-century political attitudes is that it leads to both the obfuscation of more basic ideas [12] and a misrepresentation of the class bias of optimist literature.

The consequence of ignoring the idea and the real threat in Shaftesbury's youth, of royal absolutism, is the distortion of the polemical intention of optimism. A distinctly moderate position by the standards of its time is made into a radically conservative one by assuming that the primary aim behind the formulations of optimist politics was to attack liberal egalitarians. The heart of the problem this assumption poses for the interpretation of Shaftesbury in particular is the relation of his political attitudes to those of his own tutor, John Locke, the greatest theoretical opponent of royal absolutism of his age. Locke's political theory has been characterized in widely, not to say wildly, differing ways.[13] For the present purpose, it will be sufficient to remark that in attacking divine-right monarchy, Locke taught a doctrine of individual rights that constituted an outline of a genuinely egalitarian political philosophy; but he left intact, to say the least, the property rights that form the basis of class. The question then becomes: was Shaftesbury's optimism propounded as a conservative antidote to the alleged threat of Locke's very moderate individualism and egalitarianism, or did the differences between the two involve, instead, a dispute between liberals about the proper foundation of liberal theory?

Since Shaftesbury expressed admiration for Locke's writings on government explicitly in one of his letters,[14] claims to discern hidden polemics against Locke's political theory in the *Characteristics* must be viewed with great caution. Barry M. Burrows has claimed that the clearest example of such covert opposition is Shaftesbury's insistence that contract could not be the source of political morality; for contract itself rests upon the sanctity of promises, a sanctity that must precede, not follow, the contractual act.[15] We have, however, no evidence that Shaftesbury had Locke in mind on this point. Furthermore, Locke himself believed that natural law derives from God, and antedates the social contract: "truth and keeping of faith belongs to men as men and not as members of society."[16] When, on the basis of such imaginary conflicts between Locke and Shaftesbury as this, we are urged to believe that Shaftesbury meant to assert the claims of cosmic tory hierarchicalism against Lockean individualism,[17] the same style of counterargument must be employed again. Locke did not deny, and we have no reason to believe Shaftesbury thought Locke denied, the importance of civil society for human fulfillment or the indispensability of hierarchy in the bare sense of makers and enforcers of law. But if respect for "hierarchy" in this sense be Cosmic Toryism, the phrase is meaningless.

Shaftesbury expressed disagreement with Locke on two points only: he believed that moral and aesthetic judgments were objective and their truth not dependent merely upon God's will,[18] and he believed that we should do the good for its own sake without being induced by fear of punishment or hope of extrinsic reward.[19] Let us leave aside the complex question of whether these propositions were in fact anti-Lockean. It is indubitable that Shaftesbury thought they were. But the passion with which Shaftesbury could assail Locke's name on these points in some of his letters does not justify us in inferring any opposition to Locke in the *Characteristics* beyond what can clearly be derived from these points themselves. There are, I believe, only a few possibilities of such covert opposition that relate to politics. By insisting that even God has no authority over us but that which stems from his goodness toward the whole,[20] Shaftesbury may have had both a political and a religious point about "monarchy" in mind, although the context is purely religious. And in attacking the submission to God's mere will, as opposed to his objectively defined goodness,[21] supposedly advocated by Locke, Shaftesbury may have sought to undermine the last vestige of authoritarianism in Locke out of the conviction that slavish principles in religion have more than purely religious consequences, and the belief that Lockean political liberalism could only be adequately safeguarded by a comparably free-spirited religion. At the very least, one can say that anyone wishing us to believe that Shaftesbury was more authoritarian than Locke must surmount the insurmountable obstacle presented by Shaftesbury's theology.

Another point is equally plausible. In assailing rewards and punishments as the foundation of ethics, Shaftesbury surely wanted to insinuate a spirit of generous devotion toward the social whole in the English people as opposed to a selfish individualism some have discerned in Lockean principles. But noble-hearted patriotism has nothing to do with hierarchy as such, and a belief in such patriotism is not tantamount to a call for stronger government, but merely for that public spirit which seeks a just balance between the welfare of the individual and of the whole. Shaftesbury, in other words, thought that the inner moral spirit of Lockean liberalism could be improved for the sake of freedom itself. But this is a Cosmic Toryism that looks suspiciously like the thought of Jean-Jacques Rousseau.

The third earl of Shaftesbury was not, of course, a perfect modern democrat. He believed in the distinction between the philosophically refined and the "mere vulgar,"[22] and in the need for a liberal education remote from "mean employments" in order to attain true "perfection of grace and comeliness in action and behavior."[23] But these beliefs, however important they were in his total outlook, do not mean that optimism was taught specifically in order to strengthen hierarchy against anarchy. There is no reason to believe that Shaftesbury feared anarchy; rather, there is every reason to believe that he sought in the writings of his maturity to counter what was left of the dangers of absolutism, so real in his youth, and sought, also, to purify legal equality itself of any meanness of spirit.

This does not mean that Shaftesbury's optimism, to say nothing of Pope's and Bolingbroke's, so far from being especially conservative, can be viewed unqualifiedly as a stage in the development of modern progressivism. The need for caution on this matter does not rest on Shaftesbury's political complacency at the end of his life, for that complacency derived in no small part from his conviction that the authority of the Crown had finally been reduced in a satisfactory fashion.[24] The true reason Shaftesbury's optimism, liberal as it was, has a profoundly conservative or, as I should prefer to call it, traditionalist and premodern flavor, is that it favored the view that the solution to the human problem lies more in things internal than external, or, as Pope put it:

> What nothing earthly gives, or can destroy
> The soul's calm sun-shine, and the heart-felt joy,
> Is Virtue's prize: A better would you fix?[25]

There is no question that this view was Shaftesbury's: no question, also, that the very spirit of such a Stoic doctrine works toward the acceptance of the external social, economic, and political conditions of man because it asserts the primacy of the goods of the soul.[26] Nor is there any inconsistency between this spiritual emphasis and the importance of optimism for the obligations of the higher as well as the lower classes. On the contrary, to the degree that the higher deserved their position, to that degree they would exemplify the conviction that their virtue was their true essence, and not the accessories of rank upon which Shaftesbury and Pope both poured their scorn. So understood, optimism did indeed possess a meaning for which the phrase "Cosmic Toryism" is too frivolous, but not otherwise entirely misleading, provided we remember that men were asked to submit to the basic principles of the English political order, not simply because that order was ordained by God, and not simply because of the difficulty of attaining a better one, but also because of the large measure of genuine freedom it was thought to embody.

But we cannot stop here. A doctrine of the primacy of the goods of the soul is a relative concept, not an absolute one, so long as the soul is connected to the body. In order to complete this survey of the social implications of optimism in the broadest sense of the word social, we must ask whether there was anything in optimism which could actually encourage certain kinds of change. Since modern progressivism draws most of its strength from hopes for beneficial change in politics, science, and economic productivity, it is necessary to address the relation between optimism and progressivism in each of these areas.

Two things can be said to qualify the static, if liberal, complacency of Shaftesbury's politics. First, the obvious point should be made that despite the relative political contentment of Shaftesbury's politics, a contentment based upon specifically English conditions, his views could have explosive effects where those conditions did not obtain. The esteem in which Diderot and Montesquieu held Shaftesbury's writings doubtless owed much to his criticism of despotism.[27] And Voltaire, in his optimist phase, admired optimism in part because of the spirit of tolerance that informed its natural religion, a spirit which, he was well aware, had sharply critical political implications for eighteenth-century Catholic France.[28]

Mention of religion leads to a second point. As is well known, the optimism of Shaftesbury, Pope, and Bolingbroke, though emphatically not that of Leibniz and Jenyns, implied a criticism of original sin, a fact noted during the age of optimism itself. No political implications follow automatically from this attack on original sin. The relation between opinions of human nature on the one hand and opinions about desirable forms of government on the other is very complex. But there is a particular aspect of Shaftesbury's implicit criticism of original sin that does have great force of a potentially progressive character. When he singled out religious hatred as one of the principal causes of human evil,[29] he suggested the possibility of a remediable historical cause of such evil. In the eighteenth century, the structure of this argument concerning evil could easily be transferred to the more strictly political sphere. Bad government could then be viewed as a cause of the evil it was supposed to control. More equitable government, like more tolerant religion, could then emerge as a means for the improvement of human behavior. The implicit interweaving of political and religious themes in Shaftesbury's work hints at such lines of thought, which were to be more powerfully developed in the French Enlightenment.

Hope for political improvement, like hope for religious improvement, was not a radical novelty in Western thought. The specifically modern project of perpetual progress probably owes more to scientific and economic advances than to anything else. The two are not easily separated, for progress in science depends upon a degree of emancipation from a subsistence economy, and the possibilities of economic progress unaided by technical advance must always remain strictly finite. If I discuss science briefly in substantial separation from trade and manufactures, it is in order to deal fairly with what appears to be, and in some ways *is*, an antiscientific bias in Shaftesbury and some other figures of his age.

Shaftesbury was more Platonist than empiricist in his theory of knowledge. There is no equivalent in the *Characteristics* of either Pope's praise of Newton or Bolingbroke's Lockean empiricism. There is, furthermore, a denunciation of any purely mechanical understanding of the universe that excludes a governing mind.[30] More important, and more at variance with the scientific spirit of his age, there is a strong hint of Swift's snobbish deprecation of the laboriously *manual* character of experimentation,[31] and, most important of all, a denunciation of the irrelevance to the Cartesian mechanistic understanding of man's emotional life in comparison with philosophic introspection and moral self-control.[32]

Shaftesbury, then, was no particular friend of the new mechanical philosophy. But before drawing excessively sweeping conclusions from this fact, we should remember the defensiveness of his remarks. He wrote to counter what he viewed as a threat to sound morals, philosophy, and religion, and to counter, as well, what he took to be the obnoxious arrogance of the militant propagandists of the scientific method. The very fact that some of his arguments might still be used in defense of the eternal indispensability of what we term the humanities is no proof that he wished to eradicate the spirit of scientific projects, but merely proof that he rejected the all-encompassing claims of the intellectual ancestors of B. F. Skinner. Neither Shaftesbury nor, so far as I know, any other major figure of his time attacked modern science and technology precisely for their *successes* in alleviating the ills of life; indeed, Shaftesbury wrote in praise of mathematics specifically for its utilitarian "advantage to mankind."[33] Jonathan Swift, whose *Tale of the Tub* is certainly an onslaught on science, attacked what he took to be the uselessness of science by its own materialistic criteria, not its success. Swift, after all, wrote in *Gulliver's Travels* that "whoever could make two ears of corn or two blades of grass to grow upon a spot of ground where only one grew before, would deserve better of mankind, and do more essential service to mankind than the whole race of politicians put together."[34] His lifelong concern for the wretched poverty of the Irish peasantry makes it likely that these words express Swift's own view, and that he had no intention of rejecting the agricultural revolution, to say nothing of the life work of Pasteur, Lister, and Ehrlich, in advance.

Seventeenth-century English science developed in no small part under the inspiration of Puritanism; its values, as R. F. Jones, Robert K. Merton, and others have emphasized, were often explicitly opposed to the aristocratic spirit of contemplative idleness. Perhaps, as Jones has claimed, one can see the late seventeenth and early eighteenth centuries as something of an interruption of the Puritan utilitarian ethos.[35] But the gulf between the humanistic and the scientific spirit, great though it was, should not be exaggerated. Shaftesbury, much more a friend of pure contemplation than Swift, inveighed against the excesses of contemplative ecstasy that, as he put it, "render the devout person more remiss in secular affairs, and less concerned for the inferior and temporal interests of mankind."[36] Such sentiments are entirely incompatible with the pure aestheticism for which Shaftesbury has been blamed,[37] incompatible, also, with the pure Platonism for which he has been praised,[38] and incompatible, finally, with the pure otherworldliness of religious devotion, which his readers have not cared about sufficiently to do either. But such sentiments are entirely compatible with *some* aspects, at least, of the Puritan attack on the aristocratic uselessness of contemplative and monastic withdrawal and with the practical bent of the French, Scottish, and English Enlightenment during its mid-eighteenth-century heyday.

Finally, it is necessary to discuss purely economic matters, which exhibit the ambiguity of optimism with the greatest clarity of all. The attitude of writers to the general question of economic progress is obviously central to the entire complex of issues raised here. The spirit of grand antithesis in the secondary literature against which this essay is directed has led to two errors: the confusion of indictments of outright dishonesty and corruption with indictments of capitalism in toto; and the analogous confusion of the indictment of ruthless and selfish individualism with a devout insistence that nobody should ever try to become richer than his great-grandfather was before him.

These confusions are in some ways understandable. In 1720, the South Sea Bubble provided a traumatic proof of the instability of a new economic age. Had Shaftesbury lived to witness the event, he might have reacted as negatively as Pope, Bolingbroke, and Swift did. Shaftesbury, to be sure, regarded the war against Louis XIV in the reign of Queen Anne as a holy war for liberty,[39] the view of the trading interest and not the country Tories; and he gave still other indications of holding views comfortable to the trading interest above and beyond his membership in the Whig party. But these facts constitute no certain proof that he would have taken the Bubble in stride. It is also important to note, with Isaac Kramnick, that while Bolingbroke often praised trade, he had a passionate desire to keep the landed interest in control of political power.[40] There can be no question that Bolingbroke's political convictions offer a clear example of a desire to keep out "new men," a desire that led to apparently sweeping denunciations of ambition that were woven into the fabric of his optimism.

But these considerations should not be blown out of proportion even with respect to Shaftesbury's optimist successors. They should not lead us to exaggerate the contrast between alleged heroes of untrammeled capitalist individualism, like Defoe, Addison, and most falsely of all, Locke, on the one hand, and supporters of an essentially premodern conception of the economy and of social relations on the other. No doubt the South Sea Bubble magnified for all to see an unsavory quality in an age beset with economic ambitions and delirious with economic opportunities. No doubt, also, men balefully proclaimed generalized condemnations of a new order that seemed to look back to an earlier age of economic innocence. But the Bubble was not the essence of capitalism and was not defended as such, any more than the writers supporting the "monied" interest defended peculation and fraud.[41] Furthermore, Bolingbroke's defense of both trade and manufactures was too frequent and too extensive to be adequately comprehended within the terms of Kramnick's almost parenthetical observations that political considerations required a measure of such defense, and that Bolingbroke merely defended them as an adjunct of state power.[42] At the very least, one should add that Bolingbroke was guilty of extraordinary naiveté if he expected manufactures and trade to grow ad infinitum while the directors of this growth were kept out of the seats of power. But one can also add that Bolingbroke's theology provides an example of a form of thinking which was to characterize later writers who specifically blessed economic expansionism in almost entirely wholehearted terms. He noted, in an implicit confutation of any strictly static interpretation of optimism, that God gave mankind the means with which to *improve* its creature comforts and evidently expected men to use them.[43]

This apparently innocuous piece of piety was destined to help destroy traditionalism entirely, though Bolingbroke's own influence was not important in this matter. We should not be misled by Bolingbroke's concomitant tendency, shared by so many in his age, to inveigh against "luxury"; for by "luxury" he meant, not economic prosperity,[44] but a mode of life that corrupted the capacity for action with a stupor of perfumes and soft Lydian airs, not the life of hard work and well-merited comfort that characterized the ideal of Defoe.[45]

Shaftesbury's own attitude toward the pursuit of wealth was best expressed in a nuanced statement that typifies what Bernard Mandeville scornfully termed his "boasted middle way,"[46] but which less ardent advocates of acquisitiveness than Mandeville could find suitable enough for their purposes:

> Now as to that passion which is esteemed peculiarly interesting, as having for its aim the possession of wealth, and what we call a settlement or fortune in the world: if the regard towards this kind be moderate and in a reasonable degree; if it occasions no passionate pursuit, nor raises any ardent desire or appetite; there is nothing in this case which is not compatible with virtue, and even suitable and beneficial to society. The public as well as private system is advanced by the industry which this affection excites. But if it grows at length into a real passion, the injury and mischief it does the public is not greater than that which it creates to the person himself. Such a one is in reality a self-oppressor, and lies heavier on himself than he can ever do on mankind.[47]

Shaftesbury expresses here about as well as anyone else did the basic attitude toward wealth of most major writers of his century. He is no more enthusiastic about it than Dr. Johnson or Swift, not much less so than Hume, Smith, or Ferguson, none of whom raised a banner in praise of truly soul-destroying greed. At the same time as he condemned greed, however, Shaftesbury hinted at the social utility of a moderated desire for wealth. It might be foolish to treat this commonplace as an anticipation of Smith's invisible hand, but one can certainly say that, as with Bolingbroke's theology, even the most apparently static optimism possessed, in its economic aspect, the suggestion of a potential dynamism, which later, indisputably progressive theodicists were to make clearer with only a few new additions of principle.

In sum, optimism was not a movement of thought that simply tried to strangle progressivism in its cradle. However different its spirit was from the restless dynamism of later periods, however great the disgust with certain features of emergent capitalism felt by Pope and Bolingbroke, there were elements within the writings of all the major optimists that directly or indirectly furthered and blessed the hope of progress. These elements, on balance, were almost as prominent as those that sought to inculcate an entirely static vision of the world. One reason things were pronounced good was that God and the genius of England had provided the means whereby they might be bettered, if only men remembered the eternal principles of virtue.

The possibility of another, more tentative, but broader conclusion also presents itself. Scholars of eighteenth-century thought have categorized Shaftesbury in remarkably various ways, and the writers and belief aligned with or opposed to him in the secondary literature have been similarly diverse. Most of these disputes concern variations on a single dichotomy expressed in different ways: ancients versus moderns, Augustan humanists versus sentimentalists, Tories versus Whigs, agrarian hierarchicalists versus individualistic, egalitarian capitalists. The fascination of scholars with these dichotomies is entirely justified. Everyone recognizes the pivotal importance of the Age of Enlightenment. Most, of course, see it as the blessed triumph of hopeful, progressive reason. Others see it as the transition from Dante, Shakespeare, and Milton to Gino's, MacDonald's, and Burger King. Because of the importance of the Enlightenment as a transition, it is natural for polemical writers to separate sheep from goats, and for less polemical ones to separate fish from fowl. But it may be that, in reading back into eighteenth-century England conflicts that became very violent in the age of the Industrial Revolution and the French Revolution, we exaggerate the extent to which the lines of battle were sharply drawn before those revolutions occurred. I would caution against this exaggeration, without wishing to imply that the conflicts did not exist at all. Above all, I would caution against any temptation to align authors in opposing groups defined by entire systems of beliefs. This has the consequence, disastrous because of the number of convictions involved, of implying that agreement on one point of ethics, politics, religion, society, the economy, or the nature of man means agreement on the rest. One may, for instance, if one should choose, call a group of writers Augustan humanists. But most of those writers often shared a great deal in common with those whom Paul Fussell, in his brilliant book on the humanists, has aligned against them.[48] My own doubt as to whether Shaftesbury should be included in the Augustan humanists because of such things as his praise of moderation, or excluded, as Fussell emphatically would prefer, because of such traits as his mild encouragement to emotionalism in ethics, urges upon me the conviction that all attempts to divide eighteenth-century English writers into separate camps must procede entirely issue by issue, belief by belief. The bewildering ambiguities of optimism and its implications demonstrate the pitfalls awaiting the unwary definers of mutually exclusive schools.

NOTES

1. See Basil Willey, *The Eighteenth Century Background: Studies on the Idea of Nature in the Thought of the Period* (London, 1940), 43–56, and Barry M. Burrows, "Whig versus Tory—A Genuine Difference?" *Political Theory* 4 (1976): 455–69, a study of Shaftesbury's political views in part inspired by Willey.
2. Soame Jenyns, *A Free Inquiry into the Nature and Origin of Evil* in *Works* (London, 1790; facsimile reprint, 1969), 3:257–78.
3. See "On Mutual Subjection" and also "On the Poor Man's Contentment" in *Irish Tracts and Sermons, 1720–1723* (Oxford, 1948), 139–49 and 190–98.
4. Thomas R. Edwards, Jr., *This Dark Estate: a Reading of Pope* (Berkeley and Los Angeles, 1963), 30–31.
5. Jenyns, *Free Inquiry*, 264.
6. Anthony, Earl of Shaftesbury, *Characteristics of Men, Manners, Opinions, Times*, 2 vols., ed. John M. Robertson (Indianapolis, 1964), 1:142–43. Hereafter cited as *Ch*.
7. See the classic treatment of this idea in Arthur O. Lovejoy's *The Great Chain of Being: A Study of the History of an Idea* (Cambridge, Mass., 1936).
8. John Locke, *An Essay Concerning Human Understanding*, III.vi.12. For Jefferson, see Garry Wills, *Inventing America: Jefferson's Declaration of Independence* (New York, 1978), 210.
9. For Shaftesbury, see *Ch*, 2:22 and 74. For Pope, see *An Essay on Man*, 1:237–94. For Bolingbroke, see *Works of Lord Bolingbroke* (London, 1844; facsimile reprint, 1967), 4:337–39. Isaac Kramnick, in his illuminating study, *Bolingbroke and His Circle: the Politics of Nostalgia in the Age of Walpole* (Cambridge, Mass., 1968), 101, completely misrepresents the meaning of this section.
10. See W. H. Greenleaf, *Order, Empiricism and Politics: Two Traditions of English Political Thought 1500–1700* (Oxford, 1964), passim.
11. Daniel Defoe, *The Compleat English Gentleman*, ed. Karl D. Bülbring (London, 1890), 19–20.
12. Cf. Jacob Viner, *The Role of Providence in the Social Order: An Essay in Intellectual History* (Philadelphia, 1972), 94.
13. Compare, to name some of the most oustanding works, Leo Strauss, *Natural Right and History* (Chicago, 1953), 202–51; C. B. Macpherson, *The Politics of Possessive Individualism* (Oxford, 1964); John Dunn, *The Political Thought of John Locke: an Historical Account of the Argument of the 'Two Treatises on Government'* (Cambridge, 1969); and, for a compellingly sympathetic account, James Tully, *A Discourse on Property: John Locke and his Adversaries* (Cambridge, 1980).

14. Benjamin Rand, ed., *The Life, Unpublished Letters, and Philosophical Regimen of Anthony, Earl of Shaftesbury* (London, 1900), 402.
15. Burrows, "Whig versus Tory," 460–61.
16. Locke, *Second Treatise on Government*, 2:14.
17. Burrows, "Whig versus Tory," 466.
18. Anthony, Earl of Shaftesbury, *Second Characters, or the Language of Forms*, ed. Benjamin Rand (Cambridge, 1914), 104–5, where Locke is specifically mentioned. This general point, however, is basic to Shaftesbury's entire philosophy.
19. See Rand, *Life, Unpublished Letters*, 345, where Locke is castigated on this point, one which, again, is basic to all of Shaftesbury. It is only just to remark here that Shaftesbury's interpretation of Locke's meaning is highly questionable. Locke had written, in a letter that came to Shaftesbury's attention: "All the use to be made of it is that this life is a scene of vanity that soon passes away, and affords no solid satisfaction but in the consciousness of doing well, and in hopes of another life." Shaftesbury declared to the forwarder of this innocuous passage as follows: "*Consciousness* is, indeed, a high term, but those who can be conscious of doing no good, but what they are frightened or bribed into, can make but a sorry account of it, as I imagine." This implies, as Locke's conventional if elegant piety does not, that only the thought of hell stood between John Locke and a life of vice, a crude and cruel misconstruction refuted by, among other things, all of Shaftesbury's own, deeply devoted letters to Locke. But the view that virtue should be done for its own sake was one of Shaftesbury's most passionately held convictions; and his intention may have been not so much to impugn the character of Locke but rather to take another opportunity to propound his idée fixe.
20. Implicit in *Ch.*, 2:92.
21. *Ch.*, 1:264.
22. Ibid., 139.
23. Ibid., 125.
24. As Burrows himself shows, "Whig versus Tory," 467. Burrows's general thesis that the differences between Whig and Tory often appear minimal or at least hard to define is one with which I heartily agree. The reason, however, is less that the Whigs were like Tories, as Burrows alleges, than that the Tories, in their comparative "liberalism," were like Whigs. For a good general discussion of the relation between Whigs and Tories, which supports though it certainly qualifies, this generalization, see H. T. Dickinson, *Liberty and Property: Political Ideology in Eighteenth-Century Britain* (New York, 1977), 57ff.
25. *An Essay on Man*, 4:167–69.
26. For this reason, I would still subscribe to my claim that "adaptation to a preexisting order . . . not the creation of a new order, was the burden of [Shaftesbury's] message." *Shaftesbury, Rousseau, and Kant: An Introduction to the Conflict Between Aesthetic and Moral Values in Modern Thought* (Cranbury, N.J., 1980), 55. Nevertheless, the present essay is to some extent a qualification of the brief treatment of the political and social implications of Shaftesbury's thought on that book.

27. In addition to the well-known claim in Montesquieu's *Pensées Diverses* that "the four great poets are Plato, Malebranche, Shaftesbury, and Montaigne," one can note the pervasive reminiscences of Shaftesbury's theological and moral attitudes in *The Persian Letters*. For Diderot, see R. Loyalty Cru, *Diderot as a Disciple of English Thought* (New York, 1913; reprint, 1966), 119ff.

28. Voltaire, *Mélanges* (Bibliothèque de la Pléiade, 1961), 302.

29. *Ch.*, 1:292.

30. *Ch.*, 2:93–94.

31. *Ch.*, 2:8. For a discussion of Swift's satire on science, see Miriam Koch Starkman, *Swift's Satire on Learning in "A Tale of a Tub"* (Princeton, 1950), 64–86.

32. *Ch.*, 1:191.

33. *Ch.*, 1:188.

34. "Voyage to Brobdingnag," *Gulliver's Travels*, chap. 7. This work as a whole, of course, continues Swift's onslaught on the new science, but not because of its utility.

35. Richard Foster Jones, *Ancients and Moderns: A Study of the Rise of the Scientific Movement in Seventeenth-Century England*, 2d ed. (St. Louis, 1961), 268–72. Jones does not mention Shaftesbury, whose writings both illustrate and suggest modest qualification of the sharpness of Jones's antitheses between opponents and proponents of science.

36. *Ch.*, 1:287.

37. For example, by John Dunn, *Political Thought of John Locke*, 255.

38. For example, by Thomas L. Pangle, *Montesquieu's Philosophy of Liberalism: A Commentary on "The Spirit of the Laws"* (Chicago and London, 1973), 323.

39. *Ch.*, 1:145.

40. Kramnick, *Bolingbroke*, 199.

41. See the very balanced and subtle discussion of Augustan attitudes toward trade and finance in J. G. A. Pocock, *The Machiavellian Moment: Florentine Political Thought and the Republican Tradition* (Princeton, 1975), 423–61, esp. 446ff.

42. Kramnick, *Bolingbroke*, 199.

43. Bolingbroke, *Works*, 4:433.

44. Cf. James William Johnson: "Sometimes conjoined to ideas of climate, 'luxury' meant economic prosperity and cultural affluence" (*The Formation of English Neo-Classical Thought* [Princeton, 1967], 48).

45. See Bolingbroke's "On Luxury," in *Works*, 1:474–77.

46. Bernard Mandeville, *The Fable of the Bees: or, Private Vices, Publick Benefits* (Oxford, 1924), 1:333.

47. *Ch.*, 1:326.

48. Paul Fussell, *The Rhetorical World of Augustan Humanism: Ethics and Imagery from Swift to Burke* (Oxford, 1965).

CHAPTER 5

Who's Afraid of Christian Wolff?

THOMAS P. SAINE

CHRISTIAN WOLFF: IN DEFENSE
OF PHILOSOPHY

For more than two hundred fifty years it has been difficult for any two people to agree about Christian Wolff.[1] This is a response that began during his own lifetime (1679–1754), whenever there was an attempt to classify or characterize his philosophy. Some considered him to be an eclectic philosopher, to which Wolff was accustomed to reply that it was simply not possible to discard all of earlier philosophy—something to which the Moderns on the whole were all too inclined. On the other hand, having received his early education in Breslau, Wolff early on became acquainted with both Protestant and Catholic Scholasticism,[2] an acquaintance that contributed not a little to his urge to philosophize in a systematic fashion. During his lifetime Wolff was already viewed as a disciple and successor to Leibnitz, and his philosophy was tagged as "Leibnitz-Wolffian," an adjective rejected by Wolff himself in no uncertain terms, because it was applied to him by his opponents and therefore not exactly a badge of honor.[3] Without going into further detail on this question, we can conclude that Wolff owed much to Leibnitz and that it is often necessary to refer to Leibnitz when elucidating Wolff, without, however, Wolff's philosophy being identical to that of Leibnitz in all respects. Simply from the point of view of the systematic ambition, even if there were no other point of comparison between the two philosophers, Wolff, by relating all the disciplines of philosophy closely to each other, proves himself no mere disciple of Leibnitz but indeed goes far beyond him. Because of the tight cohesion of his system, which was based on the mechanistic view of causality developed by modern mechanics and physics, epithets such as "Spinozist," "Deist," "Cartesian," and worse were applied to Wolff by his opponents, while other intellectuals, even in Catholic territories, managed long before Wolff's death to see in him a pious Christian and in his system the strongest bulwark against the flood of freethinking and atheism that threatened, in their opinion, to sweep Christianity away in the wake of modern science and the associations with Epicurean philosophy that it evoked. This was his own opinion of his work, as he never tired of stressing his own Lutheran orthodoxy, all more radical connotations and associations notwithstanding.

Wolff was the most respected and the most widely known philosopher of the eighteenth century before Kant, and he was the real inventor of the German philosophical language.[4] The main tenets of the Wolffian system became public property through the writings of countless popular philosophers from Johann Christoph Gottsched—who is remembered more for his efforts in the field of poetics and literature than for his philosophical efforts but who also wrote the most widely used compendium of Wolffian philosophy—to Moses Mendelssohn; even Kant was greatly indebted to Wolff's system and for years based his lectures on metaphysics on the textbook by the Wolffian Alexander Gottlieb Baumgarten, who was also the inventor of a Wolffian aesthetics. Since Kant and the German Romantics it has been fashionable to view Wolff's philosophy as superficial, transcended by the profound strivings and insights of German Idealism, and so on—a view that has greatly obscured our understanding of the development of German intellectual life in the eighteenth century, because the historians of philosophy and thought have all too often tended to see in Kant a radical new beginning. Nevertheless, the Romantics themselves had been steeped in Wolffian thinking from their earliest years, and the post-Kantian German reaction against Wolff seems suspiciously like that of upstart sons seeking to discredit and displace their father. Kant himself was more just when he praised Wolff in the preface to the second edition of the *Critique of Pure Reason* for his thoroughness and his strictness of method.[5] The ferments of theological controversy in the eighteenth century and the roots of Romantic and post-Romantic philosophy of religion go back in large part to Christian Wolff—for in spite of his professed orthodoxy, Wolff's philosophy itself, as well as his strict demarcation of the boundary between the realms of philosophy and theology, contained a number of elements that proved to be serious threats to the very orthodoxy he professed to espouse and defend.

In the eighteenth century the study of philosophy within the philosophical faculty of the university was conceived primarily as propaedeutic: students spent only a limited time being initiated into the philosophical subjects in preparation for the higher learning offered in the faculties of theology, law, and medicine. The highest degree conferred by the philosophical faculty was the "Magister," whereas study in the other three faculties could lead to the doctorate. Wolff was probably the first in Germany to represent tenaciously and self-consciously the claim of philosophy to be a science to be studied seriously for its own sake and not merely as a preliminary to the study of theology. Otherwise his definition of philosophy ("Weltweisheit") as a science of "all possible things, and of the how and why of their possibility"[6] would have little meaning. In his dedication to the first edition of the "German Teleology," written in September, 1723, before his hasty departure from Halle to comply with Frederick William's cabinet order threatening him with hanging if he did not disappear immediately, we see him concerned to stake out clearly the respective territories of philosophy and theology.[7] Obviously he is reacting in part to the attacks of his Halle opponents when he distinguishes between the domains of philosophy and theology, and he is not prepared to take back any of his views unless an opponent can convince him with philosophical certitude that he has erred. Until and unless he has been convinced in such philosophical fashion of the error of his ways, he is not about to allow the theologians to prescribe to him how he should think and write, for philosophy and theology should remain each in its own sphere and not interfere in the affairs of the other. Each has as its appropriate field a particular kind of truth: "There are two kinds of truths, natural and supernatural. We know the former through reason, the latter through Holy Scripture. It is the philosophers who have trained their reason who are qualified to judge of the former; and it is the theologians, who are conversant with the true meaning of the Scriptures, who are qualified to judge the latter. Whoever wishes to judge both kinds of truth simultaneously must be both a philosopher and a theologian at the same time."[8] As a philosopher Wolff is interested only in those truths about God that can be demonstrated by reason alone, the branch of theology traditionally known as *theologia naturalis*. Whatever transcends the powers of natural reason belongs properly to the sphere of the theologians, who deal with the dogmas and mysteries of faith from the perspective of Biblical revelation. When, however, theologians venture into the realm of natural philosophy or rational theology, they must be prepared to adhere to the rules of philosophy and cannot claim to have solved all problems merely by appealing to Scripture.

Actually, if we take seriously what Wolff writes in the dedication to the "Teleology," all controversies between the philosophers and the theologians must be carried out on the philosopher's home ground. In debate it is always a matter of the one convincing the other that he is in error, a proposition that assumes that the controversy will be conducted according to the rules of reason and logic even if it is the theologian who is seeking to maintain that the philosopher is in error. Wolff excludes any appeal to tradition or established authority, any claim of superior insight into God's ways that would obviate the need for reasoned argument, or any other short-circuiting of controversy by calling for the intervention of the powers that be.[9] The theologian does not have the right to claim superiority over the philosopher simply on the basis of the authority of revealed truth: "For why should there be any greater probability that the theologian has arranged his system of ideas correctly than the philosopher, and why should it be assumed that he is more likely to have reached the correct conclusions than the philosopher, who works even more with logic than he does?"[10] In order to qualify for the right to criticize the philosopher, the theologian must be as much in command of logic and the art of demonstration as the philosopher; otherwise, the best advice to each of the contenders would be not to mix in each other's affairs. At least Wolff himself respected the boundaries he had set up between philosophy and theology, for he never took it upon himself to criticize Lutheran dogma; on the contrary, he repeatedly asserted his own orthodoxy, such as he understood it, without at any rate undertaking to define it.

It is apparent that the uncomfortable situation at the University of Halle and the hostility of the Pietists and the orthodox Lutheran theologians made it advisable for Wolff to avoid the appearance of seeking to be an innovator in dogmatics. In the preface to the second edition of the "German Teleology" he claims that the readers of his "German Metaphysics," his "German Ethics," and his "German Politics,"[11] far from being inoculated with heretical or otherwise dangerous notions, would not only receive a thorough grounding in the tenets of rational religion but would also be led to a greater understanding of "revealed religion" as well, so that they would remain immune from all temptations to stray from the teachings of the established church in their thoughts.[12] As a philosopher he takes no professional interest in the dogmatic controversies of the theologians, and he would like for the theologians to leave the philosophers alone in return.[13] He is, however, of the opinion that the theologians would profit greatly from framing their arguments more philosophically than has until now been the case: "For one would then be able to see better which [revealed truths] can co-exist with each other and which ones, on the other hand, become untenable: which in truth would contribute not a little to ending confessional controversies, if not all at once, then at least little by little, for reasons which are familiar without my discussing them here."[14]

In his *Ausführliche Nachricht von seinen eigenen Schriften, die er in deutscher Sprache heraus gegeben*,[15] Wolff delivers, among other things, an impressive argument for freedom of thought and of the press. As in his discussion of the boundaries between theology and philosophy, here too it is a question of whether one should accept ideas whose validity has not been demonstrated convincingly, simply on the basis of traditional authority, or whether one should not rather have the courage and the freedom to think independently for oneself. More important than anything else, there is a purely moral problem involved, namely the question whether or not one is truthful, whether or not one is to present an argument for any other reason than for the purpose of contributing to mankind's common search for truth: "I have not sought to attain happiness in the world by practicing deceptions. I want no part of any happiness which I cannot attain through honesty."[16] Were he to abandon his sincerity and hoodwink those who are eager for knowledge, simply in order to curry favor, then he would consider the practice of philosophy to be something totally indecent, "for by doing that one would have to act contrary to one's natural obligation, and desire to harm others knowingly and with intent."[17] Since, according to Wolff's philosophy of morals, the understanding and the will are intimately connected, it would be a contradiction to be enlightened in understanding and not to act accordingly, to know what is good and proper without being able or willing to express that knowledge. One is either slave or free, decent or indecent. It is absurd ("ungereimt") to accept a truth simply on the basis of authority, but even more absurd to be forced to acknowledge a proof as convincing when one is not able to feel its power of conviction: "It is just the same as though I were to demand that someone should believe on my account that something tastes sweet like honey, when it tastes as bitter as gall to me. Reason does not allow itself to be ordered about."[18] Wolff claims, and in view of the difficulties he experienced because of his philosophical system it is not difficult to believe him, that he has only been concerned for the truth of his philosophical statements and that he has trusted to his own striving for truth rather than accommodate himself to the requirements and demands of others.[19] In another paragraph of the *Ausführliche Nachricht* he maintains that he has never concerned himself in the least whether a truth was new or old, respectable or not, whether it was embraced by everyone or by no one.[20] This willingness to consider truth no matter where it is to be found, whether or not it is popular, figures prominently in his definition of the freedom of thought contained in a more formal statement at the beginning of section 41 of the *Ausführliche Nachricht*, a statement that is one of the most impressive in all his writings and deserves to be known more widely than it is:

Freedom of thought consists in this, that in judging truth one depends not on what others say, but on one's own mind. For if one is constrained to consider something to be true because someone else says it is true, and must consider the proof of it to be convincing because someone else gives it out to be convincing, then one is in a state of slavery. [In that case] one must allow oneself to be ordered to consider something to be true which one does not recognize as truth, and to regard a proof as convincing when one does not feel its power of conviction in oneself. And just as a slave must subjugate his will to that of another and do things which he has no desire to do and which he would not do of his own free will; so here too one must subjugate one's reason to that of another and pronounce something to be true which one cannot consider to be true, to proclaim the validity of a proof regardless of whether or not that proof leaves one in doubt. And accordingly slavery in philosophizing consists in the subjugation of one's reason to the judgment of another or, what amounts to the same thing, in expressing one's approval of the authority of another.

Sixty years later Kant himself in his essay "What is Enlightenment?" got no farther than Wolff. In fact it can be maintained that the times had not progressed at all: Wolff's arguments on the freedom of thought had their impetus in his controversies with opposition theologians and his determination to stake out an area in which philosophy could claim to find its own truth; in Kant's essay, published in 1784 in the most liberal of the Berlin Enlightenment journals, the *Berlinische Monatsschrift*, it is still above all a question of the freedom to express one's views on religious doctrines, not by far a matter of freedom of thought in all things. The times were still not so far advanced in Kant's day that one could afford to proceed to the discussion and propagation of enlightened *political* or *social* views, at least not in Frederick II's Prussia.[21] Wolff's formulation can be considered rather more expressive than Kant's in "What is Enlightenment?": Wolff names the lack of freedom to philosophize by its true name, "Slavery," whereas Kant contents himself with defining Enlightenment as man's emergence from a condition of legal guardianship for which he himself is made to bear the responsibility. Kant further defines this condition of "legal guardianship" as the incapacity to use one's own reason without relying on the guidance of other persons.[22] By thus equating Enlightenment with the ending of guardianship over a child, Kant manages to put a much milder, patriarchical face on things. Besides, Wolff considers himself already to be emancipated from intellectual slavery and he acts and writes accordingly, as though he were in fact emancipated, whereas Kant is only expressing the hope that *some day* mankind will leave behind that stage of its development in which it needed the tutelage of a guardian; potentially, the slave can become truly free, while the child, when it becomes an adult, must still take into consideration the father's feelings and point of view.

It may appear that Wolff subsequently takes back some of the asserted freedom of the philosopher when he goes on to say at the beginning of section 42 of the *Ausführliche Nachricht* that what is, in the abstract, freedom of thought, like so many other good things, can be misused ("gemißgrauchet"). It is necessary, after all, to have a regard for society and other human beings and to restrict freedom of thought and expression to the extent necessary to protect religion, virtue, and the state. In the course of Wolff's analysis it turns out, however, that these restrictions are not quite as repressive as one might imagine they could be: (1) Wolff excludes from the category of "opinions opposed to religion," which are to be regulated, all those questions and problems where the theologians themselves have not attained unanimity of opinion, that is, dogmatic questions; thus it seems that very little can be prohibited (aside from the open propagation of antireligious points of view), since the theologians of the various confessions are not in agreement on a majority of the questions they argue about. (2) Wolff means under the rubric of "opinions that are opposed to virtue" in essence only the deliberate provoking of public opinion by publicists who might perversely advocate vice by calling it virtue ("das Laster und Schand-Thaten für Tugenden anpreisen"), a position with which all his contemporary and even many modern observers and critics would have agreed. And (3) he stresses that one must not rush prematurely to equate the conclusions that can be drawn from a *philosophical statement* with publicly propagated statements or claims that would be injurious to religion, morals, or the state. To be sure, Wolff is quite conservative in his political views and with regard to public order, but perhaps he is only being a loyal subject of that order: according to him no one should be allowed to preach any opinions "through which the citizens [Unterthanen] could be confused and led to disobey or even to rebel." If, however, someone were to publicize opinions that might appear suspicious from the point of view of the health of religion, virtue, or the state, then that might be cause for controversy, but not for accusing that person of the crime of having "transgressed the boundaries set to the freedom of thought in the body politic" or for claiming that he had thereby forfeited that freedom. One dangerous thought does not make a philosopher an outlaw ("vogelfrei") and intellectual controversy is not in itself an evil—at least, as long as the intellectuals do not come to blows over their assertions—for it is to be assumed that philosophers are rational people and that someone who has made proper use of true freedom of thought and has a correct understanding of philosophy can be convinced that he is maintaining arguments injurious to religion, virtue, or the state, will be swayed by the reasoning of his opponent, and voluntarily revise his views to conform with truth. Thus for Wolff there do not seem to be any truths ("Wahrheiten") that could be truly dangerous for reasonable and enlightened people.

THE WOLFFIAN SYSTEM AND THE INTERESTS OF THE THEOLOGIANS

As we have seen, Wolff defines philosophy as the "science of the possible," a definition which encompasses the whole of the intellectual realm of possibles as well as the existent world (which is obviously "possible" by virtue of the fact that it exists). In the dedication of the "German Teleology" and in the *Ausführliche Nachricht*, as we have seen, he draws the boundary between philosophy and theology in no uncertain terms: philosophy is the science of possibles and existents, while theology is the science of the suprarational, that is, of divine revelation as contained above all in the Bible. Since, however, God is to be viewed as existent, he is an object of study not only for the theologians, but also for that branch of philosophy, *theologia naturalis*, which concerns itself with the existence and attributes of God as they can be known and demonstrated according to the laws of reason. The philosopher (that is, Wolff) is not so presumptuous as to seek to intervene in the controversies of the theologians: he himself has nothing to do with the truths of revelation, but only with such truths as can be recognized and dealt with by the faculty of reason alone.

In spite of his professed determination to remain on the philosophical side of the boundary, it must nevertheless be admitted that the territory of *theologia naturalis* to which Wolff lays claim in his "German Metaphysics" leaves very little room for traditional Christian (especially orthodox Lutheran) theology, depending as that theology does to such an extent on direct revelation by God of the truths necessary for the salvation of men and on miracles to substantiate its articles of faith. Wolff limits the room for miracles drastically, as in the following passage:

> Whatever is grounded in the essence and the nature of the world and the bodies of which it consists is natural. Thus when everything in a world occurs naturally it is a work of God's wisdom. If, however, things occur which are not grounded in the essence and

the nature of things, they occur supernaturally or by means of miracles; and thus a world in which everything occurs by means of miracles is only the product of God's power, not of his wisdom. And for this reason a world where miracles occur only very sparingly is to be esteemed more highly than one in which they occur frequently.[23]

A world full of miracles would in fact be a rather bad thing, since the use of power not guided by the highest wisdom would be quite arbitrary. God's creation of the world ex nihilo is the only miracle that Wolff needs for the sake of his philosophical system; the creation miracle itself is, in fact, the only miracle that *can* take place in the world without being exposed to the critique of reason. Wolff asserts that God, through the one-time miracle of creation, has produced a world that then fulfills all the conditions for being considered a "natural" world, because it follows the laws of Nature instituted by God at the time of the creation. Everything that occurs in this world has its sufficient reason "in the essence and in the nature of the world" and such a creation miracle, in which, thanks to natural laws, the entire future course of the world has been regulated, represents a higher-class miracle than if God were to have to demonstrate his power on a continuing basis by arbitrarily intervening in the world whenever he desired or found it necessary to do so. Whereas God demonstrates his wisdom and his omnipotence simultaneously by creating a "natural" world, his later intervention could only demonstrate his power and remove a blemish caused by an apparent original lack of divine wisdom: "One recognizes from this that less divine power is necessary for miracles than for natural occurrences. For miracles demand only divine power and knowledge of a thing: whereas natural occurrences demand the knowledge by which God connects everything in the world with everything else, his wisdom, and also his power."[24]

The Christian religion depends of course on certain miracles, both to legitimize its claim to truth and to differentiate it from all other religions, including Judaism and Islam, both of which depend in part on the same traditions and the same sources. Wolff allows only the one true and great miracle of creation to go unchallenged by reason; all other putative miracles are subject to investigation as to whether they are genuine or not, that is, in the last analysis, whether they are fictitious or real:

Now we have a sign by which we can distinguish true miracles from false ones. For if it is claimed that miracles have occurred in cases where either nature is sufficient to fulfill the purpose, or an old miracle already known to us can serve the purpose just as well, then it is not possible that God should have caused such miracles, and the miracles that are claimed to have occurred are accordingly either made up or they are natural occurrences which, for lack of proper understanding, have been taken for miracles.[25]

Any theologian could be expected to have some reservations about setting up criteria according to which miracles can be explained to be impossible. The God of Christianity is a far less predictable, that is, a more complex God than the God whom Wolff has called upon to perform the creation miracle. Wolff had already demanded in a previous paragraph of the "Metaphysics" that a *genuine* miracle, in order to give evidence of God's wisdom, had to be capable of being incorporated into the natural order of the world ("Zusammenhang der Dinge"), if it was to give evidence of God's wisdom:

The natural way, as the superior way, must always be preferred over the way of miracles, and therefore miracles cannot occur except where God cannot achieve his goal in the natural way. And in such a case miracles derive not only from God's power, but also at the same time from his wisdom, for he uses them as a means for achieving his end, which end he afterward connects to natural ends; whereby the miracles are integrated into the natural order of things.[26]

Thus God does not perform miracles unless there is no other alternative—a tacit admission that God's wisdom is not all that it is claimed to be, otherwise the all-wise and all-knowing God would be thought capable of having avoided such an impasse by paying more attention to his original creation. In what manner God weaves his miracles into the fabric of nature and thus connects them with "natural ends" would also merit some attempt at an explanation, which, however, Wolff does not offer at this point.

Without himself explicitly challenging the teachings of the Church, Wolff here lays the groundwork and sets the criteria according to which miracles recorded in the Bible can be investigated and questioned. The passage of the Israelites through the Red Sea, the sun standing still at Gilead, the transformation of water into wine, above all Christ's resurrection and the miracles of the Apostles, which according to traditional theology took place precisely in order to prove the truth and the divine nature of the Christian religion, are not the kind of events that can readily be integrated into the world, the "Zusammenhang der Dinge." Even though

Wolff himself does not go any farther than to set forth criteria for rational inquiry and does not question those miracles that are central to faith as Pierre Bayle and some of the English Deists had done, this is precisely the point where Hermann Samuel Reimarus (whose anonymous "fragments" were published by Lessing in the 1770s but written much earlier, probably during the 1740s)[27] scores most tellingly against the miracles passed on by Old Testament tradition—for example, by calculating just how long it would have taken for so and so many Israelites to make the crossing through the Red Sea and the unlikelihood that the sea, in closing again behind them, would have distinguished between fleeing Israelites and pursuing Egyptians. One can also mention in this connection Lorenz Schmidt, the translator of the so-called "Wertheim Bible," and Karl Friedrich Bahrdt, toward the end of the eighteenth century, both of whom went to great lengths, at the other extreme from Reimarus, to interpret the miracles recorded in the Bible as thoroughly "natural" events in Wolff's sense. In any case, any questioning of the miracles necessary for the preservation of the faith understandably caused good orthodox theologians great concern, and it is not surprising that they were critical of Wolff's whole tendency of thought and his systematic enterprise, even though he himself did not go so far as to apply his criteria to a radical critique of dogma.

In his critique of the nature and the possibility of divine revelation Wolff proceeds according to the same principles as in the case of miracles. Even the very manner in which he approaches the question allowed for the possibility of doubting the basis of Christian revelation:

> We find . . . that at all times and among all peoples there have been claims that God had made known his will, here or there, by means of a direct revelation: and since the whole Christian religion is built upon revelation it will not be beside the point to investigate here how one should recognize a divine revelation and how one can distinguish it from false claims. For since a divine revelation, which consists in truth, is different from an empty figment of the imagination and from a false claim, then the former must have something about it which is not to be found in the case of the latter.[28]

Christian revelation is not differentiated in its essence from the revelations asserted to be the content of other religions, nor does Wolff claim that *only* Christian revelation can satisfy his criteria in order to be classified as "true" revelation. Since a revelation consists in "truth" ("Wahrheit") and there have been claims of divine revelation at all times and among all peoples, it is necessary to set up standards which can be used to investigate any revelation that may be asserted, and which thus at least in principle can also be applied to Christian revelation. Wolff allows (similar to his argument in the case of miracles) for no direct revelation by God if the knowledge to be imparted to man can be imparted in a "natural" manner, for example through reason or through observation of nature. If, in spite of this requirement, God should have had reason to resort to direct revelation, this revelation has to be integrated into the whole of the world (the "Zusammenhang der Dinge") just like any miracle: "And just as God cannot perform superfluous miracles, because they bring with them much too much that is unpredictable, and therefore he does not perform directly what he can do in the ordinary way, so too the manner of the revelation must have made use of the powers of nature as far as possible."[29] He takes for his example the sleeping prophet to whom God wants to reveal a truth in his dreams. God must bring about, through his supernatural intervention, the beginning of the revelatory dream, since the dream is not a consequence of the immediately preceding spiritual condition of the prophet. But the dream is to be integrated into the framework of the spiritual processes of the prophet by allowing it to proceed from that point according to the laws of the imagination. Wolff thus reduces God's intervention to the smallest possible traces; and in the course of time even these infinitesimal traces of divine intervention came to be explained by other thinkers in terms of the laws of the imagination alone, without reference to the divine will to provide a revelation of truth.

Wolff's "German Ethics" presented the theologians with no fewer problems than his treatment of miracles and revelation, for here was a philosopher who claimed that the happiness ("Seeligkeit") of man consisted in his uninterrupted progress to ever greater perfection and that a virtuous man has a capacity to do that which makes him and his condition more perfect than before.[30] It was all too easy to disregard Wolff's careful definition of perfection ("Vollkommenheit") as logical or natural "unity of the manifold" and to claim that Wolff meant that it was possible for *man* to attain perfection. What had happened here to the doctrines of original sin and the utter depravity of the human condition? Such an assertion would directly contradict those points of the Augsburg Confession according to which man, because of original sin, can do *nothing* that is good or pleasing to God of his own accord, and according to which moreover even God's grace, while sufficient for salvation, does not constitute a foundation for moral betterment. To be sure, Wolff makes an effort to distance himself from such imputations drawn from his ethical doctrines: "As a philosopher I am speaking of no other happiness than that happiness which can be attained in this life by natural powers." And yet Wolff does not entirely escape the suspicion of claiming the possibility of perfection, for it is clear from his definition of the soul in the "German Metaphysics" that he conceives of the stages of the soul's development in earthly life and in the afterlife as continuous, one proceeding directly and almost imperceptibly from the other. Therefore, all the perfections with which the soul manages to enrich itself on earth still redound to its benefit in the hereafter. With such a conception of the soul Wolff has taken a step that was already anticipated by Leibnitz, but which Leibnitz had not followed through to its conclusion: namely, the step from a static Lutheran conception of the afterlife to a dynamic concept according to which the soul is capable of attaining increasing perfection during earthly life and continuing uninterruptedly toward that goal after the "transformation" that is represented by death. The poetic last stage of this development is to be found at the end of the second part of Goethe's *Faust*, when Faust's entelechy is borne off toward heaven in spite of his sins.

Wolff's conception of the will represents another step in the undermining of Lutheran teaching. According to the Augsburg Confession the will is corrupt as a result of original sin and is not capable by itself of doing anything at all that is good. Wolff, however, distinguishes between sensual appetite ("sinnliche Begierde"), based on an unclear or confused idea of some thing as desirable, and true will, which he treats as an analogue of God's will. (In fact, at one point in the "German Metaphysics" he goes so far as to explain God's faculty of will as an analogue of *man's* will: "Thus we should note that we meet in the divine will with all those things which we found earlier while considering the freedom of the human will.")[31] The will of man and the will of God are alike in the fact that both are determined voluntarily by recognition of the Good. And in order to prove that God was not determined by external causes to create the present world, Wolff makes God's thought and volition processes the same as man's: "It is easy to show that God cannot be compelled to do anything, because he can only will that which is the best . . . and whatever he wills, he wills without compulsion. It is the same with us, that we gladly do what we consider to be good, and we do it all the more gladly, the better it seems to us."[32]

Such an essentially intellectualistic conception of the will represents a substantial divergence from traditional Christian moral teaching. Good and evil are retained as categories, but they are no longer absolute moral concepts. A thing is not good simply because it is pleasing to God, or evil simply because God forbids it. Instead, in the "German Ethics" Wolff characterizes good and evil in terms of their effect on the earthly condition of man: "Whatever makes our inner as well as our external condition more perfect is good; whereas whatever makes both more imperfect is evil. For this reason the free acts of men are either good or evil."[33] To be sure, the Wolffian teaching presupposes that an act that violated, let us say, one of the Ten Commandments would serve to make a person's state more imperfect than it was before (perhaps because of the punishment meted out by the worldly authorities, perhaps because of the delinquent's subsequent guilty conscience); but the moral quality of the action is appraised without reference either to God or to divine law: "Because the free acts of men become good or evil by virtue of their consequences, and because whatever follows from them is a necessary consequence and cannot fail to come about, they are good or evil in themselves and are not simply made to be so by God's will."[34] Since voluntary acts are good or bad in themselves and because of their necessary consequences, there is no more need for an external moral standard and man is made directly responsible for his actions. Wolff's ethics assumes therefore the existence of rational man, who weighs the consequences of his actions, can recognize the Good, and, in light of the nature of the will (namely, that it desires the Good), cannot fail to choose that which he has recognized as the Good, in order to make his state more perfect. From this conception of rationality and will it also follows that an evil deed does not incontrovertibly prove the evil will of man, but only that he has not clearly recognized the consequences that will follow from his action. It thus appears that the major stumbling block in the way of good actions is the understanding, and not the will. One could even maintain that in Wolff's system there is *no* evil will, because a person who could always weigh the consequences of his actions correctly would never choose anything but the Good. And because the actions of man are good or evil in and of themselves, and God's express command is not necessary in order to judge the morality of an act, one could get along in the field of ethics and morality *totally without* God: "Therefore even if it were possible that there were no God, and the present state of things could exist without him, the free actions of men would still remain good or evil."[35] Even though couched in the subjunctive, this remains a remarkable statement. Naturally, Wolff has no intention of conceding that the world could exist without God; nevertheless he is unmistakably raising the claim that reason provides men with sufficient guidance for their actions.

It is thus not God, but "Nature" which impels men to do that which is good and avoid the evil, "also to prefer the better to that which is not so good and to choose the greater good over the lesser one."[36] To be sure, the so-called "Law of Nature" ("Gesetz der Natur") can be derived, in the last analysis, from God, since it was he who created the world and the laws of nature which are necessary for it to remain in existence. But according to Wolff's system the divine law is *nothing other than* the "Law of Nature" and can thus in no way contradict it.[37] Thus there are no absolutes and the calculus of relative consequences (to prefer "the better" over "the less good," "the greater good" over the "lesser good") is expressed in Wolff's summation of the "Law of Nature": "[The rule], 'Do what makes you and your state more perfect, and refrain from what makes you and your state more imperfect,' is a law of Nature. For since this rule applies to all the free actions of men there is no need for any other law of Nature. . . . And therefore this rule is complete as the basis of all natural laws."[38] The "Law of Nature" is of course to be comprehended by means of reason, which has the ability and the task of providing "insight into the connection of things" ("Zusammenhang der Dinge"), that is, also into good and evil: "And therefore reason teaches us what we should do and not do, that is, *Reason is the teacher of the Law of Nature*."[39]

In and of themselves, such statements were more than enough to have generated trouble for Wolff among the Lutheran theologians, since the orthodox Lutheran standpoint maintained that reason was so corrupted by original sin that it could no longer serve man as a proper guide, let alone serve as a "teacher of the Law of Nature." But Wolff arrives at even more uncomfortable conclusions, once he determines that reason is capable of directing the will. An important question that surfaces repeatedly in the philosophical and theological discussions of the time concerns the treatment of the so-called "atheist" in Christian society. Without doubt the question is raised most often to rhetorical effect, as an expression of the fear that modern thinking could lead to a contagion of atheism and freethinking, rather than as a reasoned response to people who actually existed and called themselves "atheists," since at this time (the 1720s) there were probably few who would have identified themselves publicly as anything other than devout believers in God. (At any rate the frequency and vehemence of this type of discussion and controversy would have been enough to convince any true atheist, or even a moderate Deist, that prudence was the better part of valor and that it would be better to continue going to church for the sake of appearances.)[40] Usually one attempts first to demonstrate convincingly that it would be impossible for anyone to be a true atheist at all, because there are so many compelling reasons for believing in the existence of God (that is, if one is already predisposed to believe in God—as the eighteenth-century thinker still was for the most part). But *in case* it should happen that someone should claim to be an atheist, the question immediately arises whether or not such an individual should be tolerated in Christian society. Would not the atheist, if he were tolerated, immediately infect his fellow citizens with his disbelief and cause the whole society to fall away from God? Out of this fear the conclusion was usually drawn that the atheist constitutes a social, moral, and political menace and cannot be tolerated by Christian society because he confesses no acceptable faith that could serve to guarantee his morality (this type of argument disregards frequent controversies about the condition of morals within the society of the time and, if one is to believe the sharpest critics, the utter depravity of many of the clergy themselves). It would be impossible, according to this line of reasoning, to place any trust in the atheist, even under oath, since an oath would have to be sworn in the presence of a God in whom he did not believe. (On the other hand, there seems to be little or no discussion of the question whether *hypocrites* are capable of swearing a credible oath, or whether perjurers are to be viewed in the same terms as atheists.)

After Wolff, however, has finished transforming morality into a province of the understanding and made the will dependent on insight into the good and evil consequences of actions, he draws a further conclusion with regard to atheists. It is his opinion that, if it were possible for there to be such people as atheists, they would prove to be rational human beings and act just as morally as any Christian. That Wolff considers this conclusion to be important and worthy of attention is attested by the fact that he emphasizes the following passage in its entirety:

> And thus those people are in error who imagine that an atheist would live as he wanted and that he would actually give himself over to vice and commit all manner of evil deeds, if he were only free of the fear of punishment: for this is true only if an atheist is not a rational person and does not correctly understand the nature of free actions. Therefore it is not atheism which leads him into evil ways, but his lack of knowledge and his error with regard to good and evil; and this is the same source from which spring a disorderly life and immorality among other people who are not atheists.[41]

It would be possible to equate immorality with atheism only if one could presume that all Christians and other believers always acted morally. Since, however, one cannot prove that believing Christians always act more morally than atheists, there is no call to exclude atheists from society, at least before they have proven, by immoral actions that spring from their atheism, that they do not deserve to be allowed to live among Christian people. But even if the atheist is immoral, that immorality is not necessarily to be attributed to his atheism. His immorality has the same source as the actions of an immoral Christian: in both cases what is really lacking is a fruitful insight into the relationship between good and evil and into the consequences of one's actions. After all this, however, Wolff tries (it is probably obligatory!) to escape the reproach of having put in a good word for the atheists: "Perish the thought that I should want to speak for the atheists. But I still cannot go against the truth."[42]

Because of the orthodox dogma of original sin, the theologians could only panic at the idea that even an atheist could be a moral person. If the heathen Greeks and Romans had not been blessed with belief in the proper God and in the proper dogmas, at least they had not exactly been atheists. But the ancient Chinese had been an *atheistic* heathen people (at least as far as anyone knew at that time) and it had to arouse a certain amount of hostility when Wolff, in a famous lecture delivered in 1721,[43] passed favorable judgment on the morals of Confucian society. Wolff found that the Chinese philosophers had acted and taught according to their own secular ethics, and had thus practiced the Wolffian philosophy long before Wolff's time:

> I have demonstrated elsewhere [i.e., in his "German Ethics"] that the highest good of men consists in daily unimpeded progress toward greater perfections. And because the Chinese stressed so strongly the idea that one must continually advance along the path of virtue and not rest at any degree of perfection less than the very highest degree, which of course no one can attain, it is my opinion that their philosophers, too, subscribed to the view that man cannot achieve happiness unless he seeks to attain more perfections day by day.[44]

To what extent Wolff's philosophy had detached social ethics and morality from the traditional Christian context can be seen in his use of the expression "the highest good of men." In philosophy and theology God himself or man's relationship to God had always been the "summum bonum," but Wolff transfers that transcendental relationship into the earthly sphere and uses it to designate man's life journey, man's process of becoming more and more perfect, which, according to Wolff's teaching, begins here on earth and is only *continued* in the afterlife.

CONFLICT WITH THE THEOLOGIANS AND WOLFF'S EXPULSION FROM HALLE

It was not Wolff's praise of Chinese philosophers, however provoking that may have been, but rather the suspicion that he taught a thoroughgoing determinism that led to the famous cabinet order of Frederick William I expelling him from Halle on pain of death. Wolff had the most difficulties with the doctrine of the preestablished harmony between body and soul that he had explicated in the "German Metaphysics" as Leibnitz's solution to the problem of the relationship between body and soul. According to Leibnitz's doctrine, body and soul are so in tune with each other, even though the soul or monad has no "windows" or any way of being affected directly by what goes on outside it in the universe, that nothing can touch the body without also simultaneously affecting the soul, and vice versa. What is more, the movements of each body and the affects of each soul in time follow inexorably from all the preceding moments in history, so that Leibnitz more than once claims that a spirit with God's omniscience and powers of understanding can foresee, in the moment of creation, everything that will ever take place in the world. For God each moment of history becomes a déjà vu.

If, later on, Wolff defended himself against the charge that he himself was an advocate of preestablished harmony, his denial hardly represented the full truth. At the same time, one must consider as totally unfounded the reproaches made against Wolff by later philosophers and intellectual historians, namely that he had turned the Leibnitzian conception of the preestablished harmony into a superficial or one-sided idea by limiting Liebnitz's expansive theory of a universal pre-established harmony exclusively to the relationship between body and soul. In the first place, it is clear from the "German Metaphysics" that Wolff maintains the same doctrine of universal harmony between all the individual parts of matter and the universe that Leibnitz had propounded in the *Theodicy* and the *Monadology*, with the one crucial difference that Leibnitz had been a Cartesian in his physics and had thus maintained that the universe is a *plenum*, full of matter with no empty spaces at all,[45] whereas in the meantime the Newtonian system had displaced the Cartesian: Wolff, a good Newtonian, no longer believes that the universe is a *plenum*. In the Leibnitzian version of monadology there is a direct cause-and-effect relationship between motions in one part of the universe and the whole of the universe, because there is no empty space, and the monad can thus with some justice be termed a "mirror" of the whole universe; Wolff, on the other hand, has drawn the conclusion from Newtonian physics that the individual monad (or, as Wolff terms it throughout, the soul) can no longer be viewed as a mirror of the *entire* universe, but that it still has a somewhat more limited power of representing or mirroring the world: "The soul represents to itself" a part of the world, or as much of the world as the position of its body within the world allows; and, since the acts of the soul stem from its power, the soul has the power to represent the world to itself according to the position of its body within the world."[46] In the second place, Leibnitz himself had expressly conceived his doctrine of preestablished harmony as the preestablished harmony between body and soul, and had presented it thus in his "Système nouveau de la nature et de la communication des substances, aussi bien que de l'union quil y a entre l'âme et le corps" of 1695, where he still conceives the soul or "unity" as a sort of "substantial atom" in an effort to combat new theories of atomism that had started to appear in the wake of modern mechanism. It was only later, with the development of his system of monadology, that he explicitly expanded the system of preestablished harmony to include all the monads in the whole universe in one system, a system in which the harmony of body and soul represents only a special case. If, therefore, Wolff takes over from the "Système nouveau" and other Leibnitzian writings a conception of preestablished harmony as the harmony between body and soul, he is not thereby doing violence to Leibnitz's system but rather adhering to it in its strictest and narrowest formulation.

It may very well be that in the "German Metaphysics" Wolff does not expressly proclaim loudly his own adherence to the Leibnitzian teaching with respect to preestablished harmony. But he rejects all the other possibilities of explaining the communication between body and soul that have been put forward by other thinkers, and in the end he can only say: "And thus we come to Herr von Leibnitz's explanation of the union between the body and the soul, to which he gave the name of 'preestablished harmony.' . . ." After introducing the Leibnitzian conception he makes every effort over the next many pages to demonstrate how it is possible for such a harmony to exist. Since he has rejected all the other possibilities for explaining the communication between body and soul, the fact that he goes to such lengths to demonstrate the possibility of the preestablished harmony must approximate actually embracing the doctrine, because eventually he comes to the conclusion that, all in all, the doctrine of preestablished harmony offers the most natural explanation for the communication between body and soul and therefore is to be preferred over the others.

It is difficult to understand today how a philosopher of the stature of Leibnitz or Wolff could embrace such a theory as the preestablished harmony. The only explanation for this is that philosophers of the time felt themselves so obligated to maintain the originally Cartesian distinction between "material substance" and "thinking substance" that the problem of soul-body communication (and for theological reasons the soul had to be conceived as entirely nonmaterial) came to function as the Gordian knot of modern natural science and philosophy. If it had turned out to be impossible to explain the connection between soul and body without contradicting the laws of motion and without either augmenting or diminishing the sum of energy and motion in the universe,[47] then it would have been necessary to expel either the body or the soul from the philosophical system. To have reconciled oneself without further ado to the conclusion that body and soul exercise a mutual influence each on the other which is *not* capable of scientific (especially mechanical) explanation would have meant the reintroduction of just such occult qualities as Descartes and his disciples had just finished eradicating from natural science.

Although Wolff does not differ appreciably from Leibnitz in his explanations of the problem of the soul-body relationship, he occupies himself much more intensively than Leibnitz with the *reasons* why there is a problem here in the first place, and why one is practically forced to resort to the doctrine of preestablished harmony. A number of statements which today (thanks in part to Voltaire's *Candide*, no doubt) appear to us to be quite comical, hint at the deep seriousness with which the philosopher of the early Enlightenment viewed the problems, and at the fear of what would happen if the explanation which seemed to him to be the "most natural" explanation of the relationship between body and soul should not, after all, prove to be viable. According to the doctrine of preestablished harmony, the movements of the body and the movements of the soul take place with precise simultaneity and "it is not possible that the sensation should come too early or too late."[48] It is also unthinkable that desires or appetitions could arise in the soul that did not correspond to the situation of the body in the universe, because it is unthinkable that "the soul and the body . . . could get out of phase with each other."[49]

Wolff (as Leibnitz before him) makes such a radical distinction between body and soul that each could exist alone without the other, without the world being or appearing different from how it actually is—a conclusion that obviously had the potential to cause him considerable difficulty with the theologians. As we have seen, the soul contributes nothing to the motions of the body, for that would mean an addition to the total amount of motion and energy in the world. Wolff's most extreme explication of the laws of motion as they pertain to the body concludes that the body would in fact act and react as it does in the world *even if no soul existed at all:*

All the movements of the body follow in such wise—from the manner of its composition, that is, from its essence, and through its power, that is, through its nature—from the motions of other bodies which cause changes in its sensory organs, that everything occurs in the body naturally in the same way and manner as is usual in bodies, and Nature is not disturbed in her normal course either by the soul, as is predicated by the idea of natural influence, or by God, as would be the case with direct divine intervention.[50]

It is clear from this that all motions in the body would occur in exactly the same manner as is now the case even if there were no soul present, in that the soul contributes nothing through its power; only in that case we would not be conscious of what went on in our body.[51]

According to the mechanistic physics of the time, the body is nothing but a "mere machine,"[52] or, as Leibnitz had also called it, an automaton. If there were no souls, nothing would be different in the world—bodies would continue to interact and affect each other as they do now—except that there would be no consciousness.

For Wolff the *soul* is just as much a kind of automaton as the body. Again, this is nothing that Leibnitz had not previously allowed for, at least hypothetically, but Leibnitz had not written as unambiguously on this point as Wolff. Just as the body is a machine which only acts and reacts in response to external forces, the soul is a "sensation machine"[53] that registers and works upon a never-ending series of sensations that follow one from the other, each sensation being the cause or the reason for the next. These sensations and the soul's occupation with them do not cease even during sleep, the soul being thus a "machine" that reacts internally to the forces that move it *within itself*. Just as it is hypothetically possible for a world of bodies to exist even if there were no souls or spirits, so it is just as possible for a world of souls to exist without there being any bodies or other material objects, as Wolff must admit:

And since the body contributes nothing at all to the sensations ["Empfindungen"] in the soul, all these sensations would continue to occur even if no world existed: which was recognized also by Descartes and long before him by the idealists, who allowed nothing but spirits and souls to exist and left no room for the world except in thought. Indeed, it is evident from what we have demonstrated above that we would see and hear and have other kinds of sense impressions even if there existed nothing in the way of corporeal things outside of us.[54]

Thus if Wolff, on the one hand, takes a view of the role of bodies in the world that is mechanistic (and therefore seems strongly deterministic) in order to accord with the theories of mechanistic natural science,[55] on the other hand, with regard to the soul, he ends up in the vicinity of idealism.

It is not merely idealism that he seems to espouse, but idealistic determinism, since according to his philosophy events in the soul follow upon one another with the same degree of necessity and consequence as is the case with the motions of the body, which are determined by the conditions of the external world.

We can be certain that Wolff has only painted the precarious situation of body and soul in the world so drastically in order to show all the more impressively how gloriously God, through his great wisdom, has solved these great difficulties by inventing the preestablished harmony. In fact, Wolff even makes use of the situation of body and soul in the world to formulate a new kind of proof for the existence of God (a proof that Leibnitz had already hinted at):

> And now because the soul and the body, which can each exist without the other and which are therefore not bound together by necessity, cannot have come together by chance; therefore there can be no harmony between soul and body, except there be a thinking being, which is itself not a part of the world, which has brought them together. And it follows incontrovertibly from this that there is a creator of the world and of nature, that is, a God.[56]

Of course this proof assumes what was to be proven, namely that body and soul *do* act together in harmony. The more we think about the matter, the less we are satisfied by the doctrine of preestablished harmony, especially if, as was the case with Wolff, one must expose oneself to accusations of determinism, not only of the body, but of the soul, by embracing the doctrine so unreservedly.

Leibnitz had already realized that the preestablished harmony was only a "possible" model for representing the relationship between body and soul, and that in actuality one had practically no other alternative than to act *as though* body and soul had a mutual influence each upon the other.[57] Wolff, however, embraced the preestablished harmony to such an extent that, practically speaking, he could do nothing with this *as though*. He makes use of the findings of physiology to explain how the motions of the body are caused by a "subtle motion" in the brain and in the nerves, allows the soul no role at all in these motions, and refers to reflex actions that appear to take place without any action or will on the part of the soul. It would perhaps be petty to point out that Wolff's "German Ethics" still assumes, without allowing for counterargument, that the soul has something to do with the motions of the body when it wishes to estimate whether or not an action contributes to the perfection of its state.

Even though Wolff had painted the possibility of determinism of body and soul so drastically in order to prove God's great wisdom in inventing the system of preestablished harmony to deal with the problem, the doctrine of preestablished harmony itself came to be viewed among Wolff's opponents as one of his most dangerous teachings, and the question whether or not someone asserted the system of preestablished harmony came to be the touchstone for determining whether or not the said thinker was a Wolffian. A certain Friedrich Wagner was probably not the only teacher of philosophy who was unhappy about being designated a "Wolffian" (i.e., as an ally, in this case) by the more or less official contemporary historian of the Wolffian school, Carl Günther Ludovici. Wagner protested against the designation: "In my writings I have publicly rejected and attacked various teachings of the Wolffian philosophy wherever I had the opportunity, especially in the harmoniam praestabilitam along with the Monadology.[58] So I can hardly be a Wolffian at all!"[59] Johann Christoph Gottsched, one of the most influential popularizers of the Wolffian philosophy by virtue of his two-volume *Erste Gründe der gesammten Weltweisheit* ("First Principles of all the Parts of Philosophy," first published in 1733–34), at least had enough common sense to leave the doctrine of preestablished harmony aside and proceed more or less empirically when discussing the relationship between body and soul. After detailing the three most commonly taught theories pertaining to this relationship, the theory of mutual influence, the theory of occasionalism, and the theory of preestablished harmony, Gottsched comes to the conclusion: "Each [of these opinions] has its unresolved difficulties: thus everyone is free to adhere to whichever one pleases him the most. But it has always seemed to me that one has no reason to reject the oldest and most common opinion, that of the natural influence of one upon the other, before it has been completely disproven and its impossibility established. But this has not yet been accomplished by anyone."[60] In fact, Gottsched goes on in the next paragraph to express the belief that even the Leibnitzian conceptions of body and soul do not make it so impossible to assert a natural mutual influence, as some philosophers have until now believed.[61]

The doctrine of preestablished harmony presented the best point of attack by the theologians, for here was the clear proof of Wolff's dangerous determinism. As we have seen, however, that was far from the only thing in Wolff's philosophy that conservative thinkers had to reproach him for. In spite of everything Wolff maintained the courage to assert himself and defend his system, for he was conscious of his rights and advantages vis-à-vis mere theologians, since he had so clearly shown them the bounds of their "science." When he was attacked after his famous speech about Chinese philosophy, because he had allowed Confucius too many good qualities to please the theologians, and when he was attacked by nonprofessorial teachers at the University of Halle with the encouragement of the professors, he appealed successfully to the university statutes forbidding public attacks by professors on their colleagues. His flight from Halle as a result of the cabinet order of November 8, 1723, no longer had anything to do with a philosophical controversy, but rather with the passion of King Frederick William I for his so-called "lange Kerls," his oversize guard regiments recruited by hook or by crook from all over Europe. Wolff's opponents had whispered in the King's ear that according to Wolff's teaching he had no right to punish a soldier who deserted, because in deserting the soldier would have acted not by choice, but by necessity.[62] That was about the worst thing anyone could have told the King about Wolff, and Wolff's whole consciousness of his modernity, his knowledge, his certainty about the correctness of his philosophical positions—nothing was of any use against the royal threat of the noose. Even Wolff's Halle opponents acted as though they were shocked by the King's energetic reaction to the philosopher.

Leibnitz had already been exposed to criticism because of the pre-established harmony, criticism that would no doubt have intensified if he had not died conveniently in 1716. Wolff's critics were well aware that in indicting Wolff they were also attacking Leibnitz. The evaluation of Wolff's philosophy prepared by the theological faculty of the University of Jena after Wolff's expulsion from Halle[63] brings together in twenty-seven articles most of the bad things that could be said about Leibnitz and Wolff at the time: Wolff did not recognize the teleological argument for the existence of God and was a partisan, along with Leibnitz, of the so-called argument from "sufficient reason"; Wolff ceded more to the atheists than was consonant with truth. Further points made against him asserted that Wolff

(5) sees the freedom of the divine will in the fact that God chose the best world, in spite of the fact that according to his opinion God *had* to choose that world, and otherwise he prejudices the argument along with Herr von Leibnitz; . . . (7) maintains that the essence of things depends in no way on God's will, but is rather grounded in God's understanding;[64] (8) explains the so-called "wise connection of things" in such a manner that he completely agrees with the Stoic conception of Fate which is so prejudicial to divine Providence as well as to all religion and true morality; . . . (10) maintains that the present fallen world (11) is the most perfect and the best and considers the evil to be found in it not only (12) to be necessary and unavoidable, but also to be (13) a means to a greater perfection,

by which the world becomes a complete mirror of the divine wisdom; (14) totally denies the true freedom of the human will,[65] maintaining on the other hand (15) that the body contributes nothing to the sensations of the soul and that these would be present exactly as they are even if there existed no world; [16–18 have further to do with the preestablished harmony and Wolff's rejection of the possibility of natural influence]; (19) Herr Wolff does not assert the Leibnitzian teaching about monads in all details at this time, but he assumes most of it nevertheless. . . . [21 has to do with Wolff's acceptance of the idea of the preexistence of souls; 22–27 have to do specifically with objections to Wolff's ethics.]

CONCLUSION

Extreme and bitter controversy was unavoidable as soon as the "German Metaphysics" and the "German Ethics" had appeared, because it was no small part of Wolff's program to make philosophy independent of theology, an independence that threatened the claim of theology to the highest rank and authority in the whole intellectual realm (an authority and precedence entrenched above all in the institution of censorship, which was firmly in the hands of the theological faculties). It is quite arguable that in certain parts of his philosophical system, particularly in his "German Politics" and his "German Teleology," Wolff was rather conservative, or at least not opposed to the prevailing conditions of his times. There is, however, a significant difference between lack of radical thinking in politics and teleology, which are to be viewed as concrete applications of his philosophical system, and the potential for radical application of the principles themselves as set forth in the "Metaphysics" and the "Ethics": one need only recall what Wolff has to say about miracles and the possibility of revelation, about the soul as an object of metaphysical and scientific observation and investigation, and about the human will, which in his philosophy is informed by reason and understanding, not paralyzed by the taint of original sin. Such views and principles could not coexist with the interests of the theologians and the powers that ruled the contemporary world.

From the historical point of view, the controversy between Wolff and the theologians was objectively necessary as a step forward into modernity, especially if the bourgeois classes were to assert themselves and their newly awakening power and interests. It was objectively just as necessary that Wolff and his followers won this fight in the end, if the power of the Church and the dominance of religion over daily social, economic, and political life was to be broken and secularization was to proceed to become a fundamental driving force behind the modern way of life. Wolff was a practical man who knew quite well what he was doing and what he wanted to achieve. Before his death in 1754 Wolff had become "Praeceptor Germaniae" for the whole eighteenth century. A mystical dreamer or a radical eclectic such as Johann Christian Edelmann,[66] who was much more outspoken in his denunciations of Lutheran orthodoxy than Wolff and the Wolffians, would have had no lasting success. The controversy between orthodoxy and modernity would in such a case, have been decided very quickly in favor of the existing order, and the entrance of the Germans into cultural and intellectual modernity, which was already delayed at least a generation behind the British, the French, and the Dutch, would have been held up for yet another generation. That the Wolffian system quickly became a new orthodoxy was a problem for the following generations, not for Wolff himself. We know from Gottsched's encomium on Wolff, the *Historische Lobschrift des weiland hoch- und wohlgebohrnen HERRN Herrn Christians, des H. R. R. Freyherrn von Wolf* . . . published in 1755, the year after Wolff's death, that Wolff's system had appeared to a whole generation of young intellectuals to represent salvation from intellectual chaos. It was the system itself that had the most extensive influence: within ten to fifteen years after Wolff's expulsion from Halle, Wolff and the Wolffians had conquered the universities and could no longer be beaten back. Even before his death, Frederick William I was prepared to go to great lengths to get Wolff back for Prussia, an undertaking in which Wolff refused to acquiesce because he demanded to return to Halle. That was not in Frederick William's plan, no matter how much he desired Wolff's return for reasons of prestige, and it remained to Frederick II to recall Wolff to Halle soon after ascending the throne in 1740. By the middle of the eighteenth century, even the theologians found it necessary to reconcile themselves to Wolffian philosophy and make use of its system for their own arguments about God and the place of religion if they were to retain any influence at all in the modern world.

NOTES

1. This paper is taken from the Wolff chapters of my book, *Von der Kopernikanischen bis zur Französischen Revolution: Die Auseinandersetzung der deutschen Frühaufklärung mit der neuen Zeit*, to be published by the Erich Schmidt Verlag, Berlin.
2. Breslau, chief city of the province of Silesia, belonged to the Catholic Habs-

burgs, but there was a sizable Protestant population there that the rulers had been compelled to refrain from seeking to reconvert by force or by fiat. One of the favorite pastimes of Breslau students in Wolff's day was theological disputation between the Protestants and the Catholics. On the peculiar circumstances in Breslau in the last decades of the seventeenth century see Herbert Schöffler, *Deutsches Geistesleben zwischen Reformation und Aufklärung. Von Martin Opitz zu Christian Wolff*, 2d ed. (Frankfurt am Main, 1956), 153–94; also *Christian Wolffs eigene Lebensbeschreibung*, ed. Heinrich Wuttke (Leipzig, 1841), and Adam Bernd's *Eigene Lebens-Beschreibung* (Leipzig, 1738; reprint, Munich, 1973). Bernd was Wolff's schoolmate in Breslau.

3. Cf. Max Wundt, *Die deutsche Schulphilosophie im Zeitalter der Aufklärung* (Tübingen, 1945), 150: The one opponent, when speaking of Leibnitz's teachings, illustrates them with passages drawn from Wolff's writings, and the term "Leibnitz-Wolffian" can be found in the writings of Wolff's opponents as early as 1724.

4. In spite of the fact that Christian Thomasius was the first modern (Enlightenment) philosopher to write extensively in German. Thomasius's German is clumsy, to say the least, and he refrained from extensive efforts to establish a German philosophical terminology to replace the traditional Latin technical vocabulary. See Eric A. Blackall, *The Emergence of German as a Literary Language 1700–1775*, 2d ed. (Ithaca and London, 1978), 26ff.

5. *Kritik der reinen Vernunft*, B 36–38. On the history of earlier eighteenth-century philosophy see Lewis White Beck, *Early German Philosophy: Kant and His Predecessors* (Cambridge, Mass., 1969). Ernst Cassirer's *Die Philosophie der Aufklärung*, originally published in 1932 and long since widely available in English, has little to say about German thought before Kant.

6. In his *Vernünfftige Gedancken von den Kräfften des menschlichen Verstandes und ihrem richtigen Gebrauch in Erkäntniß der Wahrheit* (Rational Thoughts about the Powers of Human Reason and their Correct Use in Arriving at Truth) (Halle, 1713), sect. 1. The book is usually referred to as the "German Logic." The epithet "German" here, as in the commonly used short titles of Wolff's other major works, is meant to differentiate them from the subsequent series of Latin texts devoted to the same subjects. Wolff's system was developed in the German works, and the Latin Works did not have the same impact in Germany as did the German works.

7. *Vernünfftige Gedancken von den Absichten der natürlichen Dinge* . . . (Rational Thoughts about the Final Causes of Natural Things . . .) (Halle, 1724); the book appeared at the end of September 1723.

8. The "Dedication" to the "German Teleology" is unpaginated. All translations of titles and quoted material in this essay are my own.

9. Without an established tradition of a free press, it was common practice to claim to be a victim of libel or slander and call on the law to silence an unwelcome critic.

10. "German Teleology" (unpaginated).

11. Full title of the "German Metaphysics": *Vernünfftige Gedancken von Gott, der*

Welt und der Seele des Menschen, auch allen Dingen überhaupt (Rational Thoughts about God, the World and the Human Soul, and All Things in General) (Halle, 1720); the "German Ethics": *Vernünfftige Gedancken von der Menschen Thun und Lassen* (Rational Thoughts about Human Morality) (Halle, 1720); the "German Politics"; *Vernünfftige Gedancken von dem gesellschaftlichen Leben der Menschen und insonderheit dem gemeinen Wesen* (Rational Thoughts about the Life of Man in Society and Especially about the Body Politic) (Halle, 1721).

12. The preface to the second edition of the "German Teleology" is dated "Marburg, in September, 1726." Wolff is referring here to accusations made by his enemies, who still seek to persuade people that "the reader would be led away from God, virtue, and all sense of decency by my teachings." In his own defense he cites an anonymous learned theologian who had claimed after reading his works that he had thereby become "stronger in the truth, more competent with regard to everything that a scholar can learn, more understanding of the role of worldly authority, and more passionately devoted to God." Wolff in fact claims the distinction of being the first philosopher to turn *all* the subdisciplines of philosophy to advantage in constructing a ladder "on which one can safely ascend to God," and then leading the reader on from knowledge of and about God back to spiritual happiness and to the practice of virtue.

13. The period from the Treaties of Westphalia to the end of the eighteenth century was still a period of undiminished theological controversy, intolerance, and name-calling in the German territories, both between Pietists and Orthodox theologians and between the Lutherans and the Calvinists (not to speak of general Protestant condemnation of the "superstitions" of the Roman Church). Friedrich Nicolai's novel, *Leben und Meinungen des Herrn Magisters Sebaldus Nothanker* (Life and Opinions of Herr Magister Sebaldus Nothanker), first published in 1772, offers a not overly exaggerated picture of the tribulations of a kindly pastor whose theological notions do not all conform to the requirements of the Lutheran or Calvinist creeds, or to the specifications of the Pietists.

14. This is the opinion expressed by Wolff in his *Ausführliche Nachricht*, sect. 36. (See n. 15, below.)

15. Detailed Report about his own Writings which he has Published in German (published in Frankfurt am Main in 1726). This apology for his works gives an extremely interesting summation of Wolff's reasons for writing, and the process of writing, his German works of the 1720s. Space does not allow for discussion of this work here (see the Wolff chapters of my book, *Von der Kopernikanischen bis zur Französischen Revolution*, referenced in n. 1 above). It was Wolff's German works which established his position in eighteenth-century philosophy and were of such great importance for the development of German thought. It would therefore have been desirable if the editors of the current Wolff edition (Jean Ecole et al.; Heidelberg: Olms-Verlag) had seen fit to begin publishing with the German texts instead of first concentrating on the later Latin versions. On the relationship of Wolff's German texts to the Latin texts see Wundt, *Deutsche Schulphilosophie*, 182ff.

16. *Ausführliche Nachricht*, sect. 39.
17. Ibid., sect. 40.
18. Ibid.
19. Ibid., the first sentence of sect. 40.
20. Ibid., beginning of sect. 39.
21. In fact, it gradually became risky to advance unpopular *religious* views in the atmosphere created after the succession of Frederick William II to the throne of Prussia in 1786 and the promulgation of new religious and censorship edicts from 1788 on. Kant himself ran afoul of the censorship in the 1790s and was forced to refrain from writing on religious subjects until Frederick William's death in 1797.
22. "Was ist Aufklärung," A 481.
23. "German Metaphysics," sect. 1039.
24. Ibid., sect. 1040.
25. Ibid., sect. 1043.
26. Ibid., sect. 1041–42.
27. Reimarus's work was notorious through the nineteenth century and formed a substantial part of the basis for the "Leben-Jesu" line of research represented by David Friedrich Strauss and, in the twentieth century, Albert Schweitzer, but it was never published in full until the 1970s: *Apologie oder Schutzschrift für die vernünftigen Verehrer Gottes* (Apology or Defense for the Rational Worshippers of God), ed. Gerhard Alexander, 2 vols. (Frankfurt am Main, 1972).
28. "German Metaphysics," sect. 1010.
29. Ibid., sect. 1018.
30. Because the text of the relevant chapters of the "German Ethics" is much more widely accessible in Fritz Brüggemann's selections in the volume *Das Weltbild der deutschen Aufklärung* (Series: Aufklärung, vol. 2) in the Deutsche Literatur in Entwicklungsreihen (hereafter cited as DLE), originally published in Stuttgart in 1930 and since reprinted, I quote where possible from Brüggemann's edition (here, 160).
31. "German Metaphysics," sect. 984.
32. "German Metaphysics," sect. 987.
33. DLE, 142.
34. Ibid.
35. DLE, 143.
36. Ibid., 144.
37. Ibid., 149.
38. Ibid., 147. A little farther on Wolff claims: "The law of Nature has determined everything and is complete in itself, although up to now it has not yet been completely recognized" (148).
39. Ibid., 148; Wolff's emphasis.
40. My book, *Von der Kopernikanischen bis zur Französischen Revolution* (see n. 1, above), contains an extensive chapter on attacks on atheism and free thinking.
41. DLE, 147.

42. Ibid. With his argument for the likelihood that the atheist will be a moral person, Wolff has differentiated between civic morality, which makes men capable of living in society and acting responsibly, and the traditional identification of laws with Christian morality, whose field he has now limited to the area of church regulations and articles of faith (i.e., sin, which is not always the same as immorality). Pierre Bayle had used a similar argument to justify the civic morality of the Protestants in Catholic society. Since belonging to an accepted faith does not guarantee moral behavior and the sanctions of religion no longer form the basis for social behavior, the atheist acts in society from the same principles as other men.

43. "Rede von der Sittenlehre der Sineser" (Lecture on the Moral Teachings of the Chinese), reprinted in DLE, 174–95.

44. DLE, 190–91.

45. In this regard see the correspondence between Leibnitz and Samuel Clarke.

46. "German Metaphysics, sect. 753.

47. Wolff writes, in order to explain the impossibility of a "natural" mutual influence of body and soul (the commonsense explanation): "I have already pointed out that, due to the laws of motion in which the order of nature is grounded, there must always be the same amount of energy in the world. If the body affects the soul and the soul affects the body, then the same amount of energy cannot be maintained. For if the soul has an effect on the body there arises a motion which has no relationship to any preceding motion, so that one is forced to postulate that the soul brings forth motion in the body through the mere exercise of its will. And since this motion possesses a measurable force, there arises new force which previously did not exist. And in this manner the amount of force in the world would be increased, contrary to the laws of nature" ("German Metaphysics," sect. 762). Thus the laws of nature regarding the conservation of energy and motion are applied so strictly that not even a soul can remain unregulated by them!

48. "German Metaphysics," sect. 775.

49. Ibid., sect. 791.

50. This is a reference to Malebranche's theory of "occasionalism," which explained the simultaneity of movements of body and soul as having been brought about directly by divine intervention.

51. "German Metaphysics," sect. 779–80.

52. Ibid., sect. 781.

53. By "sensation" we must understand not only sense impressions, but also thought and/or intuition processes which either arise from or accompany sense impressions.

54. "German Metaphysics," sect. 777.

55. See ibid., sect. 781. "In the end, everything which man does or does not do seems to be necessary. For the body is determined to its movements externally by other bodies which it cannot resist, and its movements follow from those external movements, in accordance with its essence and its nature. The body

has no intellect with which it can recognize and consider what is happening, and no power to chance anything; rather it must let everything happen, whatever and however it may be."

56. "German Metaphysics," sect. 768.

57. In his explication of the "Systéme nouveau" Leibnitz writes: "Je ne fuiray pas même de dire qu l'ame *remue* le corps, et comme un Copernicien parle veritablement du lever du soleil, un Platonicien de la realitè de la matiere, un Cartesien de celle des qualités sensibles, pourveu qu'on l'entende sainement, je crois de même qu'il est tres vray de dire que les substances agissent les unes sur les autres, pourveu qu'on entende qu l'une est cause des changemens dans l'autre en consequence des loix de l'Harmonie" (Leibnitz, *Philosophische Schriften*, ed. Hans Heinz Holz, vol. 1: *Kleine Schriften zur Metaphysik* [Darmstadt, 1965], 230).

58. Here Wagner is claiming a glory that does not properly belong to him. Wolff, too, did not want to be identified with the Leibnitzian monadology, although in his rational psychology and in his discussion of spirit and soul he assigns to the soul many of the attributes assigned by Leibnitz to the monads.

59. Quoted from Wolfgang Philipp, *Das Werden der Aufklärung in theologiegeschichtlicher Sicht* (Göttingen, 1957), 137.

60. *Erste Gründe der gesammten Weltweisheit*, sect. 1077.

61. In an earlier discussion of the dominance of the soul over the body (sect. 1002), Gottsched had even been prepared to assume that the brain was the seat of the soul, and thus to localize the nexus of the influence of the soul on the body: "For the art of anatomy teaches that the origin of all nerves . . . is in the brain; likewise, that all nerves are hollow tubes which are filled inside with a subtle fluid of the kind that is to be found in the brain in large amounts. Anatomy teaches further, that even the larger nerves which come from all the sense organs continue to the brain and end there. All of this brings us to the conclusion that the soul exercises its afore-mentioned dominance over the body from within the brain, and that it carries out its desires or decisions in all the members of the body, which are subordinated to it by means of the nerves." Needless to say, this more or less materialistic explanation of the relationship between body and soul was still problematic for orthodox theologians.

62. The full text of the cabinet order is most readily to be found in the Wolff chapter of Hermann Hettner's *Geschichte der deutschen Litteratur im Achtzehnten Jahrhundert* (numerous editions since first publication in the nineteenth century). The punishments meted out for desertion in the Prussian army throughout the eighteenth century were particularly barbarous.

63. The text of the Jena evaluation is printed in full in Hettner's chapter on Wolff.

64. This is a point in which Wolff completely agrees with Leibnitz's argument in the *Theodicy*. The result of this differentiation between God's will and his understanding is, of course, that God cannot think and create everything which he *wills* to create, but only what is in itself *possible* and consistent with *the whole of the universe* taken all together. The reason for this differentiation between the divine understanding and the divine will, as I have analyzed it in

the discussion of Leibnitz's *Theodicy* in my book, *Von der Kopernikanischen bis zur Französischen Revolution* (see n. 1, above), was precisely to assert and defend God's freedom. But this manner of defending God's freedom is looked down upon by the Jena theologians because according to the Leibnitz-Wolff position God is no longer *arbitrarily* free, free to do anything and everything he wants, but only within the limits of (1) the possible and (2) the rule of the Best as enunciated in Leibnitz's *Theodicy.*

65. That Wolff denied the freedom of the human will would be difficult to establish convincingly; on the contrary, he involves himself with the intricacies of the doctrine of preestablished harmony precisely in order to maintain and defend human freedom.

66. See Walter Grossmann, *Johann Christian Edelmann: From Orthodoxy to Enlightenment* (The Hague, 1976). I have published numerous reviews and review essays on Edelmann in the *Lessing Yearbook* and in the *Zeitschrift für deutsche Philologie*, and there is a chapter devoted to Edelmann in my book, *Von der Kopernikanischen bis zur Französischen Revolution* (see n. 1, above).

CHAPTER 6

Scientific Culture in the Early English Enlightenment: Mechanisms, Industry, and Gentlemanly Facts

MARGARET C. JACOB

> Yet was there one thing still reserved for the glory of this Age, and the honor of the English Nation, the grand secret of the whole Machine.
>
> John Arbuthnot[?], *An Essay on the Usefulness of Mathematical Learning*

Any characterization of the nature and role of science in the English Enlightenment immediately encounters two problems. The first can be put quite straightforwardly: Was there an aggressive, self-conscious movement for Enlightenment in England (as distinct from Scotland)? Or, to borrow a phrase from J. G. A. Pocock, where do we find in England the "philosophe intelligentsia," those "secular intellectuals marked by a discontent with society and its history"?[1] And, if we assume that science must play a central role in any cultural movement that claims to be part of the European Enlightenment, what are we to do with the second problem, posed quite independently by historians writing about eighteenth-century English science. They assert that by then English science had grown moribund, devoid of the dynamism and practicality characteristic of the seventeenth-century revolution that had nurtured the European Enlightenment.[2]

The answer to both problems lies in an examination of eighteenth-century English scientific culture. There we find a different kind of enlightenment from the alienated, philosophically and even politically radical version thrown up by the various ancien régimes on the Continent. The

English "philosophe," whether as Fellow of the Royal Society, or scientific experimenter, lecturer, or engineer, managed to flourish in the Whig and Erastian political order that dominated eighteenth-century England. Although it did produce its share of alienated Tory wits, that order fostered a unique intellectual movement centered upon the new science, on its cultivation and promotion. In the hands of these scientific philosophes the mechanical philosophy was grafted onto the interests of its audience in a way that helped to lay the foundations of an industrial mentality. This fusion rested upon a vision of the profits and improvements made possible by science. Its success was also contingent upon the existence of an intelligentsia sufficiently content, at least in the early decades of the century, with the larger political and ecclesiastical order that they were able to concentrate their energies on "the grand secret of the whole machine," thereby rendering scientific learning into mechanisms fit for gentlemen and entrepreneurs.

If the character of eighteenth-century science is examined closely, we find that it was neither moribund nor impractical, although it does not conform to definitions still cherished by some contemporary historians of science. And once perceived as dynamic and progressive in relation to the material order, the science of these English philosophes appears not only as a unique version of Enlightenment but also as the historical link between the Scientific Revolution in its final, English phase and the intellectual origins of the Industrial Revolution. The scientific philosophes of the English Enlightenment escaped alienation only so long as they confined themselves to promoting a vision of scientific learning tied to industrial application. When that vision expanded, late in the century and only in select philosophical circles, into a program for social and political reform, then we begin to see manifestations of political and intellectual radicalism coming from within the scientific community that could rival in intensity, and identify with, the revolutionary movements of both America and France. But to understand those later manifestations of radicalism and the direction that they ultimately took, we must first establish the character of eighteenth-century English scientific culture.

To find that culture we must look at evidence traditionally ignored by historians of ideas as well as by historians of science. We must search among the records left by the promoters of science in London and the provinces, men who offered their contemporaries a vision of progress and improvement based upon science that was as secular as the religiosity of Voltaire yet concerned almost entirely with practical application rather than with polemics against estates and churches. But to interpret these artifacts, indeed even to recognize their importance, requires that we abandon the shibboleths of an older historiography of science and turn elsewhere for methodological insights.

The major shibboleth that scholars are already demolishing asserts that the pure science of Boyle and Newton had nothing to do with the Industrial Revolution.[3] Stated this baldly, the thesis seems almost inoffensive; after all, what does the *Principia* have to tell us about the steam engine? But the methodology that lies at its heart presumes the existence, now and in the eighteenth century, of "pure science," a conception of science that would have been alien to most eighteenth-century scientific practitioners. So, predictably, the historians of that "pure science" dismiss those practitioners as either incapable of, or disinterested in, doing real science. This neglect of part of the historical record, a part singularly important for understanding the English Enlightenment as well as the origins of modern industrial society, has required that evidence readily available in the primary sources simply be ignored. The evidence to be discussed here demonstrates an active interest in, and understanding of, Newtonian physics on the part of scientists whose definition of science required them at every turn to seek its practical application while encouraging its theoretical development. For these eighteenth-century scientists, we now see, science was, perhaps above all else, useful science.

The last rites on this older "pure science" historiography have been adroitly performed by A. E. Musson and Eric Robinson, with some assistance recently from Neil McKendrick, writing on Josiah Wedgwood.[4] I wish to draw from that excellent historiography as well as to add both new evidence and new perspectives. Historians of technology and science like Musson and Robinson give us insights that help to clarify the nature of the Enlightenment in England. They also provide indispensable background for examining eighteenth-century scientific culture with an eye to establishing its own working definition of science and the scientist. The implications of studies such as these extend far beyond their boundaries. If it can be demonstrated that enlightened culture championed a mechanical science intended for application to commerce and industry decades before the so-called "take-off" of industrialization, then students of the causes of the Industrial Revolution will have to pay far closer attention to this intellectual history.[5] The scientific knowledge readily available to late eighteenth-century entrepreneurs may have provided the determining factor when decisions involving the introduction of new machinery, at considerable capital risk, had to be taken promptly and confidently.

The early Newtonians rendered their science comprehensible to an audience that could be either genteel and educated or commercial and practical. Whatever their social standing, occupation, or lack of it, members of that audience were invariably nonmathematical. In the period from 1692 (the date of the first Boyle lectures) until late in Anne's reign, the effort to reach this audience largely took the form of pulpit lectures, of which the great Boyle lectures given in London by liberal Anglican clergymen such as Bentley, Clarke, Whiston, and Derham, are justly the most famous.[6] By 1710, however, scientific promoters had also found entirely secular milieux for their lectures, which quickly turned into structured courses offered in coffee houses, taverns, and publishers' shops. Among the earliest of these were the ones given by William Whiston and Benjamin Worster, who illustrated the Newtonian universe by recourse to mechanical devices, through demonstrations using weights, pulleys, and levers.[7]

In this genre of early scientific lecture, two characteristics are immediately evident and remain present throughout much of the century: first, natural philosophical language, such as we find in the Boyle lectures, continues to be used in the opening lectures of any course, with definitions of matter, motion, space, and time freely tendered, complete with their implications for society and religion. Just as in the Boyle lectures, matter theory—to us that most abstruse of subjects—is routinely explicated so that the audience understands that it is a violation of orthodox Newtonian theory to assert, as would the materialist, that motion is inherent in matter, and thereby to sever the universe from divine control and to deny the providential harmony of the existing social order. The consumers of the new science, who might pay anything from one to three guineas for a six-week course that met two or three times a week, were repeatedly told that what they were learning sanctioned the existing social and constitutional order. Secondly, the earliest lecturers, and all of their successors, used mechanical devices of increasing complexity, especially air and water pumps, levers, pulleys, and pendulums to illustrate the Newtonian laws of motion and hence simultaneously their applicability to business, trade, and industry. It was pointless to give mathematical explications to lay audiences; that must have been obvious from the beginning. The interests of men who wished to weigh and move goods, to improve water transportation, to drain fens or remove water in mines, dictated the format of the earliest lectures. To that extent the practical interests and mathematical limitations of the audience for science profoundly shaped its articulation; at the same time, the experimental rigor of the Newtonian achievement disciplined and excited the minds of these listeners. Through these scientific lectures nature was rendered knowable; its laws could be mastered and, just as important, applied.

Surviving outlines and course descriptions make this mechanical approach to Newtonian laws absolutely clear. In December 1713 Jean Desaguliers offered a course of twenty-one lectures on Newtonian science for two guineas, and these began quite theoretically with "an experiment to show what Cartesius meant by his three elements," and proceeded in the second lecture "to shew the effect of mechanical engines in general."[8] A decade or so later Desaguliers had taken his scientific course outside of London, to the gentlemen of the first provincial scientific and literary society, the Spalding Society in Lincolnshire. There he illustrated Newton's three laws of motion, "exploded" M. Descartes's vortices, gave a demonstration of "a model of the engine for raising water by fire"—one probably based on Newcomen's steam engine, in which Desaguliers had a great interest—and explained in the section on levers and pulleys how "men or horses of unequal strength may be made to carry, or draw a burden, in proportion to their Strength."[9] Similar lectures were given at the Spalding Society by John Booth, who charged twenty persons only half a guinea each to hear about "the universal properties of matter" and "concerning motion in general"; the same topics were discussed by William Griffis, another itinerant lecturer who was all over the Midlands in this early period.[10]

In the 1720s, Benjamin Worster's London lectures were tailored "for qualifying young gentlemen for business," and he attacked those clergy who still opposed the new science as men "whose chief Merit and Trade it is to lye for God."[11] In the 1730s Isaac Thompson, a lecturer of Quaker background, gave a course in Newcastle-upon-Tyne on the mechanical philosophy specifically intended for "those in the coal trade." He repeated it a few years later because of the large number of coal owners near the river Tyne who had subscribed.[12] Both John Horsley (1685–1732) and Benjamin Martin (1704–1782), itinerant lecturers in the early and middle decades of the century, illustrated the Newtonian universe by constant reference to mechanics, going from "the method of computing the force of all sorts of engines" to the application of Newtonian physics to clocks and guns. Martin was so zealous in his desire to convert Newtonian science into universal practice that he lectured publicly to mass audiences. He also came to despise the genteel exclusivity of the Royal Society—at least that was his attitude after he was denied admittance.[13] By the 1760s itinerant scientific lecturing was everywhere in fashion and Martin, although able to make a living at it, had dozens of competitors.

Among the earliest secular occasions where science revealed its mysteries was in the new speculative Masonic lodges comprised largely of tradesmen but also frequented by gentlemen and aristocrats. Adulation of Newtonian science was an official part of Masonic belief, as revealed in the 1723 *Constitutions* published by the Grand Lodge of London—a document in which Desaguliers had a considerable hand—and Masonic rhetoric reflected quite early in the century a new enlightened definition of the gentleman.[14] In one of the most important changes wrought by the Enlightenment in England he was now defined as a man of science. Many institutions and trends, not least the scientific societies to which we shall shortly turn, wrought this transformation, but we can find evidence of it quite easily and early in Masonic literature. Lecturing to his brothers in York, a Masonic orator of 1726 gloried in the world of ordinary mortals: "Human society, Gentlemen, is one of the greatest blessings of life . . . for 'tis to it we owe all Arts and Sciences whatsoever." He condemned the "learned pedant" as an "unsociable animal . . . who has shut himself up all his Life with Plato and Aristotle." The tradesmen present in the lodge were exhorted by the orator to be faithful to their callings, but from gentlemen more was expected: "The education of most of you has been noble, if an academical one may be call'd so; and I doubt not but your improvements in literature are equal to it." Freemasonry asks, however, not only that gentlemen "by signs, words, and tokens . . . are put upon a level with the meanest brother" but also that they "exceed them, as far as a superior genius and education will conduct you. I am credibly inform'd [the orator continued] that in most lodges in London, and several other parts of this kingdom, a lecture on some point of geometry or architecture is given at every meeting. . . ."[15] There is every reason to believe that lodges in London practiced what the York orator preached. At the Old King's Arms Lodge in the 1730s an itinerant lecturer, avid Freemason, and progressive schoolmaster named Martin Clare lectured "on the history of automata . . . on the circulation of the blood . . . [and] on magnetism."[16] Other evidence suggests that Clare also gave his complex lectures on hydrostatics first to his Masonic brethren. In those lectures on the motion of fluids he drew attention to the steam engine, but issued a caution that would determine its selected use until well into the nineteenth century: "in point of profit" the engine may not answer the expectation of those who use it "where Fewel is not very cheap."[17]

Where we find the association of science with Freemasonry, or with societies whose ambiance resembled the relaxed socializing of the lodge, as did the Derby Philosophical Society of the 1780s and 1790s, then we see most clearly the democratizing tendencies within scientific culture. The Freemasons sought (though only in their private gatherings) "to meet upon the level," and in that spirit Martin Clare attempted to bring science to the lower middle class. His educational exercise book for young apprentices, which was an eighteenth-century bestseller and went through ten editions, made passing reference to the value of experimental and natural philosophy as early as its first edition of 1720; by its fifth edition of 1740 it actually gave the three Newtonian laws of motion and exercises to illustrate them.[18]

Although we do not as yet associate the Masonic lodges of eighteenth-century England with the spread of scientific learning, the historiography of the period takes for granted the important role of the Dissenters and their academies in the enterprise of scientific education. The evidence is quite convincing for this truism, and it is a necessary and useful one, provided it does not obscure the larger, more widespread, dissemination of science in Anglican or purely secular settings. Certainly the inventor of the steam engine, John Newcomen (1663/4–1729),[19] was a devout Baptist, while Philip Doddridge, the Dissenting minister of Northampton, was a leader in its philosophical society. One of the few extant diaries from the early part of the century, one which records the conscience and learning of the scientifically minded layman, reveals the great emphasis placed in the Dissenting tradition on constant attendance at both religious sermons and scientific lectures. The habit and discipline of the first led, it would seem, to the cultivation of the second. As this diary reveals, the providentialism preached at both suited the temperament of the striver and seeker after improvement and salvation:

> This Day in the Morning I attended on Domestick Affairs, went in the Afternoon to Manchester heard a Lecture concerning Attraction and Repulsion of Matter by Mr Rotheram D.D. [Caleb Rotheram, D.D. (1694–1752), minister at Market Place Chapel, Kendal] we subscrib'd our Guineas a piece each. Lord, May this and all other labor and expense for my improvement and advantage turn to a very good Account.[20]

This listener at Rotheram's lectures was a young Lancashire doctor, Richard Kaye (1716–1751), whose piety as recorded in his diary came to embrace scientific instruction as a singular means by which "may I daily grow in Wisdom and Knowledge both in Temporals and Spirituals."[21] His almost daily entries attest to the abundance of lectures already available in the shire by the late 1730s and to the theoretical as well as practical nature of these subscription courses in mechanics, optics, hydrostatics, geography, electricity, and pneumatics.

Fortunately, a manuscript copy of one set of lectures transcribed by a listener, and almost certainly heard by Kaye at the Angel Inn in Manchester, has been preserved. These "Observations and Memorandums of the Philosophical Experiments in a Course of Lectures; begun August 15,

1743 . . . by Mr John Rotheram, Jr of Kendall" are notes taken from memory by someone present at lectures given by Caleb Rotheram's son, John, and they are extremely useful for illustrating both what was actually said, as opposed to what was printed, and better still, what could be absorbed by the careful listener. Physics, theology, and Newtonian science were effortlessly combined with mechanical devices and experiments to illustrate a wide range of natural phenomena. At every turn it was emphasized "how the all Wise Ruler and Governour of the World has given particular rules and laws to all bodys of every sort and kind whatsoever,"[22] and the lecturer also made frequent reference to Newton's published works, to recognition of ideas or experiments given by the Royal Society, and to Newtonian explications by Desaguliers and Whiston. The person recording these lectures is doing so from memory (f. 45v) and whenever possible he (or just conceivably she) eschews mathematical illustrations, "as mathematical experiments are strange to me."[23] The lecture on motion or gravity quickly moves to a discussion of weight and velocity, explaining that the "very principle and foundation stone on which depends all the Laws of Mechanicks" is the relationship between weight and velocity "where a weight of 6 pounds is to be balanced by another of 3 it will require twice the velocity as twice three is six to bring it to an equilibrio."[24] The rest of the lecture concerns beams and the brachia of a pendulum; the audience is even treated to an explanation of how goldsmiths and shopkeepers might fiddle their scales to deceive their customers. Pulleys and inclined planes are also examined, with the understanding that "compound machines are the same in effect as the simple machines with this difference only, that simple machines are only smaller in their powers and in their weights, than the compound machines and therefore less force is required. . . ." The measuring of the force of projectiles for "bombarding and cannonading" is explained, with the method currently in use among military engineers criticized as "not mathematically true." A pyrometer for measuring the heat needed to expand metals is demonstrated and an entire lecture devoted to "how fluids gravitate upon one another, and from some other experiments to show probable causes for the arising of some phenomena such as the ebbing and flowing wells at [?] in Yorkshire and at . . . in Derbyshire."[25] A generation later, engineers in Derbyshire were to attempt to harness water power to windmills and install steam engines where cheap coal was available. Is it not possible that they and the entrepreneurs who paid them understood the risks and rewards involved by virtue of the scientific knowledge first transmitted in lectures such as these?

By the second half of the eighteenth century, however, this new scientific culture had permeated so deeply into the lives of the nominally

Anglican and genteel elite that it would be quite mistaken to associate it primarily and exclusively with the Dissenters and their academies. This is not to deny that all existing evidence seems to show the Dissenters to have been inordinately active, in relation to their actual numbers, in the enterprise of disseminating science to the commercial and the industrious. Richard Kaye's knowledge of the new science was undoubtedly superior to that of a contemporary Cambridge or Oxford graduate, institutions from which Kaye, who was a Dissenter, was excluded by virtue of his religion. Yet even in the traditional universities some evidence can be found from early in the century of scientific lecturing intended for industrial application. In 1716 Thomas Whiteside, the keeper of the Ashmolean Museum, gave a course of lectures described as excellent by contemporaries in Oxford, and the existence of a copy of these lectures in Cambridge implies that they may have been given there as well. "A Course of Philosophical Lectures" deals almost entirely with mechanics, specifically with the assertion that

> there is a universal law to which all the forces of mechanical powers may be reduc'd (viz) The power and ye Burden are reciprocally proportional to ye velocities. This is evident in all kinds of leavers. Now this Law is applicable to all ye other mechanical powers since they are reducable to the leaver. The whole effect then of mechanical engines consists in diminishing the velocity of the weight to be raised, so that its momentum be no more than the momentum of the power that raises it. . . .

Whiteside concentrated on levers, pulleys, inclined planes, pendulums, and screws, but it should be added that his lectures, at least in Oxford, required a subscription of one and a half guineas and may have been intended for a wider audience than simply undergraduates.[26] Other scientific lectures given at Cambridge on Newtonian science appear to have been more overtly theoretical but no less clear or polished.[27] Yet at mid-century Oxford offered little hospitality to Dr. Nathan Alcock (1707–1779) who had gone to Leyden to learn his Newtonian mechanics from s'Gravesande. Returning to Oxford where in his opinion "little or nothing" was done for the scientific education of the students, he managed to secure a lecturing position "against all opposition."[28] But the deficiencies of the universities could be compensated for by attendance at public lectures, membership in the Royal Society or one of the provincial philosophical societies, or simply by reading one of the many new scientific books then pouring from the presses.[29]

By the last quarter of the century, a new ideal of the English gentleman had been proposed and ratified by polite society, and foreign writers grasped it as a standard to which their audience, envious of English prosperity, should now aspire. As the Dutch became increasingly alarmed by the evidence of their own economic decline, they looked obsessively to the English, searching for what it was they were doing "right" in much the same way the English had done a century earlier when they pondered the prosperity of their Dutch rivals. The epistolary novel of the Dutch writer, Marie de Gertruida de Cambon, created for her readers (both in Dutch and in popular English translations of the 1790s) the fictional ideal of the contemporary English gentleman, one Sir Charles Grandison, whose favorite toy as a child was a microscope with which he studied the insects that crawled about his feet. His tutor, a Dr. Bartlett, the veritable English Pangloss, wished to make him wise, "to shew kindness to the insects . . . to let my love mount up from them to the beings, who, while they enjoy the blessings of heaven, can recognize the hand which bestows them."[30] Grandison combines science with sentiment and benevolence; he is a true aristocrat of his age, one worthy of emulation for his sense of order, industry, and fair play.

As the popular English translation of this novel proclaimed, Grandison's lessons from Dr. Bartlett rendered him socially tolerant: "I recollected I have often seen labouring men very compassionate. God takes care of the meanest insect."[31] It is altogether possible that a real-life Sir Charles would have been eagerly welcomed as a Fellow of the Royal Society or as a member of one of the provincial philosophical societies, to which we shall now turn.

The itinerant lecturers were the purveyors of scientific culture, but they neither initiated it nor sustained it. For a continuous history of the diffusion of scientific enterprise and scientific learning to the genteel and the mercantile we must look to the philosophical and literary societies of the period, from the Royal Society of London to the Spalding Society, the Northamptonshire Philosophical Society, and later in the century the Lunar Society and the Derby Philosophical Society, among others.[32] No historian writing in English has, to my knowledge, attempted to understand the role of these eighteenth-century private societies in fostering a new enlightened culture. Like its continental counterpart, the English Enlightenment flourished in the milieu created by secular fraternizing for the purpose of personal improvement and social intercourse. This culture was public and secular in that it was neither family oriented nor in attendance at the feet of pulpit preachers. Yet it was private in that its elite membership was restricted by income and dues, education and occupation, and the meetings were always held behind closed doors, although not necessarily in secret, with the exception of the Freemasons.

Preeminent among the European historians who have attempted to explain the significance of the eighteenth-century philosophical societies of the French Enlightenment is Augustin Cochin (d. 1916), a French Catholic whose writings, published posthumously in the 1920s, are just beginning to receive the attention they deserve.[33] He saw the philosophical society on the Continent as the outgrowth of a new political order, originally English and based upon parliamentary and constitutional systems that required constant communication within the political nation. It seems altogether appropriate that we apply Cochin's insights to the original culture, out of which came the objects of his historical studies. Surely it is simply a confirmation and extension of Cochin's insight to note that the first English philosophical society in the provinces began among a group of gentlemen in Spalding who gathered each week to read the *Tatler* as it arrived off the London coach. A similar society was also started in Edinburgh, also late in Anne's reign, as the outgrowth of a group formed to read the *Spectator*.[34] The printed word was essential to the new scientific culture, and it was the ferment of party politics that gave unprecedented circulation and importance to the press. Cochin further argued that the continental societies came into existence to meet the social needs of new men who defined themselves as individuals, divorced, at least psychologically, from the old corporate structures of kinship, guild, or religious confraternity. For such men, a minority in any European society of the eighteenth century, the philosophical society composed of individuals dedicated to the world of ideas provided identity and conviviality, as well as ideology.

Being a student of the French Revolution and a conservative, Cochin lavished attention on the Masonic lodges, not to assert their conspiratorial nature, which he denied, but to understand their meaning in the lives of their brothers. As in the continental Enlightenment, the English Masonic lodges are but another type of philosophical society, although undoubtedly less controversial in their country of origin than they were to prove on the Continent. Yet the English lodges, frequented in noticeable numbers by men from the Royal Society or the provincial philosophical societies, help us to understand one aspect of the larger phenomenon of philosophical socializing intended for self-improvement. Only in the Masonic lodges did ritual and mystery reinforce fantasies about the perfectability not only of self but of society, and those fantasies, if overindulged, could lead to a profound discontent with the corruption and inertia of the existing political order. The lodge provided a secret temple wherein the God of Newtonian science, the Grand Architect, could be worshipped by his most enthusiastic and increasingly more knowledgeable followers. Predictably, lodges on both sides of the Channel reinforced the work of the scientific lecturers and societies, with the Dutch lodges even distributing translations of the Boyle lectures.[35]

Cochin did not emphasize the importance of surplus wealth and its public display in permitting these philosophical societies to flourish,[36] but that element must be reckoned with when we try to understand why certain cities or towns, and not others, might sustain such gatherings. In England, among those who possessed excess wealth or, just as important, those who aspired to do so, the perception that science would contribute to their aspirations was arrived at quite early in the eighteenth century. As the century wore on, the proportion of time in those societies devoted to science increased, at the expense of history or literature; utility intended for profit must have become increasingly paramount.

As the most prestigious English philosophical society, the Royal Society of London offered extremely prosperous gentlemen, not unlike Sir Charles, an intimacy with science unrivalled by any other eighteenth-century forum. All the early provincial philosophical societies recognized that fact and sought copies of its minutes, even before publication, so as to be abreast of the latest scientific advances. But despite the enthusiasm of contemporaries, the Royal Society's dalliance with "amateurs," its insistence upon science as useful science, and its gentlemanly membership have cost it dearly with historians of eighteenth-century "pure science." They have simply refused to write its history, lamented its decline, and hinted at its corruption.[37] Although it is not possible here to write that history, some passing reference must be made to the sources out of which it could be constructed.

Throughout most of the century candidates for membership in the Royal Society had to be proposed well in advance by three or more members, who wrote and publicly displayed at meetings "certificates" stating the reasons why a man should be voted in by the Fellows, each of whom possessed one vote. After 1730 the affirmative vote of two-thirds of the Fellows present at a meeting, rather than a vote in the society's Council, was required for admittance. It seems reasonable, when we consider those extant manuscript certificates for the period 1731 to 1766,[38] for example, to suppose that they were intended to impress the membership, to reflect the society's best conception of itself and its science in such a way as to court a Fellow's affirmative vote for a candidate. Negative votes were occasionally given, however, and it is also worth speculating why some men and not others were admitted.

The society's rhetorical formulations about itself in the vast majority of cases emphasized the ideal of electing "a gentleman well skill'd in all parts of the mathematicks, natural and experimental philosophy, and most branches of curious and useful learning." But one category was no more important than another. A gentleman from the Navy Office could be skilled in mathematics and have written a treatise on gunnery.[39] Alternatively, one could either possess useful learning or simply be "useful," for example, by defending or explicating one of Newton's works,[40] especially for a foreign audience, or by "being a great promoter of Natural Philosophy," or by supplying the society with foreign contacts, as in the case of Myrheer Hop, the Dutch ambassador.[41] It was sufficient for a squire to be "well-versed in natural knowledge" or to be a "great lover of natural knowledge" without possessing any particularly noteworthy scientific achievement.[42]

Philosophical lecturing on the circuit was never held against a man, as Benjamin Martin's rejection might have implied. Martin Clare, who was recommended by his Masonic brothers Desaguliers and Ephraim Chambers, was described, obviously with approval, as "a good mathematician well skilled both in natural and experimental philosophy, and a great promoter of the same. . . ."[43] Being a mechanic as well as a merchant was also no shame, as Jonathan Fawconer, a lapidary in London, was described as having "a knowledge of precious stones [while being] well-versed in most branches of mathematicks, and more particularly in mechanicks, having invented an engine of great service to him in his profession."[44] In 1735 the society honored a man with election who presented before it "curious experiments relating to the damp of coal mines";[45] another was admitted because as a sea captain he had made many geographical and navigational enquiries on the Society's behalf.[46] His admittance stands in contrast to the rejection of a doctor of physics and a surgeon, the latter being recommended by Martin Folkes, Sir Hans Sloane, and Jean Desaguliers.[47]

Generally speaking, men with such prominent Fellows as their sponsors did not suffer rejection, and one task facing the historian of this period would be to try to determine why certain men were turned away when their reputation, occupation, and sponsorship were apparently acceptable. The rejection of Diderot in 1752 should not, however, be surprising. His reputation as a philosophical radical and a materialist would have doomed him. What is fascinating, however, is to see one of the highest turnout of Fellows for any meeting in the century where a membership vote was to be taken. Diderot was rejected by 50 to 18.[48] Obviously there were other criteria for membership beyond those stated in the certificates, and these would eventually lead to dissension within the society.

In the 1780s a rift opened publicly between the president, Sir Joseph Banks, and Fellows who felt that Banks was using his personal influence excessively, "making himself the sole master of the admissions, in other words, the *Monarch* of the Society."[49] Banks was not trying to restrict membership to the "pure scientists"; he would not have understood the nature of the society or science in those terms. Rather, he was trying to keep out the less socially prominent and those of republican leanings, some of whom were friends of Dr. Priestley. Neither were his opponents trying to admit the "pure scientists"; they too would not have accepted the distinction. Instead they argued that "for whatever we ought to be, (which is another question,) we are not an Academy of Sciences, i.e. a receptacle for the Great in Science, but a Society of Gentlemen, of all ranks and professions, all opinions, and, we must add, all kinds of learning (or no-learning) paying 52s. a year for the encouragement of literature."[50] The reformers said what the certificates for admission confirm to have been the Royal Society's conception of itself and the variety of its membership.

And what the society honored as good science is revealed through the annual Copley awards, which in 1738 went to a watchmaker "for his useful engine contrived for the driving of piles of the new bridge"; and in 1739 to Stephen Hales "for discovery of dissolents of the stone, and preservation of Flesh in long sea voyages."[51] The pattern of those awards for the rest of the century does not deviate significantly from that criterion of usefulness broadly conceived. In 1759 when the President of the Royal Society, Lord Macclesfield (1697–1764), awarded the Copley medal to the famous engineer, John Smeaton, to whom I shall return, he noted that while the medal should be for papers presented to the society "yet much honor" belonged to Smeaton for his extraordinary achievement in constructing the Eddystone lighthouse. Macclesfield in turn praised Smeaton for his papers submitted to the *Philosophical Transactions* on water wheels and windmill sails, for displaying in them "so clear and scientific method" to produce "a chain of close reasoning, that depends upon many computations and numeral proportions arising from the results of a considerable number of very accurate experiments."[52] In short, Macclesfield and the committee that awarded the Copley medal thought that Smeaton was a very fine scientist. As we shall see from his private letters, Smeaton also thought this of himself and so, too, did his friends. It is only historians who have somehow failed to record and understand these contemporary perceptions of what constitutes true science. The definition of science employed by the Royal Society, although laying greater emphasis on the mathematical and experimental than was common in the other philosophical societies of the period, was held in admiration by those societies and never seen as demanding an enterprise that was either intimidating or foreign to their aspirations.

But organizing natural philosophical learning in the provinces, given London's preponderance and the difficulties in transportation and communication, was seen as a delicate and fragile business. The success rate for the early part of the century was not high, but even that fact has not, until recently, prompted scholars to attempt a history or prosopography of any one or any group of the survivors. The Cambridge doctoral dissertation of R. J. Evans, a geographer interested in the spatial boundaries within which ideas are transmitted, is a valuable recent attempt to write the history of the first English provincial society of a philosophical sort. My brief discussion here of the Spalding Gentlemen's Society, which from as early as 1712 introduced gentlemen to natural philosophical, literary, and historical subjects in more or less equal proportions, is largely indebted to his work.[53]

From 1712 to 1755, 374 men joined the Spalding society, located in a town of some 500 families, although only about twenty or so members in every decade formed its core. Its organizer and guiding light, Maurice Johnson, belonged to the top stratum of genteel society, was a J. P. in the shire, an active Fellow in the Royal Society, and a devotee of London club and pub life. He meant to export that easy socializing to the county, to the gentlemen of quality but also to clergymen, who were to form nearly a fourth of the society's membership, and to doctors, lawyers, surveyors, even tradesmen, the last of whom made up $3\frac{1}{2}$ percent of its total.[54] The Spalding Gentlemen's Society's manuscript minute books, which I have surveyed, show a remarkable interest in Newtonian science as explicated by s'Gravesande and Desaguliers—provided the explanations were not too mathematical—and in natural artifacts and natural history in general, as well as in antiquities.[55] At the inner circle of the society's leadership were that ubiquitous medical man, later turned clergyman and antiquarian with an interest in the mystical, Dr. William Stukeley (1687–1765), and John Grundy (1696–1748), one of the most important engineers in the period between Newcomen and Smeaton.[56] Both, incidentally, were Freemasons; indeed, Grundy was master of the lodge at Spalding, one dedicated to the improvement of each brother "through natural philosophy" among other disciplines, and Johnson may also have been a lodge brother.[57]

The Spalding Society is important not simply because its very existence demonstrates the widespread interest in the new science among the genteel, the educated, and the mercantile of the provinces, but also because its understanding of science, as documented in its archives and extant library catalogues, was mechanical and experimental as well as "useful." In this society the itinerant lecturers made their mark on men interested in the draining of the local fens, in the improvement of agricultural technique, in surveying for enclosure and canal building, in using pumps, pulleys, levers, and the new steam engines, wherever practical, and in finding labor-saving devices of a mechanical sort. But did this science of the lecturers, to be found in Spalding as well as in London, ever actually inspire technological innovation of the kind essential to the early stages of industrialization?

The water engineer, John Grundy, for instance, has always been described as self-taught; his important innovations as a surveyor of the fens and instigator of various successful canal routes through Lincoln, Chester, and Lancaster have never been connected in the historical literature with his interest in natural philosophical learning. He is known to have taught mathematics and may even have been an itinerant lecturer early in his career; perhaps most important, he educated his son of the same name to such a degree of excellence that he became an important engineer of the next generation. But the manuscript minutes of the Spalding Society reveal Grundy's interest in the industrial and agricultural application of the new science:

> Mr Grundy communicated his proposals for draining lands that lie near the sea, showing the necessity of mathematical and philosophical knowledge thereto required, approved by J.T. Desaguliers, D.D., F.R.S.[58]

Desaguliers, we know, had actively campaigned for the industrial application of science in England and the Low Countries,[59] but Grundy had gained more from him than simply an interest in machines; he had learned the principles of Newtonian science as an experimental and mechanical system. When Grundy's machines pumped efficiently they did so in part because their inventor obtained through the Spalding Society a theoretical and correct understanding of the natural order that enabled him to channel nature into the service of human productivity.

Other philosophical societies from this early period also sprang up in Stamford, Northampton, Peterborough (1730), and Edinburgh. But the Peterborough society, started by a clergyman from the Spalding Society, Timothy Neve, refused to admit tradesmen, "which makes some who set themselves up for gentlemen the more desirous of becoming members, as piqueing themselves upon their quality or profession."[60] Although modeled on Spalding, the Peterborough society barely survived ten years. The one at Stamford did not do much better, despite the occasional appearance of an original Newtonian, William Whiston, at its meetings.[61] Evans believes that these other societies lacked dynamic leadership, and this is undoubtedly a critical factor, since both Northampton and Spalding succeeded for a time and both possessed nationally connected organizers of the stature of Johnson, or in the case of Northampton, of Thomas Yeoman, the engineer, and Philip Doddridge, the Dissenting minister. Yeoman was an itinerant lecturer and a manager of a cotton mill in Northampton who turned his skill to surveying for turnpikes and enclosures as well as to water engineering. Indeed, in 1743 he erected the machinery in the world's first water-powered cotton mill.[62] In these and other projects he had the encouragement of Doddridge, who extracted from the Newtonian legacy both its mechanical and ethical applications.[63]

More than enthusiasm for Newtonian science was required to create and sustain these societies. All evidence suggests that their membership was drawn entirely from the ranks of voting freeholders—those newly empowered individuals who so fascinated Cochin—and where we can find political affiliations for the leadership of these societies, whether in London or Northampton, it is court and Whig. As J. H. Thornton has discovered, the Northampton society was filled with supporters of the Whig Hanbury, whose 1748 election was one of the most hotly contested of the period. The Whig leadership of the Royal Society in this period is, of course, well known. The societies eschewed politics, yet they were dependent upon political life for the social network that sustained them. Other social factors, however, were equally important in giving dynamism to these gatherings. As the quick demise of the Peterborough Society would suggest, exclusivity, if carried too far, brought with it boredom. Those societies that permitted the mixing of the genteel and educated with the mercantile and prosperous seem to have kept both their attendance and intellectual content reasonably high.

What, however, was a man, and certainly a woman, to do if he or she did not have access to, or could not be admitted to, one of these societies? For both there were, of course, the travelling lecturers who specifically appealed to ladies to attend their courses, occasionally even doing a special course solely for them. Lecturers preferred daylight for their demonstrations and therefore needed leisured customers to pay the fees as well as to attend these afternoon sessions. After all, a course in science at two guineas would be no more than a gentleman would pay for his children to attend lessons with a dancing master. Aside from these public lectures a woman could also read about science, and by midcentury the finest scientific journal for a lay audience was the *Ladies' Diary*. It set complex mathematical puzzles for its female readership, and copies of solutions offered by members of the Spalding Society turn up in its archives.[64].

One such lone reader and student of the new science, who became a close friend and admirer of the younger John Grundy, was the Yorkshire engineer John Smeaton, F.R.S. (1724–1792). With him we move from the general cultural background, the intellectual origins of the Industrial Revolution, into the very center of that economic and social upheaval. Recognizing as we do now that water power was more important in the first decades of industrialization than steam, Smeaton must be seen as singularly important for his perfecting of the atmospheric engine, indeed as the most important industrial engineer in the years between Newcomen and Watt.[65] Like the older Grundy he has also been described in the literature about early industrial technology as not only "self-taught" but also as being without "any system of conceptual or theoretical knowledge."[66] The evidence proves otherwise.

Like so many other minor, or major, philosophes, Smeaton's earliest intellectual interests began with religion, as his unpublished letters to Benjamin Wilson testify. Wilson, who was an early electrical experimenter and theorist, acted for a time as Smeaton's mentor in matters religious and scientific. Both, it would seem, sought a rational Christianity, and in the context of either eighteenth-century Anglicanism or Dissent that meant discarding the doctrine of the Trinity. Smeaton believed that "this is doing service to religion. . . . Jesus Christ [is] the greatest of all created beings and mediator between God and man. . . . I think it is observable there is no direct mention of a Trinity . . . in the Scripture."[67] Throughout his life Smeaton paid little attention to formal religiosity, maintained his belief in divine providence, and regarded the Catholicism he witnessed on the Continent as "calculated for striking the minds of the vulgar."[68] Indeed, other people's prejudices and superstitions fascinated him,[69] and he and his engineer friends prided themselves on their willingness to follow wherever the new science led, even in the dangerous business of allowing their children to be inoculated against smallpox.[70] As a young man Smeaton sought to become a "philosopher," to use his word, and he cultivated a sophisticated understanding of Newtonian science. He offered Wilson both theoretical and experimental criticism for his ideas on electricity, but he also believed that learning must serve society:

> If I were so far to abstract my self from the world as to consider myself without either friends or enemies or any person to take any measure of notice of me . . . I should quickly lay aside toyling and noyling in ye sciences, and industry of all kinds any farther than so much food as to provide me from starving. . . .[71]

Smeaton, like so many enlightened men, believed that the love of society was implanted in Everyman and that knowledge must serve human needs and bear reference "to the opinion of [our] fellow creatures." Yet amid this idealism reality dawned harshly on this would-be philosopher. His parents objected to his betrothal to an impecunious woman, and around the same time Smeaton realized that even a coveted membership in the Royal Society cost a great deal of money. Its admittance fee of 22 guineas led Smeaton to complain bitterly that "I think only rich philosophers can afford to pay: so that I suppose ye popish proverb will fit them 'no penny no pater noster.'"[72] Although "we ought all of us to be philosophers," this young scientist who wanted to become a professor of physics became instead an engineer.[73] His earliest efforts at building mechanical devices, for example, an air pump with which to create a better vacuum, had been prompted by their usefulness in electrical experimentation.[74] Smeaton, however, was "as poor as a church mouse,"[75] and he was forced to abandon the purely theoretical and experimental. He was to struggle for many years to build canals, bridges, and machines for industrial application. Throughout his mature years he sought to attain solvency and respectability, as would any rising professional in a world obviously dominated by the well-born and the genteel. "My profession is as perfectly personal as that of a Physician or councillor at Law," he declared to a local schoolmaster seeking to place a pupil, while to a customer Smeaton tersely explained, "The construction of Mills, as to their Power, is not with me a Matter of Opinion it is a Matter of Calculation. . . ."[76]

Throughout his life Smeaton's friends frequently addressed him as "my great philosopher,"[77] but how did he perceive himself? Not only did Smeaton invent the profession of the civil engineer—indeed, he and the younger Grundy corresponded with one another as early as 1764 as members "of a profession"[78]—he also possessed a finely honed definition of his place in the scientific world, one with overtones of the supposed split between technicians and "pure scientists." Only in his own mind, Smeaton is the theorist, the "pure" scientist. In a long letter to a friend prompted by the failure of the London projectors to compensate promptly and adequately the architects and surveyors who designed Blackfriar's Bridge, Smeaton wrote:

> there are few masons but have time enough to draw lines by a ruler and make circles with a pair of compasses, while their journeymen are bringing in a considerable profit, both upon their own labour and the materials they are working up . . . The proper business of a master, then, is to get in regular payments, to keep his accounts . . . but to take up the time of an artist whose sole profession is design who must apply his own head and hands to every thing he

undertakes; whose resources in time of sickness . . . are totally stopt; I say to possess ourselves of this man's time without an equivalent is comparatively speaking, not only to take away the lines and paper but the timber stone and mortar for nothing; or more strictly speaking the profits arising from the manufacturing thereof; which is the basis of trade and commerce.

Although not directly involved in designing the bridge, Smeaton identifies with the "artists" whose time has been effectively stolen. Writing in 1764, he then draws out the political meaning of this insult to professional dignity and the right to profit from one's labor:

> I have heard a mighty bustle of late about the securitys of our libertys and *properties;* pray sir is not the *time* and *skill* of any artist employed in design, his property, his estate, the good and manufacturers of his shop; the means by which himself and family are maintained [,is] not any man therefore that forces or cheats him out of this an Invader of his property? If any man by fraudulent pretences gets possession of another's goods the British Law has provided a remedy; but are the men whose superior ingenuity is capable of furnishing employment for thousands, the only men whose property is left defenceless; better to be born a Blockhead of any denomination than be plagued with ingenuity on such terms. . . .[79]

Smeaton the scientist, who also had to be an entrepreneur if he was to survive, could identify—if only momentarily—with the "country" and Wilkesite agitation when the dignity of his profession was maligned and his right to profit thwarted by his far richer employers. Generally, however, Smeaton directed his entrepreneuring energies into the discovery of labor-saving mechanical devices that could replace human labor. He, even more than his scientific predecessors like Desaguliers, perceived that replacing human power with mechanical power increased profits.[80] So long as he could keep his dignity, exercise his talents, and profit, Smeaton never railed publicly against the existing order. He was too busy being one of the most successful entrepreneurs and scientists of his generation.

The Whig and Erastian order that enabled men like Smeaton, Grundy, Desaguliers, and all their philosophical associates to pursue science for its profitable application to industry rendered them at most times politically complacent. In general the historian searches their meeting books or private letters in vain for a hint of political disaffection from the ruling oligarchy, for an attack on "corruption" or the evils of placemen or paper credit.[81]

These men are Court Whigs by default. When alienation does appear within the mainstream of the scientific community, it comes from men of merit rather than birth, like Smeaton, who think that their skill and talent have not been sufficiently appreciated and rewarded.

But suppose that this scientific culture of the philosophical societies and engineers, with its extraordinary sense of what could be achieved through study and experimentation, were to turn its energies in a socially reforming direction, and suppose that the pursuit of profit through mechanical ingenuity were put in the service of opposition to existing authority for the purpose of republican, even democratic, reform. No general portrait of English scientific culture in the eighteenth century would be complete without discussing its radical underside. Public education through lectures and books and philosophical societies intended to make the genteel practical and the meritorious genteel—with all the optimism that those activities imply—could and did have levelling tendencies, even if most of their earliest propagators self-consciously sought to reinforce the existing social hierarchy. The English republic of letters could also be republican, even, or perhaps more especially, when it was busy being entrepreneurial and industrial.

Of the many philosophical societies that sprang up in the later decades of the century, the one at Derby deserves our special attention for what it can tell us about the potentiality and perimeters of enlightened scientific culture. In that society established by Erasmus Darwin in 1784 for the pursuit of "gentlemanlike facts," we find the same useful and mechanical science practiced in Spalding, London, or Birmingham, as well as the same desire for industrial application. Now, however, there are industrialists present in goodly numbers. Suddenly the whole burden of scientific culture has also been shifted in a politically and socially radical direction by the addition of two ideological ingredients: philosophical materialism and republicanism. Since the late seventeenth century both could be grafted quite easily onto the new science—however hard the Newtonians had worked to prevent the hybrid—and now in the Derwent Valley, at the very center of the Industrial Revolution, we find pioneering industrialists like William Strutt (d. 1830), Darwin's closest friend and founder-member of their philosophical society, distributing copies of Thomas Paine's *Rights of Man* to his factory workers. Indeed, Derby's radical corresponding society of 1791[82] was a direct outgrowth of its philosophical society, and revolutionary ardor, first of the American and then of the French variety, ran through Darwin's society and among some of its members, even surviving the disillusionment brought on by the Terror.[83]

In the Derby Philosophical Society many strands found in enlightened scientific culture are once again present, only now rewoven into an entirely different tapestry. As Cochin saw, the philosophical society had become a testing ground for democratic ideas and even a center for the expression of revolutionary ideals. There still remains the omnipresent emphasis on mechanisms and utility, in this case revealed in the extant catalogue of the society's carefully chosen scientific library, but this improving science is now also channelled into creating mechanisms for domestic comfort and home improvement, as well as into town planning and the construction of more efficient factories. The Dissenters and Unitarians are also present in exceptionally large numbers, although the irreligious like Darwin seem particularly comfortable among the inner coterie of the society's members. They are devoted to books and print culture in general, collecting as many of the proceedings of scientific societies from anywhere in the world as they can lay their hands on.[84] And finally there are the medical men, the engineers, and industrialists, some of whom, like Strutt, are so idealistic and confident about the future being prepared by science and industry that they are ready to promote republican ideas among their workers.

Erasmus Darwin, more a philosopher than an organizer, nevertheless deserves to be seen as the guiding force in Derby's philosophical society. He was a full-blown pantheist and materialist devoted to drawing from the new scientific culture of his age all of its apparently infinite possibilities. And therein lies the root of his political radicalism. His passion for scientific learning, born out of his conviction that Nature is All, gave him an optimism about human nature and the future that demanded the transformation of existing social and political institutions. His faith in material progress wedded to an egalitarian ideal, although undoubtedly born of a more radically materialist metaphysic, is remarkably similar to that of his near-contemporary, Thomas Jefferson, who could, however, act out his ideals in a much more congenial political context.[85] Indeed, Darwin was on close personal terms with Dr. William Small (b. 1734), who had taught natural philosophy and mathematics to Jefferson at the College of William and Mary in colonial Virginia, before returning to Birmingham in 1765, where he, Matthew Boulton, the industrialist, James Watt, of steam engine fame, and Darwin formed their own collegium.[86]

In his opening address to the Derby Philosophical Society Darwin waxed eloquent about the material and intellectual benefits promised and already delivered by science as transmitted by the printed word, which has "scattered among the great mass of mankind the happy contagion of science and of truth."[87] In a letter to a friend he compared the new society to Freemasonry, as simply another form of congenial fraternizing, but Darwin does not appear to have been drawn to that particular form of secretive philosophical socializing. Nor were other members of the Derby society—only one, a Dr. Pigot, was active in the local lodge.[88] But Darwin and his society were well-acquainted with other aspects of the radical tradition; they were republicans of a kind. Historians such as J. G. A. Pocock have emphasized the ambivalence within classical republican thought around the issues of capital and credit. While that ambivalence is undoubtedly present in the writings of so many eighteenth-century English republicans, it is absent from the thought, and most especially, from the actions, of Darwin and his friends. Science could work profound transformations within the radical tradition. Inspired by a powerful faith born of science, and reinforced by the wonders of industrial productivity, these Derbyshire republicans put their trust in capital harnessed to machinery, indeed in mechanisms of every sort.

But faith was not enough to save institutions, whether traditional or radical, from experiencing a difficult time in the decades after 1790. Not only did the Masonic lodges in Derby decline, so too did the Anglican churches in the shire.[89] The new population drawn to the district in search of factory work had little use for either institution. They also seem to have had little faith in Strutt—his books or his projects—and his schemes for enclosing the town green, enacted through a parliamentary bill of 1792, were violently attacked by ordinary folk as another form of enclosure.[90] In that decade the Philosophical Society also came in for severe criticism: the clergy attacked it and the Dissenters for their supposed Jacobinism, and all the reforming societies, in particular the corresponding society, were attacked as followers of Thomas More, Harrington, Milton, Sydney, and Locke.[91]

In the face of local opposition to their politics, the members of the Derby Society simply turned their attention away from political reform and busied themselves in improving their town, its factories, canals, and even its homes. In the 1790s these Derby republicans concentrated their reforming instincts on canal building, on the protection of their industrial secrets from foreign spying and competition from the Irish, on public works such as town lighting, on domestic improvements such as central heating and the water closet,[92] and on projects to build the ideal factory with a central observation point from which all workshops and workers could be overseen. No amount of popular or clerical opposition could deter Strutt and his philosophical allies from the pursuit of material progress and profit based upon science. In the end that revolution took precedence over all others. Although personal letters, particularly from the female members of the Strutt and Darwin families, bear witness to the survival of republicanism, utopianism, and irreligion within the family,[93] these receded increasingly into the realm of the private and the domestic.

The pursuit of scientific learning and its industrial application also continued uninterrupted at the meetings of the Derby Philosophical Society; nothing could shake its faith in the improvements made possible by science, even if these now had to be confined entirely to the material order. By 1820 the mechanisms championed by the society and its members had indeed conspired with capital and surplus labor to transform Derbyshire in ways that the mechanists of earlier generations could never have imagined. What had begun in the London coffeehouses and taverns during the reign of Anne, and then been spread by itinerant lecturers and philosophical societies, had finally produced a new kind of entrepreneurial and philosophical gentleman. He championed a particular type of science, which had to be applied mechanically in order to be understood, and which had within its power the capacity to transform both nature and society.

NOTES

1. J. G. A. Pocock, "Post-Puritan England and the Problems of the Enlightenment" in Perez Zagorin, ed., *Culture and Politics. From Puritanism to the Enlightenment* (Berkeley and Los Angeles, 1980), esp. pp. 106–8. The tract from which my opening quotation is taken has been variously attributed to Arbuthnot, Martin Strong, and John Keill; hence my question mark. The BL copy attributes it to Arbuthnot in a note written in a contemporary hand.
2. Margaret 'Espinasse, "The Decline and Fall of Restoration Science" in Charles Webster, ed., *The Intellectual Revolution of the Seventeenth Century* (London, 1974), 347–68 (reprinted from *Past and Present*, no. 14, 1958).
3. For a succinct statement of the thesis see A. Rupert Hall, "Engineering and the Scientific Revolution," *Technology and Culture* 2 (1961): 334: "The great discoveries of mathematical physicists were not merely over the heads of practical engineers and craftsmen; they were useless to them."
4. A. E. Musson and Eric Robinson, *Science and Technology in the Industrial Revolution* (Manchester, 1969); cf. A. E. Musson, ed., *Science, Technology and Economic Growth in the Eighteenth Century* (London, 1972), in particular 14, citing Simon Kuznets (*Secular Movements on Production and Prices* [Boston, 1930]) for a theoretical background to this approach; and Neil McKendrick, "The Role of Science in the Industrial Revolution: A study of Josiah Wedgwood as a scientist and industrial chemist" in M. Teich and R. Young, eds., *Changing Perspectives in the History of Science* (London, 1973), 274–319, in particular 274–79, for an excellent introduction to the historiographical problems; and in the same vein, D. S. L. Cardwell, "Science, Technology and Industry" in G. S. Rousseau and Roy Porter, eds., *The Ferment of Knowledge* (Cambridge, 1980), 449–83, esp. with good intuition on Smeaton, 470; and finally Peter Mathias, "Who unbound Prometheus? Science and technical change, 1600–1800" in Peter Mathias, ed., *Science and Society 1600–1800* (Cambridge, 1972), 54–80, where

I think the problems posed do not bear up against the archival evidence presented by Musson, Robinson, and the rest. For a recent example of rearguard action supporting the "pure science" perspective see Michael Fores, "Francis Bacon and the Myth of Industrial Science" in *History of Technology* 7 (1982), 57–75.

5. Comparative studies of differing rates of industrialization fail almost entirely to speak about the mentality of the elites being compared. Yet there is growing discomfort with this failure and the way in which it has impoverished the entire question of why industrialization might occur in one area of Europe and not another; see Joel Mokyr, "Industrialization in Two Languages," *Economic History Review*, 2d ser., 34 (1981): 143–49.

6. See my *The Newtonians and the English Revolution, 1689–1770* (Ithaca, 1976); Larry Stewart, "The Structure of Scientific Orthodoxy: Newtonianism and the Social Support for Science, 1704–1728" (Ph.D. diss., Univ. of Toronto, 1978).

7. Benjamin Worster, *A Compendious and Methodical Account of the Principles of Natural Philosophy: As they are explain'd and illustrated in the Course of experiments; perform'd at the Academy in Little Tower-Street* (London, 1722), and Francis Hauksbee, *A Course of Mechanical, Optical, Hydrostatical, and Pneumatical Experiments. To be perform'd by Francis Hauksbee; and the Explanatory Lectures read by William Whiston* (London, n.d. [probably 1714]). The first lecture is on Newton's laws of motion; the second on "the ballance and stillyard . . . All the various Kinds of Levers . . . Pulleys"; and those from the third on, respectively, on the wheel, the wedge, the screw and "a compound engine. . . ."

8. See British Library, C.112.f.9, *A Collection of Medical Advertisements*, no. 181. I owe this reference to Peter Wallis; see his paper "Ephemera issued by the early lecturers in experimental science" (available from the author, University of Newcastle-upon-Tyne).

9. John Theophilus Desaguliers, *A Course of Mechanical and Experimental Philosophy. Whereby anyone, although unskill'd in Mathematical Sciences, may be able to understand all those Phaenomena of Nature . . .* (London, 1725). It is preserved in the archives of the Spalding Gentlemen's Society; my thanks to its curator, Mr. Norman Leveritt.

10. John Booth, *Course of Experimental Philosophy* (n.d.); a flyer from the archives of the Spalding Society on which are listed the names of members who subscribed; and Will. Griffis, *A Short Account of a Course of Mechanical and Experimental Philosophy and Astronomy* (n.d., but 15 August 1748 written in as the date the lectures were first announced to this society).

11. Benjamin Worster, *A Compendious and Methodical Account of the Principles of Natural Philosophy: As they are explain'd and illustrated in the Course of experiments, perform'd at the Academy in Little Tower Street* (London, 1722), preface and 230.

12. F. J. G. Robinson, "A Philosophic War: An Episode in Eighteenth-Century Scientific Lecturing in North East England," *Transactions of the Architectural and Archaeological Society of Durham and Northumberland* 2 (1970): 101.

13. See John R. Millburn, *Benjamin Martin, Author, Instrument-Maker, and Country*

Showman (Leyden, 1976), 40–41, 64. In general, see F. W. Gibbs, "Itinerant Lecturers in Natural Philosophy," *Ambix* 6 (1960): 111–17. See also John Horsley, *A Short and General Account of the Most Necessary and Fundamental Principles of Natural Philosophy* (Glasgow, 1743); and Benjamin Martin, *A New and Comprehensive System of Mathematical Institutions Agreeable to the Present State of the Newtonian Mathesis*, vol. 2 (London, 1764). Dutch translations of Martin's lectures were bound with those of Desaguliers. See B. Martin, *Filozoofische Onderwijzen; of Algemeene Schets der hedendaagsche Ondervindelyke Natuurkunde* (Amsterdam, 1737).

14. For copy of the *Constitutions* and a discussion of Desaguliers's role, see my *The Radical Enlightenment: Pantheists, Freemasons and Republicans* (London, 1981), appendix and 109–13, 122–27.
15. A Junior Grand Warden, *A Speech deliver'd to the Worshipful and Ancient Society of Free and Accepted Masons. At a Grand Lodge, Held at Merchant's Hall, in the City of New York, on St. John's Day, December 27, 1726* (York, [1726]). This tract is extremely rare and I am grateful to the assistant librarian Mr. Hamell of the Grand Lodge in London for drawing my attention to it. See in particular 2, 14–15.
16. W. K. Firminger, "The Lectures at the Old King's Arms Lodge," *Ars Quatuor Coronatorum* 45 (1935): 255–57.
17. Martin Clare, *The Motion of Fluids* . . . (London, 1735); dedicated to Thomas Thynne, Viscount Weymouth, Grandmaster of the Freemasons. According to the *Advertisement*, these were "some lectures, privately read to a set of gentlemen," with the mechanical drawings done by Isaac Ware, an architect. Desaguliers is thanked profusely. For the steam engine, see 67–70.
18. Martin Clare, *Youth's Introduction to Trade and Business*, 5th ed. (London, 1740), 97, 109–10.
19. John S. Allen, "Thomas Newcomen (1663/4–1729) and his Family," *Transactions of the Newcomen Society* 51 (1979–80): 19.
20. W. Brockland and F. Kenworthy, eds., *The Diary of Richard Kaye, 1716–51 of Baldingstone, near Bury. A Lancashire Doctor* (Manchester, 1968), 3d ser. (22 June 1743), 16, 63.
21. Ibid., 26; 24 Feb. 1738/9.
22. "Observations and Memorandums," ff. 1–2 and f. 8, Chetham's Library, Manchester. These are sometimes cited as being by John Rotheram, but the writer makes it clear that he is a listener; cf. Musson and Robinson, *Science and Technology*, 103n.
23. Ibid., ff. 20–21; f. 24, where a mathematical illustration of the moon's effect on the tides was given but the listener records "but whether or no my ignorance as to mathematicks may not be the reason that I don't form a just notion of this calculation I'll rather allow than Dispute." In f. 35 we are told that "I have in this as well as in all the observations I made on Mr. Rotherham's Lectures omitted inserting the mathematical experiments and only deduced such rules from them as were servicable to conducting me through the nature of others."
24. Ibid., ff. 12–14.

25. Ibid., f. 57.
26. Cambridge, University Library, MSS. Add. 6301, f. 6.
27. For notes taken on the lectures of Gervase Holmes (M.A. 1722) at Emmanuel College see U.L.C., MSS. Add. 5047.
28. N. Alcock, *Some Memoirs of the Life of Dr. Nathan Alcock, lately deceased* (London, 1780), 7–9.
29. See the excellent treatment of this literature in G. S. Rousseau, "Science books and their readers in the eighteenth century" in Isabel Rivers, ed., *Books and their Readers in Eighteenth-Century England* (Leicester, 1982), 197–255. This brings up the whole *genre* of subscription literature; see Peter Wallis, "British Philomaths—Mid-eighteenth Century and Earlier," *Centaurus* 17 (1973): 301–14; and F. J. G. Robinson and P. J. Wallis, "A Preliminary Guide to Book Subscription Lists: Part 1, pre-1801," in *History of Education Society Bulletin*, no. 9 (1972): 23–54.
30. Madame de Cambon, i.e., Maria de Gertruide de Cambon, *Young Grandison. A Series of Letters from Young Persons to their Friends*, 2 vols. (London, 1790; translated from the Dutch), 78.
31. Ibid., 32.
32. There is no general study of these societies. See, however, Roy Porter, "The Enlightenment in England," in R. Porter and M. Teich, eds., *The Enlightenment in National Context* (Cambridge, 1981), 1–18; R. E. Schofield, *The Lunar Society of Birmingham* (Oxford, 1963); Guy Kitteringham, "Science in Provincial Society: The Case of Liverpool in the Early Nineteenth Century," *Annals of Science* 39 (1982): 329–34; Roger L. Emerson, "The Philosophical Society of Edinburgh, 1737–47," *British Journal for the History of Science* 12 (1979): 154–91; J. H. Thornton, "The Northampton Philosophical Society, 1743" (Lecture given to the Northamptonshire Natural History Society; available from the author, to whom I am grateful for assistance); and by way of comparison: James Meenan and Desmond Clarke, eds., *The Royal Dublin Society*, 1731–1981 (Dublin, 1981); J. H. Buursma, *Nederlandse Geleerde Genootschappen opgericht in de 18ᵉ eeuw* (Discom, 1978). Studies that are somewhat related to this topic and should be consulted are F. W. Gibbs, "Robert Dossie (1717–1777) and the Society of Arts," *Annals of Science* 7 (1951): 149–72; David D. McElroy, *Scotland's Age of Improvement. A Survey of 18th Century Literary Clubs and Societies*, (Seattle, 1969); Kenneth Hudson, *Patriotism with Profit: British Agricultural Societies in the Eighteenth and Nineteenth Centuries* (London, 1972), esp. 18–23; R. S. Watson, *A History of the Literary and Philosophical Society of Newcastle-upon-Tyne* (1897), and D. G. C. Allan, *William Shipley, Founder of the Royal Society of Arts* (London, 1979), esp. 30–39.
33. For the introduction to Cochin, see François Furet, *Interpreting the French Revolution* (Cambridge, 1981), chap. 3; of Cochin's various writings, I have found *La Révolution et la libre pensée* (Paris, 1924), to be the most useful.
34. David D. McElroy, *Scotland's Age of Improvement*, 14–15.
35. For example, the Dutch Masonic manual, *De Vrye Metselaar* (Dordrecht, 1754), contains advertisements for Dutch translations of the Boyle lectures. For the

concerted campaign to spread liberal Protestantism in Holland see V. van den Berg, "Eighteenth century Dutch translations of the works of some British latitudinarian and enlightened theologians," *Nederlands archief voor kerkgeschiedenis*, n.s., 49 (1979): 178–207.

36. Peter Borsay, "The English urban renaissance: The development of provincial urban culture, c. 1680–1760," *Social History* 5 (1977): 593.

37. There is no modern account of the eighteenth-century society; see Charles R. Weld, *A History of the Royal Society*, 2 vols. (London, 1848); T. E. Allibone, *The Royal Society and Its Dining Clubs* (Oxford, 1976); H. Lyons, *The Royal Society, 1660–1940* (Cambridge, 1944); Charles Lyte, *Sir Joseph Banks, Eighteenth Century Explorer, Botanist and Entrepreneur* (London, 1980) (largely useless); H. Hartley, ed., *The Royal Society* (London, 1960). One approach to the society by a critic can be discovered in G. S. Rousseau, ed., *The Letters and Papers of Sir John Hill 1714–1775* (New York, 1982); cf. L. Trengove, "Chemistry at the Royal Society of London in the 18th Century," *Annals of Science* 19 (1963): 183–237.

38. Royal Society MS Certificates, vol. 1, 1731–50; vol. 2, 1751–66 (approximately 1,000 folios).

39. Royal Society MS Certificates, vol. 1, f. 21.

40. Ibid., ff. 50, 66.

41. Ibid., f. 62.

42. Ibid., f. 163.

43. Ibid., f. 85.

44. Ibid., f. 95.

45. Ibid., f. 118.

46. Ibid., f. 139.

47. Ibid., ff. 167, 248, a Robert James, Doctor of Physick, rejected. In general, surgeons did not fare well in the voting process.

48. Ibid., vol. 2, f. 467.

49. [P. H. Maty et al.], *An History of the Instances of Exclusion from the Royal Society* (London, 1784), 3.

50. Ibid., 10.

51. Royal Society MS. 702. I wish to thank A. Clark, librarian at the society, for his assistance.

52. Royal Society MS. L + P. III, f. 403.

53. Raymond James Evans, "The Diffusion of Science: The Geographical Transmission of Natural Philosophy in the English Provinces, 1660–1760," (Cambridge University Library, D. Phil., no. 12208, 1982). Cited with the kind permission of the author.

54. Ibid., 172–75.

55. The manuscript minutes are currently housed at the Spalding Gentlemen's Society, 9 Broad Street, Spalding. Maurice Johnson's MSS, Drawer 1, are particularly interesting on the scientific content of the society's meetings and his contacts with Cromwell Mortimer and the Royal Society.

56. On Stukeley see Stuart Piggott, *William Stukeley, an Eighteenth Century Anti-*

quary (Oxford, 1950); see also his MS commonplace book at the Spalding Society, entry for 15 August 1730 on Daniel's prophecies; and for an unadulterated sampling of his mystical tendencies, see Stukeley MSS, The Library of the Grand Lodge, London, MS. 1130, "The Creation," f. 171 on experiments done by Newton "by cutting the heart of an Eel into three pieces," but that is incidental to the text; and his many manuscripts there on Solomon's Temple. On Grundy, see R.S. LBC. 25, f. 138, Grundy to Senex, 1739, who was also a Freemason; and minutes of Spalding Society and the Institution of Civil Engineering John Grundy MS, "Surveys, levels, etc." vol. 2 (1740).

57. Evans, "Diffusion of Science," 288–90; A. R. Hewitt, "A Lincolnshire Notable and an Old Lodge at Spalding," *Ars Quatuor Coronatorum* 83 (1970): 96–101.

58. Evans, "Diffusion of Science," 243.

59. G. J. Hollister-Short, "The Introduction of the Newcomen Engine into Europe," *Transactions of the Newcomen Society for the study of the history of engineering and technology* 48 (1976–77): 11–22.

60. Evans, "Diffusion of Science," 269.

61. Ibid., 278.

62. See Eric Robinson, "The Profession of Civil Engineer in the 18th Century: A Portrait of Thomas Yeoman, F.R.S. (1704?–1781)", *Annals of Science* 18 (1962): 195–216; A. W. Skempton, "Early Members of the Smeatonian Society of Civil Engineers," *Transactions of the Newcomen Society* 44–45 (1971–73): 23–47. There are some Yeoman letters at The Institution of Civil Engineers, John Smeaton's Letter Book.

63. See Philip Doddridge, *A Course of Lectures on the Principal Subjects in Pneumatology, Ethics and Divinity* (London, 1763) [published posthumously], esp. 43–53, for an attack on Toland and materialism drawn straight from Clarke's Boyle lectures. Cf. Malcolm Deacon, *Philip Doddridge of Northampton, 1702–51* (Northampton, 1980).

64. Spalding Gentleman's Society, Spalding, Lincs., a loose flyer entitled "Answer to the Question the Sixth in the *Ladies' Diary* for the Year MDCCLI" from William Burwell, a school master in Norfolk. Cf. Gerald D. Meyer, *The Scientific Lady in England, 1650–1760* (Berkeley and Los Angeles, 1955), *English Studies* 12.

65. H. W. Dickinson, *A Short History of the Steam Engine, With a New Introduction by A. E. Musson* (London, 1963), chap. 4, esp. 62.

66. Terry S. Reynolds, "Scientific Influences on Technology: The Case of the Overshot Waterwheel, 1752–54," *Technology and Culture* 20 (1979): 285; cf. A. E. Skempton, ed., *John Smeaton, F.R.S.* (London, 1981), where none of the contributors discusses Smeaton's theoretical interests or religious beliefs or political values.

67. BL MSS. Add. 30094, f.10 Smeaton to Wilson, 20 July 1745.

68. John Smeaton, *Diary of his Journey to the Low Counties 1755, from the original manuscript in the Library of Trinity House, London* (Leamington Spa, 1938), 14; and on providence, Skempton, *John Smeaton*, 22.

69. *Diary*, 5–6, 40.
70. The Institution of Civil Engineers, London, John Smeaton MS Letter Book, ff. 47, 50, 58.
71. BL MSS. Add. 30094, f. 46; Smeaton to Wilson, 23 July 1747.
72. Ibid., f. 42.
73. Ibid., ff. 46, 69.
74. Ibid., f. 74.
75. Denis Smith, "The Professional Correspondence of John Smeaton: An eighteenth-century consulting engineering practice," *Transactions of the Newcomen Society* 46–47 (1973–76): 181.
76. Ibid., f. 112.
77. The Institution of Civil Engineers, f. 50, Thomas Maud to Smeaton on an eclipse.
78. Institution of Civil Engineers, John Smeaton Letter Book, f. 132; cf. Smith, "Professional Correspondence of John Smeaton," 179–89; and A. W. Skempton, "Early Members of the Smeatonian Society of Civil Engineers," *Transactions of the Newcomen Society* 44–45 (1971–73): 23–47.
79. The Institution of Civil Engineers, Smeaton Letter Book, f. 39. The letter is clearly by Smeaton but he signs it "Agricola"; it is to a Mr. Ledger.
80. Skempton, *John Smeaton*, 4, 54, 249; and for Smeaton's own concern for the cost of labor, see The Institution of Civil Engineers, Smeaton Letter Book, f. 32. Cf. Royal Society, MS. L + P. VII, no. 11, ff. 4–5, for Smeaton's interest in water and steam engines as replacements for horsepower.
81. Only the Rev. Timothy Neve, founder of the Peterborough Society, had little trust in "the religious capacity of the Court," but dined with Walpole at Houghton Hall and liked it. See Spalding Society, Maurice Johnson MS, drawer 1, no. 14, letter from the late 1720s.
82. E. Fearn, "The Derbyshire Reform Societies, 1791–93," *Derbyshire Archaeological Journal* 83 (1968): 48–55.
83. See Henry Redhead Yorke, *Reason urged against precedent* (London, 1793), for a full statement of radical sentiments commonplace in these circles, but Yorke eventually grew disillusioned with the Derby corresponding society and moved on to the more radical one at Sheffield. On Darwin see Brian Easlea, *Science and Sexual Oppression* (London, 1981), 94–99.
84. See the printed *Rules and Catalogue of the Library Belonging to the Derby Philosophical Society* (Derby, 1815); and even more interesting the manuscript list of acquisitions numbered in order of acquisition; the list of borrowing shows that members also attempted to read, as well as buy, the society's books. Derby Borough Library, MS. BA 106.
85. Joyce Appleby, "What is Still American in the Political Philosophy of Thomas Jefferson?" *William and Mary Quarterly*, 3d ser., 39 (1982): 308–9.
86. Desmond King-Hele, *Doctor of Revolution: The Life and Genius of Erasmus Darwin* (London, 1977), 60–62. Jefferson described Small as having given him "my first views of the expansion of science and of the system of things in which we are placed."

87. *Address to the Philosophical Society . . . July 18, 1784*, by Doctor Darwin, President, found in *Rules and Catalogue of the Library Belonging to the Derby Philosophical Society* (Derby, 1815), ix–xiv.

88. Eric Robinson, "The Derby Philosophical Society," *Annals of Science* 9 (1953): 360. On Pigott, see James O. Manton, *Early Freemasonry in Derbyshire* (Manchester, 1913), 21; D. King-Hele, ed., *The Letters of Erasmus Darwin* (Cambridge, 1981), 128.

89. M. R. Austin, "Religion and Society in Derbyshire During the Industrial Revolution," *Derbyshire Archaeological Journal* 93 (1973): 75–89.

90. *William Strutt—Memoir*, typescript in Derby Local Library, no. 3542, 27.

91. Philo-Filmer, *Encomiastic advice to the Acute and Ingenious Personage who parodied the Address from the Derby Societies to the Rt. Hon. Charles James Fox* (London, 1793), 4, and 13: "At the epithets Leveller, and Republican, they smile." This is a satire by someone actually in favor of the societies, probably William Ward. Cf. *The Derby Address. At a Meeting of the Society for Political Information held at the Talbot Inn, in Derby, July 16, 1792:* "To the Friends of Free Enquiry, and the General Good."

92. M. C. Egerton, "William Strutt and the Application of Convection to the Heating of Buildings," *Annals of Science*, 24 (1968): 73–88; cf. *William Strutt—Memoir*, 17–20, and Charles Sylvester, *The Philosophy of Domestic Economy* (Nottingham, 1819), dedicated to Strutt.

93. *William Strutt—Memoir*, 60. The poet, Thomas Moore, found them "true Jacobins" in 1814; see 10 for copy of a letter by Elizabeth Evans, Strutt's sister, on Godwin; 47 for a letter of condolence from Elizabeth Darwin to William Strutt in 1804 never mentioning God or providence. I wish to thank Margaret Hunt for assistance with this archive, and also the excellent staff of the Derby Local Library, Ms. Karen Smith and Ms. Sylvia Gown.

CHAPTER 7

Science and Literature in the Early German Enlightenment

UWE-K. KETELSEN

It is impossible, of course, to produce a completely satisfactory discussion of this topic in any brief format. The topic is, however, one of decisive importance in any attempt to form an accurate description of the development of the German Enlightenment. In order, then, to present at least a few of the basic concepts that I consider to be of greatest importance, I have decided to concentrate on the following three points—and, even so, I find myself forced to speak in very broad terms:

1. Hermeneutic difficulties involved in dealing with the topic of natural science and literature in the early German Enlightenment.
2. Literature as a purveyor of natural scientific knowledge in the eighteenth century.
3. The significance of literature as ideological resistance to mechanical materialism.

HERMENEUTIC DIFFICULTIES INVOLVED IN DEALING WITH THE TOPIC OF NATURAL SCIENCE AND LITERATURE IN THE EARLY GERMAN ENLIGHTENMENT

If one of those mythological "men from Mars" were to pay a visit to our world (or, perhaps more appropriately, to the so-called "Western world"),

Translated by James Bean.

the intellectual community would no doubt seem strange to him. He might even think it to be schizoid upon discovering that it is divided into two strictly separate parts. He would find two groups of thinking human beings inhabiting one world but severed into distinct camps. One group is composed of practically oriented realists and rationalists, whose thought processes are formed empirically by their experiences in a strange, at times even a threatening, environment; they concern themselves with the material world of nature as it supposedly "actually" exists. The other group—the philosophers, the aestheticians, the dreamers—occupies itself with speculation about material phenomena, with the problem of "ordering the universe," with the potential of the human mind for attaining knowledge and controlling actions.[1] It is characteristic of our age that this basic split in the intellectual world has resulted in the division of our social and educational institutions into two separate communities: the humanities and the natural sciences. These two scientific communities have developed differing basic scientific concepts, differing methods and procedural systems, and they pursue differing intellectual goals. In 1959 Charles Percy Snow characterized the situation with the phrase, "two cultures."

The book that bore this title and the animated debate that was, at least in West Germany,[2] triggered by it, made it vividly clear that the "two cultures" do not peacefully coexist as two possible intellectual alternatives. The fact is that whereas the natural scientists show in general little interest for the humanities and social sciences (or only a token interest, perhaps on ceremonious occasions), the humanists adopt a sceptical, even an inimical attitude toward the natural scientists. (There has been, it is true, a recent awakening of interest in the natural sciences on the part of historians and social scientists, even the beginnings of such an interest in literary-critical circles.[3] And, of course, a small group of philosophical "friends of the natural sciences" has existed for a long time. Such curiosities, however, seem of little significance when viewed in the light of the general situation.) There is nothing new about this mutual aversion; on the contrary, it is a fundamental part of the modern European consciousness. It can be observed as early as the beginning of the seventeenth century in, for example, the attitudes of Galileo Galilei. After his famous failure to convince his philosophical colleagues in Padua of the validity of his description of the heavens, Galilei wrote on 19 August 1610 to Johannes Kepler: "Odysseus closed his ears; these men have closed their eyes to the light of truth. Men of this type think philosophy (*Philosophia naturalis*) is a book, like the *Aeneid* or the *Odyssey*."[4] The uncompromising battle cry of the natural sciences" has existed for a long time. Such curiosities, however, seem of little significance when viewed in the light of the general situa-

From the perspectives of our age, the struggle between the two cultures seems to have been settled. The natural sciences and their intellectual methods have gained the field. *They* determine what is to be considered truth, and above all, *they* set the standards for judging what is to be accepted as "scientific." The practice of humanistic sciences seems to be possible only in areas where the natural sciences have not (yet) laid their claims, or, perhaps, in areas where natural scientific endeavours have proven to be the origin of devastating results that the humanities might possibly be able to repair.

If we now turn our attention to an examination of the relationship between natural science and literature in the German Enlightenment, then it must be with the realization that this cannot be done in a straightforward, positivistic manner. For not only is our knowledge of this relationship extremely fragmentary; much more serious is the fact that since we are all members of a society split into two cultures, our insights into historical relationships are limited. This limitation becomes immediately apparent when we try to inform ourselves about the position of the natural sciences in the eighteenth century. For our historical analysis of the last five hundred years of Western intellectual history is influenced by our interpretation of our own divided society. Both the natural scientists and the humanists are affected: the one group writes the history of their triumph, the other the history of their adjustment. The present situation is, in a way, imposed upon the past. The process is much too complicated for me to do more than merely refer to it here.

"Tanta vis est veritatis," Kepler's frequently quoted phrase, which occurs in his letter to Galilei of 13 October 1597, is, for the modern historian, a prophetic signal of the historical triumph of the natural sciences. This triumph is portrayed from two different points of view: as a process in which the knowledge of nature and of the methods by which nature can be understood becomes continually more detailed and precise;[5] and as the progressive subjugation of larger and larger areas of human existence to the claims of the natural sciences, an encroachment which has been extended in our own century even to the traditional humanistic disciplines such as psychology, sociology, and philosophy. This process is interpreted in global proportions: the sun of reason rises first in Europe, then in the entire world; "man" eventually becomes master of his own fate; heroes and basic plots are endowed with mythical dimensions—comparable to the heroic chronicles of "primitive" societies—the heroic human will is described as prevailing against obscurantism and ignorance. The most famous of these basic scenarios is the "Eppur si muove" ("But it does turn"), which Galilei is said to have murmured under his breath after having been forced by the Holy Inquisition to renounce his theory of planetary motion. Since the nineteenth century, this dramatic tableau has represented the heroic self-confidence and missionary spirit of the natural sciences.

I introduce this discussion only in order to indicate the special complexity of the material with which every historian who takes on a topic like "science and literature" has to deal. Because of the situation that I have just described, too many historians of natural science are unaware of the extent to which they simply attribute to the past the limited and reduced concepts of natural science characteristic of our present-day mentality. Textbooks accept in the history of their own disciplines only those theories that can be interpreted as forerunners of the modern natural-science consciousness: the mechanistic interpretation of nature; empiricism as the basis of scientific methodology; and mathematics as the basic scientific system of representation. Whatever does not come under these headings is either relegated to the history of philosophy or simply rejected. Thus, scientists doing their own history often fail to realize how extremely narrow our concept of natural science is, compared to what its practitioners originally hoped it to become. And, more importantly, they understand nothing at all about the vast disagreements and contradictions among prior natural scientists themselves. Are they aware that the renowned physician and biologist Albrecht von Haller in the last years of his life wrote works that were intended to defend Christian revelation against the attacks of the so-called freethinkers?[6] Are they aware that Isaac Newton took an extraordinary interest in metaphysics, that his intellectual development was to a large extent influenced by philosophical principles, that he considered himself a theologian, and that he wrote a large number of works on theological problems (which, however, were not published)?[7] These examples are characteristic of the reduction process by which natural philosophical science was contracted into the scientism of the nineteenth and twentieth centuries, a process of which some would-be historians of natural science are completely unaware.[8] The fact is that what scientists and their contemporaries around 1700 understood as "natural science" was decidedly more than what their successors of later generations were willing to accept. And what is far more important: their natural-science questions were inextricably connected with metaphysical, religious, and philosophical problems.[9] The process which I have been describing is so complex and its details so contradictory that only very general statements can be made about the relationship between science and literature in the German Enlightenment. In this transition period between two ages of world history, it is possible only in the case of individual authors to make completely accurate and definite pronouncements.

It is, however, not only historians of natural science who project the present-day intellectual situation onto the past; literary historians, as well, follow slavishly in the footsteps of their counterparts, only not as the victors in the historical development. They too begin with the basic division into natural sciences and humanities and interpret natural science—at least in connection with the seventeenth and eighteenth centuries—only as mechanical materialism, empiricism, and the body of knowledge known as *more geometrico*. Thus, in general, they completely neglect the topic "science and literature"; the notion that Newton or Christian Huyghens could have inspired a poem about nature is unthinkable to many of them. Or they treat the topic principally within a framework that was (supposedly!) not penetrated by natural science as they understand it. They even ascribe to the nature poetry of the first half of the eighteenth century the appropriation of that sphere which they suppose natural science to have gradually banished from the realm of man's intellectual pursuits.[10] "Nature" is defined as "landscape," "feeling for nature" becomes important, and specific genres of landscape description like those that occur in rococo poetry are explained as reactions to the natural sciences.[11] The hypothesis of the existence of a pre-Romantic cult of nature in the eighteenth century, which has been discussed for a long time, has its origins in this interpretation. Anglo-American scholars[12] and, subsequently, German specialists on English philology[13] have produced informative but unfortunately one-sided studies in this area. The sentimental portrayal of nature is emphasized, its sources sought in the Cambridge Platonists, and its antirationalistic and antiscientific characteristics exploited.[14] The fact that natural science and poetry, mechanical explanations of the universe and metaphysics can be closely connected with each other, that there was poetry which dealt with natural-science problems, that natural-science methodology influenced the literary language, that both latent and manifest contradictions between the two areas could be resolved in one individual—all such insights have been attained only very recently.[15]

The origins of this extreme limitation of the scope of the natural sciences, which has characterized European thought since the nineteenth century, reach back to a far earlier period. What was already a well-established historical tendency has merely reached its full maturity during the last two centuries. The nineteenth-century mentality looked back to older traditions that originated in the late Middle Ages, to the nominalists and the school of Ockham. These philosophers were characterized by the tendency to see material nature as isolated from a more comprehensive universal being and as controlled by specific laws (those very laws which later became the basis of the "mechanical universe" of the Enlightenment). [16] This inclination to interpret material nature as an isolated part of the cosmos gained strength and influence in each succeeding period between the late Middle Ages and the nineteenth century. René Descartes gave this concept an almost proverbial formulation in his convenient differentiation between the "thinking" object and the "extended" object (*res cogitans, res extensa*). [17] As the origin of far-reaching problems of vast significance, this idea received extensive attention throughout the early modern period. As a problem in the history of philosophy, the debate can be seen as a controversy between two scientific-philosophic explanations of nature: the medieval-universal interpretation, on the one hand, in which nature exists as God's creation and part of his plan for salvation; and the modern particularistic interpretation, on the other, in which nature, as *machina mundi* (the material machine) is autonomous.

Because of this controversy, enormous complications arose for the age in general and especially for the German Enlightenment, and literature played a significant role in the attempts to unravel them. Only against this very broad background can a discussion of the topic "Science and Literature" be profitable, a fact that I am delighted to admit, since it exonerates me of long-windedness and ineffectuality in offering these introductory remarks. For in Germany, a controversy reaching back for centuries into the past culminated in discussions centering around this topic. Unfortunately, one cannot say that the German Enlightenment carried on this debate on a level commensurate with its importance. Quite the contrary.

The multifaceted relationship between natural science and literature in the Enlightenment can be reduced to a simple formula: literature had a twofold function. On the one hand, it popularized the knowledge attained by natural science and contributed to an extent that is difficult to overestimate to the dissemination of this knowledge among those classes of society which had previously been deprived of it because of the system of education. On the other hand, literature helped to win a bitter but extraordinarily successful battle against those very reductionist tendencies that gained ascendency later in the history of natural science. I shall try, briefly, to analyze this paradox in more precise terms.

An examination of the other perspective, namely, the question of the importance of literature in the sphere of natural science, seems appropriate first. Did literature, for example, ask pertinent questions or produce special linguistic tools which were an incentive or a help to the natural scientists? [18] Yes, indeed; but it has gone largely unnoticed ever since the division of the intellectual community into "two cultures." In the process of "maturing" (as Thomas S. Kuhn calls it), [19] the natural sciences have rejected as unscientific the questions asked by literature: for example, whether man acting in nature has a universal moral responsibility; or whether the processes of nature have as their goal the welfare of the human race; or what significance the subjective conditions of human perception can have for theories which aspire to being scientifically acceptable. A similar answer can be given to the question of the relationship of language to natural science. Although Latin was given up as the artificial language of scholarship during the late seventeenth and eighteenth centuries, vernacular European languages were used by scientists only during a short transitional period. Eventually new artificial languages were created, and a new general idiom of science was elaborated, which was generally understandable: mathematics. The last German natural scientist of significance who resisted this development was the young Alexander von Humboldt (1769–1859). In 1783 Louis-Sébastien Mercier wrote: "La règne des lettres est passée; les physiciens remplacent les poètes et les romanciers; le machine électrique tient lieu d'une pièce de théâtre." (The reign of literature is past; physicists are replacing poets and novelists; the electric generator is taking the place of theatrics.) [20]

Natural science and literature were both intimately involved in the rationalizing process that characterized the Enlightenment. For this reason, it is often difficult to determine whether phenomena typical of the literature of this period are really derived from natural scientific disciplines or whether it is simply a matter of a common occurrence of enlightened rationalism. If, for example, dramatists or novelists of the Enlightenment were increasingly conscious of the psychological plausibility of the actions of their characters, are we compelled to say that they were influenced by the natural sciences? [21] Or do we simply have here a particular instance of the general trend of the period to demonstrate logical connections?

LITERATURE AS A PURVEYOR OF NATURAL SCIENTIFIC KNOWLEDGE IN THE ENLIGHTENMENT

During the course of the seventeenth century, man's knowledge of the material world was dramatically transformed. With few exceptions, notably in the field of chemistry, the insights that had been considered valid by medieval man were almost completely discarded. New conceptions of the entire universe and of its largest and smallest phenomena had been formed, involving not only speculations but also observable facts. Not only had the telescope and the microscope led to new insights, they had also—and this was at least as important—made these new insights demonstrable. And, as we all know, there is nothing more convincing than seeing for yourself, even if appearances do sometimes deceive. The material world lay visible to the eyes of all. At first, of course, only the experts took an interest, but it is striking how quickly the new insights were disseminated beyond the narrow confines of the scholar's study. A genuine revolution occurred. Knowledge about the world (which meant, in the end, control over the world) was no longer in the hands of a traditional scholarly elite who hoarded their insights in books, preserved them only in written (and thus, because of the accepted system of education, in secret) forms, and communicated them in the artificial Latin incomprehensible to the general population. Suddenly the world became accessible to all, and knowledge of it was grounded in a common human ability, the ability to see. A mania for examining and exploring the real world took possession of certain sections of the upper middle classes who became particularly zealous in learning. Throughout Europe, but especially in the Protestant countries, a genuine passion broke out for studying the heavens, for performing optical experiments, for collecting minerals and plants, for observing flora and fauna. What had formerly been the eccentricity of princes became the sport of the middle class. There was almost nothing on the earth or in the heavens that did not become the object of burning interest. A blind humanity seemed suddenly to have attained sight. There are many documents which testify to this development: the diary of Samuel Pepys is one of the most amusing;[22] the publications of England's Royal Society are perhaps the most instructive; and the flood of moral weeklies produced for the education and edification of the German middle classes are, no doubt, the most wearisome.[23] In England, by around 1700, the formulation of man's new interpretation of the world had been completed in outline form. The transformation of the old research-oriented system into a system of advanced education had also been carried out. In Germany this process took somewhat longer to complete. It was accomplished in the first three or four decades of the eighteenth century by Christian Wolff and his disciples in more highly educated circles, and by the moral weeklies on a more general scale.

Popular publications of the time often illustrated explicitly this new passion of the bourgeois dilettantes. Their pictorial language often showed the same basic constellations. There would be the scholar of the old school, surrounded by all the traditional furnishings of his class; a cluttered study, rows of book shelves, a writing desk—he is, however, not lost in his books, but rather looking out of the window at Nature (often shown as an allegorical figure who is pointing the way into the far-reaching landscape). Or there would be the man of the middle class (recognizable by the characteristic dressing gown and nightcap), examining natural objects (like insects or flowers) with a microscope or a magnifying glass. The results of those studious inspections were shown in detailed sketches of the form and composition of animals and plants.

The sermon and the didactic poem were the two literary genres that proved to be of the greatest service in disseminating the natural scientific knowledge gained by both professionals and amateurs.[24] There was practically no insight that literature did not help to make known among the general population. Nothing was too farfetched to be made the subject of a didactic poem. Didactic pens were especially activated by problems of astronomy and human anatomy. Scholars[25] have compiled impressive lists of natural scientific topics that formed the subjects of didactic poems, and more could be added, since practically all the knowledge to which eighteenth-century man had access inspired, at one time or another, a poem.[26] It indeed would be possible to write a popular history of natural science in the eighteenth century by consulting such a list. We might be amused today by some of these topics (or perhaps we would simply be bored), but we should realize that here, for the first time in the history of Europe, knowledge about the world is being dispensed to a nonscholarly reading (and listening!) public. It really was an "enlightened" and "enlightening" literature, even more so in cases (generally occurring after midcentury) where practical instructions (concerning, for example, the care and treatment of certain plants) were included.[27] Even medical controversies of widespread interest and importance were fought out in poems of great length. The physician Daniel Wilhelm Triller (1695–1782), for example, produced two hundred pages of lyric polemic against small-pox vaccination.[28]

A brief excerpt from a typical didactic poem of this kind will give at least a vague idea of what these works were like. This poem describing the human anatomy appeared in 1759. In the section devoted to the stomach, after explaining that the stomach is partially set in motion by the diaphragm, partially by the muscular tissue, the poem continues:

With the energy thus produced the stomach exerts pressure on the food which has collected in it; nothing disturbs it in its function; it fills up, stretches, and enlarges. It has two openings: to the left the cardia, and to the right the pylorus. When the stomach is empty, folds can be observed which resemble velvet. The nutriment is liquid, basic as opposed to acidic, and warm. It is received into the duodenum in order to be decomposed by bile and gastric juices. The anatomist can here point out the Virsung canal and the accompanying mechanisms, especially the tender Kerkring valve; the glands which were discovered by Brunner produce juices which the nutriment absorbs.[29]

Nowadays such instructive material is to be found in encyclopedias (and they do not always provide much more information than we have here).

The modern reader is astounded not only at the great number of these didactic poems, but also at the amazing chaos of topics which they treated. Any and every subject could—apparently with complete arbitrariness—serve as the theme for a "physical" (as they were then called) poem of a didactic nature. All sense of order was overcome by the desire to inspect and understand the real. Nature seemed to be an immense concatenation of physical phenomena, reminiscent, perhaps, of the antiquated exhibition rooms of a natural science museum. Ordering criteria are only rarely detectable; an absolute arbitrariness is the rule. The dominant principles are spatial proximity and temporal simultaneity. The genetic principle introduced by Lamarck and Cuvier shortly before 1800 was, for metaphysical and religious reasons, totally unthinkable in the German Enlightenment. There were, it is true, models and paradigms that were intended to order the universe, but none of them proved very effective. At times didactic poets tried to use them, as was the case with Barthold Heinrich Brockes (1680–1747), the most remarkable poet of the early Enlightenment in Germany, who attempted to explain the entire material universe in a poem of mammoth proportions; but he didn't get very far. Generally, they selected arbitrary objects, turned their interest temporarily to one area, and then leapt without apparent reason to another.

The readers of these poems did not demand systematically explained or even innovative insights; they did not even insist on a complete version of the information presented in the popular descriptions of nature. What they expected was to find the abstract and scholarly knowledge of the experts retold to them in a pleasant and entertaining fashion. The purpose was, on the one hand, to charm those readers who were already familiar with the material by presenting it in an imaginative guise; and, on the other hand, to educate in a pleasurable fashion those who were not inclined to or capable of more extended intellectual exertion. These tasks were taken up with great enthusiasm by the didactic poets, and accomplished with more or less success depending on their abilities. This meant, however, that priority was given in these poems not to scientific knowledge, to completeness of information, and to technically correct explication, but rather to beauty of form. The content of the poems was subjugated to the poetic process, a practice generally characteristic of the poetry of the Enlightenment. That is, the poet had to present his theme in concrete images (which, of course, was not extremely difficult, since the theme itself was concrete); he had to arrange these images according to the principle of "a pleasing succession of sensuous impressions" (the so-called *beau désordre*); he had to find charming words and use them to create appealing rhymes and verses which were meant to induce his readers and hearers to conceptualize his theme.[30] This can be shown by comparing a didactic poem to a corresponding nonpoetic text that treats the same theme. To many didactic poets this necessity to couch their material in pleasing and pictorial, but inaccurate terms seemed to be too great a detriment to the truth, and they emended their poems with lengthy and scholarly footnotes, hoping in this way to produce works of a more complete and reliable nature. The editors of one of Brockes's works in which a description of a sunrise occurs felt themselves called upon to assure their readers that, apart from this temporary lapse, the author remained faithful to the Copernican explanation of the organization of the solar system.[31] It was, however, they continued, in this case permissible to deviate from the scientific truth, since the purpose of the poem was to appeal to the emotions and the conceptual abilities of the readers. An extensive discussion took place, by the way, among the literary critics of the German Enlightenment as to whether the necessity to educate and inform did not force didactic poets to neglect poetic style to far too great an extent. In the end these critics (among them Johann Jakob Breitinger, Lessing, and Goethe) succeeded in gaining general acceptance for their opinions.

To give just a brief impression of the aesthetic quality that these didactic poets strove to achieve, I would like to quote a few lines in the original. I choose an English equivalent to the continental fashion (which is nowadays almost as unknown as the German text). The verses come from a poem entitled *Universal Beauty* by the Irish poet Henry Brooke (1706–1783) and deal with Newton's theory of the diffusion of light:

> The subtile mass its copious mantle spreads,
> Its mantle wove of elemental threads;
> Th' elastic flue of fluctuating air,
> Transfus'd invisible, enfolds the sphere;
> With poinance delicate pervades the whole,
> Its ear, eye, breath, and animating soul.[32]

It has to be admitted, however, that only a very few writers achieved such skill in imparting facts in a pleasant and appealing style. Even less frequent was the intellectual independence of a poet like Lessing who composed for a moral weekly a parody of the popularizing tendencies of such periodical publications. Lessing's poem was called *The Three Realms of Nature*, and was based upon the well-known scientific division of nature into three kingdoms: animals, which drink and make love; plants, which only drink; and stones, which neither drink nor make love. Lessing ended the poem with irresistable logic by remarking that a moralist who neither drinks nor makes love would indeed be a stone.[33] But such a stroke of genius is a rare high point of ironic reflection; in general, such topics are treated very seriously in the Enlightenment.

In addition to being a major theme of the poetry of the German Enlightenment, natural science also exerted an important (and diverse) influence on the *way* in which the theme "Nature" was treated poetically. The influence is immediately recognizable if we look at the poems against the background of tradition; we need only to compare a didactic poem of the Enlightenment to a baroque poem in which the theme of nature occurs. Let us take the famous *Now All Forests Are Quiet* of Paul Gerhardt (1607–1676). In the first stanza, we are told that it is evening; the second stanza (in prose translation) goes like this: "O Sun, whither have you fled? Night has banished you, Night, Day's rival. But go—another Sun, Christ, my joy, shines brightly in my heart."[34] You can see it immediately: night indicates death; the sun is related to another sun, the Son of God, who brings salvation. The natural phenomenon points to something else, something metaphysical; nature is, as it were, transparent; it can be used to explain the relationship of things in the universe in their saving, moral, anagogical dimensions.[35] Creation is like a huge book in which information can be obtained about the order of the universe and the meaning of all existence. This conception of nature has a long tradition reaching back to the medieval thinkers and their ideas of universal order.[36]

This analogical technique became, under the influence of natural science (but also under the influence of theological developments), less and less feasible (which does not mean, however, that it did not continue to be possible to talk about God in connection with a theme from nature). For the Enlightenment, the sun is the sun and nothing else. It is a ball of fire and the center of the field of gravity for our solar system. Thus it must be described as a natural phenomenon, as, for example, Brockes does in a poem of 72 stanzas in which he explains the importance of the sun for the earth's vegetation, for the times of day and the seasons, and for our solar system's gravitational field; even the problem of empty space is discussed.[37] Images from nature were not allowed to serve as allegories for something else (as the night, for example, is an allegory for death for Gerhardt); the poets were compelled to describe natural phenomena as it was presented for human observation; descriptive words and phrases could not be metaphors for farfetched or hidden ideas, they had to characterize accurately the objects to which they referred. Words, said Leibniz, are comparable to tokens: they are exactly representative of objects. However, only a very few writers were content to remain at this level.

THE SIGNIFICANCE OF LITERATURE AS IDEOLOGICAL RESISTANCE TO MECHANICAL MATERIALISM

Actually it was only very seldom that the poets of the German Enlightenment limited themselves to such a narrow conception of nature. They were, on the contrary, constantly attempting to encorporate "mechanical nature" into a larger metaphysical context.[38] The haunting fear that this might prove to be impossible is either openly expressed in their works or inherent in their attitudes.[39] The best known lyric poet of the German Enlightenment, Friedrich Gottlieb Klopstock, devoted one of his most frequently quoted poems, *Rural Life*, to an expression of this fear. In these verses, written in 1759, Klopstock praises God's creation in noble terms; his feeling for the majesty of the deity seems to him to prove that man is more than a mechanical machine. Then he happens to see a glowworm, and the idea that the living world of nature might in the end be indeed merely mechanical shocks him deeply: "O, spring-time creature, green and golden, playing here beside me: you live and are perhaps—alas, not immortal!" Then a mighty thunderstorm arises. "But look, the golden worm takes note! Does it perhaps not lack a soul? Is it immortal?" The very possibility of asking these questions at all gives the poet hope and inspires him to even more enthusiastic praise of God.[40]

The same doubt that so deeply disturbs Klopstock in this poem filled the entire German Enlightenment with anxiety: Was it possible that the *machina mundi* was not a part of a divinely created and inspired universe? Germans did not embrace the materialist doctrines of French thinkers like La Mettrie, Diderot, or d'Holbach—or at least not publicly. Even Deists were rare in Germany and were not orthodox representatives of this movement. On the contrary, every attempt was made by the Germans to avoid having to draw the possible philosophical consequences that were implied by the natural advances of the "new science."[41] The numerous and extremely contradictory attempts to resist this interpretation were often of little intellectual significance and have hardly any influence at all as far as philosophical history is concerned. Yet in the eighteenth century they were powerful enough to prevent mechanical materialism from gaining a foothold in Germany, although it dominated the intellectual life of France (and partially of England) at this time. Goethe's recollection, in *Dichtung und Wahrheit*, substantiates this assertion quite effectively.[42] Goethe describes the disappointment that he and his friends experienced when—in the 1770s—they had finally managed to get hold of a copy of d'Holbach's forbidden *System of Nature*. They were profoundly disappointed with it, and found it "pale"; they were unable to take its ideas seriously; indeed, they failed to understand them in their philosophical context. Goethe ends with an unfavorable comparison of d'Holbach to his revered Shakespeare![43] This confrontation of German intellectuals with contemporary French materialism shows only too clearly how successful the attempts to subvert the influence of the "new science" in Germany had been.

Let us take a brief look at one of these attempts, one that exerted a major and more or less persistent influence on the popular nature poetry of the German Enlightenment. It was called "physicotheology"[44] and its one basic and relatively simple principle, which had been fully developed in England by the end of the seventeenth century, went something like this: The more complicated the insights of the "new science" demonstrate material nature to be, the more necessary it becomes to posit the existence of a God who has 'invented' this mechanism; the more detailed and involved the functional system of material nature proves to be, the more inevitable the necessity of a God to keep it going; the more extensive and complex the functioning of the cause-and-effect processes within the world of nature, the more compelled we are to acknowledge a God who has produced its design. On the basis of this kind of argumentation, the "new science" took on an apologetic function! It was employed to prove the existence of a creating, conserving, and planning God—a God whom it was trying—at least in its actual historical tendency—to take out of circulation![45]

The physicotheologians, like their opponents the materialists, turned the "new science" into the basis of an ideology by putting the newly attained knowledge about physical nature into a metaphysical context. Paradoxically the physicotheologians, in their struggle against mechanical materialism, popularized exactly those insights of the "new science" that later were to contribute most significantly to its triumph. Johann Albert Fabricius, the "father" of the German physicotheologians, wrote in 1730 that nature was to be studied "not merely for the sake of curiosity and the thirst for knowledge (as many physicists and anatomists do), but for the glory of the Creator."[46] Thus natural science itself came to be used as a weapon against atheism. One of the German physicotheologians, the aforementioned physician Daniel Wilhelm Triller, gave his collection of poems of 1725 the significant title *Poetic Observations on Various Objects Taken from Nature and Moral Philosophy, for the Preservation of the Christian Religion and in Defiance of Atheists and Naturalists [Deists].*[47]

The physicotheological nature poetry of the German Enlightenment lacked originality and was highly imitative of the English physicotheological literature fashionable at the end of the seventeenth century.[48] Numerous translations of works of this kind appeared in Germany and it is significant that the religious authors (John Wilkens, John Tillotson, William Derham, Nehemia Grew) were more strongly represented than the natural philosophers (John Ray and Robert Boyle). The Boyle Lectures, financed through the legacy of the chemist, were received in Germany with enthusiasm over the course of many decades. Through this method the existence of God could be proved to each and all in defiance of the atheists. Within a short time there was an immeasurable throng of theologies—astro-, chiono-, chorto-, cosmo-, hydro-theologies, and many more—which had taken on the task of the precise study of the stars, thunder, snow, and so forth, "in order to inspire men to admiration, love, and adoration of the most powerful, wisest and most benevolent Creator" (as a typical formulation of the title page of such a book might assert).[49] In contrast to their English models, the German writers failed to develop originality of thought. They added nothing thematically or argumentatively innovative to the basic model.[50]

What was, however, an innovative contribution of the Germans—at least of the poets among them—was accomplished in the area of presentation: the particularly effective persuasive power that was attributed to poetry by traditional humanistic rhetoric was placed by the poets at the disposal of the physicotheological doctrines (whereas the English writers had preferred the tract or the sermon). This process indeed was necessary, for it had become apparent that the hopes which the English thinkers—Newton, for example—had harbored of maintaining the unity of universal nature, despite the potential materialistic tendencies of the "new science," were becoming less and less feasible. It had for a long time ceased to be possible on a purely logical level to continue to believe in the realization of these dreams. The nominalistic conception of the universe continued unchecked to unfold its own inner logic. It was then that poetry assumed the position of logical argument. The attitudes called forth by the immensity and complexity of nature and the emotional enthusiasm heightened by poetry went hand in hand: both were intended to aid in preserving the possibility of an advance from the *machina mundi* to the one universal nature which was the creation of God.[51] Frequently, the affective capabilities of poetry were heightened through the use of music.[52] This description of the ideological background of the first stages of the German Enlightenment makes plausible the alliance between natural science and poetry that other-wise might seem unlikely. This alliance was neither paradoxical nor acci-dental: literature took on a particular polemical function that could not have been performed so well by any other means of communication.

Finally, I should like to demonstrate the argumentative technique to which I am referring by discussing briefly a poem by Pastor Albrecht Jacob Zell, *Wild Violet*, published in 1735. The 134 stanzas of this poem begin with an introduction which, by the way, is untypical for such works. The poet asserts that God must also be praised by observing the beauty and complexity of everyday objects. The poem itself, which is composed in the madrigal form, begins with a brief description of a particular situa-tion: during the course of a walk the poet takes notice of a wild violet growing on the side of the road. A detailed description of the plant, which comprises the major part of the poem, follows. The form of the plant, the leaves, and the flower are precisely described. The explication could come from a popular botanical study. Since the poet is striving to create concrete images, no technical terminology is used; he tries, rather, to employ every-day speech. He also avoids metaphors and other "poetic" devices. He emphatically resists in his description any metaphysical interpretation of phenomena and limits himself strictly to the facts. But—and this is impor-tant for him—by emphasizing the complex formation of the parts of the plant, their observable relationships to each other, and the nuances of color, he is trying to call forth in the reader a very definite admiration for its functional and differentiated structure and beauty of coloration. A con-cluding section in the form of a religious hymn ends the poem. The culmi-nation of the poem occurs in these final verses: they represent its ultimate purpose: "O, Creator! Made beautiful by the omnipotence of Your hand, the low-lying land rises up with golden blossoms, which are splendid, though in all their splendor only small. O, let me, Creator, remember this; for the golden brilliance of Your grace will make me beautiful as well."[53] With this turning towards God, the material world becomes analogous to the world of grace. Material nature is integrated into the unity of God's *one* creation. And this is exactly what the poet intends.

Further developments within German nature poetry of the eighteenth century took their cue from poems of this kind. Our last example demon-strates that poetry had the function of rendering material nature aesthet-ically appealing; it also makes clear that nature itself was considered an aesthetic phenomenon. In the following decades—that is, the 1740s and 1750s—we can observe a characteristic sentimentalizing of the concept of nature in German poetry.[54] How this beauty of nature ("das Naturschöne") was to be interpreted, how it acted upon the perceptive and emotional as-pects of man's personality—these problems occupied thinkers throughout the century, right down to Novalis and Hegel. Whether natural science (above all, physiology) played a role in this process is a question which has been asked as yet only in regard to the Weimar Classicism of a Goethe or a Herder.[55] It also would be a question of some importance to the topic of "Natural Science and Literature in the Early German Enlightenment."

NOTES

1. Charles Percy Snow, *The Two Cultures and the Scientific Revolution* (New York, 1959); see also Aldous Huxley, *Literature and Science* (London, 1963).

2. Helmut Kreuzer, ed., *Literarische und naturwissenschaftliche Intelligenz* (Stuttgart, 1969).

3. Lewis Mumford, *The Myth of the Machine*, 2 vols. (New York, 1964–66); Wolf Lepenies, *Das Ende der Naturgeschichte. Wandel kultureller Selbstverstaendlichkeiten in der Wissenschaft des 18. und 19. Jahrhunderts*, 2d ed. (Frankfurt am Main, 1978).

4. Galileo Galilei, *Sidereus Nuncius*, ed. Hans Blumenberg (Frankfurt am Main, 1965), 9 (with an instructive introduction by Blumenberg, 7–75); Paul Feyerabend, *Against Method: Outline of an Anarchistic Theory of Knowledge* (Berkeley, 1975), esp. 6–12.

5. Cf. for example, Stuart F. Mason, *A History of the Sciences* (London, 1953), esp. part 3, which deals with the "revolution" of the natural sciences; James Jeans, *The Growth of Physical Science* (Cambridge, 1947); see the epistemological formulation of this constellation by Werner Heisenberg, "Der Begriff 'abgeschlossene Theorie' in der modernen Naturwissenschaft" in *Schritte über Grenzen* (Munich, 1971), 87–94.

6. Cf. Richard Toellner, *Albrecht v. Haller* (Wiesbaden, 1971); also Toellner, "Mechanismus—Vitalismus. Ein Paradigmenwechsel? Testfall Haller," *Studien zur Wissenschaftstheorie* 10 (1977): 61–72.

7. Cf. Fritz Wagner, *Neue Diskusionen über Newtons Wissenschaftsbegriff* (Munich, 1969).

8. Cf. Max Horkheimer and Theodor W. Adorno, *Dialektik der Aufklärung* (Amsterdam, 1947); Jürgen Habermas, *Erkenntnis und Interesse* (Frankfurt am Main, 1968); Karl-Otto Apel, "Szientistik, Hermeneutik, Ideologiekritik," in Apel, et al., *Hermeneutik und Ideologiekritik* (Frankfurt am Main, 1971), 7–44.

9. Cf. Thomas P. Saine, "Natural Science and the Ideology of Nature in the German Enlightenment," *Lessing Yearbook* 8 (1976): 61–88.

10. Cf. Joachim Ritter, *Landschaft. Zur Funktion des Ästhetischen in der modernen Gesellschaft* (Münster, 1963); Hans-Joachim Possin, *Natur und Landschaft bei Addison* (Tübingen, 1965).

11. Alfred Anger, "Landschaftsstil des Rokoko," *Euphorion* 51 (1957): 151–91.

12. Arthur O. Lovejoy, *The Great Chain of Being*, 2d ed. (Cambridge, Mass., 1950); and Lovejoy, "'Nature' as Aesthetic Norm," in his *Essays on the History of Ideas*

(Baltimore, 1948), 69–77. See also Marjorie Hope Nicolson, *Mountain Gloom and Mountain Glory*, 2d ed. (New York, 1963).

13. Bernhard Fabian, "Pope und die goldene Kette Homers," *Anglia* 82 (1964): 150–71; Ria Omasreiter, *Naturwissenschaft und Literaturkritik im England des 18. Jahrhunderts* (Nuremberg, 1971).

14. Basil Willey, *The 18th Century Background: Studies on the Ideas of "Nature" in the Thought of the Period* (New York, 1940).

15. Cf. Karl Richter, *Literatur und Naturwissenschaft. Eine Studie zur Lyrik der Aufklärung* (Munich, 1972); Wolfgang Harms, "Allegorie und Emperie bei Konrad Gessner. Naturkundliche Werke unter literaturwissenschaftlichen Aspekten," in *Akten des V. Internationalen Germanistenkongresses* (Bern, 1976) 2:119–23.

16. Cf. Hans Blumenberg, *Die kopernikanische Wende* (Frankfurt am Main, 1965).

17. Cf. Etienne Gilson, *Etudes sur le Rôle de la Pensée médiévale dans la Formation du Système Cartésien* (Paris, 1951).

18. Some scholars have devoted attention to this question, especially in respect to English literature. See Wilda C. Anderson, "Translating the Language of Chemistry: Priestley and Lavoisier," *Eighteenth Century* 22 (1981): 21–31; John Arthos, *The Language of Natural Description in 18th Century Poetry* (Ann Arbor, 1949); Donald A. Davie, *The Language of Science and the Language of Literature, 1700–1740* (London, 1963); see also n. 25, below.

19. Thomas S. Kuhn, *The Structure of Scientific Revolutions* (Chicago, 1966).

20. Louis-Sébastien Mercier, *Tableau de Paris*, new ed. (1782/83) cited by Wolf Lepenies, *Das Ende der Naturgeschichte*, 2d ed. (Frankfurt am Main, 1978), 137.

21. Cf. Horst Thomé, *Roman und Naturwissenschaft* (Frankfurt am Main, 1978).

22. Marjorie Hope Nicolson, *Pepys' Diary and the New Science* (Charlottesville, Va., 1965).

23. Pamela Currie, "Moral Weeklies and Reading Public in Germany, 1711–1750," *Oxford German Studies* 3 (1968): 69–86; Wolfgang Martens, *Die Botschaft der Tugend. Die Aufklärung im Spiegel der deutschen Moralischen Wochenschriften* (Stuttgart, 1968).

24. Christoph Siegrist, *Das Lehrgedicht der Aufklärung* (Stuttgart, 1974).

25. Cf. Ralph B. Crum, *Scientific Thoughts in Poetry* (New York, 1931); William Powell Jones, *The Rhetoric of Science: A Study of Scientific Ideas and Imagery in the 18th-Century English Poetry* (London, 1966); Marjorie Hope Nicolson, *The Breaking of the Circle: Studies in the Effect of the "New Science" upon 17th-Century Poetry* (New York, 1960); and above all, Walter Schatzberg, *Scientific Themes in the Popular Literature and the Poetry of the German Enlightenment, 1720–1760* (Frankfurt am Main, 1973). Since 1966 the MLA has published a voluminous periodical bibliography on the topic of relations of literature and science.

26. To give only one brief but characteristic example: in 1725 the poet and physician Daniel Wilhelm Triller published a poem of 240 madrigal verses dealing with the propagation of frogs in *Poetische Betrachtungen*, part 1 (Hamburg, 1725), 139ff.

27. Cf. Bernhard Tscharner, "Von der Wässerung," *Der Schweitzerischen Gesellschaft*

in Bern Sammlungen Von Landwirtschaftlichen Dingen, part 2 (Zurich, 1761), 11–28.

28. Daniel Wilhelm Triller, Geprüfte Pockeninoculation (Frankfurt, 1766).

29. Johann Siegmund Leinker, *Die Körperwelt und ihr Einwohner der Mensch: Zwey Oden* (Frankfurt, 1759), 82ff.

30. Cf. Uwe-K. Ketelsen, Afterword to the reprint of Carl Friedrich Drollinger, *Gedichte* (1743; Stuttgart, 1972), 452ff. In England Alexander Pope articulated comparable thoughts. They were the European standard.

31. Barthold Heinrich Brockes, *Auszug der vornehmsten Gedichte* (reprint, Stuttgart, 1965), 182ff.

32. Henry Brooke, *Universal Beauty, a Philosophical Poeme in Six Books* (1735), part 1, verses 352–57. (Cf. Alexander Chalmers, *The Works of English Poets* [London, 1810], 17:340.)

33. Gotthold Ephraim Lessing, "Die Drei Reiche der Natur," in *Werke*, ed. Fritz Fischer (Cologne, 1965), 1:97.

34. Paul Gerhardt, "Nun ruhen alle Wälder," in Albrecht Schöne, ed., *Die deutsche Literatur*, vol. 3: *Barock*, (Munich, 1963), 190.

35. During the Middle Ages this idea was brought into the mnemonic verses: "Littera gesta docet, quid credas allegoria, / Moralis quid agas, quo tendas anagogia."

36. Cf. Wolfgang Harms, "Der Übergang zur Neuzeit und die Wirkung von Traditionen," in *Der Übergang zur Neuzeit und die Wirkung von Traditionen* (Göttingen, 1978), 7–14.

37. Barthold Heinrich Brockes, "Die Sonne," in *Auszug der vornehmsten Gedichte* (reprint, Stuttgart, 1965), 180–204.

38. Cf. Reijer Hooykaas, *Religion and the Rise of Modern Science*, 2d ed. (Edinburgh, 1973).

39. Cf. Uwe-K. Ketelsen, *Die Naturpoesie der norddeutschen Frühaufklärung* (Stuttgart, 1974), esp. 43–97.

40. Friedrich Gottlieb Klopstock, "Das Landleben," in Karl August Schleiden, ed., *Ausgewählte Werke* (Munich, 1962), 85–89.

41. Recent studies emphasize the Hermetic traditions since the Middle Ages: Antoine Faivre a. Rolf Zimmerman, ed., *Epochen der Naturmystik. Hermetische Tradition im wissenschaftlichen Fortschritt* (Berlin, 1979). The authors treat Jacob Böhme, Johannes van Helmont, Daniel Czepko, Emanuel Swedenborg, Blake, Newton, and others. (Some of the articles are in English); Hans-Georg Kemper, *Gottebenbildlichkeit und Naturnachahmung im Säkularisierungsprozeß*, 2 vols. (Tübingen, 1981), esp., 1:310–61.

42. Johann Wolfgang Goethe, "Dichtung und Wahrheit," *Goethes Werke: Hamburger Ausgabe*, ed. Erich Trunz (Hamburg, 1955), 9:490.

43. Paul-Henri Thiry d'Holbach, *Système de la Nature, ou Des Loix du Monde Physique et du Monde Moral* ([Amsterdam], 1770).

44. Wolfgang Philipp, *Das Werden der Aufklärung in theologiegeschichtlicher Sicht* (Göttingen, 1957); Hans-Martin Barth, *Atheismus und Orthodoxie* (Göttingen, 1971), 251–80; Sara Stebbins, *Maxima in minimis. Zum Empirie- und Autori-*

tätsverständnis in der physikotheologischen Literatur der Frühaufklärung (Bern, 1980; with a summary in English).

45. Uwe-K. Ketelsen, "Naturpoesie als Medium bürgerlicher Ideologiebildung im frühen 18. Jahrhundert," in Norbert Mecklenburg, ed., *Naturlyrik und Gesellschaft* (Stuttgart, 1977), 51.

46. Johann Albert Fabricius, Preface to his translation of William Derhams *Astro-theologia*, 3d ed. (Hamburg, 1739), xv.

47. Daniel Wilhelm Triller, *Poetische Betrachtungen, über verschiedene, aus der Natur- und Sitten-Lehre hergenommene Materien zur Bewährung der Wahrheit christlicher Religion, denen Atheisten und Naturalisten entgegen gesetzet,* 6 vols. (Hamburg, 1725–55).

48. This dependence upon a broad tradition reviews in the case of B. H. Brockes: Ida M. Kimber, *B. H. Brockes, a Transmitter of Germinal Ideas in his "Irdisches Vergnügen"* (Ph.D. diss., Edinburgh, 1969).

49. Cf. Lois Armour Westen, *Melitto-Logia: The Mythologia of the Bee in 18th-Century German Literature* (Ph.D. diss., University of Illinois, Urbana, 1952).

50. The only difference between English and German physicotheologists one may see in the circumstance is that some of the German authors seemed to be influenced by mystical and Hermetic traditions (see n. 41, above).

51. Gerolf Fritsch, *Das deutsche Naturgedicht* (Stuttgart, 1978).

52. See Harold P. Fry, "B. H. Brockes und die Musik," in Hans-Dieter Loose, ed., *B. H. Brockes: Dichter und Ratsherr in Hamburg* (Hamburg, 1980), 71–104.

53. Albrecht Jacob Zell, "Feld-Viole," in *Erweckte Nachfolge zum Irdischen Vergnuegen in Gott* (Hamburg, 1735), 231.

54. Cf. Gerhard Sauder, *Empfindsamkeit*, vol. 1 (Stuttgart, 1974); Helmut J. Schneider, "Naturerfahrung und Idylle in der deutschen Aufklärung," in Peter Pütz, ed., *Erforschung der deutschen Aufklärung* (Koenigstein, 1980), 289–315.

55. Hugh Barr Nisbet, *Herder and the Philosophy and History of Science* (Cambridge, 1970); Nisbet, *Goethe and the Scientific Tradition* (London, 1972); Wolfgang Duesing, "Kosmos und Natur in Schillers Lyrik," *Jahrbuch der deutschen Schiller-Gesellschaft* 13 (1969): 196–220.

CHAPTER 8

The Gallant Novel and the German Enlightenment, 1670–1750

JOHN A. MCCARTHY

> ". . . it is often the mediocre writers, who are eventually forgotten, who foreshadow the great statements to be made later by authors of genius. . . ."
> —Geoffroy Atkinson, *The Sentimental Revolution: French Writers of 1690–1740*

Not many people would take exception to the argument that the emergence of a new, increasingly middle-class, increasingly secularized world view is most discernible in the prose writings of the period of transition from a predominantly aristocratic, dogmatic society to a predominantly bourgeois, individualistic one. The novel and the journal were characteristic instruments of instruction in the Enlightenment and they have continued to dominate the literature of the nineteenth and twentieth centuries. Gallant style, on the other hand, is widely considered most typical of the period of transition from Grimmelshausen's *Simplicissimus* to Gellert's *Schwedische Gräfin*, or roughly 1670–1750. In 1643, before the beginning of our time frame, H. M. Moscherosch, a seventeenth-century satirist, had commented: "As the times change, so does the written word; and conversely: as the written word changes, so do the times change."[1] After the conclusion of this period, Christian Friedrich von Blanckenburg aptly observed in his celebrated *Versuch über den Roman* (*Essay on the Novel*) (1774): "Novels were not created by the genius of their authors alone: the social values of their period of origin also gave birth to them."[2]

Until relatively recently it has not been customary in literary histories to date the beginnings of the German Enlightenment before Gottsched, that is, before 1720–30.[3] Because little interest has been shown for the pre-1730 period, the history of German prose literature between 1670 and

1750 is still a bit murky. So clouded is the history of the German novel in this period that one leading expert called the period terra incognita.[4] In the twenty years since then, we have not made much progress. After some reflection we might come up with a modest list of novels, most of which represent exceptions to the general fare:

Hans Jakob Christoffel von Grimmelshausen, *Der abenteuerliche Simplicissimus teutsch* (1669)

Christian Reuter, *Schelmuffsky, Curiose und sehr gefährliche Reisebeschreibung zu Wasser und Lande* (1696)

Johann Gottfried Schnabel, *Wunderliche Fata einiger See-Fahrer . . . Insel-Felsenburg* (1731–43)

Johann Michael von Loen, *Der redliche Mann am Hofe* (1740)

Christian Fürchtegott Gellert, *Das Leben der schwedischen Gräfin von G**** (1747)

In literary histories these works are usually considered as high points in an otherwise uninteresting period and atypical of the state of the art. However, these titles represent only the tip of an iceberg. Many novels were written in the late seventeenth and early eighteenth centuries. Between 1670 and 1724, for example, 315 original novels and 151 translations of foreign ones were published. Although the combined figure of 466 does not compare all that favorably with novel production in France, where 347 novels were published in the twenty years between 1680 and 1699, and although the German figure of 466 represents less than 3.2 percent of the absolute book production in the last quarter of the century, the 466 novels signify a relatively high figure for the fifty-five-year period in Germany.[5] The implication of a relatively high production rate is underscored when we consider that the reading public around 1700 numbered only about eighty thousand persons, drawn mainly from the lower nobility, patrician, and artisan classes, and predominantly university trained. Of that number, probably only a few thousand were potential novel readers, many of them university students. Thus only a very small portion of the German populace (estimated at twenty million) was engaged in novel reading. But they were apparently very active readers.[6]

Concurrent with the rise of the novel from approximately 1670 is the phenomenal rise of periodic literature, especially of the moral weekly. Wolfgang Martens estimates that there were about 230 moral weeklies published in Germany in the eighteenth century.[7] Although other forms of journals were founded in the course of the century, the moral weekly was one of the earliest types, experiencing a flowering between about 1720 and 1760. Additionally, it was aimed at a general, middle-class audience. In other words, the moral weeklies began their rise more or less simultaneously with increased activity in the novel, coinciding to a large degree with the numerous imitations of Defoe's *Robinson Crusoe*.[8] The interconnection between the moral weekly and the novel form is especially intriguing, one in need of detailed study. Obviously that interconnection must figure prominently in an examination of the spread of early Enlightenment thought, since both kinds of writing coincide with the ascendancy of the middle class and its moral-social values.

Finally, the concept of "gallant style," which originally referred to the polished manners and correct demeanor of aristocrats toward others, especially women, underwent important connotational changes between 1670 and 1750. These shifts in meaning are mirrored not only in the novel but also in the moral weeklies and theoretical writings of the time. Thus the concept can serve as a unifying focus in my deliberations.

Among the critics who have examined the prose of this period, Eric A. Blackall has attempted to trace the mature German prose style clearly evident after midcentury in the writing of such men as Lessing back to the efforts of the first half of the eighteenth century. His conclusion is important for us: namely, that the first half of the century produced a prose style that followed a middle course between a consciously artistic, extravagant manner and a completely natural, unadorned tenor. The new synthesis was a "plain, lucid style avoiding both flatness and extravagance."[9] Although the gallant mode was a dominant style in early century, Blackall does not accord it a central position in his study of the various kinds of prose writing.

In light of this situation, a reexamination of the question of continuity in the literary development of the prose forms of the late baroque to those of the early Enlightenment would appear to be in order. I will argue that there was a continuous evolution that proceeds from the "decaying" forms of the baroque novel via the popular gallant novel of 1700–1720, and the journalistic writing of the early eighteenth century to the novelistic production of the 1740s and after. Most critics of the novel contend that German prose begins the process of refinement under the influence of English models such as periodicals like *The Spectator* and *The Tatler* and Richardson's novels *Pamela* and *Clarissa*. In fact, it is widely held that the modern German novel is indebted directly to these imports.[10] To them there seems to be a gulf separating the achievements of Grimmelshausen and Johannes Beer on the one hand, and those of Loen, Gellert, and Wilhelm Ehrenfried

Neugebauer on the other. In those brackish waters, however, there was fresh life germinating, life engendered by the "decaying" Baroque novel and first reaching full flower after 1740. The maturation process was promoted by, but was not entirely due to, the literary influx from England. That developing embryo of a "new" literary taste and ideal was contained above all in the so-called "galanter Stil" of the popular novel. Although logical sounding, this assumption of continuity is not widely shared. That is to say: critics generally agree that the moral weeklies prepared a "broad" reading audience via style and theme for the morally tendentious novel after 1740. But they also tend to concur that the gallant novel left no legacy.[11]

In the early part of the eighteenth century we are confronted with a dizzying array of types of novels. In his dissertation on the early bourgeois novel, Max Götz identifies no fewer than eighteen kinds of narrative prose: "Abenteuerroman, Amadis-, Avanturier-, Bildungs-, Brief-, Familien-, Künstler-, Maler-, Reise-, Ritter-und Räuberroman, historischer Roman, Robinsonade, satirischer Roman, Schäfer-, Staats-, Schelmen-, Studenten-, moralischer und sentimentaler Roman."[12] From these he attempts to isolate what he considers to be the most progressive: "der frühbürgerliche Roman," that is, a subcategory of the adventure novel. Since these types are designated for the most part on the basis of content, the list could be continued indefinitely. Obviously a fine division into types is scarcely fruitful to our purposes, especially if the categories are based on extrinsic characteristics that often exist in the elaborate titles alone.[13] We would be better served with more general categories that unite rather than separate, such as "der galante Roman" and "der moralischer Tendenzroman."[14] These two types are based on evolving ideological tendencies within them rather than on form or narrative content alone. Moreover, we should bear in mind that the Enlightenment novel is probably best approached via the question of ethics.[15] What more judicious way to determine the relationship between the gallant novel and the morally tendentious novel than by comparing their ethical ideals (or "seelische Haltungen")?

The most substantial and influential contribution to our understanding of developments in the novel between 1670 and 1700 is Arnold Hirsch's *Bürgertum und Barock im deutschen Roman*.[16] He was the first to demonstrate that the so-called modern novel of the eighteenth century had its roots in the picaresque, anticourtly novel of the late seventeenth century; that is, in such works as Johann Christian Ettner's *Des getreuen Eckharts Medicinischen Maul-Affens Erster Theil* (1694); Johann Kuhnau's *Der Musicalische Quack-*

Salber (1700); and Johann Beer's *Der Verliebte Österreicher* (1704). Additionally, many of Christian Weise's novels (most notably *Der politische Näscher*, 1678) and of Johann Riemer's works (e.g., *Der politische Maul-Affe*, 1679) could be considered in this same connection. This particular strain, however, seems to have died out around 1700 and only reemerged in a muted form around 1720 under the influence of Defoe.[17]

From the outset Hirsch intended to describe a "second wave of 'middle-class' novels" written between 1700 and 1720 and which represented a kind of continuation of the first wave of "verbürgerlichter Romane" occurring between 1670 and 1700. The second study was to have traced the descent of the courtly-historical (also known as "heroic-gallant") novel of the baroque style into a supposed world of relative values and trivial, erotic love affairs in which adaptability was the highest virtue. That "degenerate" form of the baroque novel was the gallant novel. Unfortunately, exile and the Second World War prevented Hirsch from following through with his plan.[18]

Coincidentally, Heinrich Tiemann completed his dissertation on the gallant novel under the direction of Fritz Brüggemann at about the same time that Hirsch was finishing his study of the picaresque form. Entitled *Die heroisch-galanten Romane August Bohses als Ausdruck der seelischen Entwicklung in der Generation von 1680 bis 1710*, his study endeavors to trace attitudinal changes in the "Welt- und Lebensanschauung" of Bohse, but also of Eberhard Werner Happel, Riemer, Hunold, Georg Christian Lehms, and Johann Leonhard Rost. Through an analysis of several gallant novels, Tiemann successfully demonstrates that the generation of writers 1680–1710 gradually moved from a fatalistic to an optimistic view of man's lot in the world. Additionally, the protagonists of the novels examined begin to place ever greater emphasis on a subjective, contemplative life that proved more sensitive to the beauty of nature and the quiet promptings of the heart. The resultant candor in human relations stands in contrast to the previous ideal of political manipulation and vindictiveness. Tiemann concludes: "Decidedly new is the rejection of political activity; the new goal is a completely relaxed attitude; the exercising of patience is the highest ideal."[19] Although this reorientation was not completed until well into the eighteenth century, one is justified in speaking of a growing reliance on feeling, a kind of "Vorsubjektivismus," in the period 1680–1710.[20] One of the most salient features of this attitudinal shift is the preservation of virtue as the new motive for "political" action instead of the desire for revenge or for personal advancement.[21] The result of all these changes is to place the personal and social values of the high baroque in a skeptical light while foreshadowing ideals of the Enlightenment.

189

Herbert Singer picked up where Hirsch left off, but not where Tiemann left off. In his two books on the gallant novel—*Der galante Roman* (1961) and *Der deutsche Roman zwischen Barock und Rokoko* (1963)—Singer takes little note of Tiemann's work, according it no critical analysis. Singer endeavors to bridge the gap in the history of the novel between the last novels of Johann Beer (c. 1700) and the ascendancy of the robinsonade and the moral weeklies (i.e., after c. 1720). The focus of his studies is the gallant novel, which flowered between 1700 and 1720 and then rapidly died out. Singer thus comes to the same conclusion concerning the "non-continuity" of the gallant novel as Richard Alewyn had reached regarding Johann Beer's "Folgenlosigkeit" or Hirsch's conclusions regarding the "sudden death" of the political novel (Riemer, Weise) around 1700.[22] There seems to have been a lot of discontinuity going on in the first part of the century!

Singer is unable to detect a continuing, vital tradition of the gallant novel after 1720, stating that there is a "missing link" between Hirsch's "first wave of bourgeois novels" and the modern, psychological, middle-class novel of the post-1740 era.[23] Nevertheless, he concludes that there is "an unmistakeable congruity of numerous characteristics of the gallant novel with those of Wieland's narrative art—despite the historical break in continuity."[24] The gap 1720–40 is filled, Singer continues, by the moral weeklies which, however, can scarcely be considered the missing link—although they appealed to the same kind of reading public as the gallant novels at the beginning of the century—because of their supposed rejection of the gallant novel.[25] Consequently, he is unable to explain how those salient characteristics of the gallant novel survived to the 1760s and Wieland. But what if the moral weeklies *were* a missing link in the continuity of narrative prose from Beer to Loen, Gellert, and beyond? What if the moral weeklies were not as ill disposed toward the gallant novel as is generally thought?

Dieter Kimpel remarks in his *Der Roman der Aufklärung* (1977) that Singer's attempt to trace the domestication of the cavalier novel produced "unexpectedly modest results."[26] Kimpel suggests that the outcome was less than satisfactory because the novels examined are so inaccessible. Like Kimpel I am startled at Singer's early disclaimer that the novels of the early eighteenth century are "historically insignificant and aesthetically unimportant" and that to study them is an exercise in "the science of that which is not worthy of being known."[27] I agree with Kimpel that we must guard against treating the gallant novel and other narrative forms from the late baroque lightly because they would appear to be an art form in decline.[28] Singer seems intent only upon demonstrating that the gallant novel was a short-lived genre. For example, he repeats Alewyn's view that Beer's progressively bourgeois novels were unique and untypical, implying that they (like the "political" novel) are therefore of no consequence for the narratives of the early eighteenth century.[29] Hunold's highly successful, extremely popular satire of the gallant lifestyle in Hamburg, his *Satyrischer Roman*, is characterized as an "interesting" book "difficult to categorize because it contains elements of the gallant novel, the adventure story, the scandal sheet, and even pornography." However, it is rejected as inconsequential because it is "an atypical work" of the period, although it was reprinted eleven times between 1706 and 1744.[30] Perhaps there is good reason to downplay the significance of extraordinary works for literary developments. But then why does Singer suggest a new category of novel, the so-called "Komödienroman" (a descendant of the lower line of seventeenth-century style), even though he can locate only one work which bears the marks of this whole new category, Melissus's *Adelphico* (1715)?[31] Why should this singular work, supposedly the purest form of the gallant novel, be any more "typical" than Hunold's *Satyrischer Roman?*

Moreover, Singer argues with Richard Newald that the moral weeklies—in contrast to the novel—were harbingers of the new because they were free of the strictures of tradition. The novel "was surprisingly tenacious in its adherence to traditional forms."[32] In isolation the argument might seem convincing. However, only a few pages earlier Singer had contended that the situation in the novel of the early eighteenth century was extremely confusing because all kinds of genres, "totally alien" to the novel were intermingled with it; for example, satire, historical report, biography, devotional literature, and pamphlets were published under the guise of the novel.[33] In the same vein, he criticizes Hunold's gallant novel, *Adalie* (1702), as being an impure "Komödienroman" because it includes a blatantly moralizing section dealing with the conversion of a shameless miscreant. Such a passage, Singer avers, "has no place in a comic novel and would be much more at home in a devotional work."[34]

Singer's treatment of the gallant novel is only moderately successful because his attempt to isolate a pure form of that type fails. It fails for two reasons: first, he relies too heavily on the aesthetic criteria of the later eighteenth century and, second, not enough novels from the early period fit into the narrow category. Like Max Götz's attempt to discern a genre of "the early bourgeois novel" in certain robinsonades and adventure novels in the years 1720–50, Singer's attempt to identify one kind of gallant novel also miscarries. The shortcomings of both these treatments of the novel in the first half of the eighteenth century are traceable, I submit, to their obsession with the need to categorize everything into narrowly defined classes. The difficulty with trying to identify types is the fact that the novel form was in a definite state of flux. Novelists were not just slavishly following poetic practices of the seventeenth century but were groping for new forms of expression in prose. Because of the increase in motifs and narrative strategies, it is not possible to speak of a "unified form."[35]

In 1906 Max von Waldberg published an informative treatise on the development of the sentimental novel in France during the seventeenth century in the wake of such writers as Madame de La Fayette (*La Princesse de Clèves*, 1675), Madamoiselle Bernard (*Eleonor d'Yvrée, ou les malheurs de l'amour*, 1687), and Madeleine de Scudéry (*Clélie*, 1654–60, *Artamène ou le grand Cyrus*, 1649–53, and *Conversations sûr divers sujets*, 1680).[36] This development is characterized by a growing sensibility to the psychology of the individual and represents a shift of emphasis to private concerns. The growth of sensibility to individual, emotional states complements the tendency of the roman comique (e.g., Charles Sorel, *La vraye Histoire comique de Francion*, 1623; German translation, 1662) to depict antiheroic, courtly attitudes. Singer feels that Waldberg's important study cannot be applied to the German situation between 1670 and 1720 because the novels discussed by Waldberg "apparently found no direct echo in Germany."[37] I would suggest that there is a need to reexamine the possible impact of the emergent psychological novel in seventeenth-century France (e.g., *La Princesse de Clèves*) on the development of the gallant novel in Germany from approximately 1670 on. On the one hand, there is a likely connection between the gallant attitude and psychological sensitivity. It is a connection which Waldberg made and to which Max Götz has drawn attention.[38] On the other hand, there is a relationship between the movement away from the heroic stoicism of the seventeenth-century courts and the emergence of the sentimental burgher, a development greatly advanced by the growth of Pietism. For example, Fritz Brüggemann—following Waldberg's lead— had argued such a metamorphosis of attitudes in his influential study, "Der Kampf um die bürgerliche Welt- und Lebensanschauung."[39] Brüggemann's attention was focused primarily on the novel around 1730, predominantly on Schnabel's *Insel-Felsenburg*. However, as implied by Götz (for the adventure novel) and Tiemann (for Bohse and his generation), this development is discernible even earlier. In Hunold's *Satyrischer Roman*, for example, we find extended reflections on the nature of true love (prompted by graveyard musings) which are best expressed in terms of "edle Liebe" and which would seem to foreshadow the sublimated love of a later "schöne Seele" (Iphigenie, Maria Stuart). Moreover, we also encounter an interpretation of "Galanterie" as being complementary to virtue.[40]

In wishing to place greater emphasis on Waldberg's approach than

Hirsch, Singer, or Jacobs have done, I am aligning myself with Ernst Weber, who feels that the importance attached to the English influence for the emergence of the modern German novel has tended to overshadow the equal significance of an "indigenous" tradition.[41] In his investigation Weber allots special status to theoretical reflections on the nature of the novel between 1700 and 1750.[42] It is not my intent to deny Richardson, Fielding, and Sterne, among others, their just distinction as stimulators of a first-rate novelistic literature in Germany, but rather to place the early history of the German novel in proper perspective. Thus there is a need to reiterate the argument that the "modern" novel, which is marked by qualities of "sentimentality" and domesticity, experienced a continuous, gradual development in Germany, first under the influence of the French model, then under the impact of the English novel. Because "sensibilité" is associated with the emotion of love, the concept of gallantry and its expression in the gallant novel is central to any study proposing to trace the roots of the Enlightenment novel.

Thus, we might do well to take seriously the gallant novelist's statement of intent as formulated in his prefaces. One such salient remark concerning the earnest aspect of the *Satyrischer Roman* (1706) is found in Hunold's introduction to the *Academische Neben-Stunden* published seven years later in 1713. Here Hunold refers emphatically to the morally didactic intent of his earlier work, especially in the graveyard scene where the lovelorn hero, Selander von Amalienburg, is confronted with the reality of death. The tombstone inscriptions cause Selander to review in a dialogue with his own soul the connotations of love. The author's purpose in presenting this "inner monologue" is didactic, "because the reader is induced to reflect upon the consequences of vanity, and that was [the work's] main purpose."[43] Regarding the well-made novel in general, Hunold cites the need for variety in order to maintain the reader's interest. Above all, he concludes "such a work must prove edifying by dint of the interpolated moral lessons, the behavior of the personae, the unusual descriptions, the retribution of vice, the chaste narrative style, and by dint of scrupulous character delineation."[44] The recitation of these "modernistic" qualities by one of the greatest practitioners of the gallant novel tends to lend greater substance to the art itself.

An echo of these conceptions, derived from the actual practice of them, is found in Johann Leonhard Rost's (Meleaton) remarks in the preface to his gallant novel, *Der verliebte Eremit Oder des Gravens von Castro Lebens und Liebes-Geschichte Der Galanten Welt in einem Roman* (reprinted five times between 1711 and 1741). After praising Menantes's (Hunold's) esprit and style, which he has tried to emulate, Rost suggests that any book written in that manner is worthy of serving as a conduct guide to young readers who do not intend to stay tied to mother's apron strings.[45] Furthermore, he indicates that his enraptured *Hermit* is intended for middle-class as well as aristocratic readers, for the charm of its diction and flow of language cannot help but "appeal to the high and the low."[46] The mention of the middle class implies the increased participation of that group in literary life as consumers and potential models.

There is no doubt, for example, that middle-class representatives began to play major roles in narrative fiction around 1740 and that moralizing works such as *Pamela* and *Der redliche Mann am Hofe* pursued a clearly didactic purpose. Richardson and Loen hoped to benefit their readers by offering them models for virtuous and refined behavior. We would do well in this regard to recall that the didactic strain of the Enlightenment novel is—as research on the theory of the novel has demonstrated—a direct result of the theories of the nature and purposes of the novel as expounded during the seventeenth and early eighteenth centuries.[47] Thus we should probably treat with some skepticism Singer's claim that the gallant novel had no impact after 1720.[48]

A peripheral concern of M. Götz's study of the early bourgeois novel is highly relevant in this regard. In noting a bourgeois "domestication" of the gallant novel especially when placed in a university town setting, Götz provides fuel for an argument to assign the gallant novel in general and the student variation in particular a pivotal role in the development of a modern novel form.[49] Götz perceives the essential qualities of the gallant novel to be an extensive use of dialogue and letters in depicting the vissicitudes of two lovers who ultimately achieve an operatic happy ending with all their friends and acquaintances assembled. In depicting the lovers' exploits, gallant authors of the student novel show a marked preference for familiar scenes drawn from bourgeois life and reveal a growing awareness of the complexity of the human personality.[50] Although the gallant novel, such as Hunold's *Adalie* or his *Satyrischer Roman* with its student milieu, cannot be strictly equated with the likes of *Der redliche Mann am Hofe* and *Pamela*, the qualities of the former would seem to point forward to similar characteristics of the latter.[51]

Finally, with regard to the early reflections on the nature of the gallant novel in general, I want to take a close look at Christian Thomasius's views on the subject. His opinions are doubly important, since he was not only the "father of the Enlightenment" but also an astute literary critic. Together with Pierre-Daniel Huet (*Traité de l'origine de roman*, 1670; translated into German in 1682 by E. W. Happel), Thomasius stands at the beginning of an intense debate concerning the relationship of the novel to the wondrous on the one hand and to history on the other.[52] Important milestones in this discussion, which reached a high point in Germany with Blanckenburg's *Versuch über den Roman* (1774), were Du Plaisir's *Sentiments sur l'histoire* (1683) and Abbé Lenglet du Fresnoy's *L'Histoire justifiée contre le roman* (1735). However, I will focus on Thomasius's ideas as seminal to the role of the gallant novel within that overall controversy.

Writing in his journal, *Freymütige Lustige und Ernsthaffte iedoch Vernunfft- und Gesetz-mäßige Gedancken: Oder Monats-Gespräche*, Thomasius published his views on the personal and social benefit of novel reading. His various comments—published in January 1688, and in August-September 1689—revolve around two basic questions that are central to our undertaking: (1) what kinds of novels are there and (2) what are the appropriate qualities in a good novel? In pursuing his subject, Thomasius intends to argue "that we cannot write anything more useful and simultaneously more amusing than decorous tales of love in the German tongue modelled on any number of famous novels of this type."[53] Acknowledging that there is no disagreement concerning the entertainment value of novels, he sets about his task of demonstrating that they are useful as well. He begins by differentiating between two broad categories.

Whereas the first group is made up of brief love stories that follow the tribulations of just one pair of lovers (such as the French novels presumably written in the wake of *La Princesse de Clèves*), the second group is composed of those works that treat the history of an entire nation. The latter works entail a confusing series of interrelated tales and episodes. Both kinds of novel are similar in that "they not only please the imagination by their inventive ploys, but also sharpen the reader's understanding. Thus it can be expected that frequent reading of such books will lead to the acquisition of knowledge which the reader can apply with benefit to everyday situations" (*TuT*, 1:44). If the novel is to prove useful as well as amusing, Thomasius emphasizes, both kinds of narrative require substantial poetic genius.

In order for his work to be beneficial, a novelist must abide by the principles of verisimilitude, and that is not easy. It is more difficult to come up with something entirely new yet plausible than it is to retell an actual occurrence. In addition to the historian's ability to perceive relationships and structure experiences, therefore, the novelist must also possess the ability to create fictional realities that seem as convincing as the real thing. The implicit goal for the writer of fiction is to write in such a manner that the reader cannot distinguish between fact and fiction in his composition (*TuT*, 1:44). Moreover, Thomasius asserts that the poetic element enhances the utility of the composition because it draws more on examples and images than on rules. The imagery stimulates the reader's imagination and causes him immediately to comprehend the author's intention. Consequently, novel reading proves in the long run to be more beneficial to the young reader than straight expository writing. The educational value of a novel rises, therefore, in relation to the amount of creative exertion on the novelist's part, for his talent determines the degree of judicious integration of "political, moral, even philosophical and theological discourses" in the narrative fabric (*TuT*, 1:45). Imperceptibly, the reader learns to appreciate this harmonious union of charm and instruction. Because he is enticed by the author's poetic inventiveness to read on, even to reread works of that nature, the reader stands to gain "greater benefit from the reading of these love stories than from studying other kinds of writing" (*TuT*, 1:44). In short, well-written novels are instruments of instruction. Those who stand to profit the most are those young people "addicted" to novels who would otherwise not be exposed to any kind of moral or intellectual improvement but for the interpolated discourses, for it would never enter their minds to study didactic treatises on learned subjects.

And what novels would Thomasius place in this august category? He lists Andreas Heinrich Buchholtz's *Hercules and Herculiscus* as an exemplary novel of integration. In it we find a history of the Thirty Years War plus the whole scale of theological and philosophical discussion (45). Additionally, he mentions Johann Philip Ferdinand Pernauer's adaption (1688) of La Calprenède's *Faramond* (1661–70), Barclay's *Argenis* (in Opitz's translation of 1626), and several others. However, the best examples of the longer novel are Duke Anton Ulrich's *Die Durchleuchtige Syrerinn Aramena* (1669–73) and *Die Römische Octavia* (1685–1707). *Aramena*, the Old Testament story of the three patriarchs (Abraham, Isaac, Jacob), is praised for its treatment of ancient customs and manners and for its depiction of virtuous as well as wicked behavior among the high and the low (*TuT*, 1:45). *Octavia*, for its part, encompasses the whole of Roman history as told by Suetonius, Tacitus, Dio, Velleius Paterculus, and others.

All these views on the novel Thomasius presents through Herr Christoph, one of the regular interlocutors in the *Monats-Gespräche*. What is striking about his argument is its similarity to the more mature dicta of a Blanckenburg, a J. C. Wezel, or a Wieland in the later stages of the Enlightenment. The most notable criteria of the well-written novel cited by Thomasius in 1688 are as follows:

1. Its fulfillment of (Horace's) demand for improvement as well as amusement (*delectare et docere*).

2. The instruction mediated by the novel is of a practical nature, applicable to the reader's own life.
3. The assertion that novel reading is capable of refining the reader's critical acumen.
4. The demand that the causal relationships apparent in the flow of historical events be reflected in the fictive work; that is, the standard of verisimilitude must be observed.

Although we can acknowledge the fact that Thomasius developed his ideas of the purpose of the novel from his study of various kinds of prose fiction, we should also bear in mind that Madame de Scudéry, who was very popular in Germany at the end of the seventeenth century and was cited as an authority by Thomasius himself, had formulated similar views on the need for social and psychological authenticity in the novel.[54] Her opinions were based more on the practice of the novel in the wake of *La Princesse de Clèves* than on her own more remote *Clélie* and *Cyrus*. Scudéry's remarks on the novel are to be found in her *Conversations sur divers sujets* (1680).[55]

Toward the conclusion of his initial discussion of the relationship between the novel and history, Thomasius elaborates upon the standard of authenticity. Regarding the shorter love novels assigned to category one, Thomasius contends—through his spokesman, Herr Christoph—that the advantage of this shorter form over its more intricate sister, the courtly historical novel, lies in its greater psychological detail. The focusing on two lovers under stress "allows the reader an opportunity to study the workings of their psyche" (*TuT*, 1:46). In the long run, such insights enhance our understanding of political action which to Thomasius's (as well as Christian Weise's) mind appeared most important.[56] Placed in this light, the art of these shorter, amorous tales is comparable to Moliére's. The Frenchman was esteemed as a progenitor of the psychological Tartuffes and Misanthropes.[57] Therefore, Thomasius's concluding shift to psychological verisimilitude is even more remarkable as a distinct foreshadowing of the call for psychological veracity in the later Enlightenment under the shadow of such writers as Richardson, Rousseau, Diderot, Fielding, and Sterne.

Perhaps most notable for our purposes is the fact that this early defense of the novel form is formulated by an unmistakeable representative of the middle class: Herr Christoph, a businessman. After all, the Enlightenment (and its first cousin, Sensibility) attained its full fruition through the support of the "Bürgertum," especially in England and Germany. We need only recall George Lillo's *The London Merchant* or Lessing's *Nathan*.[58]

In August 1689, Thomasius used a review of Lohenstein's *Großmütiger Feld-Herr Arminius oder Hermann* (1689–90) to classify novelists into four separate groups: (1) those who cater to coarser tastes; (2) the creators of literary meringue; (3) the preparers of exquisite dishes for the most discriminating connoisseurs; and (4) the "hot tamale" artists (*TuT*, 1:47–49).

The first group of writers produce nothing of value, for their highly fanciful tales of love and adventure serve no purpose beyond titillating the reader's literary taste buds. And their works—the so-called Volksbücher—lack all sense of decorum. As examples he cites *Melusine*, *Amadis*, and *Ritter Pontus*.[59] For this reason, Thomasius calls them "Sudel-Köche" (bad cooks; *TuT*, 1:47). The second group is likened to court master chefs accomplished in the art of "haut goût" and culinary delicatesse. But, unfortunately, their exquisite dishes are all fluff and outward show, lacking in substance. The third group receives Thomasius' unqualified approbation. They are the masters of wholesome yet tasty delights. Their works are inviting as well as nutritious. In this connection, Thomasius mentions Barclay's *Argenis*, Madame de Scudéry's *Clélie* (1654–60), and Anton Ulrich's *Aramena* and *Octavia*. The most appealing quality of these works is the realism with which the past ages are drawn. For this reason Thomasius recommends them to untraveled readers as a reliable introduction to the ways and manners of the world (*TuT*, 1:48). The fourth class of authors serve their readers sharply seasoned dishes in an effort to whet abated appetites with different kinds of spices. In this class belong Cervantes's *Don Quixote*, Scarron's *Roman Comique*, and Charles Sorel's *Francion* (1623–41). Thomasius rejects this last group in favor of the third class because the too explicit depiction of vice and wickedness in satirical writing frequently does the young reader more harm than good (*TuT*, 1:49).

Thomasius's use of the extended metaphor of the novelist as cook further aligns him and his early assessment of the novel with the tenor of High Enlightenment writers and their fare, for the allusion to the author as chef was popular not only with prominent writers like Fielding and Wieland, but also with anonymous popularizers of middle-class values like the author-publisher of the moral weekly, *Der Mensch*.[60]

Even more fruitful for our purposes is the review of Eberhard Werner Happel's (1647–90) novel of gallant romance, *Africanischer Tarnolast* (1689), published in the *Monats-Gespräche* in September 1689. Happel's exotic tale of two lovers on the African continent serves Thomasius as a springboard into a discussion of what topics are appropriate in a novel, even a gallant one. In the popular style of the *Monats-Gespräche*, the views on the subject are rendered in dialogic style. Thomasius's spokesman grants that a book can never find universal acclaim. Although he and a friend read *Tarnolast* together, they had decidedly differing reactions. His friend rejected the novel as not true to life, as fanciful. By implication Thomasius informs us that that particular reader rejected the novel because it did not fit into the scheme of the gallant novel as then practiced. Thus its themes and descriptions were inappropriate. Asked what then *was* appropriate to this kind of novel, the interlocutor replied: that which has been done by other "galante Autoren" (*TuT*, 1:50). Conversely, the fact that Happel had not tread the trodden path was precisely the quality that so appealed to Thomasius's spokesman.

The alter ego's first argument is that his opponent's rule-bound orientation curtails the right of an author to innovate. What right does one poet have to prescribe form and theme to any other poet? Hans Sachs is cited as an example of a poet who did not fit the classic mold but is nevertheless considered a classic. The objection that Hans Sachs was a cobbler by profession, not a poet, is shrugged off as immaterial. Style and theme in the novel are an individual matter and are more or less unlimited in scope.[61]

The second main objection to Happel's novel is psychological in nature. Specifically, the objection is raised that Tarnolast, a prince by birth and education, frequently speaks and acts in "a manner more suitable to the low born" ("und schicke sich eher vor einen Kerl von geringer Extraction," *TuT*, 1:51). Through his spokesman, Thomasius replies that, on the contrary, such characterization epitomizes Happel's artistic talent, for he depicts his hero "as a genuine 'politician' and a man for all seasons who is capable of adapting to those conditions in which he finds himself" ("als einen rechten Politicum und omnium horarum hominem, der sich allezeit nach dem Zustande richtet, darinnen er lebet," *TuT*, 1:52). (The echoes of contemporary ideas regarding public behavior [Christian Weise's "politicus"] and "ius decorum" [Thomasius's] are clearly audible in this passage.) Consequently, Tarnolast acts entirely appropriately for his various roles as prince, slave, lutist, ordinary foot soldier, knight, young scholar, lover, and so forth. The guiding principle is fidelity to human nature, which is everywhere the same; human weakness is as much at home among the very high as among the very low (*TuT*, 1:52).

This latter claim leads to the further objection that novels should depict the ideal not the real: "Aber doch, streuete mein Freund ein, soll man in Romanen nicht das vorstellen quid fiat, sed quid fieri debeat, und also allezeit eine ideam hominis perfectissimi im Sinne haben" (*TuT*, 1:53). In rather amusing fashion, Thomasius's representative parries this new thrust. Fine, he retorts, but do these "ideas" have to be so subtle that they can nowhere be found in real life? What good is gained, he continues, by a slew of "entia rationis" which have no counterpart in reality: "Was [hülfe es] einem Politico, wenn er gleich des Platonis libros de Republica auswendig könte, und könte die Bürger, die darzu gehöreten, nirgend als in des Mori Utopia antreffen. . . ?" (*TuT*, 1:53). For this reason Thomasius concludes his argument with a plea for moderation in the demand for the depiction of the ideal in art: "Man müste freylich vorstellen quid fieri debeat, aber auch zugleich bedacht seyn, quid fieri possit, und homo perfectissimus wäre nicht perfectissimus, wenn er nicht zugleich homo bliebe" (*TuT*, 1:53). This argument is strikingly similar to the idealism versus realism debate fought out in the later eighteenth century (*Der Mensch*, Neugebauer, Bodmer/Breitinger, Wieland, Merck, among others). A perfect description of man must necessarily include human imperfections. In fact, Thomasius adds as the clincher the assertion that novels which depict only perfect people cause more harm than good since young people are frustrated by their inability to achieve the fictional ideal in their own lives (*TuT*, 1:53). In Wilhelm Ehrenfried Neugebauer's *Der teutsche Don Quichote* (1753), now widely recognized as an early example of the modern German novel, we find a parallel argument: ". . . ein Roman muß den Menschen und seine Leidenschaften zum Original haben: er schildere ihn nach der Natur, oder so wie er ist, allezeit sich selbst gleich, er sey tugend- oder lasterhaft."[62] However, Neugebauer took his lead not from Thomasius, but rather from Marivaux and Prévost (who in turn were following de Scudéry and de LaFayette!).[63] Regarding Thomasius's warning that unattainable models of virtue can pose problems for the inexperienced, we need only recall the skepticism which met the appearance of Richardson's *Pamela* on many fronts (cf., for example, Fielding's caustic satire, *Shamela* [1741]).

Analogous to his argument for psychological verisimilitude in characterization, Thomasius defends Happel's exotic milieu and social descriptions as logical and appropriate (*TuT*, 1:54–55). In doing so he appeals to his reader's common sense ("gesunder Menschenverstand"), citing cultural differences among Western European nations to underscore his point. For example, he comments: "Hier zu Lande wäre ein Leben, wenn ein artig Frauenzimmer eine Toback-Pfeiffe im Munde hätte; in Engelland wäre es grand mode" (*TuT*, 1:55). We think nothing of ridiculing the country bumpkin, he continues, who can conceive of the opulent wealth and majesty of the king only in naive terms of the very modest standard of living of the local country squire. There is, of course, no comparison. By extension, Thomasius avers, we readily criticize the description of Oriental and African customs as exotic and untrue to life solely because *we* are accustomed to *European* ways. In judging Happel's descriptions in *Africanischer Tarnolast*, therefore, we must guard against applying European standards to non-European cultures. As in the case of his argument regarding the art of characterization, Thomasius also calls for realism in the depiction of external circumstances. The poet's cardinal preoccupation in creating a novel must be with authentic psychological and sociological description. Only by observing this dictum will a novel assume appropriate form and prove beneficial to the reader.

It is truly striking how similar Thomasius's views of 1689 on the composition and function of the novel are to the perceptions of other literary critics and novelists ranging from Madame de LaFayette and Huet to Blanckenburg and Wieland. The innovative feature of Thomasius's ideas of greatest consequence in the emergence of so-called Enlightenment ideals is the realism of the characters peopling the novelist's world. The distance between reader and character is greatly reduced. Superhuman monarchs are replaced by the Tarnolasts who convincingly play middle- and lower-class roles. As a result, the social barriers to identification between the reader and the hero are gradually broken down. This demythologizing of characters is clearly evident in Thomasius's positive review of Happel's gallant novel long before 1740. Moreover, an investigation of Hunold's gallant novel, *Die liebens-würdige Adalie* (1702, 1714, 1731, 1752), has demonstrated the further humanization of the love story. In *Adalie* the German prince, Rosantes, falls in love with the merchant's daughter, Adalie, and eventually marries her. The Cinderella-like rise of a commoner to the rank of duchess is considered unprecedented at the time in the late baroque courtly novel. In addition the miscreant, Curton, is ultimately won over to virtue when confronted with the reality of death.[64] Surely we must attribute some significance as well to the fact that Hunold's adaption of the theme went through four reprintings, while the French original, Sieur Jean de Prechac's "histoire galante et veritable," *L'illustre Parisienne* (1679), was translated several times into German (1680, 1686, 1722, 1734). Apparently, the German reading public found the topic rather intriguing.[65]

Perhaps we can find an explanation for the clear popularity of the theme in Thomasius's explanation for preferring the shorter type of novel, which deals with the experiences of two lovers. That preference is rooted in his perception that all men partake of a universal equality regardless of one's station in life. Thomasius remarked: "Men are after all men and even the greatest of heroes is still subject to human frailty. They eat, drink, sleep, experience feelings of hate, love, anger, etc., just like other people. It would not be quite right, therefore, to depict heroes in those novels as if they had scarcely any human quality about them. Thus we are compelled to praise Herr Happel for consistently drawing his heroic characters complete with their human frailty" ("Menschen wären allezeit Menschen, und auch die grösten Helden wären menschlichen Schwachheithen unterworfen. Sie ässen, träncken, schlieffen, liebten, hasseten, erzürneten sich, u.s.w. wie andere Leute. Solcher gestalt aber wäre es ja gantz nicht recht, daß man die Helden in denen Romanen fürstellte, als wenn sie beynahe nichts menschliches an sich hätten; und sey dannenhero der Herr Happel vielmehr zu loben, daß er von seinen Helden überall Menschheit vorblicken lassen" [*TuT*, 1:52–53]). The new catchword is "Menschheit," and it obviously points forward to an essential ingredient of Enlightenment thought. I cannot help but be reminded of the social misalliance which is at the root of Richardson's *Pamela* and of the heroine's insistence on her human dignity. Although a conduct book in the guise of a novel, *Pamela* does recount in essence the Cinderella-like rise of a lower-class girl to the highest aristocratic circles. Perhaps Richardson's novel was an immediate success in Germany because the German reading public had been schooled on the likes of Hunold's *Adalie*. A comparison of the two novels would surely turn up many parallels right down to the use of letters, intrigue, the sudden alteration of the miscreant into a man of consummate virtue, the use of the death (or suicide) motif to reinstate a character's equilibrium, and the happy ending with the entire cast assembled. There are, of course, major differences, but they should not blind us to the similarities. With regard to the importance of the criterion of "Menschheit" in the theory of the novel and social mores, we need only recall the premise of Blanckenburg's *Versuch über den Roman* (1774), namely that the novel as the "bürgerliche Epopöe" treats of the "Mensch" not the "Bürger."[66]

Historians of the gallant novel have largely ignored Thomasius's views on the genre. Instead, they tend to follow the lead of the Swiss Calvinist pastor, Gotthard Heidegger, who vociferously polemicized against the evils of the novel form (especially the novel of love) in his famous *Mythoscopia Romantica* (1698). The entire category of the gallant novel is judged by the undeniably large number of poorly executed, superficial treatments of the love theme. A great number of erotic tales of intrigue were composed in the early stages of the eighteenth century that do warrant labels such as insipid, trivial, or even distasteful. However, Singer and his followers have failed to distinguish between two very important aspects of the gallant style. In his criticism of Singer's work, Kimpel argues cogently for a differentiation between gallant style as a theory of social education and gallant style as a fashionable literary mode.[67] If we were to observe this distinction, we would have little trouble in discerning a parallel between the serious intent of novels written in the gallant mode and the educational designs of the moral weeklies. We would also have less difficulty in accepting the claims of authors in their prefaces that they wrote their novels for the moral, social, and/or intellectual improvement of their readers.

Christian Thomasius is important to us not only because of his judicious reviews of late seventeenth-century novels, but also because of the connection he saw between novel reading, the acquisition of a gallant attitude, and the perfection of the social graces. This movement toward the practice of social graces is not devoid of a substratum of virtue. This later point is revealed on several occasions when Thomasius addressed himself to the question of the "galant homme" (i.e., man of honor)[68] in lectures at the University of Leipzig. In passing, I might remark that the fact that we find these discussions imbedded in university lectures would indicate that the question was a serious matter. Moreover, the titles of many of these lectures point to an earnest aspect of polite behavior in the gallant mode. For example, a lecture of 1689 in which Thomasius claims to treat the topic of gallantry for the first time in systematic fashion is entitled: "Christian Thomasius eröffnet Der Studerenden Jugend Einen Vorschlag, Wie er einen jungen Menschen, der sich ernstlich fürgesetzt, Gott und Welt dermahleins in vita civili rechtsschaffen zu dienen, und als ein honnet und galant homme zu leben, binnen drey Jahre Frist in der Philosophie und singulis Jurisprudentiae partibus zu informieren gesonnen sey."[69] The title openly speaks of the acquisition of social graces as essential to a life of virtue; that is, a "honnet und galant homme" is suited to serve God and man in an honorable way. A later lecture of 1693 draws an even more distinct parallel between Christ's teachings and the life of a "galant homme."[70]

But already in his celebrated inaugural lecture of 1687 in Leipzig, Thomasius raised the issue of "galanterie," expressing his dismay at the widespread misuse of the term "galant," which was being used to describe all sorts of things such as dogs and cats, slippers, tables and benches, quills and ink, and who knows what else.[71] Appropriately used, the term describes that social behavior which derives from a combination of "understanding, learning, a sense of good judgment, politeness, and a cheerful disposition which abhors all stiffness, affectation and coarse bluntness."[72] In sum, gallant behavior is based on the golden mean and is integrally related to a commonsense, rational way of life. Instead of imitating the French willy-nilly in externals, Thomasius contends, the Germans should adopt above all the essence of the graceful manner so characteristic of the Gauls. He considers that essence to be "honnéte [*sic*] Gelehrsamkeit, beauté d'esprit, un bon goût und galanterie." When all these "individual parts" are combined in one person, the ideal of "the perfect, wise man" is realized.[73] The "galant homme" in the world of the novel is a descendant of the

22

"parfait homme sâge." The term "homme galant," on the other hand, designated the degraded, trivialized version of the ideal.

Four years later, in 1693, Thomasius elaborated on the difference between true and false gallantry. The catalyst for his remarks was the pervasive shallow behavior among students toward the fair sex. Thomasius begins by distinguishing three categories of people: animals, men, and Christians, which correspond to three ways of life. He then argues that false gallantry marks only the first category: animals, which is equated to a life of dissolution. Categories two ("men") and three ("Christians") are characterized by true gallantry and correspond respectively to a life of common sense and a life of elegant politeness.[74] On the basis of such distinctions Thomasius develops a whole doctrine of "ius decorum." "Decorum" is the Latin equivalent of French "galanterie"[75] and is later defined as "the soul of human intercourse, a human frailty but not a vice."[76] The clear implication is that "galanterie" in its purest form is a social and moral good, but when misused leads man away from the path of virtue. The distinction strikes me as significant for a judicious appraisal of the nature of the gallant novel between 1700 and 1720 and for its relationship to the moral weeklies and Enlightenment novels having a moral tendency, such as Johann Michael von Loen's *Der redliche Mann am Hofe* (1740). An examination of the intent and style of that novel—widely recognized as the first novel of the German Enlightenment—would reveal the continuity of thought from Thomasius and his contemporaries.[77]

The continuity of development from Thomasius to the likes of *Der redliche Mann* becomes even more manifest when we look at a poetological work such as Benjamin Neukirch's *Anweisung zu Teutschen Briefen* (A Guide to Writing German Letters, 1721), in which the poet defines the gallant style as a felicitous combination of the sagacious, comic, and satiric modes.[78] This combination ultimately expresses a manner of social interaction that clearly foreshadows the ideal of the well-mannered burgher; that is, a person free of pedantry and coarseness.[79] For example, Herr Damis, the idealized virtuous lover in Gellert's *Die zärtlichen Schwestern* (1747) is lauded from the outset as: "Ein Mann, der so vernünftig, so reich und so galant ist . . . und doch ein armes Frauenzimmer heiratet, kann in seiner Wahl mit Recht auf diejenige sehen, die die meisten Annehmlichkeiten hat" (1:i). Moreover, gallant behavior also acts as a social equalizer, for gallant men measure others not according to social station ("Stand") but according to breeding ("Verstand").[80] This latter claim seems to have found literary expression in both *Der redliche Mann am Hofe*[81] and in *Pamela* (especially regarding Pamela's breeding, which is much beyond her age and station and which assures her acceptance in the highest circles). There is much to the argument that the beginning of the Enlightenment novel is best comprehended in terms of a set of ethics. Even those beginnings have their roots in earlier manifestations.

A link between gallant style, the gallant novel, and the moral weeklies must still be established if the chain of continuity from the declining baroque age to the emerging Enlightenment is to be complete. We will have to be content with a few representative examples.

A connection between the practitioners of the gallant style and authors of moral weeklies has already been perceived by critics. Ulrich Wendland has argued persuasively, for example, that the theoreticians and practitioners of the gallant style—most notably Christian Friedrich Hunold and Erdmann Neumeister—were immediate precursors of the stylistic and literary views propounded by Johann Christoph Gottsched.[82] Similarly, Ekkehard Gühne has demonstrated that Gottsched's first moral weekly anticipated the literary and linguistic reforms of the *Critische Dichtkunst* (1740).[83] Wendland is interested neither in the gallant novel per se nor in a comparative study of gallant style and the "loose, Senecan style" of Gottsched's moral weeklies, and Gühne does not deal at all with the possible influence of the gallant style on Gottsched although he does know and does cite Wendland's work on the pre-Gottschedian theoreticians.[84] For his part, Eric Blackall is only peripherally interested in the gallant novel and style despite his commendable delineation of stylistic developments from 1700 to 1770. In fact, he explicitly downgrades the significance of that novel type.[85]

Of the research on the relationship between narrative fiction and the moral weeklies, Wolfgang Martens's *Die Botschaft der Tugend* (1968) is the most acute study. After reviewing innumerable articles from the early journals, he concludes that the moral weeklies all in all rejected the novel form: "With the exception of very few novels, the entire genre is depicted as being unsuitable reading for readers interested in furthering virtue, religion, good breeding, taste, and reason."[86] The only kind of prose narrative considered beneficial is the historical report ("histoire," 505). In fact, the moral weeklies very frequently recommend the study of history as the best means of getting to know the world and eventually, therefore, of mastering the art of living (506). History is a "reservoir of virtuous as well as degenerate deeds and characters from which a reader can learn much" (506). Because of such views, Martens concludes, "actually history is a handbook full of moral truth" (506).

The emphasis placed on historical accounts was an effort designed to stem the reading of novels, especially seductively gallant ones. In addition, the weeklies attempted to present themselves as an alternative to novel reading (cf. the titles listed by Martens, 508). Perhaps it *was* due to these efforts that the type of "galanter Roman" so popular between 1700 and 1720 began to wane after 1720, as Martens and Singer argue.[87] In any event, the moral weeklies did seem to advance the interests of later enlightened novelists by preparing an audience capable of a more psychological and aesthetic taste. Martens concludes his section on the novel and the weeklies by suggesting that the attitude of the journal toward the novel genre began to change around 1745 because of the influx of such foreign novels as Prévost's *Manon Lescaut* and *Paysan parvenu*, Marivaux's *Marianne*, and Richardson's *Pamela* and *Clarissa* (519). Like Singer's argument concerning the significance of the gallant novel, Martens's assessment of the relationship between novel and moral weekly has set the tone for subsequent research.

However, Martens does not address himself to the phenomenon of the continuing wide popularity of the gallant novel after 1720 (as evidenced by the frequent reprintings) and of the robinsonade (cf. 511f.). Nor does he draw attention to the fact that theoreticians of the novel form were as intensely involved in the debate on the relationship between historical and fictional reality as were the authors of the moral weeklies. Although it is customary in novel research to point out the English influence on the German form, no one stresses the fact that *Pamela*, for instance, took its story line from a moral weekly, Addison and Steele's *The Spectator*.[88]

Instead of seeing the relationship between the two writing modes as antipathetic, we might do better to look for reciprocal influences between the two genres, as has been the case in English research.[89] Thus we might argue that not only did the moral weeklies prepare the reading public for the morally tendentious novel after 1740, but that the earlier novel forms, especially the stylistically more adroit shorter form, helped create a receptive audience for the "'loose' manner of Senecan style" adopted by the journals in contrast to the stilted, effusive Ciceronian style of the chancery and university.[90] In his study of the Hamburg moral weekly, *Der Patriot* (1724–26), Jörg Scheibe suggested, for example, that the constitutive factors ensuring the success of the moral weeklies on the continent were already more or less in place by the time Germans began to imitate Addison and Steele's undertaking.[91] Above all, the reading public was prepared to accept the tone and moralizing tendencies of the new breed of journal. Since the German journals prior to the weeklies were so few and geographically restricted, the preparatory influence must have come from other quarters. Although Scheibe does not elaborate on those sources and is himself not concerned with the role of the gallant novel, he does recognize the fact that a receptive audience could not evolve overnight. Scheibe is most impressed by the active reaction of readers to the *Patriot*, and he consequently depicts the creation of a participatory public as a special mark of the moral weeklies.[92] This reaction was evoked, of course, by the choice of style and themes. In this regard, a stylistic comparison of the two forms of prose work, gallant novel and moral weekly, is revealing. Martens and Blackall list the major traits of the "new" journalistic style that allegedly prepared the way for the modern novel. Their major points are that (1) the narrator adopts a personal tone; (2) the characters are fuller, more rounded; (3) there is a tendency toward realistic milieu descriptions; and (4) tales with an Oriental motif are interpolated to emphasize a moral point.[93] Except for the personal narrator, all the other major characteristics were already advocated by Thomasius in his review of Happel's *Tarnolast*.

Martens himself supplies us, paradoxically, with yet another reason to look more closely at the possibility of a reciprocal influence between the early novel and weekly. He pointed out, namely, that the so-called gallant reader was not restricted to reading just gallant novels. He also "consumed" seventeenth-century novels of heroic virtue and idealism (*Octavia*, *Banise*, for example) (501f.). If the presumed dandy was capable of intermingling the sublime and the banal, what would have prevented him from perusing a popular journal as well?

After all, the moral weeklies—for all their preaching and practical teaching—were also known to print discourses on the lofty and the routine side by side. An example of the kind of reciprocity intimated here is provided by Thomasius in his aforementioned discussion of what constitutes a useful book. In arguing that entertaining literature can also be useful, Herr Christoph cited the popular French journal, the *Mercure galant* (1672–1724), as a model of the felicitous intermingling of fact and fancy in the manner of the short novel.[94] Somewhat later in the discussion one of the interlocutors suddenly asks why Herr Christoph is suddenly citing a journal when they are discussing the novel? Herr Christoph replies without missing a beat that the *Mercur galant* is "the most gallant and most ingenious work he could think of."[95] Obviously, the two writing modes must have had common thematic and stylistic elements. Given the ease with which Herr Christoph moved back and forth between journal and novel in 1689, there was probably more ease of interchange between moral weekly and entertaining novel in the period 1714–40 than previously surmised.[96]

Finally, Martens specifically addresses the reaction of the moral weeklies to the phenomena of true and false gallantry in a subchapter entitled

"Galantes Wesen und Äusserlichkeit" (354–70). Citing Thomasius's distinction between authentic and empty gallant behavior, he says that "it is full of the middle-class doctrine of virtue which was later advocated by the popular weeklies" (*Bot.*, 356). He then concludes with a quotation from the journal *Der Mensch*, which states, "On the one hand we call a gallant man an honest, candid, well-behaved and respected individual and that is something very virtuous. On the other hand, the term also designates a ladies' man, a dandified apron-chaser, and in his behavior we can find nothing worthy of praise."[97] The fact that the quotation stems from a moral weekly that only began publication in 1750 attests to the tenacity of the gallant code and to the accuracy of Thomasius's perceptions.[98]

But we need not look to midcentury for a positive appraisal of the benefits of the much maligned social code. Johann Christoph Gottsched recognizes the beneficial value of the gallant style for creating pleasant, useful members of society. On 15 September 1727, Gottsched published an ironic, half-serious proposal in his *Der Biedermann* for attracting students back from a dissipated life in their drinking haunts and whorehouses to a serious pursuit of their academic studies.[99] His proposal is to replace all the dry, pedantic, boring professors at the universities with "gallant, erudite women." The presence of these women on the faculty and in the administration of the universities would certainly be most effective in drawing the masses of students back to the lecture halls. The students would readily leave their dissolute street life and return en masse to diligent pursuit of their studies in an effort to gain the approval of their "gallant 'Professorinnen und Doctorinnen.'" Not only would students pursue their academic goals with zeal, Gottsched suggests, but they would also learn proper manners and moral behavior from the good example of their new mentors. In this ironic vision, Gottsched discerns the essential difference between the false (profligate) and the authentic (virtuous) gallant code outlined by Thomasius in 1693.[100] Gottsched's distinction remains, regardless of how one might interpret his ironic purpose.

Beyond the benefit for the students themselves, other advantages could be realized from such a judicious application of the gallant style. For example, academic positions would become available for those learned women who had no previous prospects for useful employment. And Gottsched leaves no doubt that there were enough qualified women in 1727 who equalled or even surpassed men in erudition and aptitude (1:82). In time other women would be encouraged by the example of these successful, gallant women to seek academic careers, careers hitherto unfairly denied them (1:82). Thus the benefit of combining gallant behavior in its authentic form and academic studies is seen as twofold: (1) boorish, indolent students would begin to pursue their studies with rare enthusiasm and (2) new social opportunities would be created for women whose numbers would perceptibly swell the ranks of the useful and diligent members of society.

Finally, let me cite but one example of the apparent impact of the gallant style on the manner of writing in the moral weeklies. I take an example from Gottsched's *Der Biedermann*. In the twenty-fifth number of the weekly (20 October 1727) Gottsched elaborates upon the style he has chosen for his journal. In so doing he describes two other writing modes then current. The first is a journalistic style, indeed, his own, which seeks an unaffected natural manner of expression (1:97). This manner would appear to be closely related to the French ideals of "clarité, facilité, and simplicité." [101] The second is an "Old Frankish" style, which is a distinct descendent of the Ciceronian ideal of elaborateness. [102] Third, there is the newest fashion in writing, which is highly affected and dependent on foreign words (1:99f.). On the basis of our previous considerations we readily discern a clear similarity between Gottsched's ideal of a natural, balanced writing style and the moderation of the true gallant mode. The second type is unquestionably aligned with late baroque extravagance (e.g., Lohenstein), while the third kind is clearly symptomatic of an affected or false gallantry concerned only with externals and not with the inner person. In other words, the distinction between styles 1 and 3 is the difference between the "galant homme" ("Ehrenmann") and the "homme galant" ("Modekavalier" or "Libertin"). We seem to have here a clear parallel between an important doctrine of the gallant epoch and the urgings of a popular moral weekly.

The only way to determine the ultimate accuracy of the contested thesis of a natural, uninterrupted evolution (read "domestication") of language and ethos in the narrative prose of the late seventeenth to the novel of the eighteenth century is by augmenting the few studies of narrative technique of the period 1670–1750 with additional, comparative studies of authors and their works. Tiemann, Hirsch, and Götz—for all their supposed shortcomings—have shown that an unbiased approach to that period of transition can produce positive results. In this essay, I have endeavored to indicate how their methodologies could be expanded in order to help dissipate the still widely promulgated philosophical and literary view that the transition from Baroque to Enlightenment is marked by discontinuity and contrast. If we bear in mind that the blurring of clear demarcations between the literary genres was characteristic of the spread of Enlightenment, [103] we could better appreciate the significance of such transitional forms as the gallant novel and its relationship to the moral weekly. Moreover, studies of their respective readerships would help determine whether their audiences were as mutually exclusive as hitherto surmised.

NOTES

1. H. M. Moscherosch, *Der Unartig teutsche Sprach-Verderber* (1643), 5: "Wie die Zeiten sind / so sind auch die Wort; und hinwiederumb sie die Wort sind / so sind auch die Zeiten."
2. Friedrich von Blanckenburg, *Versuch über den Roman* (1774; reprint, Stuttgart, 1965), xiii: "Die Romane entstanden nicht aus dem Genie der Autoren allein; die Sitten der Zeit gaben ihnen das Daseyn."
3. See Rolf Grimminger, ed., *Hansers Sozialgeschichte der deutschen Literatur*, vol. 3, no. 1: *Deutsche Aufklärung bis zur Französischen Revolution 1680–1789* (Munich, 1980), 33.
4. Herbert Singer, *Der galante Roman*, 2d ed. (Stuttgart, 1966), 7. In his *Der deutsche Roman zwischen Barock und Rokoko* (Cologne and Graz, 1963), 1–2, Singer speaks of the neglect this period has experienced. Cf. also Arnold Hirsch, *Bürgertum und Barock im deutschen Roman: Ein Beitrag zur Entstehungsgeschichte des bürgerlichen Weltbildes*, 2d ed. (Cologne and Graz, 1957), 1f.
5. For the entire seventeenth century in France the total was 1,220, compared to the total of 553 for Germany between 1615 and 1724. Cf. Alberto Martino, "Barockpoesie, Publikum und Verbürgerlichung der literarischen Intelligenz," *IASL* 1 (1976): 114. See also Marianne Spiegel, *Der Roman und sein Publikum im früheren 18. Jahrhundert, 1700–1767* (Bonn, 1967), 32, and Albert Ward, *Book Production, Fiction, and the German Reading Public: 1740–1800* (Oxford, 1974), 64.
6. Martino, "Barockpoesie, Publikum und Verbürgerlichung," 111–15.
7. Wolfgang Martens, *Die Botschaft der Tugend: Die Aufklärung im Spiegel der deutschen Moralischen Wochenschriften* (Stuttgart, 1971), 162.
8. Max Götz, "Der frühe bürgerliche Roman in Deutschland (1720–1750)." (Ph.D. diss., Munich, 1958), 24, reports that more than forty robinsonades appeared between about 1720 and 1750.
9. Eric A. Blackall, *The Emergence of German as a Literary Language, 1700–1775* (Cambridge, 1959), 149f.
10. See Hans Gerd Rötz, *Der Roman des Barock, 1600–1700* (Munich, 1972), 133; Jürgen Jacobs, *Prosa der Aufklärung: Kommentar zu einer Epoche* (Munich, 1976), 64; Peter Uwe Hohendahl, *Der europäische Roman der Empfindsamkeit* (Wiesbaden, 1977), 65.
11. Singer's dictum (*Deutscher Roman*, 2, 5) that it has proven impossible to substantiate a hypothetical, direct line of development from the novel of the seventeenth century via the gallant novel to the novel form of the age of Goethe has apparently been quite persuasive. A similar argument is found in Spiegel, *Roman und sein Publikum*, 22–31. A notable exception to this view is Dieter Kimpel, *Der Roman der Aufklärung (1670–1774)*, 2d ed. (Stuttgart, 1977), 57–61.

12. Götz, "Früher bürgerlicher Roman," 21, 23.
13. Ibid., 24.
14. Cf. Singer, *Galanter Roman*, 50ff. and Spiegel, *Roman und sein Publikum*, 18–21. See moreover K.-I. Flessau, *Der moralischer Roman: Studien zur gesellschafts-kritischen Trivialliteratur der Goethezeit* (Cologne, 1968), esp. chap. 1.
15. Gerhard Kaiser, *Aufklärung, Empfindsamkeit, Sturm und Drang*, 2d ed. (Munich, 1976), 81.
16. Hirsch's study was first published in 1934 and was reissued with some emendations in 1957 by Singer (cf. v–vi).
17. Cf. Hirsch, *Bürgertum und Barock*, 115–17.
18. Ibid., 3.
19. Heinrich Tiemann, *Die heroisch-galanten Romane August Bohses als Ausdruck der seelischen Entwicklung in der Generation von 1680–1710*. (Ph.D. diss., Kiel, 1932), 75: "Das entscheidend Neue ist die Überwindung des Aktivismus; man strebt nach völlig gelassener Lebenshaltung; Übung in der Geduld ist das höchste Ideal."
20. Tiemann, ibid., 116.
21. Tiemann (ibid., 75–76) discerns three kinds of motivation for "political" action, which correspond to three stages of movement away from a high baroque attitude: (1) desire to inflict injury (pure individualism); (2) desire to procure personal advantage (utilitarianism); (3) desire to preserve virtue (idealism). The motivation for "political" action also mirrors other changes in the writers' world views (e.g., "Naturgefühl, wahre Frömmigkeit").
22. Cf. Singer, *Galanter Roman*, 19.
23. Singer, *Deutscher Roman*, 155.
24. Singer, *Galanter Roman*, 52.
25. Singer, *Deutscher Roman*, 155; Jacobs, 64, avers that the gallant novel contributed to the fall of the novel genre into disrepute; Martens, 357, notes the rejection of extreme forms of gallantry.
26. Kimpel, *Roman der Aufklärung*, 36–37.
27. Singer, *Galanter Roman*, 11: "die Wissenschaft des Nichtwissenswerten."
28. Kimpel, *Roman der Aufklärung*, 39.
29. Singer, *Galanter Roman*, 19; cf. also Singer, *Deutscher Roman*, 1–9.
30. Singer, *Galanter Roman*, 38–39.
31. Ibid., 53–54.
32. Ibid., 23.
33. Ibid., 19.
34. Ibid., 54: "Selbst Hunold . . . scheut sich nicht . . . eine Episode aufzunehmen, die von der Bekehrung eines Bösewichts handelt: ein krasses, überdeutliches Exempel, das im Komödienroman nichts zu suchen hat, vielmehr seinen Platz in einem Erbauungsbuch hätte."
35. Jacobs, *Prosa der Aufklärung*, 64. Wilhelm Vosskamp, *Romantheorie in Deutschland* (Stuttgart, 1973), 121, avers: "Gerade der Roman treibt seine Entwicklung dadurch voran, dass er mit herkömmlichen Formen und Traditionen entschieden zu brechen versucht, und jede 'Krise des Romans' ist eine Voraussetzung seiner Renaissance." Finally, Kimpel (*Roman der Aufklärung*,

42, 45, 52), arguing that classification of the novel is not possible, moves to expand the boundaries of narrative prose.

36. Max von Waldberg, *Der empfindsame Roman in Frankreich* (Strasbourg and Berlin, 1906). For the tradition of the sentimental novel in France before 1600 see Gustave Reynier, *Le Roman sentimental avant L'Astrée* (Paris, 1908). For a consideration of the overall development in our time frame see English Showalter, *The Development of the French Novel, 1641–1782* (Princeton, 1972).
37. Singer, *Galanter Roman*, 17.
38. Götz, "Früher bürgerlicher," 42, 52n. Götz even suggests that August Bohse (1661–1742), the highly successful author of many gallant novels and mentor to Hunold, had early incorporated elements of the French "sensibilité" into his works between 1700 and 1720 (41f.). In his afterword to *Texte zur Romantheorie I (1626–1731)* (Munich, 1974), 624, Ernst Weber notes a distinct parallel between the French and German theories of the novel around the turn of the century.
39. Fritz Brüggemann, "Der Kampf um die bürgerliche Welt- und Lebensanschauung," *DVJS* 3 (1928): 94–127. See also Tiemann, *Heroische-galante*, 115f.
40. Christian Friedrich Hunold, *Satyrischer Roman* (1706; reprint, Bern and Frankfurt am Main, 1973), 97–116 (nature of love) and 79 (gallantry as virtue).
41. Ernst Weber, *Die poetologische Selbstreflexion im deutschen Roman des 18. Jahrhunderts* (Stuttgart, 1974), 16–19. Hirsch, *Bürgertum und Barock*, 2, had argued on the basis of sociological considerations against the assumption that there was no similar development in Germany prior to the influx of English models.
42. Weber, *Poetologische Selbstreflexion*, 19–85. See also Lieselotte E. Kurth, *Die zweite Wirklichkeit: Studien zum Roman des achtzehnten Jahrhunderts* (Chapel Hill, N.C., 1969), 36–64, who includes comparative glances at the novel in both France and England in our time frame. For a discussion of "sentimentality" and the novel esp. after 1750, see Georg Jäger, *Empfindsamkeit und Roman* (Stuttgart, 1969) and Hohendahl, *Europäischer Roman*.
43. "weil der Leser zu erbaulicher Betrachtung der Eitelkeit gezogen wird; und dieses ist das Haupt-Absehen gewesen." Reprinted in Weber, *Texte*, 415.
44. Hunold, *Academische Neben-Stunden*, in Weber, *Texte*, 417.
45. Johann Leonhard Rost, *Der verliebte Eremit* (Jena[?], 1711), v.
46. Ibid., v–vi.
47. Cf., for example, Weber, *Texte;* Vosskamp, *Romantheorie;* Eberhard Lämmert, *Romantheorie* (Cologne/Berlin, 1971); Dieter Kimpel and Conrad Wiedemann, eds., *Theorie und Technik des Romans im 17. und 18. Jahrhundert*, vol. 1: *Barock und Aufklärung* (Tübingen, 1970).
48. Singer (*Deutscher Roman*, 153–54) argues that the "rational, moralistic, and heroic qualities of the French and English style" were alien to the easy manner of the gallant novel. In conjunction with the campaign of the moral weeklies against unreason, insipidity, and superfluity, the French and English qualities allegedly drove the gallant style from the field.
49. Götz, "Früher bürgerlicher Roman," 128. However, Götz was intent upon showing how the gallant novel was unlike the more progressive "early bourgeois novel" of the period 1720–50, which he would see as a prefiguration of

the later "Entwicklungsroman" (see also 131). Hirsch (*Bürgertum und Barock*, 98ff.) also cites progressive features of the novel with student milieu.

50. Götz, "Früher bürgerlicher Roman," 40ff., 140f.

51. Perhaps it would be useful in this regard to compare in greater detail the chief characteristics of the gallant novel with those of the so-called "moralischer Tendenzroman" (Jacobs's "Typ des aufklärerischen Romans," 64). The following summary of the general features of the gallant novel is based on Götz, "Früher bürgerlicher Roman," 43–50; Spiegel, *Roman und sein Publikum*, 11–14; and Hans Wagener, *The German Baroque Novel* (Boston, 1973), 154–57:

1. The social emphasis is that of private love affairs.
2. These involve members of the lower aristocracy and patrician classes with an occasional dipping into the bourgeois, artisan, or agrarian classes.
3. The setting is moved from exotic locales to well-known ones; that is, there is a shift toward greater realism.
4. In place of teleological and cosmological concerns, author and reader are interested in social behavior; gallant novels take on the function of conduct books, yet we do not have true psychological development.
5. The most lauded virtue is commonly that of adapting to new circumstances; virtue is a matter of education, not necessarily of divine origin.
6. Although the old Heliodoric scheme of late antiquity is maintained, the number of characters is greatly reduced.
7. The composition is often very loose and is frequently marked by model epistolary interpolations and dialogic interludes or first-person narrative.
8. The heroic, stoic attitude of the hero in the baroque courtly historical novel gives way to a more human response, one which recognizes man's susceptibility to temptation and fall from virtue.
9. Intrigues are not infrequent.
10. The conclusion is normally a "happy ending" at which all the major characters are gathered to celebrate the final union of the lovers.

The novels from which these traits are drawn are Hunold's *Adalie* and Rost's *Die unglückseelige Atalanta* (1708). The moralizing novel of the Enlightenment is the consequence of a demand for moral veracity and pragmatic applicability (Jacobs, *Prosa der Aufklärung*, 64). It is thus characterized by a shift toward:

1. Verisimilitude of social action and moral behavior within the lower aristocracy and middle classes.
2. The moral improvement of the reader either by providing exemplary models of virtue or frightening examples of extreme vice.
3. Greater psychological delineation of the protagonist whose behavior is motivated primarily by a love relationship; the Heliodoric scheme is still very much intact.
4. Greater use of prefaces and interpolated passages to guide the reader's

interpretation of the novel; the focus is on psychological analysis, and the mixed characters choose the side of virtue.

5. First-person narrative.
6. The ultimate rewarding of virtue and retribution of vice.
7. The narration of the hero's upbringing and early experiences because virtue is considered the result of education.
8. An anticourtly stance: the aristocrats are villains, the virtuous are mostly middle class; the action is removed from the court atmosphere; the happy ending frequently involves a sudden change of heart in the villainous nobleman who marries a commoner and moves to the country.
9. Concrete suggestions for morally upright behavior; the moralizing novel thus assumes the function of a "handbook of morals."

These general characteristics are based on Jacobs (ibid., 64–66) and Spiegel (*Roman und sein Publikum*, 18–21). Despite obvious contrasts, there would appear to be a surprising number of similarities between the two allegedly opposing types of novel.

52. Vosskamp, *Romantheorie*, 72–176, details that debate, according Thomasius special recognition (see esp. 103–120).
53. Christian Thomasius, *Freymüthige Lustige und Ernsthaffte iedoch Vernunfft- und Gesetz-mässige Gedancken Oder Monats-Gespräche* (1688 and 1689) (Halle, 1690). Reprinted in Kimpel and Wiedemann, *Theorie und Technik*, 1:43–56; here, 43. Hereafter cited in the text as *TuT*, with volume and page number.
54. Christian Thomasius, "Christian Thomas eröffnet Der Studierenden Jugend zu Leipzig in Einem Discours, Welcher Gestalt man denen Frantzosen in gemeinem Leben und Wandel nachahmen solle?" (1687), reprinted in Conrad Wiedemann, ed., *Der galante Stil: 1680–1730* (Tübingen, 1969), 1–2.
55. Cf. Waldberg, *Empfindsamer Roman*, 185–88. Scudéry's discourse on the novel is reprinted in Weber, *Texte*, 31–60.
56. Cf. Dieter Kimpel, "Frühaufklärerische Sprachkritik und Literatur, 1670–1730," in Victor Žmegač, ed., *Geschichte der deutschen Literatur vom 18. Jahrhundert bis zur Gegenwart* (Königstein/Ts, 1978), vol. 1, no. 1, esp. 15–31; and Gerhard Sauder, "'Galante Ethica' und aufgeklärte Öffentlichkeit in der Gelehrtenrepublik," in Grimminger, *Hansers Sozialgeschichte*, vol. 3, no. 1, esp. 219–227.
57. *TuT*, 1:46. Cf. Singer's argument regarding the gallant novel having taken its cue from classical French comedy in *Galanter Roman*, 51.
58. This is not to say that France's middle class was ineffective in influencing the direction of literary effort. See, for example, Geoffrey Atkinson, *The Sentimental Revolution: French Writers of 1690–1740* (Seattle and London, 1965), and G. Atkinson and Abraham C. Keller, *Prelude to the Enlightenment: French Literature 1690–1740* (Seattle and London, 1970).
59. Regarding the popularity of these "Volksbücher," see Rötz, *Roman des Barock*, 31–32. The *Amadis* cited by Thomasius surely refers to the adaptions of Garci Rodríguez's famous courtly novel, *Amadís de Gaula*. Cf. Weber, *Texte*, 566, 579.

60. *Der Mensch* (Halle, 1753), 5:401–8 (217. Stück).

61. Cf. *TuT*, 1:51. We must bear in mind that Thomasius offered his views on gallant prose fiction a good ten years before the so-called type reached the status of best seller between 1700 and 1720.

62. Wilhelm Ehrenfried Neugebauer, *Der teutsche Don Quichotte* (1753; reprint, Stuttgart, 1971), 264.

63. Ibid., 263f.

64. Christian Friedrich Hunold, *Die liebenswürdige Adalie* (1702; reprint, Stuttgart, 1967), 328–35. See also Wagener, *German Baroque Novel*, 152–53; Singer, *Galanter Roman*, 39–43; and Singer, *Deutscher Roman*, 29–86.

65. See Singer, *Galanter Roman*, 40.

66. Blanckenburg, *Versuch über den Roman*, xiv–xvii. In this connection we should point out that one of the connotational differences between "gallant" and "political" is that the former is private while the latter is public. Ulrich Wendland, *Die Theoretiker und Theorien der sogen. Galanten Stilepoche und die deutsche Sprache* (Leipzig, 1930), 13, notes: "Kommt es dem homo politicus, der das Ideal des neuen, zeitgemässen Diplomaten ist, in erster Linie auf das öffentliche Leben, die staatsmännische Karriere und das, was heute (im verengten, präzisen Sinn) Politik genannt wird, an, so richtet der galant homme, der vollendete Gesellschaftsmensch und Lebensmeisterer, zunächst sein Augenmerk auf die persönliche, private Lebenstaktik, auf seine eigene Geltung in Gesellschaft und Leben."

67. Kimpel, *Roman der Aufklärung*, 39–40.

68. Cf. Kimpel's equation in ibid., 53, 57.

69. Reprinted in Wiedemann, *Galanter Stil*, 4.

70. *Chr. Thomasens Erinnerung Wegen deren über seine Grund-Lehren, Bissher gehaltenen Lectionum* (1701?), reprinted in Wiedemann, *Galanter Stil*, 22f. Other thinkers drew a close connection between gallant behavior and a Christian life by arguing the complementary nature of the qualities of "justus," "honestus," and "decorus" in the pursuit of happiness, which is intimately bound to the perfection of a Christian life. Cf., for example, Christoph Heinrich Amthor, *Collegium Homileticum de Jure Decori . . .* (1730). Reprinted in Wiedemann, *Galanter Stil*, 6–10.

71. "Christian Thomasius eröffnet der Studierenden Jungend . . . ," in Wiedemann, *Galanter Stil*, 1.

72. Ibid.: ". . . dass es etwas gemischtes sey, . . . aus Verstand, Gelehrsamkeit, einen guten judicio, Höfflichkeit, und Freudigkeit zusammen gesetzet werde, und deme aller Zwang, affectation und unanständige Plumpheit zu wieder sey."

73. Ibid., 4.

74. "Christian Thomas Entbietet der studierenden Jugend in Halle, Seinen Gruss und Dienste . . . (1693)." Reprinted in Wiedemann, *Galanter Stil*, 18.

75. "Christian Thomas eröffnet der Studierenden Jugend . . . ," in Wiedemann, *Galanter Stil*, 4.

76. *Christian Thomasens Errinnerung Wegen deren über seine Grund-Lehren . . .* , in Wiedemann, *Galanter Stil*, 22.

77. Cf. Max Wieser, *Der sentimentale Mensch gesehen aus der Welt holländischer und deutscher Mystiker im 18. Jahrhundert* (Gotha, 1924), 186–218. Wieser approaches the question of continuity in the period 1670–1740 from a religious-cultural point of view.

78. Benjamin Neukirch, *Anweisung zu Teutschen Briefen (1721)*, in Wiedemann, *Galanter Stil*, 40.

79. Ibid., 42; see also Thomasius, "Christian Thomas," in *Galanter Stil*, 1.

80. Neukirch, *Anweisung*, in Weidemann, *Galanter Stil*, 32.

81. Johann Michael von Loen, *Der redliche Mann am Hofe* (1740; reprint, Stuttgart, 1966), 533: "Der Bauer ist so wohl gebohren, wie der Edelmann: Die Natur gibt beiden gleiche Rechte; Nur alsdann hat der Adel etwas voraus, wenn er Geld und Güter besitzet, wenn er wohl erzogen ist, und wenn er bessere Sitten hat, als der gemeine Mann. Hieraus erhellet, dass der wahre Adel nicht in einer edlen Geburt bestehet, sondern in einem edlem Leben." See, moreover, the entire section, 537–76.

82. Wendland, *Theoretiker und Theorien*, 234.

83. Ekkehard Gühne, *Gottscheds Literaturkritik in den 'Vernünftigen Tadlerinnen' (1725/26)* (Stuttgart, 1978), 388–405.

84. Blackall, *Emergence of German*, 187 (Senecan style); Gühne, *Gottscheds Literaturkritik*, 60, 63, 92, 97, 243, 246.

85. Blackall, *Emergence of German*, 196–200 and passim.

86. Martens, *Botschaft*, 505. Hereafter cited in the text as *Bot.*, with page number.

87. Martens, *Botschaft*, 510; Singer, *Galanter Roman*, 62.

88. See, for example, Hohendahl, *Europäischer Roman*, 33.

89. Cf., for example, Charlotte Elizabeth Morgan, *The Rise of the Novel of Manners: A Study of English Prose Fiction between 1600 and 1740* (New York, 1911); Natascha Würzbach, ed., *The Novel in Letters: Epistolary Fiction in the Early English Novel, 1678–1740* (Coral Gables, Fla., 1969). Research on this relationship has started in Germany. For example, Hans-Gerhard Winter, *Dialog und Dialogroman in der Aufklärung* (Darmstadt: Thesen, 1974), 41–56 and 71–74, has perceived a mutual enrichment regarding a staple of narrative fiction. Ute Schneider, *Der moralische Charakter: Ein Mittel aufklärerischer Menschendarstellung in den frühen deutschen Wochenschriften* (Stuttgart, 1976), has also thrown light on the similar function of the moral character in both moral weekly and novel.

90. Cf. Blackall, *Emergence of German*, 149–77.

91. Jörg Scheibe, *Der 'Patriot' (1724–1726) und sein Publikum* (Göttingen, 1973), 12–24.

92. Ibid., 24.

93. Martens, *Botschaft*, 519ff.; Blackall, *Emergence of German*, 49–101, esp. 83–101.

94. Christian Thomasius, *Monats-Gespräche* (1688): "Oder wenn man ja an was wahrhafftiges sich belustigen will, so delectiret mich der bekandte *Mercur Galant* über die massen, als in welchem man sich auf vielerley Art vergnügen

kan . . . ja es werden mehrentheils etliche kurtze Historien von artigen inventionen auf Art der Romainen mit beygefüget." Reprinted in Peter von Düffel, *Christian Thomasius: Deutsche Schriften* (Stuttgart, 1970), 90.

95. Düffel, *Christian Thomasius*, 99–100: "Aber was gehet mich dieses alles an, deshalben kan man sich doch wohl an einen galanten oder sinnreichen Buch delectiren, und deshalber kan wohl der *Mercur Galant* vor ein davon passiren." Cf. also 98.

96. Two other similarities between popular journal and gallant novel must be mentioned here. One is the necessity for both the novelist and the journalist to act at times as a hack writer in order to survive. There is much hack writing in both the gallant novel and the moral weekly: cf. Wendland, *Theoretiker und Theorien*, 232; and Pamela Currie, "Moral Weeklies and the Reading Public in Germany, 1711–1750," in *Oxford German Studies* (1968): 181–83. In addition, the authors of gallant novels, like those of the moral weeklies, were fictitious or anonymous. Martens, *Botschaft*, 30, has cited the fictive author as a major criterion. Just how important it is as a characteristic of that kind of journal is questionable when we consider that the practice was widespread. Cf. Margot Lindemann, *Deutsche Presse bis 1815: Geschichte der deutschen Presse, Teil I* (Berlin, 1969), 233f.

97. "Einmal bezeichnet man durch den galanten Mann einen redlichen, offenherzigen, gesitteten und angesehenen Menschen, und das ist etwas Tugendhaftes. Ein andermal verstehet man darunter einen dem weiblichen Geschlecht besonders ergebenen, dem Frauenzimmer unterthänigen, zärtlichen, und zierlich geputzten Menschen, und hierin ist nichts lobenswürdiges zu finden." Cited by Martens, *Botschaft*, 357–58.

98. Similarly Wendland (*Theoretiker und Theorien*, 6–7 and passim) argues for a connection between "galantes Wesen" and the Pietistic concept of the "schöne Seele." Moreover, Max Wieser (*Sentimentale Mensch*, passim) traces the development of a central concept—that is, sentimentality—from its religious-mystical origins to the secularized fashion of the later eighteenth century.

99. Johann Christoph Gottsched, *Der Biedermann* (1727–29; reprint, Stuttgart, 1975), 81–82. Hereafter cited in the text by volume and page number.

100. Gühne nowhere notes this connection.

101. See Kimpel, *Roman der Aufklärung*, 53.

102. See Blackall, *Emergence of German*, 150f., 158ff., 165.

103. Cf., for example, Winter, *Dialog und Dialogroman*, 66–71.

CHAPTER 9

The Pattern Is Perceived and the Seed Is Sown

P. M. MITCHELL

We understand the eighteenth century because our metaphysical world rests upon its assumptions. We believe that problems can be solved by reason. We admire the accumulation of knowledge presented in encyclopedic or specialized form. We share the teleological assumption.

In the Middle Ages, the world was viewed as in essence chaotic, for order was divinely superimposed and subject to the vagaries of the supernatural. This idea was eroded with the coming of the Reformation, however, and suffered further during the growing secularism of the late seventeenth century in Western culture. The great discovery of philosophy and therewith also of the sciences was that the world was ordered in a pattern, to be sure, a divine pattern—but chaos there was not. Ultimately, every aspect of physical existence contributed to the overall pattern. Man had but to seek, to experiment, to investigate, in order to see how the many and multiple parts of the teleological universe were joined and made a perfect whole. The divine system was clearly reflected in the firmament: the starry patterns of the heavens bespoke the fixed pattern of the universe and formed an elegant and elaborate design that provided evidence of a vast and infinitely complex entity.

This assumption does not seem strange to us today, for it is still our assumption based on our own observations. Whether we be churchmen or not, whether we accept Judeo-Christian theology or not, we do not doubt that the world obeys a pattern. We refuse to acknowledge the existence of chaos in the physical world: what has not yet been explained in the universe we feel will be explained in the course of time. By reflection, by experimentation, and by deduction, questions pertaining to chemistry, physics, or medicine are all viewed as answerable, given time. First and last, our tool is reason and we hope that reason will suffice to solve social and economic problems, too, although on this count we are not so sure. Rational man has brought the social order and the economic order into being, but rational man's most important tool, reason, does not seem able to solve the problems that human beings themselves have generated. We deny chaos in the eternal structure of the universe—but we come near to creating it ourselves.

Even though we are faced with an imperfect world, judged from the standpoint of an ideal situation for all men, we share another idea with the Age of the Enlightenment, and also with numerous thinkers and prophets before that age, namely that some kind of utopian social order is possible and that human beings can reasonably plan a society that will exist without the evils of war, poverty, and greed. That is to say, we are optimistic. The eighteenth century was optimistic, more optimistic than the centuries that preceded it and in many ways more optimistic than our own century, if we leave campaign rhetoric aside. (Utopia approaches every four years in the United States but dissolves very quickly when candidates become governing officials and try to translate promises into action and programs.) Nevertheless, we do remain optimistic, so it is not accidental that we can modify our concept of teleology and speak of teleological optimism or optimistic teleology. Teleological optimism was the philosophical basis for early-eighteenth-century thought—and we still partake of it. To be sure, the social order has changed. Generally speaking, republican forms of government have replaced various forms of monarchy; what has been called enlightened despotism seems no longer to be with us. Where there is despotism we are today unable to apply the mitigating adjective "enlightened." The cut-and-dried class system of feudal Europe has, however, been transmuted into a floating class system based chiefly on the possession of negotiable wealth or of political power.

The secularization of culture was not a new phenomenon begun around 1700, but rather a tendency that continued into the eighteenth century and grew stronger. It then overcame the dominance of revealed and organized religion that still had obtained in the seventeenth century. While the monumental architecture of Western Europe, particularly of France, during the seventeenth century might seem to attest the conquest of the secular over the spiritual, imaginative literature was still predominantly subservient to religious needs in 1701. Any statistical examination of printed matter at the beginning of the eighteenth century shows an overwhelming predominance of religious writing. A rapid change occurred, however, in the first half of the eighteenth century. Not only did architecture, painting, and design establish themselves outside the pale of the church, but imaginary literature also blossomed beyond the pale. In his *Geschichte des deutschen Buchhandels*, Johann Goldfriedrich has provided some interesting statistics based on an analysis of the Leipzig book fair catalogues from various years.[1] In 1701, works either in the Latin language or books in German dealing with theology comprised 79 percent of the titles offered for sale. Of the remaining 21 percent, less than 3 percent comprised imaginative literature. To be sure, the percentage of theological works listed in the book fair catalogues of half a century before had been still higher—87 percent—but by 1740 the theological and Latin share was down to 58 percent, while imaginative literature had risen to nearly 6 percent. By 1800 it was to reach over 21 percent.

During the late seventeenth century, popular drama in France had led the way toward a secular literature. German writers were more reticent. The position of Latin as a means of learned and poetic communication was questioned really only toward the end of the seventeenth century in Germany. The symbolic break in attitude and tradition came with Christian Thomasius, who in 1687 at the University of Leipzig became the first German professor to lecture in the indigenous language. He championed the ideas that indigenous language and literature were meritorious and that poetry which did not wholly reflect Graeco-Roman classical values also had possibilities. Gradually, the literature of entertainment, which may be exemplified by the lowly chapbook of 250 years ago, came to be seen in a new light. Symbolic of this new attitude is the Faust chapbook that the leading critic of the day, Johann Christoph Gottsched, had specifically rejected in 1729, but that Gotthold Ephraim Lessing was to view with sympathy by the mid-eighteenth century when he suggested that the Faust legend could be a basis for a German drama—and he made overtures to write such a drama—although it was Goethe at the end of the century who was to form that same legend into the monumental epic drama of German literature.[2]

Essential to the creation of a new culture was the formal philosophical background, which had as its basic convictions the superiority of reason and the existence and primacy of *ratio* within the strictures of Christianity. The foremost new philosopher was, of course, Leibniz, who died in 1716 and who is remembered today primarily as a forerunner of the atomic theory, although his contributions in many other fields—he also invented the calculus, for example—were more important to his own times. As far as worldly culture and the new philosophy of the times is concerned, his most significant book was the *Theodicée*, which was published first in French in 1710.[3] The *Theodicée* is the corporate expression of the teleological concept. The justification of the existence of God by means of secular rather than theological argument meant the triumph of teleology. Curiously enough, Leibniz's book was intended in part to repudiate what were felt to be the dangerous assumptions found in Pierre Bayle's historical and critical dictionary, the useful, radical, and stimulating cyclopedic reference work that had been issued fourteen years previously.[4] If one kept merely to the main entries in Bayle's dictionary, there was no cause for alarm, but if one read the many footnotes, as indeed one was meant to, there were numerous dangerous thoughts and possibilities suggested by Bayle, any one of which was sufficient to put his dictionary on the index of the Church of Rome. In particular, Bayle had had the audacity to suggest that a society of atheists might live in a state of harmony—a quite intolerable thought to all defenders of the faith. Although Leibniz meant his *Theodicée* as a reply to Bayle, in reality he built on Bayle, extended many of Bayle's ideas, and provided in fact a worldly philosophy. Leibniz found a voluble and systematic disciple in the philosopher Christian Wolff, who wrote his many philosophical works in the German language and who, in turn, found an effective popularizer in Johann Christoph Gottsched, who not only was an arbiter of taste and himself a dramatist, but was professor of philosophy and poetry at the University of Leipzig. Gottsched published a two-volume synthetic philosophy based on Wolff that went through no fewer than seven editions between 1734 and Gottsched's death in 1766.

Pierre Bayle, like the encyclopedists as a whole, exemplified the striking universality and breadth of knowledge that could be accepted as a norm around 1700. To us it seems almost incredible that an encyclopedic work like Bayle's could be the work of one man, or that philosophers like Wolff and Gottsched could deal confidently and authoritatively with so many subjects. Moreover, it seems ludicrous to us that professors might be advanced at universities not so much by rank but by moving from one discipline to another, but that was an accepted means of promotion at eighteenth-century universities.

The universality of knowledge was accepted as a possibility for a century more. Goethe, who died in 1832, still spoke with authority on a multitude of subjects, although not as diverse as they might have been a hundred years previously. The well-educated man, the intellectual of the eighteenth century, had a command of "knowledge-in-general" and not merely of one discipline. He could evoke respect or dismay when he spoke or wrote, no matter what the subject. He would not be dismissed easily as an outsider or a dilettante. If, indeed, the world was to be understood teleologically, then no subject was without connection to all other subjects, and it did not seem strange that one and the same scholar could make pronouncements about ethics, poetry, physics, and astronomy. Philosophy still embraced the world and illuminated all facets of man's existence; it had not yet been pushed into a corner as is the case today, when the professional philosopher cannot often at the same time be a theologian, an educator, a poet, or a critic, not to mention a physicist or an astronomer.

At the beginning of the eighteenth century, the theologians dominated the world of the book and defined the limits of all other disciplines. The situation changed rapidly, however, so that during the eighteenth century the theologians gradually came to take a position comparable with that held by philosophers today. Province after province was taken from their jurisdiction—to become autonomous within the then larger realm of philosophy. How rapidly the change came about is demonstrated in the lives of both Christian Wolff and Johann Christoph Gottsched.[5] Wolff had lost his position as professor of philosophy at the University of Halle because of exercising his freedom of speech, while Gottsched, a teacher of poetry and philosophy at the University of Leipzig, had been called before a Saxon ecclesiastical court because of a comment about homiletics he had made in his rhetoric, *Deutsche Redekunst*, in 1728. Some seventeen years after his dismissal, Wolff received a call back to the university that had dismissed him, while at the same time there was no longer an ecclesiastical authority that felt the need to censor the works of Gottsched. Precisely, then, Wolff and Gottsched marked the beginning of the end and the end of a beginning respectively, as it were. Wolff, following Thomasius's example, helped bring national pride into the German academy and gave to the German language an element of dignity that it hitherto had lacked. Gottsched, also writing in the German language, produced a coherent philosophy and a poetics that marked the arrival of modern imaginative literature, the awareness of which has remained in German cultural consciousness ever since.

The literary theory that is embodied in the new poetics, exemplified primarily by Gottsched's *Critische Dichtkunst* (this was originally published in 1729 and a fourth edition was issued in 1751) was based on two principles. The first principle was the philosophical one that belles lettres, in depicting man and the world, must necessarily be an organized whole with no loose ends. The second was that writers employing the German language could produce works of a quality equal to those written either by the French in the seventeenth century or by the Romans in classical antiquity—to be sure, keeping to the same genres that both the French and the Romans had used. The new poetics was not willfully innovative. This is apparent when we examine Gottsched's Poetics and find that he proclaimed it on the one hand to be an imitation of nature and on the other to adhere to the principles contained in the *Ars Poetica* of Horace, a translation of which served as the introduction to the *Critische Dichtkunst*. Poetry is not seen to be divinely inspired but to be peculiarly human. "Die Poesie . . . hat ihren Grund im Menschen selbst . . . ; sie hat ihre erste Quelle in den Gemütsneigungen des Menschen. So alt also diese sind, so alt ist auch die Poesie." ("Poetry has its basis in the human being . . . it has its primary source in the shifting emotions of the human being. As old as these are, so too, poetry.") Thus spake Gottsched in the first paragraph of the first chapter of his Poetics in 1729.

The new poetics of the eighteenth century did not advocate a literature of entertainment. On the contrary, it was basically didactic: it both established aesthetic goals and outlined the means that must be employed to achieve those goals. Belles lettres were seen to be a new, effective way of achieving the ideals for which first theology and then philosophy had been laboring. Imaginative literature had a characteristic that both theology and philosophy lacked, however: it was entertaining despite itself. While such literature did not disseminate facts, it made man more responsive to the reception of encyclopedic information and more receptive to the idea that a certain kind of organization was necessary within society if society was to be perfected in the sense of the perfection of the teleological universe. The primary instrument of imaginative literature was the drama. More than the printed word read in one's own chambers, the spoken word of the scenic drama was observed to affect men's minds both immediately and potently. Moreover, the drama fulfilled the human need for diversion. Various kinds of performances already existed to answer that need. There were puppet shows, slapstick comedies, school plays, and liturgical drama, for example; yet none of these seemed comparable in effect to the Latin or Greek drama of antiquity—and, as far as Germany is concerned, the drama extant at the beginning of the eighteenth century did not possess the sophistication of the French drama of the seventeenth century. German-speaking Europe lacked a serious drama in the indigenous tongue. There was a gradual awakening to the desirability of not only a national drama but a national theater. There was not even a corpus of plays on which a theater might draw. The plays that were given by troupes of traveling actors seemed accidentally chosen and without benefit of a literary philosophy or literary theory behind them. It was not until the 1740s that such a corpus of plays in the German language appeared, when Gottsched published his six-volume collection called *Die deutsche Schaubühne.*[6] The establishment of a national theater had to wait still longer.[7]

The philosophers and aestheticians of the early eighteenth century in all of Europe were much concerned with inculcating the populace with a concept of good taste. Good taste became the criterion in judging any imaginative work—but there were naturally differences of opinion as to whether a given work was or was not in good taste. The concept of taste seemed to be to the times something of a discovery, and discussion of taste in the abstract was à la mode. There was unequivocal agreement regarding the desirability of good taste, and whatever might further good taste was per se commendable.[8]

As far as imaginative literature is concerned, good taste could be measured by the adherence to given rules that could be extrapolated from classical literature that was held to be unimpeachable and to be quite exemplary. The rules for the new literature were thus derivative; they were not invented but extracted. As a consequence, the literature of the early eighteenth century is understandably labeled neoclassical. That there are many elements that are foreign to classical literature is beside the point; the intent was neoclassical. Similarly, the professed objective of eighteenth-century literature was the imitation of nature; and whether or not we now see that literature to be accurate representation of nature when viewed from our own naturalistic point of view is a different matter.

Not only do we share the basic philosophical assumptions of the eighteenth century, but also that century's metaphors. While archaic biblical metaphors still permeate modern Western tongues, and we accept without blinking such images as the wolf descending upon the fold or the cubit that is added to our stature, we never really expect to experience the wolf or to measure in cubits. Similarly, we do not consider the imagery that dominates the eighteenth century quaint, antiquarian, or exaggerated. The argumentation of Addison and Steele in *The Tatler* and *The Spectator* is our kind of argumentation, not too far removed in its sophisticated tone from the style of the present-day *New Yorker* magazine. The greatest difference between the English and the German moral weeklies—that were indeed ultimately all derived from English models—was simply one of language. Similarly, the modern novel has Richardson and Fielding as its point of orientation in Germany as well as in England. An older, more fantastic and grotesque type of narrative was more closely related to the Spanish tradition symbolized by Don Quixote, but that type gave way to what was assumed to be more nearly a representation of reality, notably in the novel of development and the epistolary novel that achieved rapid popularity in the early eighteenth century and is still with us in the twentieth.

The new currents of the early eighteenth century led to the establishment of a modern German university in 1736. This was the University of Göttingen, which provided a distinct contrast to the earlier, medieval universities of Germany and bespoke a trend toward specialization and experimental science. The new idea that Göttingen exemplified and embodied was strong and bright enough to attract several sterling minds, including that of the Swiss polymath Albrecht von Haller. With the appointment of Haller, it was clear that the university had accepted the teleological assumption and the philosophical justification of secular culture. There are many facets to Albrecht von Haller, but it will suffice to point to three of his achievements: First—to mention the work for which he is remembered in particular today—he was the author of the poem "Die Alpen," written in 1729 and included in his *Versuch schweizerischer Gedichten*, first published in 1732. Almost overnight, Haller changed the attitude of his countrymen and many contemporaries in Western Europe toward natural phenomena. He was among the first to declare the beauty of mountains. What formerly was fearful was now looked upon as sublime and idyllic. Life in the Swiss Alps seemed no longer an isolated and dreadful existence but admirable and harmonious.

The attitude toward the Swiss Alps is not the only remarkable feature of Haller's poetry. If one compares it with the poetry of the late seventeenth century, Haller's verse is seen to be more serious in intent, more appreciative of nature, with less of the usual combination of the *topoi* that dominated what we identify as baroque poetry. Personal impressions and emotions played a greater role in Haller than in earlier poetry. He is not writing occasional poetry to celebrate mundane events. He is, rather, a natural scientist who is able to give his thoughts lyrical expression. One may make a fruitful contrast between the poems of Haller and those of a slightly older contemporary, Barthold Heinrich Brockes, whose multivolume collection *Irdisches Vergnügen in Gott*—"earthly delight in God"—was for many years among the unquestioned German literary masterpieces of the first half of the eighteenth century. Haller and Brockes had much in common. Both were didactic and both wrote nature poetry extensively. Their basic attitudes were, however, different. Despite the fact that Brockes included a German translation of James Thomson's *Seasons* in his collected work, his primary inspiration came from Italy and France rather than England, and his intent was a rhetorical one. There was much of the playful in Brockes, as is evidenced, for example, by his poem about a violet, where the reader is expected to draw a breath while sniffing a violet between each syllable of the text, or in a poem about the coming of a thunderstorm in which the letter *r* does not appear in all those verses prior to the arrival of the storm and then overtakes the poem when the storm does arrive. The professional backgrounds of the two men suggest their difference in orientation. Brockes was a local dignitary and politician in the city of Hamburg, while Haller was a dedicated scholar, a man of science, widely traveled, and, like a true academician, capable of functioning in several environments that could provide him with the necessities for his scholarly endeavor. Both Brockes and Haller had many readers. In addition to the several editions of the work itself, an abbreviated one-volume anthology based on Brockes's *Irdisches Vergnügen in Gott* was published in 1738, and during Haller's lifetime no fewer than eleven editions of his *Versuch Schweizerischer Gedichten* were issued.

Another of Haller's major achievements was the creation of the botanical garden in Göttingen, which to this day is visual evidence of his genius as well as of his belief in the orderly design of nature and his comprehension of a pattern in physical existence. Visitors to Göttingen still walk through Haller's botanical garden—to be sure, most of them unaware that it was Haller's creation and unaware of the philosophical implications of eighteenth-century botany that it represents. Third, Haller, helped found the *Göttingsche Gelehrte Anzeigen*, an encyclopedic scholarly periodical published in the German language and the forerunner of innumerable other periodicals consisting primarily of reviews of scholarly books. As significant as this particular journal was and has remained, it was not a new departure. It was, rather, the continuation of a tradition that went back to the late seventeenth century. As early as 1690, Christian Thomasius had published a journal entitled *Monatsgespräche* that had a function similar to Haller's periodical. More notable than the German periodical by Thomasius, the distribution of which was limited, were periodicals issued around the turn of the century in the Netherlands, and edited by Pierre Bayle and Jean Le Clerc. Bayle's *Nouvelles de la république des lettres* (1684–87) and Jean Le Clerc's three successive periodicals, each beginning with the word *bibliothèque*, were monuments to indefatigable scholarly industry and diligence in the last decades of the seventeenth and the early decades of the eighteenth century. The many reviews that the journals contained, however, tended to the perfunctory, although their tolerance and mere distribution were of incomparable importance in the search for truth and the dissemination of information at a time when one could not speak of freedom of belief and expression in other parts of Western Europe. By espousing the principle that the function of reviews was not primarily to pass judgment or to express an opinion, this new type of critical periodical was able to flourish and enjoy widespread circulation. Numerous other periodicals had appeared in the brief hiatus between the cessation of Jean

Le Clerc's last *Bibliothèque* and the establishment of the *Göttingsche Gelehrte Anzeigen*, but none enjoyed the authority and respect that immediately accrued to Albrecht von Haller's publishing venture.[9] Both Haller's botanical garden and the periodical *Göttingsche Gelehrte Anzeigen* are still with us today, and we feel quite as at home in the botanical garden or with a copy of the periodical in our hands as did our antecedents well over 240 years ago in Göttingen, which was the principal place of activity for the Swiss thinker, physician, poet, botanist, and editor. Albrecht von Haller embodies the interplay of philosophy, natural science, and imaginative writing that was an ideal for the thinking man in an age of reason.

While one can characterize and delimit the era of the Enlightenment by pointing to such monumental works as Boileau's *L'Art Poétique*, Christian Thomasius's lectures, Pierre Bayle's *Dictionnaire*, Leibniz's *Theodicée*, and Gottsched's *Critische Dichtkunst*, these phenomena were more signposts and guides, easy to recognize as points of orientation, than effective means of regularly and progressively enunciating the ideas of enlightened thought to the reading public. This function was rather the task of the popular periodical, and the popular periodical was almost exclusively the moral weekly between about 1710 and 1740, although the genre continued in vigor after that time. The rise of the moral weekly went hand in hand with the rise of the bourgeoisie. A moral weekly was a bourgeois publication speaking to the bourgeoisie—it addressed itself neither to the nobility, about which it frequently made wry and satirical comments, nor to the simple laborer or servant who could not be expected to pay even the small sum the individual issues of a moral weekly cost, or probably even to read or understand them had they been accessible free of charge. The moral weeklies served didactic purposes. They were attempting neither to advance scholarship after the manner of such a periodical as the *Acta Eruditorum* of Leipzig, nor merely to entertain, although much of the effectiveness of the moral weekly depended upon the invigorating quality of the writing, upon anecdotes, hyperboles, and satire, which so often are the devices of effective argument. The moral weeklies consistently agitated for the natural man, that is, for the application of reason, and for both deportment and appearance consonant with nature and with reason. In part unconsciously, the moral weeklies also were serving the goals of a new aesthetic education. If we contrast the basic principles that inform Gottsched's Poetics in 1729 (as well as later editions), with incidental remarks pertaining to literature in the moral weeklies Gottsched himself had edited and of which he was the primary if not generally the sole contributor, we observe congruence and parallelism. Ideas that were expressed wittily in the periodical *Der Biedermann*, for example, undergo a simple transformation into parts of a formal system in the *Critische Dichtkunst*— the Poetics.[10] The spiritual proximity of the *Biedermann* to the *Critische Dichtkunst* is evidenced by the quotations in Latin at the head of the first page of the individual numbers of the periodical. Moreover, the selection of Latin quotations indicates not only the neoclassical commitment of the day but the philosophical identification with those classical writers who themselves were champions of a rational and even ascetic stance—such writers as Seneca, Marcus Aurelius, Epicurus. To the present day these thinkers have been able to supply ethical nourishment for thirsting souls and even to substitute as a religiophilosophical basis for individuals who are disillusioned with the forms assumed by organized Christian religion.

There is a danger in the "museum" approach to the past. To the historian it is a temptation only to call attention to the best, the choicest, the monumental that has been preserved from many eras. It is difficult to ascertain what the average man, if there indeed is such a thing, had at his disposal or how he lived; only here and there do we discover some sources of information on what might be called everyday life in the seventeenth or eighteenth centuries. Examples are the open-air museums in several places in Europe, which attempt to reconstruct at least the habitations of rural and sometimes urban dwellers of a past era. The danger is more apparent, indeed is unavoidable, in the study of literature. We have neither time nor patience to go through all that was written in any decade or indeed in any year in the seventeenth or eighteenth century. If we are to read works from a given century, we wish them to be intrinsically significant and to grant us some insights or intellectual satisfaction. As a consequence, there is a discrepancy between what we read from any given time in the past and what was read then. The only simple solution to this puzzle is provided by statistics that may help us overcome the preconceived ideas with which we necessarily approach the past and indeed change the past by our own dynamic views. Statistics on books published by categories, books owned, and where possible by books read might help us answer the important questions, who read what and who learned what. The historians of a national literature are also beset by an additional prejudice in attempting to derive the development and progress of that literature solely from indigenous sources. If we view German literature during the first half of the eighteenth century, we find many sources of information that are extra-German. The dominance of French drama is apparent to all at the beginning of the century. Indeed, the role of the new English literature is nearly overwhelming. This is demonstrable through an investigation of the so-called "Spectator" literature, that is, the moral weeklies published in German that derive directly or indirectly from the English *Spectator* at the beginning of the century. There were more than five hundred periodicals published in the German language in the eighteenth century that may be said to be in the wake of the English *Spectator*.[11] That is to say, Addison and Steele are quite as significant in the development of German literature in the eighteenth century as any German one might mention. Similarly, the novel in Germany found a major source of inspiration not in indigenous writing but in the prose fiction of Defoe, Swift, Fielding, Richardson, and a few other English writers. What the correct balance is between native German literature on the one hand and English or other foreign literatures on the other, we are unable to say. The scholarly tendency is always to emphasize whatever aspect of a writer one has identified and, at least for a time, to invest that writer with more importance than probably is due him. Here as elsewhere we are busy changing the past, trying to replace one reality with another. Since this sort of dialectic is inescapable, we shall never reach a balance of views that allows us to perceive the reality.

Mention of the rise of the novel suggests a type of literature that was little represented at the beginning of the eighteenth century but which came to the fore at the end of that century: the intimate sort of communication found in the autobiography or in autobiographical narrative. The writer in the early eighteenth century was not expected to share his moods, his fears, or the details of his private life with some impersonal body of readers. The poetry, the lyric of the day is seldom an expression of actual, identifiable emotion. It tends rather to be stylized and formal. This was the heyday of the occasional poem, which made much use of certain *topoi* and well-worn images. Even what might be designated as love poetry or erotic poetry at the time is characterized by a mass of clichés. If one has not read such poetry before, a single poem may seem striking, original, and even daring. If, however, one leafs through such a work as Benjamin Neukirch's anthology, which appeared in half a dozen volumes, several times reprinted between 1696 and 1727, and which contains much so-called gallant poetry, the impression of freshness received from the first poem will quickly fade.[12] Similar situations, phrases, and descriptions recur, quite possibly skillfully wrought with careful attention to diction, rhythm, and rhyme—but without any real disclosure of feeling on the part of the poet. From this fact one may conclude that the individual with his own emotional life was less important in society in 1700 than a hundred or two hundred years later.

No time has ever lacked great men or notable writers, and we are not at a loss to identify them from the early decades of the eighteenth century. Such individuals were, however, more unusual, more the exception, than would be the case today, when every individual feels he or she has a right to make a mark in society and to be judged more or less on an equal basis with other individuals. The men and women of the early eighteenth century still felt themselves to be members of a community, primarily a community of believers, but also members of some amorphous political or at least a municipal community. The rights of the individual were, generally speaking, considered to be subject to a superior power, either the state or the church. He who willfully set himself out beyond the pale of state or church was carelessly disregarding the consequences. At the end of the seventeenth and in the early part of the eighteenth century he had best seek out the republic of the Netherlands as the refuge where an individual had the greatest chance to enjoy freedom of the press and freedom of speech. And many were the independent minds that indeed sought refuge in the Netherlands, such men as John Locke, Pierre Bayle, Jean Le Clerc, and a host of others, some for shorter, some for longer periods of time.

One is inclined to identify revolutionary thought and activity with the end of the eighteenth century, because the late eighteenth century is the time of both the American and the French Revolutions. The political and social activities that we identify as revolutionary were, however, the end-products of much radical thought that had gone before. The new thought, the new philosophy, was really the revolution that would occasion the downfall of an established, but no longer viable, political order. To over-simplify, one might say that Divine Right no longer could be upheld if people no longer believed in it. And if one accepted the thought of Locke, Hume, Bayle, and Leibniz, one could no longer accept a religious or political establishment, so many elements of which seemed to be unreasonable or which contradicted observations that the teleologically inclined naturalist was making. The thinkers of the early eighteenth century were not what we would call activists; in fact, they tried hard to work within the limitations of the state and the church into which they were born. Cataclysmic change held no promise of a better future for them. Compromises between ideal and reality, between thought and practice, seemed to be the only way. Compromises could not be made indefinitely, however, and the necessity or danger of greater change became imminent, as ideas that first were the property of lonely thinkers and then of publicists were translated into a common persuasion.

NOTES

1. See Johann Goldfriedrich, *Geschichte des Deutschen Buchhandels* (Leipzig, 1908), 2:16ff.
2. Johann Christoph Gottsched, *Versuch einer Critischen Dichtkunst vor die Deutschen,*

1st ed. (1729). See *Ausgewählte Werke*, ed. Joachim Birke, 5/1 (Berlin, 1973), 217. In the "Siebzehnter Brief" of 16 Feb. 1759 in which Lessing attacked Gottsched, in Friedrich Nicolai, ed., *Briefe die neueste Litteratur betreffend*, Lessing suggested that the legend of Dr. Faust was a proper subject for a German national drama. He himself began to write such a drama, "D. Faust." See "Theatralischer Nachlaß" in Lessing's *Sämtliche Schriften*, ed. Karl Lachmann (3d ed., ed. Franz Muncker; Stuttgart, 1887), 3:380–90.

3. Gottfried Wilhelm Leibniz (1646–1716), *Essais de theodicée sur la bonté de Dieu, la liberté de l'homme et l'origine du mal* (Amsterdam, 1710). The first German translation is from the year 1720 (also Amsterdam).
4. Pierre Bayle (1647–1706). *Dictionnaire historique et critique*, vols. 1 and 2 (Rotterdam, 1697; 2d ed., vols. 1–3, 1702). Gottsched edited the German translation, vols. 1–4 (Leipzig, 1741–44). The first English translation appeared in London in 1710.
5. Christian Wolff (1679–1754) was dismissed as a professor of the University of Halle in 1723 because of his liberal views. He then received an appointment at the University of Marburg. After his recall to Halle in 1740, he was the recipient of many honors. Johann Christoph Gottsched (1700–1766) was at first associate professor of poetry, then also professor of philosophy at the University of Leipzig. He was sentenced to censorship by the dean of the philosophical faculty. The court was apparently not aware that Gottsched himself was currently dean.
6. *Die Deutsche Schaubühne nach den Regeln der alten Griechen und Römer eingerichtet*, 2, 3, 1, 4–6 (Leipzig, 1741–45).
7. In 1767–69, an effort was made to establish a "national" theater in Hamburg. Thereafter various theaters called themselves "national" but were national in name only.
8. A commendable outline of the complex history of the concept "good taste," especially in German literature (by Bruno Markwardt), is found in the *Reallexikon der deutschen Literaturgeschichte*, 2d ed. (Berlin, 1958), 1:556–69.
9. The final volume of Le Clerc's *Bibliothèque ancienne et moderne* was issued at The Hague in 1726. The *Göttingische Gelehrte Anzeigen* (the title of which has varied) began publication in 1739. Haller was editor between 1747 and 1753.
10. *Der Biedermann* was published in 1727–29. The first edition of the *Critische Dichtkunst* appeared in late 1729.
11. The most important work about the German moral weeklies is that by Wolfgang Martens, *Die Botschaft der Tugend* (Stuttgart, 1968).
12. *Herrn von Hoffmannswaldau und andrer Deutschen auserlesene und bißher ungedruckte Gedichte*, 7 vols. (Leipzig, 1685–1727). The first six volumes were edited by Benjamin Neukirch (1665–1729).

CHAPTER 10

Sappho, Souls, and the Salic Law of Wit

JOCELYN HARRIS

A queer little flurry of interest in clever women occurred in the middle of the eighteenth century.[1] Samuel Johnson, who never missed anything, remarked upon the phenomenon in *Adventurer* (no. 115; 11 December 1753). In former times, he wrote, the pen like the sword was considered as consigned by nature to the hands of men, and the ladies contented themselves with private virtues and domestic excellence. A female writer, like a female warrior, was considered a kind of eccentric being that deviated, however illustriously, from her due sphere of motion, and was therefore to be gazed at with wonder rather than countenanced with imitation. But now, it seemed to him, all was changed: "The revolution of years has produced a generation of Amazons of the pen, who with the spirit of their predecessors have set masculine tyranny at defiance, asserted their claim to the regions of science, and seem resolved to contest the usurpations of virility." In this brief passage, Johnson manages to include issues vitally important to clever women then and now: custom's power to consign women to domesticity, the planetary image to illustrate the divinely ordained order of things, the consequent shock when women, however brilliant, step out of their sphere, their outrage at being denied, and their claim of disinheritance by men.

Johnson's acute summation of a midcentury mood shows how much he must have read. One of the items he could not have missed was John Duncombe's poem, *The Feminead, or Female Genius*, written in 1751, though not published until 1754.[2] Duncombe, whose father made Johnson proud by coming to him,[3] was a young friend of Samuel Richardson and future husband of Susanna Highmore. In his poem he calls the roll of female genius, arguing in terms similar to Johnson's that the usurpations of tyrant custom and its agent, man, must not hinder women's freedom to write. (He boasts, however, that the British gallery of female genius compares well with the Turks, who enslave their women.) The pen is well suited to the domestic life, he thinks; no husband need fear a genius in the house. Fame, writes Duncombe in hopeful conclusion, outlasts beauty and draws the sting from age; it will preserve his female geniuses as exemplars to save the world from folly.

When Johnson and Duncombe outlined current attitudes to female writers and sketched the means of reply, they drew upon ideas already considered by the twenty-one women listed in *The Feminead*.[4] These women, whom Duncombe thought the most notable representatives of their time and kind, had often, as I shall show, been forced to defend the possession and use of their gifts. They themselves had attacked what Duncombe calls the Salic law of wit, first by arguing that women had indeed a right to stand upon Parnassus, and second by calling upon religion and education to discover what it meant to be a genius and female in a world largely hostile to their efforts.

THE SALIC LAW OF WIT

The assumption, reinforced by ridicule, that literature held no place for women, understandably attracted the bitterest retorts. The Matchless Orinda, Katherine Philips, was in fact admitted to the company of poets, the first woman to be so, but she remained matchless, without inheritors. Aphra Behn was more typically excluded from the Society of Poets because "none of her Sex has any Right to a Seat there."[5] As Mrs. Centlivre's biographer later explained, "the Custom of the Times discountenanced poetical Excellence in a Female." "See here the Effects of Prejudice, a Woman who did Honour to the Nation, suffer'd because she was a Woman. ... Hold! let my Pen stop, and not reproach the present Age for the Sins of their Fathers."[6]

The women of *The Feminead* were quick to resent the injustice. "What has poor Woman done," asked Mrs. Behn angrily, that she must be "Debar'd from Sense, and sacred Poetry?"[7] Lady Winchilsea knew the reason: "All Arts are by the *Men* engross'd," because "Our few Talents [are] unimprov'd or cross'd."

> Alas! a woman that attempts the pen,
> Such an intruder on the rights of men,
> Such a presumptuous Creature, is esteem'd,
> The fault, can by no vertue be redeem'd.

Men argue, she says, that women's sphere is different and distinct:

> They tell us we mistake our sex and way;
> Good breeding, fashion, dancing, dressing, play
> Are the accomplishments we shou'd desire;
> To write, or read, or think, or to enquire
> Wou'd cloud our beauty, and exhaust our time,
> And interrupt the Conquests of our prime;
> Whilst the dull mannage, or a servile house
> Is held by some, our utmost art, and use.

Like Mrs. Behn, she demands to know what rule forbids her to follow her muse and choose feigned ideas for her pleasures, asking "Why shou'd it in my Pen be held a fault / Whilst Mira paints her face, to paint a thought?" No wonder that the "black Jaundice" conditions all she sees, when her lines are decried, and her employment thought "An useless Folly, or presumptuous Fault." Made to feel singular, Lady Winchilsea pointedly disdains traditional female activities:

> My Hand delights to trace unusual Things,
> And deviates from the known, and common way:
>   Nor will in fading Silks compose
>   Faintly th'inimitable Rose. . . .[8]

She was, in short, eccentric, one who stepped out of her due sphere, out of her fixed astronomical path, as Johnson had said (even in 1803 one finds a work entitled, *Eccentric Biography: or Memoirs of Remarkable Female Characters, Ancient and Modern*). Implied here is a curious association of notable women with comets and meteors, that is, short-lived wonders and prophets of doom. As Bathsua Makin had complained, "A Learned Woman is thought to be a Comet, that bodes Mischief, when ever it appears."[9]

Clever women are then freaky, special cases that prove nothing about the abilities of the sex. If any woman ventures to speak sense, says "Philo-Philippa," in a poem to compliment Orinda, Katherine Philips, the wise "make that, and speaking Oxe, like Prodigies." Also attempting to praise Philips, Abraham Cowley even argues that she is noticeable only because she is unique. Trade brings little profit when shared:

> *Orinda* in the female Coasts of fame
> Engrosses all the Goods of a Poetique Name,
>   She does no Partner with her see;
> Does all the Business there Alone which we
> Are forc'd to carry on by a whole company.[10]

Pope employs exactly this same trick of complimenting one woman at the expense of all in his praise of Lady Winchilsea when he says she is the sun that puts out all the lesser stars. If women who write are exceptions rather than forerunners, they need the condescension, it was thought, of special pleading. Orinda's editor wrote of her verses that "there are none that may not pass with favor, when it is remembered that they fell hastily from the pen but of a Woman."

The topics allowed to women were restricted. Lady Winchilsea withheld her translation of Tasso out of her "desire not to give scandal to the most severe," hoping that the subjects of her other poems were "at least innofensive; tho' sometimes of Love." She added mildly that "while keeping within these limmitts which I have observ'd, I know not why itt shou'd be more faulty, to treat of that passion, then of any other violent excursion, or transport of the mind" (*Poems*, 10). Mrs. Behn complained more fiercely that things that "are never taken Notice of, because a Man writ them . . . they blush at from a Woman" (*Works*, 3:185).

Nor could a woman display her learning without inviting ridicule. Much of the derision echoed traditional attacks upon pedants, for instance Bacon's criticism of the immoderate pursuit of learning for its own sake and the possibility of vanity in the scholar. Such lessons the educationalist Hester Mulso Chapone absorbed unquestioningly. "The danger of pedantry and presumption in a woman . . . of her exciting envy in one sex and jealousy in the other, of her exchanging the graces of imagination for the severity and preciseness of a scholar, would be, I own, sufficient to frighten me from the ambition of seeing my girl remarkable for learning."[11] The learned lady, the *précieuse*, the blue-stocking, is, like Mrs. Cockburn in *The Female Wits*, a frequent source of fun. A clever woman was thought to be unsociable—Mary Leapor's neighbors expressed concern lest "the Girl should over-study herself, and be mopish."[12] And probably unmarriageable. Elizabeth Carter, the *Doctissima Virgo*, who cultivated her wisdom in chaste retirement like her namesake Minerva, was confirmed in her youthful choice by attitudes such as Warburton's, when he asked for "one particular that perhaps is of more importance to her than all her Greek and Latin[:] that is whether she be handsome."[13] When Hester Mulso Chapone hard pressed Richardson in a debate, Colley Cibber swore to her face she would never be married;[14] Mrs. Pilkington after bitter experience with Mr.

Pilkington advised that "even Men of Sense discountenance Learning in Women, and commonly chuse for Mates the most illiterate and stupid of the Sex; and then bless their Stars their Wife is not a Wit." [15]

In short, a learned woman was thought to be a terror. Lady Irwin was "so learned that I believe she knew as much Latin as a second form boy does at Eton; she wrote poetry, and every body was afraid of her"; [16] Mary Leapor, vastly her social inferior, still met with a similar response:

> *Pamphilia's* Wit who does not strive to shun,
> Like Death's Infection, or a Dog-Day's Sun?
> The Damsels view her with malignant Eyes:
> The Men are vex'd to see a Nymph so wise:
> And Wisdom only serves to make her know
> The keen Sensation of superior Woe.
>
> (*Poems*, 2:65–66)

Why this extravagant fear of learned women? One cause must be the story of the Fall, where Eve's vain desire of knowledge brought evil to the world. Theologically, then, intelligent women are indeed ominous portents, and their aspirations hold dangers far beyond the local and individual. This I think lies behind Sir William Temple's odd compliment to Katherine Philips (high praise if a learned woman were the cause of all our woe): Orinda, he said, created a new dispensation for women, making "rich amends" for all "The faults her Sex committed since the Fall."

The women of *The Feminead* flinch from the name of poetess, knowing like Lady Winchilsea that they will be ridiculed "through all ranks, down to the Carman": "they say she writes, and 'tis a common jest" (44–45). How much they took to heart *The Dunciad's* representation of the pattern of a female poet in Mrs. Centlivre, a slipshod muse traipsing along in lofty madness, meditating song, with tresses staring from poetic dreams and never washed but in Castalia's streams, may be seen in their self-denigrating apologies for themselves. Each seemed to acccept uncritically that in abandoning the awful rites of pride she inevitably turned herself into a fright. "I dress just as awkwardly, I look just as silly, and I talk just as silly as ever," wrote Miss Carter; [17] Hester Mulso Chapone spoke ironically of herself as "a poor gentlewoman that never was guilty of more than four poor odes, and yet is as careless, as awkward and as untidy as if she had made as many heroic poems as the great and majestic Blackmore." [18] Most explicit is Mary Leapor's re-creation of herself as Pope's slut possessed by a dubious Muse (in his Cave of Spleen too, women's inspiration came, grotesquely, from hysteria, the effluvium of the womb):

PHILLARIO.

But who is she that walks on yonder hill,
With studious brows, and night-cap dishabille?
That looks a stranger to the beams of day;
And counts her steps, and mutters all the way? . . .

CORYDON.

What though some freckles in her face appear?
That's only owing to the time o' th' year.
Her eyes are dim, you'll say: Why, that is true:
I've heard the reason, and I'll tell it you.
By a rush-candle (as her father says)
She sits whole ev'nings reading wicked plays. . . .
Come, come; you view her with malicious eyes:
Her shape—

PHILLARIO.

—Where mountains upon mountains rise!
And, as they feared some treachery at hand,
Behind her ears her list'ning shoulders stand.

CORYDON.

But she has teeth—

PHILLARIO.

—Consid'ring how they grow,
'Tis no great matter if she has or no:
They look decay'd with posset and with plums,
And seem prepar'd to quit her swelling gums.

(*Poems*, 1:124–26)

Women writers either accepted the ridicule so damaging to their self-esteem and denied that their work mattered to them, or they defiantly resisted it, asserting that wit and duty were indeed compatible. Miss Carter, who would not read a French book in a stagecoach for fear of shocking her fellow travelers, believed that "a perpetual capacity for the pleasures of merely intellectual life, would too much withdraw our attention from the duties incumbent on us . . . and would weaken, if not totally destroy, all the sympathies of humanity." Miss Carter, having talents, hid them under a bushel, for which she was praised by her editor-nephew Pennington: "to her native town, Mrs. Carter was not a woman of letters; and many persons saw her in company, who had no idea that her pleasures were of any higher order, than such as whist or quadrille could afford, or the society of a country town impart" (*Letters*, 2:302, 63–65). Although a brilliant linguist, she ostentatiously demonstrated her accomplishment in such feminine activities as needlework, music, cooking, dancing, gardening, and benefaction to "above an hundred illegitimate children" of Deal.[19] She always called her work idle indulgence, never the passionate profession it truly was.

Concealment easily became self-censorship. Mrs. Behn threatened that if she might not tread in the successful paths of her predecessors, if she might not "because of my Sex, have this Freedom, but that you will usurp all to your selves; I lay down my Quill, and you shall hear no more of me" (*Works*, 3:187). Katherine Philips often believed her poetic employment "so far above my reach, and unfit for my Sex, that I am going to resolve against it for ever." When Mrs. Cockburn married she "bid adieu to the Muses, and so wholly gave myself up to the cares of a family, and the education of my children, that I scarcely knew, whether there was any such thing as books, plays or poems stirring in Great-Britain."[20] Lady Hertford was glad to accept from Pope's friend Martha Blount lines describing her desertion of poetry and such "manly works, for ladies' hands unfit" in favor of silks, thread, and worsted,[21] but Duncombe argued strongly that such a choice need never be made:

> And ye, our sister choir! proceed to tread
> The flow'ry paths of Fame, by Science led!
> Employ by turns the needle and the pen,
> And in their fav'rite studies rival men!

Women who excel either in sewing or in writing are he says superior beings, and he quotes approvingly from a poem where Pope shows his most generous understanding for the female condition, the *Epistle to Miss Blount with the Works of Voiture*:

> But lives there one, whose unassuming mind,
> Tho' grac'd by nature, and by art refin'd,
> Pleas'd with domestic excellence, can spare
> Some hours from studious ease to social care,
> And with her pen that time alone employs
> Which others waste in visits, cards and noise;
> From affectation free, tho' deeply read,
> "With wit well natur'd, and with books well bred?"

Duncombe sympathizes, however, with the nervous husband of a clever woman:

> Nor mean we here to blame that father's care,
> Who guards from learned wives his booby heir,
> For oft that heir with prudence has been known,
> To dread a genius that transcends his own:
> The wise themselves should with discretion chuse,
> Since letter'd nymphs their knowlege may abuse,
> And husbands oft experience to their cost
> The prudent housewife in the scholar lost.

Mr. Pilkington, for one example, was no match for his learned wife. "'P——x on you for a Dunce, [said Swift] were your Wife and you to sit for a Fellowship, I would give her one, sooner than admit you a Sizar.'" From then on Mr. Pilkington looked on her, wrote Mrs. Pilkington, with "scornful, yet with jealous eyes" (*Memoirs*, 1:120). Mrs. Centlivre's biographer dwelt rather on the consequences when a woman marries beneath her capacity. "We have been depressed and taught to entertain an humble Idea of our Genius. . . . Oft have I seen, in private Life, an illiterate churlish Fool of a Husband tyrannize over the Will, and with barbarous Insult, compel the Reason and good Sense of his Wife, to give Place to his Folly, and this on no better Foundation than Custom, established by Laws, the Handyworks only of Men."

In their professional as in their personal lives the women expected ostracism on the grounds of sex. Garrick, having rejected Mrs. Brooke's play *Virginia*, reeled back from what he called her "female Spite" in suggesting that he did so because it was a woman's; "there's brutal Malignity for You."[22] Mrs. Manley braced herself for a similar reaction.

> The first Adventurer for her fame I stand,
> The Curtain's drawn now by a Lady's Hand,
> The very Name you'll cry boads Impotence.
> To Fringe and Tea they shou'd confine their Sence,
> And not outstrip the bounds of Providence.

She remained convinced that "the bare Name of being a Woman's Play damn'd it beyond its own want of Merit."[23] Lady Winchilsea dared not show her work at Court, "where every one wou'd have made their remarks upon a Versifying Maid of Honour; and far the greater number with prejudice, if not contempt." Whenever a woman meddles in things of this nature, so strong the opposing faction still appears, "the hopes to thrive, can ne'er outweigh the fears." Anticipating the probable reception of her verse, she wrote tersely,

Jocelyn Harris

> True judges, might condemn their lack of witt,
> And all might say, they're by a Woman writt.
>
> (*Poems*, 4–9)

And so it was. Mrs. Centlivre told in her dedication to *The Platonick Lady* how "a Spark that had seen my *Gamester* three or four times, and lik'd it extremely: Having bought one of my Books, ask'd who the Author was; and being told, a Woman, threw down the Book, and put up his Money, saying, he had spent too much after it already, and was sure that if the Town had known that, it wou'd never have run ten days." Mrs. Behn also knew that "the Woman damns the Poet" (*Works*, 3:186): the day her *Dutch Lover* was first acted, she wrote, "there comes me into the Pit, a long, lithe, phlegmatick, white, ill-favour'd, wretched Fop, an Officer in Masquerade newly transported with a Scarf & Feather out of France . . . A thing, Reader—but no more of such a Smelt: This thing, I tell ye, opening that which serves it for a mouth, out issued such a noise as this to those that sate about it, that they were to expect a woful Play, God damn him, for it was a woman's" (*Works*, 1:223–24).

If women did succeed they were accused of plagiarism, like Mrs. Centlivre. "Some have arm'd themselves with a resolution not to like the Play they paid to see; and if in spite of Spleen they have been pleas'd against their Will, have maliciously reported it was none of mine, but given me by some Gentleman."[24] Mrs. Manley echoed her. If the play went well, "chattering insects" would say that "Some private Lover helpt her on her way," as if "Female Wit were barren like the Moon, / That borrows all her influence from the Sun."[25]

One solution was to hide the fact of female authorship. Several of the women in Duncombe's list published anonymously, Mrs. Cockburn, for instance, "partly from an apprehension, that the public would be prejudiced against a metaphysical treatise [on Locke] written by a woman" (*Biog. Brit.*, 3:665). Mrs. Centlivre let *The Busy Body* go forth as "a Woman's Feast," but at other times concealed her name through fear "that the Work shou'd be condemned, if known to be Feminine," wrote her biographer.

Ambition was therefore pointless in a woman. Miss Carter was praised by "Constant Reader" in her *Gentleman's Magazine* obituary in 1798 for being one of those Christian women who "devoid of all vanity, seek not to be distinguished beyond a little circle of loved friends"; Lady Hertford claimed to be "perfectly indifferent to the trifles I have writ, and have at present no manner of ambition."[26] Only the rare Mrs. Behn dared to beg immortality of the laurel,[27] valuing fame "as much as if I had been born a Hero" (*Works*, 3:187). Given their anxiety about being anomalies as women

240

writers, most felt like Mrs. Cockburn in her poem for the Queen's Hermitage that

> If some adven'trous genius rare arise,
> Who on exalted themes her talent tries,
> She fears to give the work, tho' prais'd, a name,
> And flies not more from infamy than fame.[28]

If women wrote it was for themselves alone. The two best gifts of each sex, said Lady Winchilsea, were "The Skill to write, the Modesty to hide" (57), which meant that

> 'Tis for our Selves, not them, we *Write*.
> Betray'd by Solitude to try
> Amusements, which the Prosp'rous fly;
> And only to the Press repair,
> To fix our scatter'd Papers there.
>
> > (*Poems*, 4)

"Be caution'd then my Muse, and still retir'd; / Nor be dispis'd, aiming to be admir'd." She concluded pathetically that her Muse must contract its wing, knowing she is never meant for the groves of laurel. "Be dark enough thy shades, and be thou there content" (*Poems*, 6). Lady Hertford shrank likewise from publicity:

> Publick applause is what I never sought
> The World's opinion ne're engag'd my thought;
> My Muse with me in silent shades retir'd,
> No Critick dreaded nor no fame desir'd.[29]

Most strikingly, the Matchless Orinda, "having an incorrigible inclination to that folly of riming, and intending the effects of that humor, only for my own amusement in a retir'd life," was appalled when her poems were to be published without her consent, speaking of their public exposure as a kind of rape. "I . . . am that unfortunate person that cannot so much as think in private, that must have my imaginations rifled and exposed to play the Mountebanks, and dance upon the Ropes to entertain all the rabble; to undergo all the *raillery* of the Wits, and all the severity of the Wise, and to be the sport of some that can, and some that cannot read a Verse. This is a most cruel accident, and hath made so proportionate an impression upon me, that really it hath cost me a sharp fit of sickness since I heard it."

However clever they are, however accomplished, these women displayed again and again the modesty for which the world would applaud them (Hannah More wrote approvingly in *Le Bas Bleu* [1786], that Carter "taught the female train, / The deeply wise are never vain"). The painful effects of their self-denial are everywhere apparent, in Mary Leapor's self-loathing, Katherine Philips's terrors, Lady Winchilsea's melancholy spleen, Miss Carter's debilitating headaches, and the very fact that they chose to write so often about the gift which unsought had afflicted them.

WOMEN'S RIGHT TO LITERATURE

The women counterattacked either directly through poetical returns to their tormentors, or indirectly, through criticism of the patriarchy that they blamed for the tyranny imposed on wit.

Duncombe's poem provides one kind of answer to Pope by simply listing competent women. But some of them had already provided their own answers. Lady Winchilsea, whom Pope, Gay, and Arbuthnot may have been jeering as Phoebe Clinket in *Three Hours after Marriage*, threatened Pope with the fate of Orpheus at the dismembering hands of "Resenting Nymphs" in a manner more hostile than her reputation for being quintessentially feminine would allow. Lady Irwin "espoused her sex's cause," noted Duncombe, "and, in a poetical epistle to Mr. Pope, has rescued them from the aspersions cast upon them by that satyrist in his Essay on the Characters of Women":

> By IRWIN touch'd with Truth's celestial spear.
> By her disarm'd, ye witlings! now give o'er
> Your empty sneers, and shock the sex no more.

The tyranny imposed on wit is consequent upon the tyrannies of Man the Monarch at home, argued the rustic Mary Leapor:

> When our Grandsire nam'd the feather'd Kind,
> Pond'ring their Natures in his careful Mind,
> 'Twas then, if on our Author we rely,
> He view'd his Consort with an envious Eye,
> Greedy of Pow'r, he hugg'd the tott'ring Throne;
> Pleas'd with Homage, and would reign alone;
> And, better to secure his doubtful Rule,
> Roll'd his wise Eye-balls, and pronounc'd her *Fool*.

> The regal Blood to distant Ages runs:
> Sires, Brothers, Husbands and commanding Sons,
> The Sceptre claim; and ev'ry Cottage brings
> A long Succession of Domestic Kings.
>
> (*Poems*, 2:10)

Even Lady Winchilsea, happy in marriage herself, perceived its inequities for women, writing succinctly, "Marriage does but slightly tye Men / Whilst close Pris'ners we remain / They the larger Slaves of Hymen / Still are begging Love again / At the full length of all their Chain" (*Poems*, 151). Mary Leapor, always the most vulnerable of the group, wrote her *Essay on Woman* specifically to show that whatever her marital status or abilities, "Unhappy Woman's but a Slave at large" (*Poems*, 2:67). Usurpation in literature as in life is the natural theme of many writers, remarkably unjust when, as Mrs. Rowe's husband Thomas knew, the muses have often inspired their own sex, fired them with a more than mortal ardor and taught them in wit and numbers to excel, "Nor yield to man alone the praise of writing well."[30]

Women must therefore look for champions in the cause, as Mrs. Manley hoped of Mrs. Cockburn:

> Orinda [Philips], and the fair Astraea [Behn] gone,
> Not one was found to fill the vacant Throne:
> Aspiring Man had quite regain'd the Sway,
> Again had Taught us humbly to Obey;
> Till you (Natures third start, in favour of our Kind)
> With stronger Arms, their Empire have disjoyn'd,
> And snatch't a Lawrel, which they thought their Prize,
> Thus Conqu'ror, with your Wit, as with your Eyes.[31]

Each woman should act as pioneer and proof of women's abilities, commendatory verses on Judith Cowper Madan's poem in *The Flower-Piece* (1731) point out:

> Henceforth, ye women-haters, cease to rail;
> O'er sland'rous tongues let MIRA's worth prevail:
> 'Tis now by all confess'd, that woman's mind
> For high attempts indulgent heav'n design'd.

Women should support women, wrote Mr. Collier in a preface to Mrs. Brooke's play, *The Siege of Sinope*. Urging the fair to assert themselves, he demanded what did it matter that "imperious man" had assumed the right to withhold the wreath of fame from women? If women proved their powers to judge as well as write, "man, with pride reluctant, shall confess, / Each Muse may justly wear a woman's dress." And in her lines to the Queen, Mrs. Cockburn appealed to the highest woman in the land, asking "If not the work, give the attempt applause, / And patronise in her the sex's cause."

Some bold writers even claimed that the rule of wit had already passed from men to women. Once, said Thomas Rowe, no females could aspire to equal praise: then men alone possessed the envied bays. With haughty majesty they unrivalled shone, "Nor fear'd a she-pretender to the throne." The advent of Orinda changed everything, said Cowley, writing in generous hyperbole,

> We allow'd you beauty, and we did submit
>> To all the tyrannies of it.
>> Ah, cruel Sex! will you depose us too in Wit?
> *Orinda* does in that too reign,
> Does Man behind her in proud triumph draw,
> And cancell great *Apollo's* Salick Law.

Woman excels then in beauty and in wit: more, for "*Orinda* does our boasting Sex out-do, / Not in wit only, but in virtue too." The "ravish'd Bay's" have been restored to women by Orinda, crows Philo-Philippa, "*Phoebus* to *Cynthia* must his beams resigne," since "The rule of Day, and Wit's now feminine." No wonder that James Tyrell praised Orinda's humility, writing in some alarm that

> . . . were not Nature partiall to us Men,
> The World's great Order had inverted been;
> Had she such Souls plac'd in all Women-kind,
> Giv'n 'em like wit, not with like goodness join'd,
> Our vassall Sex to hers had homage paid;
> Women had rul'd the World, and weaker Man obey'd.

The overthrow of the tyranny of wit links inseparably with a larger revolution. Jealous men, said Philo-Philippa, debar women from books in peace, from arms in war, knowing that women's abilities would soon demand "Tribunals for our Persons, and Command"; women, wrote Mrs. Centlivre's biographer, deserved a larger share not only in literary decisions, but in the church and the state.

Such skirmishes between the sexes raise vital political and national concerns. Should women, said Duncombe, be only frivolous? "Heavens! could such artful, slavish sounds beguile / The freeborn sons of *Britain's* polish'd isle?" The natives of the sultry line may boast of their female parrots, but, he declared proudly, British nymphs rove through wisdom's sacred grove at freedom's call. But Elizabeth Johnson, for one, vehemently denied his claim in a preface for Mrs. Rowe. Britain cannot be superior as long as mankind determines, using "the *Brutal Advantages of Strength*," to "Monopolize *Sence*," granting to women "neither that, nor Learning, nor so much as *Wit*": women must protest against such "*notorious* Violations on the *Liberties of Free-born English Women.*"[32] Mrs. Centlivre suffered prejudice merely for being a woman, wrote her champion, and "Are these things fit and becoming a free-born People, who call themselves polite and civilised?" Justice demands that these wrongs be righted, as Mrs. Cockburn wrote to the Queen, with the additional advantage remarked by Mrs. Madan in her *Progress of Poetry*, that the restoration of liberty bestowed "the power to sing, / And bid the verse-rewarding lawrel spring."

Duncombe's indignation that in the Turkish empire the loathsome pomp of proud seraglios galls each fair neck with the yoke of slavery[33] is echoed by Centlivre's biographer: "Can the Nation be called civilised, that confines as wild Beasts that part of the Creation, always acknowledged to be the most mild and gentle. . .? These Doctrines are unreasonably inconsistent, and arise only from Prejudices which it is high Time should be exploded, and our Sex enjoy the Liberty which they have a natural Right to."

Not only do Mahometans deprive women of liberty, said Duncombe, but they teach that "level'd with the brutal kind, / Nor sense, nor souls to women are assign'd." (Pope was perhaps developing this old charge that women have no souls, or if they do, that there is a distinction in souls by sex, when he claimed that women, full of contraries and constantly metamorphosing, have no characters at all.) Several writers answer this heathen doctrine: Ambrose Philips's epilogue to Mrs. Centlivre's *The Wonder, A Woman keeps a Secret*, complains, for instance, that "Some are for having our whole Sex enslav'd, / Affirming *we've no Souls*, and *can't be sav'd*," a barbarous belief attacked by Philo-Philippa:

> That Sex, which heretofore was not allow'd
> To understand more than a beast, or crowd;
> Of which Problems were made, whether or no
> Women had Souls; but to be damn'd, if so. . . .

245

Distinction of souls by sex is equally repugnant to her. "The Soul's the same, alike in both doth dwell, / 'Tis from her instruments that we excell"; "If Souls no Sexes have, as 'tis confest, / 'Tis not the He or She makes Poems best." At issue is woman's very theological status, her gift of reason, a sparkle of the purity of her first estate, the proof that she is divinely wrought—and this only Mahometans will deny. Patriotic and freedom-loving British must resist the Salic importation from France or risk looking Turkish. As Prior wrote generously for Mrs. Manley,

> By our full Pow'r of Beauty, we think fit
> To damn this Salique Law, impos'd on Wit. . . .
> Then the She Pegasus shall gain the Course,
> And the gray Mare will prove the better Horse.[34]

THE SEX'S CAUSE

The Feminead is a progress piece, tracing the ascent of women's poetry from Sappho to Orinda and Duncombe's sweetheart Susanna Highmore. Celebratory lists had long been a feature of didactic writing for and about women, but here in Duncombe's poem is the equivalent in verse of those petrified worthies at Twickenham, Stowe, and Prior Park, modern exempla for their own time, and in this case their own sex. (George Ballard proudly pointed in his Preface to the fact that "England has produced more women famous for their literary accomplishments, than any other nation in Europe" to disprove "that vulgar prejudice of the supposed incapacity of the female sex.") To list superior women is "Fair emulation in the sex to move," Mrs. Cockburn told the Queen; the women are to one another sister muses, or mirrors (as Thomas Flatman said of Orinda) for women writers to dress themselves by. Mrs. Manley, fired by the example of Mrs. Cockburn, would try, she said, to change her sex's weaker destiny. "O! how I long in the Poetick Race, / To loose the Reins, and give their Glory Chase."[35] Philo-Philippa would let male poets chose their male Phoebus, but "Thee I invoke, *Orinda*, for my Muse; / He could but force a Branch, *Daphne* her Tree / Most freely offers to her Sex and thee"; Mrs. Pix places Mrs. Manley in a whole pantheon of inspiration, like Sappho charming, like Aphra eloquent, like chaste Orinda, sweetly innocent.[36]

Philo-Philippa points out gleefully that although Apollo, a male, was the judge of wit, the Nine Muses or "nine Female learned Troop" actually *were* it. Bathsua Makin went so far as to write sturdily, "*Minerva* and the nine Muses were Women famous for Learning whilst they lived, and therefore thus adored when dead."[37] And so her editor can say of Katherine Philips, that she "has called herself ORINDA, a name that deserves to be added to the number of the Muses, and to live with honor as long as they."

Literary women were often called muses. The *précieuses* at the Hôtel de Rombouillet used the *noms de Parnasse*, and Aaron Hill hopefully baptized his daughters by these same *noms*. Some of the *Feminead* women contributed to a poem on the death of Dryden by the nine muses, and a 1779 portrait, later engraved, of the "Nine Living Muses of Great Britain," included Hester Mulso Chapone, and Elizabeth Carter as Urania, "our British Minerva." Like the nine Elizabethan female worthies they gather to inspire their own sex.[38]

To the immortal nine was often added a mortal tenth, Sappho, so called in an early Greek epigram. Thus it could be said in compliment to Katherine Philips.

> But if *Apollo* should design
> A Woman Laureat to make,
> Without dispute he would *Orinda* take
> Though *Sappho* and the famous Nine
> Stood by, and did repine.

A long list of women poets—Jane Weston, Anne Killigrew, Katherine Philips, Aphra Behn, Hester Mulso Chapone, Catherine Cockburn, and Anna Seward—were called Sappho or claimed descent from her. (Seward called her dog Sappho.) It was a title they were proud to claim, as Mrs. Behn revealed in her address to the laurel:

> I by a double right thy bounties claim,
> Both from my sex, and in Apollo's name:
> Let me with Sappho and Orinda be
> O ever, sacred nymph, adorned by thee;
> And give my verses immortality.[39]

The association could, though, be dangerous. Sappho's reputation for lasciviousness could easily be transferred to all scribbling women—Mrs. Behn's as an "Authoress of several obscene Plays etc." (Pope's words) has always hampered a proper appreciation of her work, and early brought upon her Anne Wharton's warning that in excelling the matchless Sappho's name she should have "all her wit without her shame."[40] No one except Virginia Woolf believes it was a passion for reading that kept Mrs. Pilkington up late with a gentleman not her husband, but one has to admire her rueful plea to Richardson that he might spare the virgin purity of Clarissa, "Consider, if this wounds both Mr. Cibber and me (who neither of us set up for immaculate chastity) what must it do with those who possess that inestimable treasure?"[41] Her lamentable example prompted Mrs. Montagu to remark that "the generality of women who have excelled in wit have failed in chastity; perhaps it inspires too much confidence in the possessor, and raises an inclination in the men towards them without inspiring an esteem so that they are more attacked and less guarded than other women."[42]

Duncombe was therefore extremely careful to separate out the "bold unblushing mien" of "modern Manley, Centlivre, and Behn" from the virtuous visages of the other ladies. The dangerous sallies of their wanton muse, he wrote, deserved praise no more than Mrs. Constantia Phillips, Mrs. Pilkington, and Lady Vane "Deserv'd applause for spotless virtue gain." Mrs. Behn's very cleverness, said Thomas Rowe, made her a persuasive purveyor of adultery and incest, so that the good and chaste, abhorring "the vitious lays," must "hate the beauties they are forced to praise." Orinda's passionate friendships with women were never disparagingly remarked upon, but Mrs. Behn's friendship with the libertine Rochester and the homosexual John Hoyle, together with an ardent poem addressed "To the fair Clarinda," give some substance to the other Sapphic qualities stressed by Pope in his satires on Sappho, Lady Mary Wortley Montagu. But one can see other reasons for imagining that creative women might be bisexual. It was—and is—common to praise women by saying that they possess a masculine understanding: Mrs. Behn indeed talked of "my Masculine Part the Poet in me" (*Works*, 3:187). Women who succeed, women who act independently, are not only alarmingly Sapphic, but in Johnson's anxious phrase, Amazons of the pen, viragoes, epicenes, warrior women from Sparta.[43] Mrs. Centlivre was thus thought to share the characteristics of her own Widow Ranter, and Swift in the *Battle of the Books* called Mrs. Behn "Afra the Amazon light of foot."

Yet even these dire charges might be turned to women's benefit. "A Female Sweetness and a Manly Grace" were said to mingle in Mrs. Behn (*Works*, 6:119); in Mrs. Madan, said Duncombe, "manly strength with female softness joins." A writer who took the best from both sexes might indeed be superior to one limited by a single sex (Keats would say the same of Shakespeare). Cowley even drew on the traditional asexuality of angels to praise Orinda:

> 'Tis solid, and 'tis manly all,
> Or rather, 'tis Angelical:
> For, as in Angels, we

> Do in thy Verses see
> Both improv'd Sexes eminently meet;
> They are than Man more strong, and more than Woman sweet.

But the best answer to personal attacks was to overleap the prostituted muses altogether and claim a source (like Milton) in the godhead itself. For works of a religious tendency one could claim a divine inspiration and disarm the critics. Before the advent of Mrs. Rowe, said Miss Carter in her contribution to the *Poems*, the records of female wit were often "blackened" by immodest intrigue; now, said her doting husband, in *To Daphnis*, Mrs. Rowe came

> To bless a ruin'd age, and succour lost mankind,
> To prop abandon'd virtue's sinking cause,
> To snatch from vice its undeserv'd applause,
> To lead in piety's forsaken ways,
> By bright example, and celestial lays.

Writing on celestial subjects one could invite the intervention of the Heavenly Bard himself, and raise the work beyond mere earthly criticism:

> No—'tis in vain—attempt not to persuade!
> They were not, cou'd not be by Woman made:
> Each Thought so strong, so finish'd every line,
> All o'r we see so rich a Genius shine;
> O more than Man, we cry, O Workmanship Divine![44]

And for these sublime truths, these raptures, the female sex was eminently suited. "It could scarcely be expected that a lady should be vers'd in the arts of strict reasoning," wrote Mrs. Rowe's nephew in her *Poems*: rather than the "accuracy of a divine and philospher" one might find in her "the fire and bold license of a poet." By writing on religious subjects, women might aspire to the heights of the sublime, and by writing in the sublime mode they might discover their own heaven-born female genius.

"WITHOUT THE CRITICK'S RULES, OR AID OF ART"

Duncombe's use of the word "genius" is of the utmost interest. Genius means to him not remarkable ability, but simply the capacity to write, a sense that would grow in acceptance with the century. Among his poets Lady Winchilsea owns the truest gift: others own no gift at all. Nor does Duncombe distinguish on grounds of learning: the "native genius" of unlettered Mary Leapor ranks her with Miss Carter and her extensive wisdom. Female genius is not, it seems, the exclusive right of any social class, since it is found in the Countess as in the gardener's daughter. This democratic idea Duncombe could have found in a poem he knew well enough to parody, Gray's *Elegy written in a Country-Churchyard*.

Formal learning was for the most part denied eighteenth-century women, who thus provided fine experimental examples of unlearned or natural genius to add to those other specimens of the kind, Pope, Richardson, Stephen Duck, and Shakespeare. John Duncombe wrote of Mary Leapor that she had "lately convinced the world of the force of unassisted nature, by imitating and (perchance) equalling some of our most approved poets by the strength of her own parts [and] the vivacity of her own genius." Judith Cowper Madan's praise of Shakespeare's "rich, uncultivated soil," of his ability to sway the passions and lead captive the heart "Without the critick's rule, or aid of art," shows that her sympathies too lie with unlearned genius. Passion, the heart of the sublime itself, must not be fettered:

> Where nature warmth and genius has deny'd,
> In vain are art's stiff languid powers apply'd.
> Unforc'd the muses smile, above controul:
> No art can tune the inharmonious soul.
> Some rules, 'tis true, unerring, you may cull,
> And void of life, be regularly dull:
> Correctly flat may flow each studied rhyme,
> And each low period indolently chime.

The sublime Mrs. Rowe "read no critics, nor could her genius brook the discipline of rules: And as the pains of correcting appeared to her some kind of drudgery, she seldom made any great alterations in her composures from what they were when she first gave copies of them to her friends." Shakespeare and Milton, Jonson and Shakespeare: the old antithesis between learned and unlearned genius, pedantry and passion, is here skewed to a point where lack of learning and a disdain to blot almost *guarantee* the sublimity of genius. Duncombe could therefore write in triumph of Mary Leapor,

> Let cloister'd pedants in an endless round,
> Tread the dull mazes of scholastic ground;
> Brackley unenvying views the glitt'ring train,
> Of learning's gaudy trappings idly vain;

> For, spite of all that vaunted learning's aid,
> Their fame is rival'd by her rural maid.

Thomas Amory praised Mrs. Rowe because "No hideous pedantry with learned noise / Confounds the music of the female voice," and even the learned Miss Carter cast her weight on the side of sensibility, not sense: she valued, she said, the "wild song of an American in his native wood" far above the learned Spaniard, on the ground that "Poetry perhaps suffers less from the want of any cultivation at all, and more from an improper sort of cultivation, than any species of composition whatever. Other authors, to arrive at any degree of perfection, require much previous information, and the assistance of different arts; but a poet may strike and charm any one if he has only ears and eyes, that hear and see, and a heart that can feel."[45]

Ears and eyes that can hear and see—the claim that unlearned geniuses are superior by virtue of their realism one finds constantly among the *Feminead* women. Women often reach heights of glory which "even the schools have wanted power to teach," said Mrs. Behn,[46] for all "Your learned Cant of Action, Time and Place" must give way to "the unlabour'd Farce." "If you're drawn to th'Life, pray tell me then, / Why Women should not write as well as Men" (*Works*, 4:116). Realism is the thing, not learning, and this any woman could provide. "Plays have no great room for that which is men's great advantage over women, that is Learning," a point she proved triumphantly by the example of Shakespeare (*Works*, 1:224). Mrs. Centlivre made fun of Mary Astell's plan for a women's college in *The Basset Table*, but her betrayal was consistent with her defence of the necessarily unlearned genius of women. Being "deterred from the Advantages of a Learned Education" would not discourage her. She would write neither from rules nor from great knowledge, but from her own artless observation of human nature[47]—a gift which Pope had said distinguished great Homer himself.

It seems odd that these women, having argued so strenuously for the superiority of untutored genius, should speak out energetically for women to be educated. But Locke's representation of the mind as a *tabula rasa*, a blank slate unmarked by inherited moral ideas, had thrown the whole emphasis of the fair sex debate back upon education and opportunity. Like the rustic Miltons of Gray's country churchyard, women, they were quick to argue, may be ingloriously mute through no fault of their own.

Women, with equal souls and equal endowments of reason, must, they said, have potential equal to men's. "A Poet is born so, not made by Rules," wrote Mrs. Centlivre's biographer in echo of Sidney's commonplace "and is there not an equal Chance that this Poetical Birth should be female as well as male?" "If properly cultivated by Education, I believe those [perfections] of the female Mind would equally shine. Female Minds are . . . capable of producing literary Works, equal even to those of *Pope*." Women, confirmed Mrs. Cockburn angrily, are "as capable of penetrating into the grounds of things, and reasoning justly, as men are, who certainly have no advantage of us, but in their opportunities of knowledge."[48] But as Duncombe realized, it was the power of custom that forced women into "feminine" activities and trivialized their lives: prejudice orders women to use their beauty and enslave men, who therefore believe, wrote Philo-Philippa scornfully, that woman's "highest Contemplation" could pass no higher than her looking-glass, "And all the painful labours of their Brain, / Was only how to Dress and Entertain." Lady Winchilsea's belle shows the vacant, pretty result:

> Whilst the gay thing, light as her feather'd dresse,
> Flys round the Coach, and does each cusheon presse,
> Through ev'ry glasse, her sev'ral graces shows,
> This, does her face, and that, her shape, expose,
> To envying beautys, and admiring beaux.
> One stops, and as expected, all extolls,
> Clings to the door, and on his elbow lolls,
> Thrusts in his head, at once to view the fair,
> And keep his curls from discomposing air.
>
> *(Poems*, 40)

Worst of all, she said, is that women, "Debarr'd from all improve-ments of the mind, / And to be dull, expected and dessigned," are then unfairly blamed for what they have been made to become (*Poems*, 6). "Shall it be our reproach, that we are weak, / And cannot fight, nor as the School-men speak?" asked Philo-Philippa, pointing out that even men themselves are neither strong nor wise, if they do not exercise their limbs and parts. Lady Irwin remarked just as tartly, "By custom doom'd to folly, sloth, and ease, / No wonder Pope such female triflers sees." She argued that, although men and women were alike in their love of power, women must move in a narrower orbit:

> In education all the diff'rence lies;
> Women, if taught, wou'd be as learn'd and wise
> As haughty man, improv'd by arts and rules;
> Where God makes one, Neglect makes many fools.[49]

Mrs. Behn complained, in addition, that to deny a literary woman education is to deprive her of inspiration. Though Dryden in his preface to Ovid's *Epistles* wrote pleasantly that she [Mrs. Behn], who understood not Latin, "has given us occasion to be ashamed who do," she made a point of praising Creech for making Lucretius available to women in translation. Her birth, her education, the "scanted Customes of the Nation" forbade, she wrote,

> . . . the Female Sex to tread,
> The mighty Paths of Learned Heroes dead.
> The God-like *Virgil*, and great *Homers* verse,
> Like Divine Mysteries are conceal'd from us.
>
> (*Works*, 6:167)

Nor could women benefit from that other mode of training advised by Locke for children at home, participation in rational conversation. Miss Carter probably provided for Richardson's *Sir Charles Grandison* a plea that women be not treated as a separate species; twenty years later she must still complain of a gathering where "As if the two sexes had been in a state of war, the gentlemen ranged themselves on one side of the room, where they talked their own talk, and left us poor ladies to twirl our shuttles, and amuse each other, by conversing as we could." She added with remarkable restraint, "By what little I could overhear, our opposites were discoursing on the old English poets, and this subject did not seem so much beyond a female capacity, but that we might have been indulged with an share in it."[50]

The women did what they could, especially educating themselves in languages that they might have access to other literatures. Miss Carter, to be fair, was encouraged by her father, but what did she think about as she prepared her brother's mind for Cambridge? Women helped women: there's a charming vignette about Queen Caroline's poetical Lady of the Bedchamber, Lady Irwin, having her attention attracted to a young girl, "partly out of contradiction, for she was always exclaiming against pert forward girls"; "She really became very fond of me, and took great pleasure in expanding my ideas. The passion I had for reading, with some little taste for poetry, enchanted her." Being no prude, Lady Irwin introduced the girl to books that she had previously read "amputated."[51]

But whatever they did was done unsystematically and in secret. Mary Leapor, poring over her little library of "fifteen or sixteen books," cried out in envy of the happy few

> who Leisure find,
> With Care, like this, to cultivate their Mind:
> But partial Fate to me this Bliss denies,
> To search for Knowledge with unweary'd Eyes;
> To turn, well pleas'd, th'instructive Volume o'er;
> The secret Springs of Science to explore;
> And by the Taper's pale and trembling Light
> In useful Studies to consume the Night.

(Poems, 2:59)

Mrs. Cockburn, too, enumerates her problems:

> those restraints, which have our sex confin'd,
> By partial custom check the soaring mind:
> Learning deny'd us, we at random tread
> Unbeaten paths, that late to knowledge lead;
> By secret steps break through th'obstructed way,
> Nor dare acquirement gain'd by stealth display.

Although her poem appeals for royal patronage, women were of course barred from political rewards, being worse off even than that other natural genius, Stephen Duck. In lines queerly anticipating Johnson's *London* by six years she writes with some cause of being "By art unaided, and by want depress'd, / Whilst toils the day, and cares the night molest."

Women's education has more than social or literary consequences, however, for unless good principles are inscribed upon the innocent blank, pupils suffer a second Fall, as grave as the first. "How are we fal'n, fal'n by mistaken rules? / And Education's, more then Nature's Fools," said Lady Winchilsea (*Poems*, 6); Lady Irwin described the female mind as a rude fallow, liable to fill with weeds:

> female youth, left to weak woman's care,
> Misled by Custom, Folly's fruitful heir . . .
> If wealthy born, taught to lisp French, and dance,
> Their morals left, Lucretius-like, to chance . . .
> Unus'd to books, nor virtue taught to prize,
> Whose mind, a savage waste, unpeopl'd lies;
> Which to supply, trifles fill up the void,
> And idly busy, to no end employ'd.

Only rational education can develop the god-given faculty of reason, turn the female mind to sublime truths. Education, said Mrs. Cockburn, would save the world's Belindas:

> No more their time in trifling pleasures waste;
> In search of truths sublime, undaunted soar,
> And the wide realms of science deep explore.
> Quadrille should then resign that tyrant sway,
> Which rules despotic, blending night with day;
> Usurps on all the offices of life,
> The duties of the mother, friend, and wife.
> Learning, with milder reign would more enlarge
> Their pow'rs, and aid those duties to discharge;
> To nobler gain improve their vacant hours:
> Be *Newton*, *Clarke*, and *Locke*, their mattadores.

Here again Locke's influence is vital. His attack on corrupt public schools, his advocacy of education at home, raised the whole question of the capabilities of mothers; it rendered urgent the need to educate women to be mentors to their sons as well as to their daughters. The whole fate of the nation depended on mothers, as Lady Irwin pointed out, for we cannot expect "our modern wives" to breed heroes, when they "lead such useless lives." By training a race of mothers equal to the Spartan and Roman matrons, England would, she said, be great. Her poem answering Pope's *Characters of Women* therefore asked him

> To rescue women from this Gothic state,
> New passions raise, their minds a-new create;
> Then for the Spartan virtues we might hope,
> For who stands unconvinc'd by gen'rous Pope?
> Then would the British fair perpetual bloom,
> And vie in fame with antient Greece and Rome.

Lady Irwin offered women a public task to shape a nation; Duncombe pointed to more personal and private satisfactions. Reason, he said, made the decays of time tolerable in the female frame. He promised the women fame not as Pope had done, for their hair, but for their minds, vowing that their names would adorn our annals to latest time, and "save from Folly thousands yet unborn."

Halfway through a century that begins with Mary Astell and ends with Mary Wollstonecraft, Samuel Johnson and John Duncombe, historians of women's early attempts and harbingers of their explosion into print, look back over fifty years of pioneering endeavor. That many of Duncombe's notions in particular have precedents and analogues in the works of the women themselves shows the scrupulous and complimentary care with which he had read it. We cannot know the full effect of the arguments he gathered up: all we do know is that eventually, and with miraculous confidence and skill, Jane Austen, the Brontës, and George Eliot would exercise that female right to literature won for them by the lonely struggles of their predecessors.

NOTES

1. See, for instance, George Ballard, *Memoirs of Several Ladies of Great Britain* (1752); Bonnell Thornton and George Colman, *Poems by Eminent Ladies*, 2 vols. (1755); Thomas Amory, *Memoirs of Several Ladies of Great Britain* (1755), and his *Life of John Buncle*, vol. 1 (1756). Works by women were being sympathetically reviewed, notably by the *Gentleman's Magazine*.

   In this essay I tread gratefully in the footsteps of Myra Reynolds, *The Learned Lady in England, 1650–1760* (Boston and New York, 1920), and Robert Halsband, especially his "Ladies of Letters in the Eighteenth Century," in *Stuart and Georgian Moments*, ed. Earl Miner (Berkeley and Los Angeles, 1972), and "Women and Literature in Eighteenth-Century England," in *Eighteenth-Century Woman* (Transactions of the McMaster Association for Eighteenth-Century Studies, Vol. 4) (Toronto, 1976).

2. The poem went through two editions in 1754 and 1757, reaching thousands of readers, as Duncombe hoped, when it appeared in Dodsley's *Miscellany*, vol. 4 (1755) and a number of anthologies thereafter. Its most recent incarnation is as an Augustan Reprint Society pamphlet (Los Angeles, 1981), with my introduction.

3. Boswell, *Life of Samuel Johnson*, 6 vols., ed. G. Birkbeck Hill, rev. L. F. Powell (Oxford, 1934–50), 3:314.

4. Aphra Behn, Frances Brooke, Elizabeth Carter, Susanna Centlivre, Catherine Trotter Cockburn, Judith Cowper Madan, Hester Mulso Chapone, Susanna Highmore, Martha Ferrar, Elizabeth Pennington, Lady Frances Hertford, Viscountess Irwin, Mary Leapor, Delariviere Manley, Katherine Philips, Constantia Phillips, Laetetia Pilkington, Elizabeth Singer Rowe, Lady Frances Vane, Anne, Countess of Winchilsea, Mehetabel Wesley Wright. For further details, see my introduction to the Augustan Reprint Society reprint of *The Feminead* (see n. 2, above).

5. Correspondent to the *Gentleman's Magazine*, May 1738.

6. "To the World," preface to Susanna Centlivre, *Dramatic Works*, 3 vols. (London, 1760–61).

7. *The Works of Aphra Behn*, 6 vols., ed. Montague Summers (London, 1915), 4:115. Hereafter cited in the text as *Works*, with volume and page.

8. *Poems of Anne, Countess of Winchilsea,* ed. Myra Reynolds (London, 1713; reprint, Chicago, 1903), 47, 4–5, 13, 250. Hereafter cited in the text as *Poems,* with page.

9. *An Essay to Revive the Ancient Education of Gentlewomen,* ed. Paula L. Barbour (London, 1673; reprint, Los Angeles, 1980), 3. Something of the same idea appears in Walter and Clare Jerrold's biographical work on clever women, *Five Queer Women* (London, 1929).

10. *Poems, by the most deservedly admired . . . Mrs. Katherine Philips* (London, 1678), valedictory verses and preface.

11. Hester Mulso Chapone, *Letters on the Improvement of the Mind* (London, 1797), 179.

12. Mary Leapor, *Poems upon Several Occasions,* 2 vols. (London, 1748–51), 2:30.

13. See Edward Ruhe, "Birch, Johnson, and Elizabeth Carter: An Episode of 1738–39," *PMLA* 73 (1958): 491–500.

14. T. C. Duncan Eaves and Ben D. Kimpel, *Samuel Richardson: A Biography* (Oxford, 1971), 344.

15. Laetitia Pilkington, *Memoirs,* 2 vols. (London, 1748), 1:122–23.

16. John Nichols, *Illustrations of the Literary History of the Eighteenth Century,* 8 vols. (London, 1817–58), 5:22.

17. Montagu Pennington, ed., *Letters from Miss Elizabeth Carter to Mrs. Montagu,* 3 vols. (London, 1817), 1:47.

18. See Ethel Rolt Wheeler, *Famous Bluestockings* (London, 1910), 192.

19. R. Blunt, ed., *Mrs. Montagu, "Queen of the Blues,"* 2 vols. (London, 1923), 1:303.

20. Thomas Birch and Andrew Kippis, ed., *Biographica Britannica: or, The Lives of the Most Eminent Persons who have flourished in Great Britain,* 2d ed., 6 vols. (London, 1778–93), 3:688n. Hereafter cited in the text as *Biog. Brit.,* with volume and page.

21. *Correspondence between Frances, Lady Hertford . . . and Henrietta Louisa, Countess of Pomfret,* 3 vols. (London, 1805), 1:260–63.

22. *Letters,* ed. David M. Little and George M. Kahrl (Cambridge, Mass., 1963), nos. 360, 1109.

23. See Gwendolyn B. Needham, "Mrs. Manley: An Eighteenth-Century Wife of Bath," *Modern Language Quarterly* 14 (1951): 259–84.

24. John Wilson Bowyer, *The Celebrated Mrs. Centlivre* (Durham, N.C., 1952), 89.

25. Quoted in Needham, "Mrs. Manley," 263.

26. Quoted in Helen Sard Hughes, *The Gentle Hertford: Her Life and Letters* (New York, 1940), 137.

27. See Frederick M. Link, *Aphra Behn* (New York, 1968), 129.

28. Thornton and Colman, *Poems by Eminent Ladies,* 1:234–38.

29. Quoted in Hughes, *Gentle Hertford,* 422.

30. *Poems on Several Occasions,* 2 vols. (London, 1738–39), under Mrs. Rowe's pseudonym of "Philomela."

31. Quoted in Needham, "Mrs. Manley," 263.

32. Reynolds, *Learned Lady,* 159.

33. Robert Halsband, "'Condemned to Petticoats': Lady Mary Wortley Montagu as Feminist and Writer," in Robert B. White, Jr., ed., *The Dress of Words: Essays on Restoration and Eighteenth-Century Literature in Honor of Richmond Bond*, (Lawrence, Kan., 1978), 35–52, tells how the British were influenced by Aaron Hill's notion of the Ottoman Empire before Lady Mary's more accurate account appeared in 1763.

34. Quoted in Needham, "Mrs. Manley," 283–84.

35. Quoted in Needham, "Mrs. Manley," 263.

36. Quoted from Lucyle Hook's introduction to Mary Pix, *The Female Wits* (London, 1704; reprint, Los Angeles, 1967).

37. Barbour, *An Essay*, 9.

38. See Robert Halsband, "'The Female Pen': Women and Literature in Eighteenth-Century England," *History Today* 24 (Oct. 1974): 702–9; Miriam Leranbaum, "The Nine Living Muses of Great Britain" (Paper presented at the American Society for Eighteenth-Century Studies annual meeting, 1977); and Celeste Turner Wright, "The Elizabethan Female Worthies," *Studies in Philology* 43 (1946): 628–43.

39. Quoted in Link, *Aphra Behn*, 129.

40. See Maureen Duffy, *The Passionate Shepherdess: Aphra Behn, 1640–89* (London, 1977), 194.

41. See Eaves and Kimpel, *Samuel Richardson*, 177.

42. See Laetitia Pilkington, *Memoirs*, ed. Iris Barry (London, 1928), 472.

43. Cf. Richardson's representation of Lady Mary Wortley Montagu in *Sir Charles Grandison*, 3 vols., ed. Jocelyn Harris (London, 1972), 1:43 and 469n. She is both martial and Sapphic, her name, Miss Barnevelt, perhaps deriving from association with Pope's *A Key to the Lock*.

44. Quoted in Henry F. Stecher, *Elizabeth Singer Rowe, the Poetess of Frome: A Study in Eighteenth-Century Pietism* (Bern and Frankfurt, 1973), 182.

45. Pennington, *Letters from Miss Elizabeth Carter to Mrs. Montagu*, 1:109–10.

46. See Duffy, *Passionate Shepherdess*, 260.

47. See Bowyer, *Celebrated Mrs. Centlivre*, 138.

48. See Edmund Gosse, "Catharine Trotter, the First of the Bluestockings," *Fortnightly Review* 105 (1916): 1033–48.

49. See Anne Ingram, Viscountess Irwin, "On Mr. Pope's Characters of Women," in *The New Foundling Hospital for Wit*, part 6 (London, 1773).

50. Pennington, *Letters from Miss Elizabeth Carter to Mrs. Montagu*, 2:68; for Carter's brief essay in Richardson's novel, see Harris, ed., *Sir Charles Grandison*, 3:243–44 and 480n.

51. Nichols, *Illustrations*, 5:22–23.

CHAPTER 11

"The Young, the Ignorant, and the Idle": Some Notes on Readers and the Beginnings of the English Novel

J. PAUL HUNTER

The novel has always had its detractors. Critics, moralists, and cultural watchdogs regarded the early novels as literary disasters, worrying not so much about the failed artistry of any one work as about the bad influence of the species. A deterioration of taste, a hodgepodge of indecorum without form, a travesty of the tradition—such terms and worse greeted the early novelists as the official response to their work. And the blame, in the minds of critical observers, often fell not so much on the writers as on readers. It was the new reading public that had brought it all about; that is what happens when you let just anybody read. And so in England in the first half of the eighteenth century, the established writers and guardians of literary standards joined with traditional moralists in something of a program to expunge bad taste, recreate a sense of decorum and appropriate form, and drive the barbarians from the land of print. Much of the force of Augustan satire and of eighteenth-century moralism more generally derives from its sense of cultural mission; the reigning taste was almost unanimous in finding offensive and despicable not only the novel but the whole set of sponsoring assumptions that allowed readers to read it and caused writers to write it.[1] They objected to the subjectivity of the form, to its indulgent and sometimes solipsistic emphasis upon the individual, its devotion to contemporary detail seemingly for its own sake, its inclusivity of tones and styles in violation of standard notions of literary de-

corum. The arbiters of taste—Augustans like Pope, Swift, and Gay—
found it necessary to spend most of their careers trying to "correct" taste
back to traditional literary standards, to curb the entire literary movement
that culminates in the novel, to turn back the clock, to stop the presses.
Writers, critics, churchmen, educators, and philosophers all agreed that
the taste for novelty and innovation was a cultural menace. But by midcentury—about the time that Dr. Johnson's literary career had begun to
flower—the novel had nevertheless become (although still unnamed and
poorly defined) England's most important literary form, and novelists vied
with each other to be considered the founder of this "new Province" or
"new Species" of writing. Still, more than two centuries later, the most
crucial early objections against the novel persist, although in more sophisticated form; critical attitudes are less moralistic but even more socially
snobbish.

The original title of this essay was "The Origin of a Literary Species,"
but I'm afraid I can't live up to its pretensions. I am serious, though, about
its allusive suggestions, for I do think that literary forms evolve slowly
rather than suddenly being born to a beaming parent who can feel altogether responsible—perhaps with the collaboration of a mystical muse or
sponsor—for their creation. But I cannot hope to address here the full
complexity of the emergence of any species. What I have to say relates to a
larger study where I treat in some detail issues I can only touch here.
What I would like to do here, however, is respond to some persistent questions raised about the first readers of novels, for I believe that one way of
approaching the emergence of the novel is to look more closely at why its
readers found it—apparently quite suddenly—so appealing. Some of
what I have to offer is frankly speculative, but I will try to sort out with
what degree of certainty we can answer three questions: (1) Who were the
first readers of novels? (2) What did they want novels to do for them?
(3) How were cultural needs translated into the emergence of a new literary
species? And in answering these questions I will try to revise some historical notions about the movement of culture in seventeenth- and eighteenth-
century England.

The audience for eighteenth-century English novels is easier than most to
define because the entire reading public then was quite limited in size.
Still, it was much larger than the reading public had been a few generations before, and when novels suddenly became very popular in the 1740s,
critical observers claimed that the readers of novels were servant wenches,
sons of tradesmen, and silly young girls. "The young, the ignorant, and

the idle" was how Samuel Johnson described them.[2] Such contemporary descriptions of the readers of novels were meant, of course, to degrade the species and certify its inferior artistic status, and detractors repeatedly asserted that novel-readers were low-born, ill-bred, and incapable of appreciating better things. Much of the contemporary opposition to novels came from those who felt self-appointed to keep the lower and middle classes from evil or, if that was not possible, at least to keep the upper classes from being infected by inferior tastes and values. Out of that high-mindedness developed the great myth that the novel is a middle-class form developed for middle-class readers at the time of the rise of the middle class, that great moment that can be dated nearly anywhere in history. In some respects, the novel *is* an antiaristocratic phenomenon, but the inordinate stress on that aspect of the novel derives from literary and cultural snobbery rather than historical analysis. Many aestheticians regard it with suspicion and contempt, and in many academic circles it is still thought an upstart and not quite respectable form, still too new to be quite established, too socially involved to be quite pure, and too amorphous and digressive to be quite capable of providing high art. The novel is, for many still, popular culture, not to the manor born, no better than it should be.

Like many clichés, the statement that the novel is a middle-class form developed for middle-class readers is partly true, but enormously misleading.[3] For one thing, the term *middle class* carries for us some freight that is not appropriate to early readers of novels; for another, it implies a more homogeneous audience than the novel actually had. I shall try to describe the early readers of novels more precisely than just by social class, partly by looking at what we now know about eighteenth-century readership from the evidence of social history and partly by examining what is in the novels themselves. The recent scholarly attention to literacy offers a suggestive new perspective about what early readers were looking for, and the novels themselves look somewhat different when read in that light.

Social historians have posited a rising curve of literacy in England beginning about 1600, and Lawrence Stone's convenient summary, drawing upon the work of R. S. Schofield and the Cambridge population group as well as upon more traditional estimates, offers us (with some caution) a fair summary.[4] Stone estimates that 25 percent of adult males in England and Wales were literate in 1600, and that by 1800 the figure had risen substantially, to about 65 percent. In Scotland the gain in those two hundred years was, incidentally, from 15 percent to 88 percent. That steep rise—a two-and-one-half-fold increase in England and Wales in two centuries and in Scotland almost sixfold—means primarily that class and occupational groups such as yeomen, husbandmen, artisans, and tradesmen had become more literate between 1600 and 1800 since "higher" groups—the landed gentry, the clergy, and the professional men—were, as Stone notes, already "almost 100 percent literate" by 1600. At first glance, these figures would seem to confirm the old rise-of-the-middle-class, rise-of-the-reading-public, rise-of-the-novel thesis (a thesis that I will call for convenience the "triple rise" thesis), but even a quick second glance suggests important difficulties. In the first place, the rise of literacy from 25 to 65 percent over two hundred years is not steady, and the sharpest inclines come at precisely the wrong time for the triple-rise thesis. Between 1600 and 1675, literacy in England nearly doubled, going from 25 to 45 percent of adult males, and after 1775 another sharp rise may have occurred. But in between, from 1675 to 1775, the years immediately before and during the emergence of the novel, the growth in literacy was relatively slow, increasing only from 45 to 53 percent—in one hundred years, mind you—a severe deceleration of the earlier rate of increase. The rise in literacy during the earlier seventeenth century clearly does mean a larger reading public for the novel, but also for several generations before the novel, so that the relationship between the size of the reading public and the emergence of the novel must be less immediate and direct than we have been led to expect. The question—one I will leave open for the moment—is what that new and large group of readers did for reading material while they were waiting for the novel to rise: unaccounted for in the triple-rise thesis is a period of three full generations. Poised on the edge of social arrival, but novel-less, they must have lived and died in bitter disappointment at the slowness of the cultural yeast.

A second issue in almost all literacy figures is that, as you may have noticed, they estimate figures only for adult males, and the novel's audience has always been presumed to include a substantial female readership. Detractors in the eighteenth century in fact commonly dismiss novels as fit only for females. Swift is working from that implicit assumption when he claims that the fire in the palace in Lilliput was started by a careless maid of honor who was reading fiction there: literally, perhaps, her candle set the fire, but Swift's figurative pun implies that her passions became inappropriately overheated by her reading. In the absence of concrete figures to go on, historians of literacy have usually estimated female literacy in the early eighteenth century to be very low, lower even than a hundred years before. Such estimates are based ultimately on two kinds of sources—nineteenth-century anecdotes about how much women's education had improved since the eighteenth century, and eighteenth-century satires, which often portray women as frivolous and empty-headed. But ultimately these estimates seem very dubious.[5] The reformers of any age are understandably prone to exaggerate how bad things were before they came on the scene, and the nineteenth century's estimate of the eighteenth-century generally is not very reliable on social matters. And the satirists—while often accurate in their assessment of social problems at a particular time—are hardly reliable for historical perspective, for their strategy is always to depict the present as a deterioration from the past. No doubt the early eighteenth century had some mindless air-heads like those portrayed by Pope and Swift, but the seventeenth century and the nineteenth had their Belindas, too. Besides, Belinda's original evidently could read; Pope addresses *The Rape of the Lock* specifically to her, and in fact the presumption of female literacy is extremely common in early eighteenth-century books.

Moll Flanders could read too, as Defoe gave her to us, and she was not of Belinda's social class. Not only does her story depend upon the convention of her authorship, but she engages in wit battles with one of her lovers by scratching rhymes on a window. One might argue that Moll would not read, that she could hardly find time to work it in among her other pursuits, but she could read—and write—rhymes for her lovers, and write a novel for us. And there is Pamela who, like Moll, is supposed to have written (largely) the novel that tells her story. In his parody of *Pamela*, Fielding has a good deal of fun with the whole idea that a girl of her class could write, or at least spell. Her virtue becomes for Fielding her precious missaid and misspelled (but nevertheless written) "Vartue": "I value my Vartue more than I do any thing. . . ," writes Shamela, "and so we talked a full Hour and a half, about my Vartue."[6]

But Fielding's snobbish spoof helps to illustrate the point. It seemed funny to some people in 1740 to think that a servant girl could read, and if they were of Fielding's social class they would think comic her attempt to spell and parse and imitate the English as well as the manners of her betters. But Fielding still makes a servant girl a letter-writer and an author, just like Richardson's Pamela. Not every servant maid, at the time the novel emerged, could read—few enough that the idea still struck their betters as an outrageous usurpation of something the upper classes owned—but enough servant girls could read so that an orphan like Moll Flanders or an upwardly mobile country girl like Pamela could be realistically portrayed as the author of her own book; it was generally known that many of the contemporary "lives" flooding the bookstalls were, in fact, written by women authors. In the absence of any actual figures or reliable estimates of female literacy to go on, the expectations of the public are a more reliable index than unsupported anecdotes and satiric rhetoric. We can be quite sure that many early readers of novels were women.[7]

A third difficulty with traditional literacy figures, much alleviated by newer, more detailed studies, is that raw estimates do not suggest the geographical distribution of literacy, and I mentioned a moment ago the literacy figures for Scotland partly to astonish and partly to hint that treating all of the island of Great Britain as if it were one homogeneous unit is not justified. Stone traces different patterns and paces in different sections of England and Wales and also notes that the literacy in town and city is everywhere higher than in village and country, a fact that is crucially important to deciding the readership of novels. Whatever the literacy rate elsewhere in England, that in London for adult males was likely to have been at least 50 percent (and probably much higher) from the early seventeenth century on, and there is good evidence—evidence about the number of local items that poured from the London press, evidence that schools for the poor flourished there when they were failing elsewhere all over the island—that it continued to increase substantially there, even when literacy in the country may actually have declined, possibly reaching 75 or 80 percent in London by 1725. That fact is extremely important for defining the audience of the novel and in accounting for the reading tastes of the late seventeenth- and early eighteenth-century public more generally, for although critics and historians like Ian Watt have linked the novel with urban growth generally, we have not fully appreciated how important to the novel's emergence is the centrality of London in the consciousness of its readers.

The importance of London to the English reading public at the time the novel emerges is out of all proportion to its numerical size and to the actual number of readers there. The crucial matter is that for an Englishman or Englishwoman of 1700, London represented the relentless forward direction of English life in a way that was startling and pervasive. London had become symbolically the center of England, just as the small village had once been symbolic, and for all kinds of reasons. During the seventeenth century, London had nearly tripled in population to a city of almost 600,000 or perhaps even 700,000. Everything—products, habits, ideas—seemed to start there and then trickle into the remote countryside. No doubt there were thousands of people who, like Squire Western in *Tom Jones*, stayed firmly planted in their country estates, cursing urbanness and modernity and everything they associated with London—dirt, bad smells, corruption, sophistication, democracy—but no doubt, too, they all had relatives who had lived there and who believed (like Western's sister) that everything worthwhile was modern and ultimately only to be found in London. And, like Western himself, those most remote from London, in place or in spirit, usually found themselves as Western did, having to go there sooner or later on urgent business.

The real reach of London is, in fact, perhaps best indicated not so much by its population as by the number of people whose lives involved it directly—because they lived there for a time, because they journeyed there on visits, or because they were regularly in touch with what went on there through business or trade. E. A. Wrigley has developed a statistical model of London's significance for 1650–1750 in which he persuasively suggests that London's status relative to England during those years actually becomes far greater than the fabled importance of Paris to France.[8] That symbolic relationship to the rest of the nation begins to show up in the literature of the late seventeenth century, as London becomes the setting for work after work. *Mac Flecknoe* (1682) is one early indicator; others are Tom Brown's *Amusements, Serious and Comical, Calculated for the Meridian of London* (1700) and Ned Ward's *London Spy*, which in its detailed exploration of London for the curious, ran to eighteen issues between 1698 and 1700. Stage comedies in the later seventeenth century were consistently set in or near London, and in the early eighteenth century London is suddenly the principal setting for poem after poem: Pope's *Dunciad* takes place there, Gay's *Beggar's Opera* and his *Trivia, or Art of Walking the Streets of London;* and Swift's *Description of a City Shower, Description of the Morning,* and even crucial parts of *Gulliver's Travels.*

All the major novelists until Sterne—that is, Defoe, Richardson, Fielding, and Smollett—wrote primarily in London, and as soon as Sterne became known he immediately went there, as if his goal had been to get there all along. And the same was true of other writers of all sorts. For the first time in history, most English authors lived within a few blocks of each other, and not far away were the shops of a majority of those who published the books for the entire kingdom—books that had been commissioned, written, edited, and printed in London, with largely Londoners (and those who aspired to London) in mind. Even writers who looked nostalgically to the values of an earlier age were themselves Londoners writing for other Londoners. The literature of England in the early eighteenth century became overwhelmingly urban literature; London was its subject, and London was the place where it was read. Reading was centered there, just as writing and publishing were, for although there were readers all over England, the first readers of almost everything—the tastemakers— were in London. To define the reading public for the novel, we have to keep their location and urban assumptions in mind.

Most early readers of novels were also young. The plots of early novels—like those of many more recent ones—readily suggest by the events and crises they highlight that their authors believed they were writing for youthful readers, men *and* women. The novels are primarily about coping with a world bigger and more complicated than what one had counted on, and a disproportionate number of them deal primarily with two crises: the choice of profession and the choice of marriage partner. What contemporary people said about the readers of novels supports the claims of youth, too, not just Johnson characterizing them as "the young, the ignorant, and the idle," but those who warned of the evils of novels almost always concentrated on possible effects on the young. They worried about youths' heads being turned, their imaginations corrupted, and their passions and expectations aroused; to read the moralists, one would never guess that anyone over eighteen read novels.

Perhaps we have not sufficiently noticed the young as the major readers of novels, because literary history has placed a misleading emphasis on the difficulty of access to books, concentrating on one aspect of the economics of reading, ownership, and ignoring social habits. It is true that the price of books and of light for reading was high—the window tax meant that houses usually let in little natural light, and candles were costly—but what has been overlooked is that young people seem to have had a kind of secret network through which they passed their contraband. Up against a disapproving establishment, young people in the early eighteenth century exchanged and shared freely their private treasures, and the few copies of novels that existed moved quickly from one private closet to another.[9] The very poor would have to struggle hard to read a novel and only the most determined would be able to do so, but the young and ambitious—the ones most likely to have found the means to learn to read—could readily find a way.

One final note about the reading public, and then let me summarize what we can safely surmise about the early readers of novels. Johnson said that readers of novels were not only young and idle, but ignorant. Johnson's standard was very high. By "ignorant" he seems to have meant several things: a lack of traditional reading in the classics, an insufficient sense of the humanistic tradition, the absence of the moral regimen and stamina that supposedly resulted from proper education, and insufficient respect for tradition and received opinion. Many readers of novels in fact *sought* to be ignorant in Johnson's sense of the term; the younger generation (and many of the older generation) distrusted what they felt to be the narrowness of traditional ways of thinking and living, and they sought a broader base for both life and art, just as the novelists themselves did. The novel is a rebel form (I prefer this term to subversive because the resistance is usually close to the surface and does not always run deep or provoke erosion); it sought rebel readers, and rebel readers sought it. But if many readers of novels were ignorant in the sense that they distrusted what they knew of traditional learning and morality and in the fact that they were less well read in the classics than, say, readers of Pope's Horatian satires or Johnson's own Juvenalian imitation entitled *London*, we should not allow that truth to blind us to the fact that traditional readers read novels, too. Johnson himself apparently read, often with disapproval, the major novelists of his time, and Pope and Swift had read Defoe thoroughly, although they might not have wanted to count it as "literature." And the literary sophistication in those early novels—sometimes ignored in the cause of labeling them middle class—meant that there was a great deal there for anyone of any background and any taste. Readers of Defoe or Richardson or Fielding did not need an extensive experience of reading to respond enthusiastically and well to *Robinson Crusoe* or *Clarissa* or *Tom Jones*, but the more they knew the richer they were in their new texts. Readers who knew their Bible would certainly find more resonance in all three (for sophisticated devices of allusion and echo were employed with as much care as in Pope or Swift). Those who knew their Homer would find both Defoe and Fielding more interesting and challenging reading, and readers of Shakespeare and Milton would find a variety of interesting surprises in Fielding and Richardson. To read Fielding, in fact, was almost to sit down to a conversation about old and familiar friends; he planned it that way even while appealing to social ambition and the rhetoric of rising.

Let me now summarize what we know about early readers of novels. "Middle class" many of them were, at least in the sense that relatively few were from the very lowest or the very highest classes. But we can be much more specific. Most were young with the world just before them, at an age when the choices of life were much on their minds. Most were Londoners and those who were not had London as their goal and guide. Most identified with modern attitudes and modern life, looking to a new urban world rather than an older rural one, and most had ambitions in that world, hoping to rise above the station they had been born into. Few probably were first-generation readers, although most of them were no more than third-generation readers. And many—there is no reliable way to tell how many—were women, young women. But if these were typical readers, there is also a minority report to make: other readers included the very old, who read novels to discover what they had missed; booby squires in the country, who were a little more curious than they cared to admit about what was beyond the ten-mile circumference of their worlds; moralists of the old school, who considered it their duty to survey what they condemned; and others who read to disapprove because they found the whole new world offensive to their sense of what had been best in older, more intimate, more communal, more traditional worlds that took their values from the past. But the minority report and the majority report of readers ultimately have the same thrust in literary history: they agree that whatever its writers consciously intended, the novel was a form fitted to a new world. And the name "novel"—although not firmly established as the right name for the species until much later—was an appropriate name for the methods and values one would find there.

The question of why eighteenth-century readers read novels—and what they expected from them—is far more complex, but a satisfactory answer to that question is crucial to any attempt to describe the nature and origins of the novel. In one sense the reasons to read novels were as various—and are as various still—as the variety of individual readers and individual books. But successful authorship, then as now, involved the reading of both fundamental and immediate human needs, being in touch with the culture of one's time, recognizing the distinctive cultural consciousness of that historical moment. The first great novelists were—like the first great English dramatists, Shakespeare and his contemporaries—tuned in to their times sensitively: they knew their audience. Defoe lived by his pen, and guided it in quite a few convenient directions; Richardson was a London printer (he had come from Derbyshire to become an apprentice at age seventeen) and lived by his commercial sense of what the pens of others could do. Fielding, who came from the West to seek his literary fortune at age twenty, was a playwright in a contemporary theatre tuned to news of the moment, quickly shifting opinions and ideas, fads and trends, that demanded from authors an uncanny ability to read the public. And Smollett and Sterne, both from the North but both sensitive to London taste, blatantly sought to discover exactly what it was that the public wanted and to satisfy needs that would not necessarily sound artistically noble. Plainly the early novelists who succeeded understood public needs and desires, and knowing something about the readers of these books allows us to match up their human situations with what novels contain and do.

Of the many human needs that early novels seem to address, I want to mention four that help suggest why the novel took the directions that it did. All have something specific to do with the kinds of readership we have been considering, and all have a basis in the particular historical conditions in the early eighteenth century.

The first of these needs involves the desire for instruction in the ways of the world. How does the world work? What are the rules? How do others manage the difficult pressures and choices that the world offers? How do they cope with competing demands of love and honor, of reason and passion, of personal life and professional responsibility? How do people talk in particular circumstances? What do they think about? How do they act? How do they feel? We may never know how much of modern human history has gone the way it has because people at crucial moments have said or done a certain thing in imitation of some character in a novel who had acted that way, on the assumption that that was the way it was to be done. Life *does* imitate art, often quite self-consciously. None of us would rationally decide to turn our personal decisions over to novelists, but the desire for instruction (usually a little disguised) still remains one of the most powerful motives for reading novels, or autobiography or history, or for seeing films. The instruction we seek usually involves a larger sense of the way things are, a knowledge of human habits, rituals, and expectations, a cracking of the code. Narrative, because it purports to offer a large picture of life in several dimensions, showing us the outcomes of actions and presenting a sense of causality, provides clues in a subtle and unthreatening way. Always appearing to be about someone else, it pretends to show us what happens without forcing on us any shoulds, or musts, or shalt nots.

For early readers of novels, this kind of need was particularly intense because of the lack of models for the kind of lives they were facing. Questions about the way of the world are not exclusively the questions of youth, but for the young there is a peculiar urgency, especially when traditional sources of guidance seem to be disappearing or when the culture seems to be changing so rapidly that old rules do not apply, and for the London youth of the early eighteenth century both conditions obtained. Cut loose from family ties and the nurturing passed along from father to son and mother to daughter, young people found little in urban institutions to take up the slack. Whether the cutting off from tradition was thrust upon an individual by circumstances (being sent to London to apprentice, for example, as Samuel Richardson was) or chosen as an act of rebellion against the repression of a tight community and stifling family, the result was much the same: the individual desperately needed information, rules, guidelines; and reading was a safe, noncommittal, uninvolved way to address that need. According to Johnson, the new fiction served, for "the young, the ignorant, and the idle," as "lectures of conduct, and introductions into life." [10]

The story of how Samuel Richardson came to write *Pamela* is suggestive of how novelists saw, or half saw, that need. Busy compiling a practical guide on how to write letters for various circumstances, a volume to be called *Familiar Letters*, Richardson found himself writing letters that began to tell a story as well, thus addressing a different set of practical questions about modes of action in certain circumstances. How is an innocent servant girl to act when her wicked master decides it is his right to seduce her? How can she preserve her virtue and keep her position, or (better yet) better herself as a result? The situations and themes of early novels suggest how often novelists saw their function partly in terms of addressing readers' needs to know about the ways of the world—how others handled particular difficulties or responded to habits and rituals larger than themselves. Novels sometimes seem founded in an abstract question answered in terms of a particular character and specific situation. What is a beautiful and sensible young woman to do when she finds herself in love with a man she disapproves of? What can one do when caught in the marital middle of a family quest for prestige, money, and power? How does one conduct oneself when thrown into the arms of a libertine as the only seeming alternative to a toad-like suitor approved by one's parents? How can one retain integrity and self-respect when opposing inappropriate parental wishes? At what point does parental authority cease? How does one live with having been raped by a suitor? Or . . . what is it like to be born an orphan girl and have to live by your wits, your dextrous hands, and your attractive body? What is it like to be caught in London in the midst of a plague? What is it like to be thrust back upon the primitive circumstances of society and have to make do with only the resources of nature for food, shelter, and company? How does one cope with being utterly—totally—alone?

The questions which novels try to answer for the curious and the innocent easily slide from intellectual ones (about the ways and means of the world) to emotional ones, and I have allowed my phrasing of the questions to slide gradually from one to the other. When the question becomes "What would it be like to be a thief and a prostitute like Moll Flanders?" instead of "What does one do when faced with a choice between poverty and prostitution?" we have subtly shifted to a second need, the need of readers to transcend themselves, to participate imaginatively in another existence. Like the need for instruction in the ways of the world, this need to fantasize, to participate sympathetically in the life and situation of someone else, seems basic to novel reading in any time or place, but the need was especially intense and focused for early eighteenth-century readers because of their historical circumstance. Hobbes had described the natural life of man as "solitary, poor, nasty, brutish, and short," but it was civilized Londoners who lived out that description more literally a few years later. For those not born among the privileged, life in the country had been hard enough, as primitive life against the elements always is. But the excitement and opportunity of London brought, with its glitter and challenge, unspeakable crowding, filth, infection, and stench. Contemporary accounts of London in the early eighteenth century portray situations unimaginable to us. In the relatively roomy homes they occupied, the rich could be comfortable and feel safe, but once they entered the streets they took, just as the poor did, their lives in their hands. The mortality rate in London was so high that the population hardly grew at all between 1700 and 1750, despite the maintenance of a rate of migration that had added at least 400,000 people to a city of 200,000 during the previous century. Even when one had survived infancy, the prospect of living much beyond youth was slim, far slimmer than in the country or in earlier times. Crime was rampant, disease was everywhere; the senses were bombarded, and not just with the symmetry of Palladian designs or extensions of the line of beauty. Hogarth's drawings were, all things considered, rather restrained, and so was Swift's picture of London streets after a rain:

> Sweepings from Butchers Stalls, Dung, Guts and Blood
> Drown'd Puppies, stinking Sprats, all drench'd in Mud,
> Dead Cats and Turnip-Tops come tumbling down the Flood.

There was no sewer system, and rains came too seldom; until mid-century, Fleet Ditch was simply a pit of open sewage, and the smell was overpowering. Almost any reading, even in a small and close room, if the windows could be shut and the nostrils stopped with lavender and rue, would be a solace of some kind. But the interesting thing about the pursuit of fantasy in the early eighteenth century is that it was firmly anchored in probability and ordinary life. One might expect that romances—tales of brave knights and fair maidens, frogs transformed to princes and houses made of cake, the stories of far away and long ago—would be the standard fare of those who spent their days in squalor and in fear for their lives. But if fantasy for these readers meant an escape from the everyday, it was an escape into hope, a reaching for possibility, a fantasy influenced by a rural and communal past but firmly grounded in a complex urban present. Romance was not a viable opiate for the urban young and ambitious. If life around them was depressing and might look hopeless to an impartial observer, to the young who chose London and its promise of a new world over an older and safer world they had left behind, it still represented a future of hope, and in their reading they sought stories of success and coping, fantasies that involved real-seeming people and imaginable situations. Being stranded for twenty-eight years on a desert island may be an uncommon situation, but half a dozen people in Defoe's lifetime had in fact survived such isolation and found their way back to civilization: the story was in the coping—with physical, emotional, and spiritual situations that were understandable, possible: real metaphors. It is an urban fantasy. For those who grew up in the growingly empirical world of the late seventeenth century and ambitiously faced an urban world of getting and spending, fantasy was a practical matter of imagining some sort of personal and private triumph over the everyday and the ordinary, not a pure escape from it in the sense in which the old romances had addressed the need.

A third characteristic need of the early readers of novels stemmed from their loneliness. By the late seventeenth century, London had become a jostling and impersonal place to live. It was the second largest city in the world, soon to become the largest, and its residents were among the first in history to experience as a group the "lonely crowd" phenomenon that we now take for granted as an urban condition of life. Most Londoners were new to the city; not only had London trebled in size in a hundred years, but people passed quickly through it and thousands died young. Young and ambitious Londoners—those who constituted the largest group of readers—were almost all strangers in London and thus even more dramatically struck by the impersonal difference from their earlier communities. Intense loneliness pervaded London life; the feeling comes through loud and clear in letters, diaries, autobiographies, and private papers. The thirst for sociability and the hunger for human community were everywhere; one thinks of the frantic but impersonal gatherings at Ranelagh and Vauxhall, of interminable masquerade balls, of the London clubs, coffeehouse gatherings, and political and occupational groupings that tried to provide institutional substitutes for the old village communality, where one person's concern had been everyone's concern, but one person's business was also everyone else's. Londoners had chosen the city over the country to free themselves from the hemming in of closer ties, but they paid a psychic price, too, and the cry of the human spirit is often plaintive—always lonely—in the literature of the city.

In the early eighteenth century, the longing for some sort of human community to replace a lost intimacy is repeatedly prominent, especially in the privacy of diaries and of letters of friends to each other. Pope, hardly the most sentimental of writers and often thought (incorrectly) to be insensitive to the human ties of loyalty and friendship, often writes plaintively to his friends about his sense of broken community and deep hunger for escape from the prison of the self. "A man's chief business," he wrote once, "is to be really at home," and for him that meant connection, and emotional and spiritual sharing.[11] The myth of lost community—the nearly universal feeling in all times that the present offers less than the past in terms of its human values—is not, of course, unique to London or to the early eighteenth century, and no doubt (as Raymond Williams suggests) even the smallest gatherings of people in the most primitive ages raised the whole issue of country versus city values out of all proportion to reality.[12] But the persistent fact is that people experience urbanness and their lost heritage of rusticity in that way, always exaggerating the way it *was* and feeling a little too poignantly what *is*. And in 1700 there was a very good reason to exaggerate—and be nostalgic about—the old green and pleasant land that Londoners and time had left behind. London contained so many with parallel experiences and similar feelings, and the feelings were hardly diminished by the fact that their dispossession from the land had been, in most cases, freely chosen as a way to "improve" themselves. The young apprentice, choosing the solitude of his room to read a novel, was at once responding to urban loneliness and basking in it.

If the novel is the characteristic literary form of the modern world, as many literary critics and historians have said, it is partly because it reflects modern society and its problems of greater population density, an accelerated pace of human activity, and a sense of increasing spiritual uncertainty and barrenness, and partly because the novel's length and manner of presentation provide the appropriate form for an audience experience of modernity. The phenomenology of the novel at once mirrors and exacerbates the sense of loneliness, and early novels betray an intense awareness of both the needs of readers and the absolute limits of the species, bound as it is to bookness, to the realities of read narrative, and to the circumstances of actual readers. Fielding, for example, in *Tom Jones* repeatedly jollies his reader, talks to him (or her), pretends to be a traveling companion. He repeatedly reassures us that he is with us, talking all the time, sharing a story and offering observations, telling us that we are not alone. And Sterne carries the device even further, often addressing readers individually as this sort of reader or that, once temporarily banishing a putative lady reader until she rereads an earlier passage while (presumably) Sterne and the rest of the company move on.[13] Such a strategy of community support, repeated in one form or another by most early novelists, is born of an acute awareness that the reading of books is a lonely act, especially when one is reading a novel, a book of a certain magnitude that requires hours of solitude to experience, especially when novels were sufficiently disapproved that readers had to curl up with them surreptitiously in cramped private spaces. Sometimes the essentially private experience of reading novels has been obscured by winning anecdotes about the public reading of novels—such as the one about how people in a small village all gathered to hear the blacksmith read *Pamela* and then rang the church bells when

she was married.[14] But the evidence is that such phenomena rarely occurred, and when they did—in the nineteenth century in social groups
gathered for the specific purpose of reading novels—they were consciously
designed to subvert the limits of the form. At the center of the novel's early
popularity lies a similar experiential irony: lonely readers found in novels
the company of others, but, in achieving such imaginative experience,
they guaranteed and even intensified their solitude from other actual human beings. Few novels are, like *Robinson Crusoe*, about real solitude, but
many of them (also like *Robinson Crusoe* in its exploration of the hero's attempts to relate to cats, goats, parrots, cannibals, and even Catholics) are
about attempts to lower the wall of loneliness, to find some sort of viable
community in whatever setting. Eighteenth-century novels, even more
than novels since, center on the experience of one individual—not of a
family or larger group or even a couple—and trace that individual's attempts to relate, whether (as in the case of *Moll Flanders*) the attempt to
relate is primarily an attempt to deal with and domesticate urban strangers, or (as in the case of *Tristram Shandy*) a matter of exploring relationships
with other family members and intimates as a way of expressing oneself.
There is a double poignancy to the act of reading a novel about a character
walled up in self and trying to relate to others. It is an act of dealing with
solitude and yet extending it: it is the loneliness of the long-distance
reader.[15]

A fourth need for early novel-readers involves the pleasures of narrative itself. The need for narrative seems to be universal (or nearly so),
but English cultural history in the seventeenth century seems to have governed the form of narrative that the novel represents. About the human
need for narrative we actually know very little in detail, although story is
found so widely even in the most primitive cultures as to suggest a persistent human hunger for it.[16] In primitive (or preliterate) societies, narrative is of course oral and transmitted by human memory rather than
through the written word, and oral narratives in many cultures are performed by a designated individual for an assembled group so that the
fulfillment of narrative needs is often hard to separate from that of needs
for communality. Still, the prevalence and persistence of narrative in some
form suggests that story telling is basic to human society. Whether narrative satisfies some deep-seated human desire to believe in sequence,
causality, and wholeness, whether it offers by analogy some clue to expected patterns of behavior, whether it addressed desires for recreation,
play, and information, or whether it offers (even when read in solitude)
some sense of interconnectedness between ourselves and human patterns
of experience is finally hard to say, but theorists of narrative like Scholes

and Kellogg are probably right to assume that the need for narrative is fundamental, nearly universal.

It would be almost fair to say that there was, however, no narrative tradition in English before 1700—almost fair, but inaccurate. Almost fair because the amount (relatively speaking) of pure narrative in the accepted canon of English literature before 1700 was very small. But it is still inaccurate to say that there was no narrative tradition in England, for as in preliterate societies there was a rich fund of popular stories passed orally from generation to generation. Old wives' tales, winter's tales, fairy tales, legends and sagas, etiological myths, and stories of magic and witchcraft were told at the fireside in villages and towns, by rich and poor alike, told by parents to children and by villagers to each other at holiday festivals and market-day celebrations. The drama of Shakespeare's time is so packed with references and allusions to such stories that we would have, right there, almost enough evidence to reconstruct folk practices of pre–Civil War times, even if there were not considerable further evidence that England's heritage of oral tales was rich and resonant.

But there is a mystery about folk tales in England that relates, I think crucially, to the emergence of the novel. The mystery involves a retreat of the folk tradition, a deterioration of oral culture that appears to have no parallel elsewhere in Europe.[17] The most dramatic evidence involves the fairy tale or *Märchen*—a type of oral tale that is found throughout Europe. Everywhere there is a continuous tradition of fairy tales right down to the time when they began to be written down by antiquaries, collectors, and folklorists—everywhere, that is, except England and Wales. There, the fairy tales that Shakespeare draws upon seem to have dropped out of sight and mind, and when collectors find them much later they bear traces of having been reintroduced in written versions from other cultures.[18] Folklorists do not yet agree on why such a phenomenon occurred. The most popular theory is that the Puritans did them in: sometimes I wonder how we would explain *any* of our cultural deprivations if we did not have the Puritans as our cultural scapegoats. But whether the Puritans by themselves managed to scourge the land of all whispered traces of such powerful stories or whether Puritan suppression of such fanciful narratives had significant allies in other segments of the culture is hard to say. This much is certain: fairy tales were driven from the land in fear, like the snakes from Ireland; they did not go joyfully or because people ceased to care deeply about the kinds of issues imbedded in them. And other kinds of oral narratives went into retreat, too. Folk tales were part of the past of Merry Old England; Puritans distrusted them, and so did the learned and the sophisticated. For Puritans and protestants more generally, everything associated with oral tradition seemed pagan or devil-inspired. And, as Keith Thomas has demonstrated, magic and folk beliefs that had welded themselves to Christian tradition and ritual gradually were pried loose during the seventeenth century.[19] Intellectual efforts and cultural pride played their part as well: the scientific spirit took its toll in goblins and warlocks and tales about them, the rational spirit sought to free the English from the darkness of their old superstitions, and the spirit of sophistication and modernity sought to drive wedges between a liberated now and a rural past of ignorance, clumsiness, and error. Combined, these forces of progress took dead aim on the folk heritage, and it is no wonder that something vibrant and vital went out with the baggage. John Locke, who speaks for the new forces in culture as articulately as anyone at the turn of the eighteenth century, vigorously denounced the old tales and the nursemaids who told them, and for at least a half century his anecdote about what the stories had done to him was retailed freely. "Fear of Sprights and Hobgoblins" had, he said, been so imbedded in him by the "Prattle" of his nurse, that all his philosophy could not triumph over it, and, even in adulthood, he remained afraid of the dark.[20] It was a powerful anecdote for an usher of the new world to tell, and it is a significant one.

The evidence, then, is that the oral narratives that had been at the heart of English experience for centuries began to dry up during the seventeenth century, at precisely the time that more and more people were learning to read three full generations before the emergence of the novel. The loss of oral tradition and the rise of literacy are plainly related to the same historical forces—empiricism, rationality about social and cultural institutions, the desire for civility and sophistication in the culture, the attraction to modernity for its own sake, and (one force that was distinctively English), the continuing pressure from Protestantism (always a book-centered religion because of its every-man-his-own-priest philosophy)—that acted to make literacy universal and free people from their oral heritage by providing them a new authority in the book.

I shall be brief and only suggestive about the third question raised at the beginning, about how the needs I have described were met before the emergence of the novel. But let me mention *one* thing I considered earlier, fill *two* gaps in the argument, and offer *three* notes and *four* speculations. The reminder is that Lawrence Stone's composite literacy figures show that the steepest rise in literacy had occurred by 1675, almost a half century before Defoe began to write novels in 1719 and nearly three quarters of a century before the novel craze of the 1740s. That means that whole generations of "new" readers did not have the novel to turn to for their reading pleasure, even though the needs I have been speaking of were developed and articulated by 1675, perhaps long before.

The gaps I want to fill involve two facts that I have not mentioned about the long, apparently dry period between the growth of the reading public and the emergence of the novel. One fact is that the taste for books of fiction per se seems not to have grown substantially during that period; some fiction was read early in the seventeenth century and little more a century later, despite the much enlarged reading public and the retreat of oral tradition. Romances retained a steady but unspectacular popularity, but there was no rush to romance, no apparent feeling that romances could address the needs I have described, for they had little to offer the young, modern, urban audience.

The second fact may suggest a reason why a garrison of fiction did not move into the narrative vacuum. Guardians of morality—writers of guides for youth, conduct books, educational treatises, sermons, and all sorts of didactic treatises—repeatedly warned of the lie implicit in any fiction, and until well into the eighteenth century little tolerance was expressed for anything that stood by itself as a fiction. Illustrative anecdotes might do well enough, whether based on truth, legend, or outright imagination, but the prohibition of fiction seems to have been widely, if somewhat superficially, accepted. No doubt a good bit of surreptitious reading in violation of the prohibition took place, and the youth underground evidently did circulate copies of plays and some few romances and tales—whatever they had—but in the absence of any published fiction that actually addressed felt human needs there was not much to pass. The moralists kept the lid on, nervously.

My three notes may suggest why, for each involves a kind of literature or paraliterature that did meet needs. In a world without clocks and the human limits that they measure and record, I would try to suggest how each of these varieties of literature provided a kind of interim satisfaction for readers, a link to what novelists learn to do more comprehensively, but here I will only name the varieties: (1) Works of journalism in the literal sense of that term, that is, works whether broadsheets, pamphlets, treatises, periodicals, or books, which addressed the topics of the day, the events of the moment, works of utter and easily dated contemporaneity, the kinds of works parodied by Swift in *A Tale of a Tub* when he has his author claim to be writing words that are true this moment that he is writing them—the kind imitated with great art and sophistication in Richardson's "writing to the moment" technique. (2) Didactic works of all sorts, which attempted—sometimes woodenly, sometimes with great subtlety—

to provide direct and open guidance for life in changing times. Many of these works were not in fact treatises but rather anthologies that collected stories for some specific thematic or pedagogical point—anthologies of special providences like William Turner's *Complete History of Remarkable Providences*, for example, collections of cautionary tales drawn from written and oral sources, gatherings of anecdotes, anthologies of great wonders and of strange and surprising events. The number of such works published between 1680 and 1720 is almost as astonishing as the wonders described in these works, and their way of bringing artfully constructed narratives into a coherent thematic or ideological framework bears a noticeable relationship to what happens in the novel. (3) Longer narratives that describe actual, or supposedly actual, happenings—diaries, autobiographies, biographies, life-and-times histories like those of Dunton and Burnet, and more conventional histories like that of Clarendon—books that have authority, scope, and shape.

Finally, four speculations. *Speculation 1:* What the early novelists were able to do, cleverly, was combine together features that were developed in the various paraliterary types, thus addressing in a more or less concentrated way what a great variety of printed materials had accomplished for readers before the novel emerged. The act of putting together, of reading the public's complexity of needs through a comprehensive review of what they read, may help to account for the novel's notorious eclecticism, a feature that has always annoyed traditionalists and generic purists and that quite naturally bothered neoclassical theorists. The novel is often a basket into which authors seem to put things, whatever they have, digressive things, anecdotes, philosophy, a mixture of styles, didactic points, even other works swallowed whole, in addition to a continuous narrative. *Speculation 2:* Because the novel is a gathering of devices, styles, features, and tones, and because its mixing of them is uneven and volatile, the novel does not get "invented" or "founded" in the usual sense by some one person who can properly be called its parent or the "first" novelist. Rather, the novel evolved, accumulating features and developing an identity as time went on. This is why we sometimes argue about whether a certain book is "really" a novel when it contains several novelistic features but not others. If I am right, there is, properly, no apostolic succession, no line, no lineage, and the whole vocabulary of birth and genealogy, based upon the analogy of human biology, is misleading, if not downright wrong. *Speculation 3:* The course of events happened in the way it did largely because England was England—still quite insular, conservative, and traditional, but pragmatic, and above all Protestant. The sharp rise in literacy, and the pressure to make it rise still further when the growth began to level off, seems largely due to Protestant theological commitments, especially the belief in the primacy of written over oral tradition and the vesting of interpretative rights in the individual. The combination of commitments to literacy, individualism, and subjectivity together with a high degree of tolerance for social mobility, meant that attitudes and ideas crucial to the novel as a species had a ready public consciousness in which to come together, and, once the moral strictures against fiction could be rationalized and once approved didactic modes could be blended in, the possibilities could be realized. *Speculation 4:* Because of the peculiar combination of conditions and events in England during the late years of the seventeenth century and the early years of the eighteenth the English novel moved quickly to the artistic forefront in narrative by midcentury, and after trailing the developments in prose fiction on the continent, especially in France and Spain, for more than a century, moved for the first time into a position to influence continental narrative. Since the second half of the eighteenth century, the story of the development of narrative has been an international one. Before Defoe and Richardson, there is little to say about the English contribution, but cultural events then allowed England to push ahead and innovate in directions that continental writers imitated and then absorbed. The novel became the universal literary species of modernity, and, like modernity itself, emerged in different places at different times.

A quarter century ago, a quieter and perhaps more innocent age used to watch with rapture the several so-called epic films made by Cecil B. de Mille, a new one every year it seemed, and each one designed to be (as they say) a biblical spectacular to end all biblical spectaculars. When one of them, *The Ten Commandments*, was released, a cartoon appeared—in the *New Yorker* I think—in the Brother Sebastian series. Brother Sebastian was a playful and puckish priest, always up to timely things but with a sense of perspective, and in this cartoon he was walking in front of the moviehouse where the film was showing, wearing a sign that said, "Don't forget to read the book." I'm not sure that films and essays are modes inferior to stone tablets and scholarly books, but the translation between modes is sometimes difficult. Ultimately, I hope that the book I am writing will clear up all possible questions and provide universal historical answers: the beauty of anything not yet finished is that it allows infinite hope. But in the meanwhile I hope I have raised some disturbing questions. Like another revisionist of history and theorist of fiction, Lemuel Gulliver, I would like to think that in six or seven months all the world can be reformed by truth and sweet reason. But unlike Gulliver, I shall not, if my efforts are unavailing, "have done with all visionary schemes for ever." Rather, like his creator, Jonathan Swift, I believe that there is virtue in simply vexing a vexatious world. On her death bed, Gertrude Stein is said to have suddenly sat upright and said, "Well, what is the answer?" When she was greeted by silence, she rephrased. "Well, then," she said, "What is the question?" For the origins of the novel, that has been the issue since the rise of Ian Watt.

NOTES

1. Recent scholarship has begun to differentiate much more precisely between attitudes and postures within the "Augustan" group (see, for example, Carol Fabricant, *Swift's Landscape* [Baltimore and London, 1982]), and Howard Weinbrot has argued that the term Augustan should be abandoned because eighteenth-century figures who are often called Augustan were themselves critical of Augustus as a political model (*Augustus Caesar in Augustan England* [Princeton, 1978]). But, valuable as these distinctions and correctives are, the literary figures committed to traditional humanist values did share a suspicion and distrust of novelty and modernist values, and Paul Fussell's statement of their social and literary attitudes remains an accurate general assessment of widely shared assumptions about literary directions (*The Rhetorical World of Augustan Humanism* [Oxford, 1965]). And I continue to use the term Augustan as the most convenient shorthand for that cluster of opinions and assumptions; the term has always, or almost always, been used with a sense of its ironic political reaches, and it suggests better than any contemporary or subsequent political term available the firm sense of traditions, standards, and literary and social barriers that lie behind the suspicions of journalism, popular literature, and unconstrained subjective imagination.
2. Johnson, *Rambler*, 4.
3. The best modern statement of the thesis is still Ian Watt, *The Rise of the Novel* (Berkeley and Los Angeles, 1957). Watt himself, although often used simplistically in quasi-historical arguments, is actually quite subtle on the class issue.
4. "Literacy and Education in England 1640–1900," *Past and Present* 42 (1969): 69–139. Since Stone's summary, a number of other studies have appeared, including the detailed account of the Cambridge group's lengthy project on demography, E. A. Wrigley and R. S. Schofield, *The Population History of England, 1541–1871: A Reconstruction* (Cambridge, Mass., 1981). See also David Cressy, *Literacy and the Social Order: Reading and Writing in Tudor and Stuart England* (Cambridge, 1980), and Isabel Rivers, ed., *Books and Their Readers in Eighteenth-Century England* (Leicester and New York, 1982). The new and more detailed evidence essentially supports the Stone summary, except to question whether literacy actually rose again at the end of the eighteenth century and to demonstrate that female literacy, especially in London, was more extensive than Stone supposed.

5. Stone seems to me rather condescending on the issue of female literacy, and he is, oddly enough, willing to settle for rumor and anecdote while insisting on hard evidence about males. See especially his comments in *The Family, Sex and Marriage in England 1500–1800* (London, 1977). Evidence is scarce about women, especially before 1754, because the kinds of records used by literacy scholars and the new social historians contain little information. In 1754 Lord Hardwick's Marriage Act provided that both bride and groom sign the marriage register, and records thereafter are more reliable.

6. *Shamela*, letter 10.

7. The best new evidence is provided by Cressy, *Literacy and the Social Order*, 128ff., and by Wrigley and Schofield, *Population History of England*.

8. E. A. Wrigley, "A Simple Model of London's Importance in Changing English Society and Economy 1650–1730," *Past and Present* 37 (1967): 44–70. Except for the estimate that the London population in 1700 may have reached almost 700,000 (for which M. Dorothy George is responsible, *London Life in the Eighteenth Century* [New York, 1965]), all of the population figures for London quoted here are from Wrigley. For more detail on London's population, see Roger Finlay, *Population and Metropolis: The Demography of London, 1580–1650*, (Cambridge, 1981).

9. The evidence for the practice is widely recorded in plays and in didactic literature, especially guides for youth where the practice of sharing, and secreting, books in private closets is constantly condemned. Guidebooks are particularly critical of such sharing after the turn of the century; see, for example, Defoe's *Family Instructor*. I have discussed habits of closet-reading among the young in "The World as Stage and Closet," in Shirley Strum Kenny, ed., *British Theatre and Other Arts, 1660–1800* (Washington, D.C., 1984), 279–83.

10. Johnson, *Rambler*, 4.

11. Pope, *Correspondence*, ed.

12. *The Country and the City* (London, 1973). Williams traces the shifts in definition relative to economic circumstance. On the values attributed to country and city, see also W. A. Speck, *Society and Literature in England* (Dublin, 1983), 116–38.

13. *Tristram Shandy* I.xx.

14. See Alan Dugald McKillop, "Wedding Bells for Pamela," *Philological Quarterly* 28 (1949): 323–25.

15. I have discussed this matter and others related to the phenomenology of reading in "The Loneliness of the Long-Distance Reader," *Genre* 10 (1977): 455–84.

16. See Robert Scholes and Robert Kellogg, *The Nature of Narrative* (New York, 1966).

17. See K. M. Briggs, *The Fairies in Tradition and Literature* (London, 1967).

18. For an excellent recent discussion of the cultural significance of fairy tales, see Robert Darnton, "Peasants Tell Tales: The Meaning of Mother Goose," in *The Great Cat Massacre and Other Episodes in French Cultural History* (New York, 1984), 9–72. Unlike the recent psychoanalytic interpreters of fairy tales (who emphasize "universal" features), Darnton delineates cultural and temporal features that suggest a considerable differentiation of experience.

19. See Thomas, *Religion and the Decline of Magic* (London, 1971).
20. Locke, *An Essay on Modern Education* (London, 1747), 41–42. Locke's most concerted written attack on oral tales is in *Some Thoughts concerning Education*, especially sect. 138. For a good discussion of Locke's suspicions and their influence, see Samuel F. Pickering, Jr., *John Locke and Children's Books in Eighteenth-Century England* (Knoxville, 1981), esp. 42–44.

Contributors

JOHN ANDREW BERNSTEIN teaches European intellectual history at the University of Delaware. His books include *Shaftesbury, Rousseau, and Kant: An Introduction to the Conflict between Aesthetic and Moral Values in Modern Thought* (1980) and *Nietzsche's Moral Philosophy* (1987).

JOCELYN HARRIS is Senior Lecturer in English Language and Literature at the University of Otago, Dunedin, New Zealand. Her edition of Samuel Richardson's *Sir Charles Grandison* appeared in the Oxford English Novels series (3 volumes, 1972).

J. PAUL HUNTER is Professor of English at the University of Rochester. He has written *The Reluctant Pilgrim: Defoe's Emblematic Pilgrim and Quest for Form in "Robinson Crusoe"* (1966) and *Occasional Form: Henry Fielding and the Chains of Circumstance* (1975).

MARGARET C. JACOB is Professor of History and Dean of the College of Arts and Sciences at the New School for Social Research. Her books are *The Newtonians and the English Revolution, 1689–1720* (1976) and *The Radical Enlightenment: Puritans, Freemasons and Republicans* (1981).

UWE-K. KETELSEN is Professor of German at the Ruhr-Universität in Bochum, West Germany. Among his books are *Die Naturpoesie der norddeutschen Frühaufklärung* (1974) and *Völkisch-nationale und nationalsozialistische Literatur in Deutschland, 1890–1945* (1976).

ALAN CHARLES KORS is Associate Professor of History at the University of Pennsylvania. In 1986–87, he was a Fellow of the Shelby Cullom Davis Institute for Historical Studies at Princeton University. He is the author of *D'Holbach's Coterie: An Enlightenment in Paris* (1976).

ELISABETH LABROUSSE is a member of the C. N. R. S. in Paris. She is the author and editor of many works on seventeenth-century French intellectual life and religious history, including *Pierre Bayle* (2 volumes, 1963–64) and *Essai sur la revocation de l'Edit de Nantes* (1985).

JOHN A. MCCARTHY is Associate Professor of German at the University of Pennsylvania. His publications include two books on Wieland (1974; 1979) and a forthcoming study of the interrelationship between Enlightenment philosophy and essayism from 1680 to 1815, entitled *Crossing Boundaries*.

P. M. MITCHELL has taught at the University of Illinois, Urbana, since 1958, where he is Professor of Germanic Languages. He is a well-known Gottsched scholar whose critical edition of Gottsched's *opera* has contributed greatly to the revaluation of his significance for eighteenth-century literature.

THOMAS P. SAINE is Professor of German at the University of California, Irvine. Among his books are studies of K. P. Mortitz (1972) and G. Forster (1975). He expects soon to publish *Von der Kopernikanischen bis zur Französischen Revolution*.

DALE VAN KLEY is Professor of History at Calvin College. He is the author of *The Jansenists and the Expulsion of the Jesuits from France* (1975) and *The Damiens Affair and the Unravelling of the Ancien Regime* (1984).

Index

DATE DUE